PRAISE FOR *THE REAL TRUMP DEAL*

"Donald Trump's entire persona is wrapped up in his belief that he is the best negotiator ever. Whether or not he wrote any part of *The Art of the Deal*, it has become his personal bible of negotiation. What kind of a negotiator is Trump? How much of the puffery is real, and how much is fake? How does his success—and lack thereof—in the business world translate into negotiating skill and power in the White House? These questions are answered powerfully and systematically in this readable and cogent book."

— Norman J. Ornstein, Resident Scholar, American Enterprise Institute
Co-Author of *The New York Times* Bestseller *One Nation After Trump*

"With this book, Marty Latz has done us an intensely valuable service—carefully sifting through and assessing all the claims, hoopla, and evidence surrounding Donald Trump's talent for negotiation. The result is shockingly instructive."

— Robert Cialdini, Author of *The New York Times* bestsellers
Pre-Suasion and *Influence: Science and Practice*

"Donald Trump's negotiation skills have been on public display for 50 years. How good are they? Longtime negotiation expert Marty Latz compares Trump's negotiations to the research on what works—and what doesn't. Everyone can learn from this astute book filled with specific examples, fascinating stories, and key insights."

— Prof. Andrea Schneider, Director, Marquette University Law School's
Nationally Ranked Dispute Resolution Program

"Success in business and life often depends on your effectiveness as a negotiator. Using Trump's 100+ business deals as 'learning lessons'—good and bad— renowned negotiation expert Marty Latz here provides practical advice you can use every day to achieve better results."

— Marshall Goldsmith, International bestselling author or editor of 35 books
including *What Got You Here Won't Get You There* and *Triggers*

"Donald Trump considers himself one of the world's best negotiators. Is he? Marty Latz's expert eye-opening analysis of Trump's 50-year negotiation history answers this question. Every student of negotiation—which should be every negotiator—will learn from this important contribution to our understanding of the most impactful negotiator alive today!"

— Dr. Roy J. Lewicki, Professor, Fisher College of Business, The Ohio State University
and author or editor of over 35 negotiation-related books,
including the world's bestselling textbook on negotiation

THE
REAL
TRUMP
DEAL

AN EYE-OPENING LOOK
AT HOW HE *REALLY* NEGOTIATES

MARTIN E. LATZ
INTERNATIONALLY RECOGNIZED NEGOTIATION EXPERT
FOUNDER OF LATZ NEGOTIATION

THE
REAL
TRUMP
DEAL

AN EYE-OPENING LOOK
AT HOW HE *REALLY* NEGOTIATES

LIFE SUCCESS
PRESS

Published by Life Success Press LLC, an imprint of Brisance Books Group LLC. The publisher is not responsible for websites or their content that are not owned by the publisher.

Life Success Press LLC
21001 N. Tatum Blvd.
Suite 1630
Phoenix, AZ 85050

Printed in the United States of America

First Edition: June 2018
Hardcover
ISBN: 978-1-944194-47-5

Cover photo: AP Photo | Eric Schultz
Martin Latz photo: Dan Vermillion
Cover design: PCI Publishing Group

062018

DEDICATION

To my extraordinary wife, Linda, who put up with my long hours and late nights while I wrote this book. I constantly struggle to find that perfect balance in life, but I'm really lucky I found an amazing wife for this journey.

To my son Jason and daughter Valerie—budding great negotiators with unique and very different negotiation strengths and weaknesses—may you not only learn and internalize the strategies and tactics in here but also the more important moral and ethical lessons that drive all effective negotiators and human interactions.

To my parents, Bob and Carolyn Latz, two of the most incredible human beings I know. Mentors. Role models. Insightful thinkers. Great advice givers. Voracious readers. Emotional supporters. Loving parents and grandparents. I can't ever thank you enough for all you have given to me.

CONTENTS

INTRODUCTION

*"**Donald Trump is the greatest dealmaker our country's ever seen.**"*[1]

— Corey Lewandowski
Trump for President Campaign Manager

What motivates U.S. President Donald J. Trump, the most powerful man in the world? Millions of Americans and billions throughout the world are still trying to figure this out. We have heard his speeches, debates, interviews, tweets, promises, and press conferences. And we've watched him demolish his Republican opponents, beat Hillary Clinton, spar with the "enemy of the people" media, career his way through his first year in office, appear "presidential" in his first State of the Union address, and upend almost all political conventions and expectations.

Many have been shocked and surprised. But we shouldn't be. Why not? Because for almost 50 years Donald Trump has consistently focused on one activity to the exclusion of almost anything else: negotiating and making deals. It's a core element of his identity—*and it largely explains his behavior.* How has he negotiated? By:

- Interacting with his prep school classmates on the playground;
- Learning the residential real estate business at the feet of his dad;
- Building his commercial and residential New York-based real estate empire;
- Partnering with major financial institutions to fund his business activities;
- Buying a pro football team;
- Running casinos and dealing with New Jersey gaming regulators;
- Obtaining relief from mountains of debt owed to huge financial institutions;
- Filing, defending, litigating, settling, and trying thousands of lawsuits with partners, customers, and subcontractors;
- Creating and licensing a worldwide luxury brand with foreign investors and partners;
- Judging and firing celebrities and wannabe business titans on NBC's hit reality TV series *The Apprentice*;
- Hiring and managing thousands of employees; and
- Publicly and privately interacting with three wives and five kids.

Of course, everyone negotiates. Whether you're buying a car, selling a house, working with a business partner, or trying to convince your seven-year-old to go to bed, you're negotiating. Whenever two or more individuals are communicating, and each has interests to satisfy, they're negotiating.

Some do it brilliantly from birth. Others spend years studying it, learning from successes and failures, and improving based on the experts' proven research. Most largely wing it and negotiate instinctively and intuitively.

What does Donald Trump do? He believes *"dealmaking is an ability you're born with. It's in the genes."*[2] Are his negotiation genes good? Have they worked? And how have they worked in presidential negotiations? That's our goal—to find out.

Here's the deal. Donald Trump has a well-documented track record of hundreds of negotiations. Let's analyze them—and this self-professed great negotiator—through the lens of negotiation research.

We will then:

- better understand how well he will negotiate as President, and
- learn from his successes and failures and be empowered to more effectively negotiate ourselves.

But first we need to be clear on the parameters of this effort.

Science Matters—Not Politics

Some will undoubtedly discount the analysis and conclusions here based on their political persuasion. Others will feel validated. The goal here is neither to offend nor affirm. Instead, it is to inform and to educate about the negotiation strengths and weaknesses of the most powerful man in the world.

The 1981 publication of *Getting to Yes: Negotiating Agreement Without Giving In* by my Harvard Law School Professor Roger Fisher and William Ury[3] inspired thousands to flood into the new field of negotiation. Today almost every college, business school, and law school offer negotiation courses. And thousands of professors now teach and study this fundamental life skill.

The result? We now basically know what fundamental strategies work. And these building blocks are supported by solid science. These tenets will serve as the framework for our analysis.

Of course, some negotiation professors will undoubtedly disagree on the extent of this consensus. That is the nature of academics. As a result, I asked two of the world's leading negotiation professors to review and comment on the fundamental nature of the negotiation science underlying this analysis. Importantly, I did not ask them to agree with my analysis or conclusions, just the science. Each of the following confirmed our basic building blocks.

- **Professor Roy Lewicki**, Irving Abramowitz Memorial Professor Emeritus and Professor of Management and Human Resources Emeritus at the Max M. Fisher College of Business, The Ohio State University, and the author or editor of 39 negotiation-related books, including the bestselling negotiation textbook in business schools around the world.

- **Professor Andrea Schneider,** Professor of Law, Marquette University Law School, and the author or co-author of numerous dispute resolution books, including *Dispute Resolution: Examples and Explanations* with Michael Moffitt and, with Roger Fisher, *Beyond Machiavelli: Tools for Coping with Conflict* and *Coping with International Conflict*.

Science matters—and this book is based upon research confirmed by the best and brightest in the negotiation field.

Trump's Actions Speak Louder than His Words

Donald Trump expounds on his negotiation strategies in many of his books. He also has an extensive and well-documented record of interviews and statements relating to his deals. His words matter.

But to accurately capture the essence and full breadth of Trump's negotiation approach, we will also analyze how his negotiation colleagues, partners, and counterparts describe his strategies and tactics. The negotiation process always involves more than one party. And the strategies one uses are often viewed differently depending on where one sits.

Plus, in many negotiations it's more important to consider what someone does versus what they say. We've all heard that "actions speak louder than words." It's especially crucial here as bluffing and puffery—strategies that put a negotiator's credibility on the chopping block—are common moves. Therefore, one must sometimes discount the impact of parties' negotiation-related statements given this dynamic. And when you add the nature of politics to this equation, parties' words can become even less credible.

Objective Facts Matter

Since we are at risk of living in a "post-truth" world, with anonymous individuals trolling the internet spawning lies and false narratives, it's paramount to scrupulously document every source, element and method utilized in this book. Credibility is essential to accurate analysis. Support here is identified in Endnotes.

Regarding the facts, this book is an analysis of Trump's negotiation behavior based on facts derived from:

- Trump's books, interviews, speeches, debates, etc., over his almost 50 years of negotiating;
- Books, articles and comments by Trump's colleagues and supporters—and counterparts—from his personal, business, and political lives;
- Articles and reports on Trump by a wide variety of media; and
- Extensively researched independent biographies of Trump, several of which were published by award-winning journalists prior to his becoming a polarizing political figure.

Collectively, the factual basis for the analysis in this book is thus based on:

- Hundreds of hours of interviews of Trump—who has been uniquely accessible to journalists for almost 50 years;
- An incalculable number of hours of interviews and documents and legal transcripts of those who negotiated with and against Trump; and
- Thousands of pages of books and other documents, some original, relating to Trump and his negotiations.

This book is *not* based on any personal interviews of Trump and his counterparts. This proved unnecessary due to: 1) the extensive public record on Trump by such a wide variety of sources, and 2) the consistent nature of the independent research and reporting on Trump's negotiation strategies.

Negotiation Success Is Not Just About the Money

"Hold on," you might say. "Donald Trump has made billions, owns his own Boeing 757, has his name atop towers around the world, was elected President of the United States, and has been negotiating almost since birth. And you agree negotiation has been a fundamental part of every element of his career. Doesn't that prove he's a great negotiator?"

No. Just getting a deal done—and even profiting greatly from it—doesn't mean you negotiated a great deal. Nor does it mean you're a great negotiator. Even if you have substantially overpaid for some commercial real estate, paying well over market value, you can still profit greatly from a strong real-estate market going forward.

Monetary success is only one measure of negotiation ability.

The Harvard Program on Negotiation—the premier negotiation research-based organization that houses some of the most brilliant academics in the world—presents an annual award recognizing an outstanding negotiator in the field. Past recipients of the "Great Negotiator Award" include George Mitchell (who helped negotiate the Good Friday Accords in Northern Ireland), Richard Holbrooke (who helped negotiate the Dayton Peace Accords), and Stuart Eizenstat (who facilitated the award of $8 billion in reparations from multiple European governments, banks, and companies to victims of World War II).

None of these highly effective negotiators recognized by independent experts are worth billions. Monetary success, while a measure of negotiation effectiveness in business, is not the sole criterion underlying negotiation skills and abilities.

The Experience and Expertise Supporting this Analysis

I have devoted the last 24 years to studying, teaching, writing, and consulting in negotiation in the U.S. and around the world. I also am the founder and CEO of a negotiation e-learning software company, which I started 10 years ago. My two kids and wife also test my negotiation skills daily!

Prior to entering this field fulltime, I practiced law and worked for the White House on the White House Advance Teams. Politically, I have supported Democrats and Republicans at the state and federal levels. I also watched and enjoyed Donald Trump in all *The Apprentice* shows.

Though some will certainly be tempted to ascertain if I have a bias for or against Donald Trump, I strongly encourage readers to keep an open mind. Everyone should use critical thinking and analytical skills to evaluate this effort. Though we can't yet determine how history will judge President Trump as a politician, his negotiation skills have been on open display for almost half a century. We should learn from them—not only to understand the present, but to prepare for the Trump years ahead.

One final note: Predicting Trump has been notoriously difficult. Few have been prescient. I am confident, however, that history provides the best clues and evidence regarding the future. Applying this logic, a science-based analysis of Trump's past negotiation strategies and behavior will provide great insight into what he will do in the future.

In fact, nothing may have a more direct impact on the safety, security and prosperity of the world than Donald Trump's negotiation skills.

With these parameters in mind, the rest of the book is organized into three parts.

Part 1—Donald Trump's Top 10 Business Negotiation Strategies

Part 2—Trump's Personal Skills and Ethics

Part 3—The Trump Transition: Business to Presidential Negotiations

Donald Trump's Top 10 Business Negotiation Strategies

President Donald Trump could be the poster boy for the classic extremely competitive negotiator schooled on the streets of New York City's rough and tumble real-estate world. What does this mean strategy-wise?

The Five Golden Rules of Negotiation

1. Information Is Power—So Get It!
2. Maximize Your Leverage
3. Employ "Fair" Objective Criteria
4. Design an Offer-Concession Strategy
5. Control the Agenda

In this part, we will analyze how Trump has consistently implemented our science-based strategic framework—my Five Golden Rules of Negotiation—in his almost 50 years of negotiating business deals.

We will do it by identifying and evaluating Trump's Top Ten Business Negotiation Strategies in Chapters 1 through 10.

Trump's Personal Skills and Ethics

What you do in a negotiation—the moves you make—differ from *how* you do it—the way you implement them. Negotiation strategies (part one) differ from skills (part two). Of course, these interrelate. You cannot draw a bright line between them. But they do represent distinct elements of a person's negotiation approach. We thus address them separately.

Style-wise, the research points to certain identifiable skills that characterize effective negotiators, including assertiveness, empathy, flexibility, ethicality, and social intuition.

How does Trump stack up?

What about Trump's ethics? Few issues engender more passion than Trump's truthfulness and credibility. Trump lovers point to his blunt, unvarnished, non-PC talk.

Trump haters point to his effort to delegitimize President Barack Obama with the birther conspiracy and his false and unsupported campaign and presidential statements reported by publications like *The Washington Post* and *The New York Times*.

How will we evaluate Trump's credibility? By identifying his credibility-related tactics and assessing his reputation developed over almost 50 years of deal-making.

The Trump Transition—Business to Presidential Negotiations

Will Donald Trump's business negotiation skills stand him in good stead in presidential negotiations? Business and presidential negotiations require different skills and strategies and present almost diametrically opposed challenges. What's different? Will Trump be able to pivot and stretch his negotiation skills into a foreign negotiation environment? After all, he did not pivot in the campaign, and he won. And if he doesn't pivot, how might his political paradigm shift, business negotiation style and strategies impact his foreign and domestic negotiations?

To truly judge Donald Trump's negotiation skills, we must objectively analyze his major negotiations in business *and* as President. We do this here by evaluating his Mexico border wall funding negotiation and his congressional health care reform negotiations.

One final note. We shouldn't set up an impossible standard and then judge Trump based on it. That would be unfair to him, unwise analytically, and counterproductive. While the best negotiators implement most of these strategies, no one adheres to all of them all the time. Even the best of the best make mistakes. However, the most effective negotiators learn and improve as they gain experience and expertise. We will evaluate this in Trump as well.

Donald J. Trump styles himself as the dealmaker president. Let's evaluate his skills and his deals based on the experts' proven research.

PART ONE

TRUMP'S TOP 10 BUSINESS NEGOTIATION STRATEGIES

"I'm the first to admit that I am very competitive and that I'll do nearly anything within legal bounds to win. Sometimes, part of making a deal is denigrating your competition."[4]

—Donald J. Trump, *The Art of the Deal*

Donald Trump started negotiating business deals almost 50 years ago in his early twenties. Named president of various Trump entities by his father, Fred, he negotiated leases and repair contracts for thousands of apartments in Trump-owned buildings.

Since then, Trump has negotiated in a wide variety of business contexts and with highly diverse counterparts. He considers negotiation part of his DNA, tweeting, *"Deals are my art form. Other people paint beautifully or write poetry. I like making deals, preferably big deals. That's how I get my kicks."*[5]

He's had massive successes and failures. What negotiation strategies and tactics has he consistently used? Donald Trump's top ten most common strategies and tactics constitute the first ten chapters of this book.

To start, some preliminary notes:

- **Different Strategies Work in Different Environments.** Sometimes the most effective negotiation strategy is to build the relationship. Other times an extremely aggressive approach works better. We will analyze Trump's strategies in both contexts.

- **Trump's Credibility Will Be Addressed Later.** Trust, credibility, truthfulness, and parties' reputations impact every negotiation. Some strategies involve bluffing, puffery, exaggeration, promises, threats, and other credibility-related moves. While we describe these here, chapter 12 extensively addresses their impact and effectiveness.

- **Trump Is Not a "One-Trick Pony."** Donald Trump uses more than these next ten strategies. However, these ten consistently pop up in his negotiations. They have likely become habits—so he will almost certainly continue to use them as President.

- **The Top Ten Order Is Based on the Five Golden Rules of Negotiation.** Finally, the sequence here is *not* based on how often Trump uses these strategies, the order in which he implemented them, or their priority or power. Instead, they are organized around my Five Golden Rules of Negotiation, a strategic framework that describes the basic building blocks of the experts' proven research.

Okay, here's my Five Golden Rules structure and a short description of how Trump's Top Ten Business Negotiation Strategies fit within them.

Golden Rule One: Information Is Power—So Get It!

The first thing to do in any negotiation is get sufficient information to set your goals. You cannot negotiate strategically based on the experts' proven research without knowing where you want to end up and defining "success" at the end of the day.

In chapter one, we will evaluate a) how much Trump negotiates instinctively versus strategically and b) how and how much he prepares. These issues infuse the entire Trump approach to negotiations. We will shift in chapter two to exploring how his incredibly aggressive goal-setting and passionate expectations impact his deals.

Puffery and the role of "truthful hyperbole" will be addressed in chapter three. Trump exaggerates a lot. Does it work? Trump also regularly used the carrot-and-stick approach in his business negotiations. In chapter four, we look at the carrots he used to satisfy his interests.

Golden Rule Two: Maximize Your Leverage

Leverage—the most powerful component in negotiations—is based on two elements: 1) how much you and your counterpart need a deal, and 2) how well your deal, Plan A, stacks up to your best alternative, or Plan B. The better your Plan B, the stronger your leverage and vice versa.

Leverage makes its first significant appearance in chapter five. These were Trump's sticks. Threats and bullying take center stage in chapters six and seven. Did they work?

Golden Rule Three: Employ "Fair" Objective Criteria

One word that most aptly describes Trump to many: unprecedented. Trump smartly used independent, objective standards like precedent, market value and experts to justify the "fairness" and "reasonableness" of his deals. We address these in Chapter eight.

Golden Rule Four: Design an Offer-Concession Strategy

Timing (when he makes his moves), speed (how often he makes his moves), and size (how big he makes his moves) comprise offer-concession strategies. Each move signals an important element in the negotiation "dance" that almost inevitably takes place between negotiation parties. Does Trump know this "dance"? This will be addressed in Chapter nine.

Golden Rule Five: Control the Agenda

If and *when* and *how* and *where* issues are addressed—and the timing and deadlines involved—greatly impact negotiation results. Chapter 10 focuses on how Trump controls the agenda in his business negotiations.

These first 10 chapters constitute Trump's Top 10 Business Negotiation Strategies. Let's see how Trump puts these into practice. Here's a chart summarizing them.

FIVE GOLDEN RULES MAPPED TO TRUMP'S BUSINESS STRATEGIES

FIVE GOLDEN RULES OF NEGOTIATION	TRUMP'S TOP TEN BUSINESS STRATEGIES
1. Information Is Power— So Get It!	1. An Instinctive Win-Lose Mindset
	2. Setting the Bar High: Super Aggressive Expectations
	3. The King of Hyperbole: Exaggerate!
	4. Targeting True Motivations: Using Carrots to Close Deals
2. Maximize Your Leverage	5. The Art of the Bluff: When He Holds... and When He Folds
	6. Threats and Leverage: Real or Fake?
	7. Business Bullying
3. Employ "Fair" Objective Criteria	8. Helpful Standards Only Need Apply
4. Design an Offer-Concession Strategy	9. Outrageous Moves and Countermoves
5. Control the Agenda	10. A Towering Home-Field Agenda

CHAPTER 1

AN INSTINCTIVE WIN–LOSE MINDSET

"Some people have an ability to negotiate. It's an art you're basically born with. You either have it or you don't."[6]

—Donald J. Trump

Donald Trump made millions from his starring role in *The Apprentice* and its progeny. And the publicity and persona he derived from it formed a fundamental basis for the millions more he made from subsequent U.S. and international licensing deals.

His celebrity and brand also proved indispensable to his successful presidential run. He almost certainly would not be president today had he not first been portrayed as such a widely admired and successful business titan in the popular NBC series.

So, how much preparation did he do for his first meeting and negotiation with Mark Burnett, the creator of the hit *Survivor* reality TV series who pitched *The Apprentice* concept to Trump?

None. Trump did it all on the fly based solely on his instincts.

According to Michael Kranish and Marc Fisher in their extensively researched and well-written biography *Trump Revealed, The Definitive Biography of the 45th President*:

> Burnett walked out of that first meeting with a handshake deal to make *The Apprentice*. Trump secured not only a starring role on a show made by TV's hottest producer but also 50 percent ownership of it. Trump had consulted no one, done no research. He liked the idea; he bought it. It was a classic Trump moment, an example of the gut-instinct decision making that he had proudly touted throughout his career. [7]

How does this fit into Trump's business negotiation approach? Two consistent themes run through Trump's business negotiations:

1) his gut-level planning and decision-making, and

2) his win–lose mindset and approach to business and life.

Trump's Gut Drove His Business Negotiations—Not Strategic Homework

"I just think that you have an instinct and you go with it. Especially when it comes to deal-making and buying things." [8]

—Donald J. Trump

Lack of planning in *The Apprentice* deal was typical Trump. In 1986, Trump sought to take over Bally's, a public company that owned three casinos, one in Atlantic City, where Trump already owned two casinos. Trump eventually became Bally's biggest shareholder after investing $63 million and buying up 9.9 percent of its stock.

His interest in Bally's originated from Daniel Lee, an analyst at Drexel Burnham Lambert, the infamous Wall Street investment bank led by Michael Milken that went bankrupt in 1990 due to its involvement in illegal activities in the junk bond market.

According to Lee, who informally advised him on this effort, *"[Trump had] begun buying the stock **without even reading the annual report**."* [Emphasis added.][9]

As with *The Apprentice* deal, though, Trump's gut proved profitable. While Bally's fended him off, he made over $20 million when Bally's bought him out.

Trump acknowledges this tendency and considers it a strength. In a 1984 interview with Lois Romano of *The Washington Post* in which he discussed negotiating nuclear disarmament with the then Soviet Union, he said that—while he was no expert on missiles—"it would take an hour and a half to learn everything there is to learn about missiles....I think I know most of it anyway."[10]

President Ronald Reagan, whom no one ever accused of digging deep into the policy details of nuclear disarmament, certainly spent a lot more than an hour and a half strategic prep time before negotiating this with Soviet Leader Mikhail Gorbachev in 1986.

How important is strategic preparation before complex, significant negotiations?

> **RESEARCH:** Harvard Law Professor Robert Mnookin, Chair of the Harvard Program on Negotiation, noted in his excellent book *Bargaining with the Devil, When to Negotiate, When to Fight*, it's appropriate to spend around 90 percent of your time in these negotiations "on preparation behind the table."[11]

In my training and consulting, I usually recommend *at least* twice as much time on strategic planning as "at the table" negotiating. Here's how I describe this crucial element in my book, *Gain the Edge! Negotiating to Get What You Want* (St. Martin's Press, 2004) (*Gain the Edge!*):

The Power of Preparation Always Makes a Difference

What is the most universally ignored but most effective negotiation tool? Preparation. I conclude every one of my seminars with this statement: "Prepare. Prepare. Prepare. It's guaranteed to succeed. The more you prepare, the better you will do."… Renowned UCLA basketball coach John Wooden said: *"Failing to prepare is preparing to fail."* He's right…. Negotiation research unmistakably illustrates the concrete value of preparation.[12]

Of course, Donald Trump would dispute the characterization that he doesn't do his homework.

First, he would likely suggest he does his homework *where it's needed*. A perfect example would be his first big real-estate negotiation when he was 27—a complex deal involving multiple parties in which he redeveloped the Commodore Hotel in New York City next to Grand Central Station (now the Grand Hyatt).

He may be right. In fact, his long-time lawyer and co-star of *The Apprentice*, George H. Ross, in *Trump-Style Negotiation: Powerful Strategies and Tactics for Mastering Every Deal (Trump-Style Negotiation)*, wrote:

Donald Trump spends a great deal of time preparing himself and members of his team for every negotiation—not just for the big deals, but every negotiation he enters. He knows that by being as well prepared as he can be, there will be fewer surprises.[13]

Ross is probably right, at least for the 1970's Trump. This is confirmed in possibly the most comprehensive Trump biography by *Village Voice* investigative reporter Wayne Barrett, who met Trump in 1978 and compiled 14 file drawers of documents on Trump and his deals. In Barrett's 450-page book, *Trump: The Greatest Show on Earth* published in 1992 (*Trump Show*), he wrote about Trump's 1974 purchase of some bankrupt Penn Central railways propertics:

> [Ned] Eichler and Donald cut the deal over the next six months, winding their way through a 65-page contract and working out a timetable for the first phase of the anticipated zoning changes and housing subsidies that reached 13 years into the future.[14]

While Trump probably did his homework early on, he did less as he became more prominent in the mid-1980s and beyond.

Barrett described Trump in the mid-1980s here in two Atlantic City casino negotiations.

The Hilton Castle Casino Acquisition

> While the Plaza deal took four years, from Donald's initial lease negotiations in the spring of 1980 to the grand opening, the Castle acquisition took less than four months…. **He proudly boasted that he purchased the Hilton without ever having taken even a walk-through**….

The Taj Construction Catastrophe

> The catastrophe at the Taj was a symptom of [Trump's] sudden inability to focus—he'd visited the site rarely and **lost contact with the detail work that was once his trademark**…. By and large, he'd transcended his Hyatt and Trump Tower days of creating value and repositioned himself as a player in the far less demanding league that merely traded in it. [Emphasis added.][15]

Trump's loss of focus and attention to detail became increasingly problematic.

Second, Trump would likely indicate that negotiation leaders *should* delegate to take advantage of their team's strengths. Doing detail-oriented homework is neither his strength nor in his interest, he might note. That's why you hire experts and lawyers, right?

Ross would again agree with Trump, noting:

> To my knowledge, Donald Trump has no negotiating weaknesses except maybe the fact that he doesn't like to discuss minor details. He lacks the patience to work on unimportant paperwork, because he likes to focus on the big picture as a more productive use of his time…. Being a smart deal maker, Donald has learned to see the forest and let his subordinates see the trees.[16]

Delegation is a critical negotiation strategy. Negotiation leaders should rely on experts and others. But effective negotiation leaders still need to understand the interests, details, and interconnections between the issues to fully appreciate the strategic negotiation landscape.

RESEARCH: Professors Roy Lewicki, David Saunders, and Bruce Barry, co-authors of *Negotiation*, the world's bestselling business school negotiation textbook and the gold standard, wrote:

We cannot overemphasize the importance of preparation, and we strongly encourage all negotiators to prepare properly for their negotiations…. Preparation… should be right at the top of the best practices list of every negotiator. **Negotiators who are better prepared have numerous advantages.**[17]

One final note on preparation. So far, we have focused on the substantive preparation for negotiations. Learn the facts.

You also need to do your homework on the negotiation *process*. Most successful professionals do their due diligence on the facts. But they give short shrift to the process and wing it when it comes to preparing for the actual moves in the negotiation. Do both.

How well has Donald Trump prepared on the substance *and* process in his negotiations over the years? On a scale of 1 to 10, 10 being the most prepared, I would give him a three. I expect he would agree he's not much for preparation.

His gut dominates.

Trump's Win–Lose Mindset Impacted All His Business Negotiations

"We are going to start winning again…. We are going to win so much."[18]

"I have a winning temperament. I know how to win."[19]

"I'm not big on compromise. I understand compromise. Sometimes compromise is the right answer, but oftentimes compromise is the equivalent of defeat, and I don't like being defeated."[20]

"We [the U.S.] don't win anymore. We don't beat China in trade. We don't beat Japan, with their millions and millions of cars coming into this country, in trade. We can't beat Mexico, on the border or in trade."[21]

"I win, I win, I always win. In the end, I always win, whether it's in golf, whether it's in tennis, whether it's in life, I just always win. And I tell people I always win, because I do."[22]

"If I'm President, we will win on everything we do."[23]

"My life has been about winning. I like to win. I like to close the deal."[24]

—Donald J. Trump

Donald Trump's favorite word may be "win." Implicit in how he uses "win" is that someone must lose, get defeated, or get beaten. Merriam-Webster defines "win" as "to gain in or as if in battle or contest" or "to gain the victory in a contest."[25]

Negotiation has traditionally been viewed as a competitive contest in which you win or lose. Not both. And not win–win.

This is an essential part of Donald Trump's life. And it permeates his business deals and way of thinking.

Where did it start? It may simply be in his DNA, but this attitude first openly manifested itself at the New York Military Academy, where he was sent at age 13. As noted in *Trump Revealed*,

> Donald's competitive drive took over as he learned to master the academy. He won medals for neatness and order. He loved competing to win contests for cleanest room, shiniest shoes, and best-made bed. For the first time, he took pride in his grades; he grew angry when a study partner scored higher on a chemistry test, even questioning whether he had cheated.[26]

He learned much of this from World War II combat veteran and the Academy's baseball and football coach Theodore Dobias. As Dobias in 2014 told Pulitzer Prize–winning journalist Michael D'Antonio, author of *The Truth about Trump*, he "taught [his players] that winning wasn't everything, it was the only thing."[27]

This winning "was the only thing" quote from legendary Green Bay Packers' coach Vince Lombardi greatly impacted Trump. Dobias told D'Antonio, "Donald picked right up on this. He would tell his teammates, 'We're out here for a purpose. To win.'.... He would do anything to win.... [Trump] just wanted to be first, in everything, and he wanted people to know he was first."[28]

Trump recognized this, believing that "his ball-field experiences were formative because they made him locally famous and because they instilled in him the habit of winning," according to D'Antonio.[29]

Trump also became a lifelong sports fan, where "in Trump's zero-sum world of winners and losers, sports always held a special place."[30] Sports is the quintessential zero-sum environment, where individuals or teams win or lose.

Of course, a win–lose, zero-sum mindset can be positive or negative in negotiations and life. Sometimes both.

For instance, Donald Trump's dominant win-at-almost-all-costs attitude was reflected in his purchase of the United States Football League's New Jersey Generals in 1983 and his effort to parlay it into an NFL franchise.

Trump's Win–Lose Approach to Get into the NFL

Donald Trump bought the USFL's New Jersey Generals in 1983 with two goals in mind: own a successful NFL team and stadium, and mass market the Trump brand. How did he intend to do this? And how did his win–lose attitude figure into it?

Three elements of his effort illustrate his intentions and win–lose attitude:

- Trump needed to win games right away,
- Trump needed the USFL to compete with the NFL in the fall, and
- Trump's last shot to win—sue the NFL.

Trump Needed to Win Games Right Away

In 1983, Donald Trump had just opened Trump Tower, a 58-story tower in New York City with his name emblazoned in big gold letters above the entrance. And he was selling Trump Towers condos at a great clip and receiving loads of positive publicity for its design and as *the* luxury place to live in Manhattan. Trump Tower was a "win" right away.

Next up—he bought the Generals in late 1983 and immediately went on a spending spree with a series of high-profile negotiations for current NFL players and coaches.[31] This generated a ton of media coverage for Trump and the USFL, as the two-year-old league was about to start its second season. (It played in the spring so as not to compete with the NFL.)

As Trump said about the publicity, *"I hire a general manager to help run a billion-dollar business and there's a squib in the papers. I hire a coach for a football team and there are sixty to seventy reporters calling to interview me."*[32]

His ownership also led to his first national TV interviews. Win #1—publicity for the Trump brand. Trump also felt this publicity was good for the USFL. Some owners disagreed.

The USFL's economic plan had been to "keep salaries low, minimize superstar acquisitions, and slowly build the league."[33] Trump's public spending spree caused tensions with other USFL owners.

> Myles Tannenbaum, one of the league's founders and owner of the Philadelphia Stars, confronted Donald about the spending spree in mid-December. *"I'm in the media capital of this country,"* Donald replied. *"When you're in New York, you have to win."*
>
> *"Donald, in Philadelphia you have to win, too,"* Tannenbaum retorted. *"You have to win everyplace."*
>
> *"I need to win more,"* Trump insisted.[34]

Another USFL owner Ted Taube wrote at the time, "It may be in Don Trump's best interests to pursue [this] strategy…. But Don's best strategy for the Generals could be [financially] devastating for the USFL as a whole."[35]

But Trump didn't much care about this cost, as it would be borne by the other owners when *their* players' salaries skyrocketed. We know this as Trump shortly thereafter signed All-Pro New York Giants' linebacker Lawrence Taylor, the NFL's top defensive player.

Trump signed Taylor even though the USFL's Philadelphia Stars had the *exclusive* right to sign Taylor under USFL rules. Ironically, the Giants still had the right to keep Taylor, and they promptly gave him a big raise and paid off Trump (who made a quick profit and a lot of publicity).[36] Trump wins. USFL and the other owners lose.

Of course, some owners supported Trump and viewed his publicity as a net plus for the league.

Another example of Trump wanting only to win and not caring about the rules occurred when he signed Heisman Trophy–winning quarterback Doug Flutie to a five-year deal worth up to $7 million. *But the USFL had a $2 million salary cap.*[37] Trump didn't care. Trump "won" again.

Interestingly, Trump later agreed he "overspent" on Flutie when he didn't perform well.[38]

Trump Needed the USFL to Compete with the NFL in the Fall

Trump's aggressive push to get into the NFL also reflected his win–lose mindset.

Trump wanted to own an NFL franchise and build a New York stadium to house it. This could happen if he either a) bought an NFL team (from 1981 to 1983 he tried buying the Baltimore Colts, but they couldn't agree on the price, and he also considered buying the Dallas Cowboys in 1983.) or b) bought a USFL team and merged with the NFL.[39]

But the NFL wasn't interested in 1984 in merging with the brand-new league. What did Trump do? He convinced his fellow USFL owners to change their go-slow-and-grow strategy by promising either:

- A network TV contract for a fall season despite the USFL being in the midst of a multi-year $14 million annual ABC contract for the next few *spring* seasons. The idea? Head-to-head competition with the NFL in the fall would convince it to merge with the USFL. Or;
- A lawsuit against the NFL for antitrust violations for *preventing* a fall USFL schedule and get a massive judgment forcing a merger.

Trump's language at the January 1984 USFL owners' meeting, according to the owners' meeting notes, reflects Trump's win–lose mindset:

> I guarantee you folks in this room that I will produce CBS and I will produce NBC and that I will produce ABC, guaranteed, and for a hell of a lot more money than the horseshit you're getting right now…. I don't want to be a loser. I've never been a loser before, and if we're losers in this, fellows, I tell you what, it's going to haunt us…. Every time there's an article written about you, it's going to be that you owned this goddamn team which failed… and I'm not going to be a failure.[40]

Trump convinced the owners in August 1984 to switch, starting fall of 1986. Unfortunately for the owners, though, it took place after an aggressive media campaign highlighted a nasty personal war between Trump on one side and USFL Commissioner Chet Simmons and Tampa Bay Bandits owner John Bassett on the other.

A Bassett letter to Trump illustrates how Trump interacted with the other owners—his seeming partners with common interests. Bassett, who originally liked Trump, opposed Trump's strategy but shared interests with him in an ultimate merger with the NFL.

> Dear Donald:… I have listened with astonishment at your personal abuse of the commissioner and various of your partners if they did not happen to espouse one of your causes or agree with one of your arguments…. You are bigger, younger and stronger than I, which means I'll have no regrets whatsoever punching you right in the mouth the next time an instance occurs where you personally scorn me, or anyone else, who does not happen to salute and dance to your tune.[41]

Trump's attitude was win–lose, even with his partners.

The owners interestingly voted to move to a fall schedule despite having commissioned an independent study from McKinsey consulting which found Trump's strategy assumed events it deemed highly unlikely, including *any* new TV contract for the fall of 1986. This was because:

- NBC said it had no interest in televising the USFL in the fall;
- CBS said it wouldn't be interested for the fall of 1986, but might for 1987 if the USFL's ratings improved; and
- ABC's contract with the USFL would be breached if the USFL moved to the fall of 1986.

McKinsey's recommendation? Cut costs, stay in the spring for 1986, launch an ad campaign to drive up attendance and revenue, and consider moving to the fall of 1987 when ABC and CBS might be interested.[42]

What happened after the owners decided to move to the fall of 1986?

ABC, the only network possibly interested for the fall of 1986, was upset the USFL intended to breach its spring 1986 contract. It thus refused to sign a deal to broadcast any fall 1986 USFL games. CBS and NBC also confirmed their disinterest in televising the USFL's fall 1986 games.

"Winning" the battle to go to a fall 1986 season also meant that Trump and the USFL would lose their contractually solid deal with ABC to broadcast USFL spring games in 1986.

No television contract for the fall of 1986 basically spelled the end of the USFL, except for a possible antitrust lawsuit against the NFL.[43]

"Wait," you might say. "It's obvious the USFL should have just followed McKinsey's recommendations and waited to go to a fall 1987 season. Why did these owners vote for Trump's move for 1986?"

Three reasons. *First*, the owners were desperate financially. Many might not have even made it to a fall 1987 season. Even Ted Taube, who penned that early letter indicating "Don's best strategy for the Generals could be devastating for the USFL as a whole," came around, noting that the USFL had "no other financially viable alternative."

Second, Trump negotiates and communicates in clear and definitive language with an air of invincibility. He "guaranteed" the TV contracts. Clarity and certainty can be persuasive and convincing. The owners wanted to believe him too.

And *third*, Trump threatened that if the USFL did not move to the fall, it might find itself playing without him. Since Trump was then practically the face of the USFL, this might spell its doom sooner rather than later.

Trump tactically and smartly negotiated with the other owners to get them to vote for the move, despite their internal strife. All along he demonstrated his win–lose mindset.

One final element of this "move to the fall" effort illustrates Trump's mindset. Trump in March 1984 secretly met with long-time NFL head Pete Rozelle to discuss the NFL–USFL relationship.[44]

We know about this negotiation as it became a major element of the USFL's antitrust lawsuit against the NFL. And Rozelle and Trump testified about it under oath.

Rozelle also a) wrote a memo to his file immediately after describing what occurred, and b) discussed it later with the NFL's finance chairman. This foreshadows former FBI Director James Comey's testimony about his Trump meetings in 2016 and 2017, where he also wrote file memos about his meetings and discussed them with his FBI colleagues.

Trump wrote no such memo nor discussed this meeting with any colleagues. (According to his testimony he said, "I would have considered notes to be a very unnatural thing to do. People don't go around making notes of conversations in my opinion.")

What happened at the Trump–Rozelle meeting that illustrates Trump's win–lose mindset? We have conflicting versions of it.

According to *Trump's* testimony:

- Rozelle promised him an NFL team if he would help keep the USFL in the spring and stop an antitrust lawsuit;

- Trump responded there is "no way I am going to sell out [my fellow USFL owners]" and would only consider an NFL team as part of a merger with "four or five or six teams" coming in from the USFL (18 USFL teams then existed); and

- Rozelle told him he would explore the possibility of at most one or two teams and get back with Trump.

According to *Rozelle's* testimony:

- Trump started the meeting by threatening an antitrust lawsuit, but noting he didn't want to sue;

- Trump said he really just wanted an NFL expansion team for himself in New York;

- Trump said if the NFL did not agree right away to his demands, he would sue and would become too committed to the USFL to walk away and cut a separate deal;

- Trump offered to identify two or three other USFL owners Rozelle might reward with franchises; and,

- Rozelle would get back with Trump on the possibility of adding one or two more teams later.[45]

Regardless of who you believe, two things are clear: *One*, Trump offered to throw at least 11 of his fellow USFL owners under the bus in exchange for an NFL team in New York. And *two*, Rozelle would consider adding one or two teams—including one for Trump—and get back to him.

Both support the following conclusion: Either Trump wins and 11 or more USFL owners lose, or no one wins.

Of course, Trump might respond that those other USFL owners could not have financially qualified for NFL teams anyway. So, he wasn't "selling them out," right?

Wrong. The purpose of the meeting, which took place at Trump's request and *unbeknownst to the other USFL owners*, revolved around an NFL franchise for Trump.

Had Trump cared about other USFL owners getting NFL franchises, he would have informed at least some of them of his Rozelle meeting. By keeping the meeting secret, *even from his "partners,"* he maintained his ability to accept an NFL franchise in the future without publicly stabbing his fellow USFL owners in the back.

But Rozelle later rejected any deal. So, it was on to litigation—another negotiation strategy that reflects Trump's zero-sum win–lose mindset.

Trump's Last Shot for an NFL Team—Sue!

Litigation represents the ultimate win–lose approach to satisfying parties' interests. Why? The final judge or jury in litigation almost always has only one choice at the end of the trial: One side wins and one side loses. Any other solution to the dispute, a negotiated settlement, must be agreed upon by the parties.

Trump understands this. In fact, his love of litigation borders on the legendary. It's public record that Trump has been a party in over 4,000 litigation matters prior to becoming President.[46] He has sued over 1,900 times. Since he effectively took control of the Trump development business in his late 20s, this comes to either suing or being sued an average of over 90 times per year.

This time he and the USFL sued the NFL for antitrust violations, alleging the NFL used its monopoly power to prevent the networks from televising USFL games starting in the fall of 1986. This destroyed the USFL, they alleged.

They sought hundreds of millions of dollars in damages, hoping a favorable verdict would force a merger.

Two elements here reflected Trump's win–lose attitude. Each furthered his goal to build his brand and generate maximum publicity for Donald Trump.

Trump Chose an Attack-Dog Win-at-All-Costs Litigator

Trump pulled a fast one on his fellow USFL owners by announcing the lawsuit at a press conference with no invited USFL representative and selecting his long-time lawyer Roy Cohn to litigate it.

Other than Trump's father, Roy Cohn more than anyone contributed to Donald Trump's business and personal success.

A bit of history: Roy Cohn came to fame as U.S. Sen. Joseph McCarthy's right-hand man in the 1950s. McCarthy made headlines then by leading a public and political witch hunt to ferret out alleged Communist Party spies and subversives who had supposedly infiltrated all levels of the U.S. government and society.[47]

"McCarthyism" became one of our country's most embarrassing historical episodes. Sen. McCarthy was ultimately censured by the Senate, and Cohn forced to resign as McCarthy's Chief Counsel of the Senate's Permanent Subcommittee on Investigations.

Cohn would later say he "had never worked for a better man or a better cause."[48]

Cohn subsequently returned to practice law in New York City and became one of its most influential men, wielding enormous political influence and representing clients ranging from the Catholic archdiocese to the mob.

He was no saint either. Cohn, according to *Trump Revealed*, "in the two decades following the McCarthy hearings…was indicted on charges ranging from obstruction of justice to bribery to extortion, but he always seemed to get off. To fight his legal battles, [he] honed a set of hard-boiled tactics and a rhetorical style that would serve him far beyond the courtroom."[49]

Trump biographer Barrett called Cohn "a walking advertisement for every form of graft, the best-known fixer in New York."[50]

The point here is not to impugn Trump's character by associating him with Cohn. Instead, it is to illustrate that Trump—who had first hired Cohn in 1973 to defend him in a U.S. Justice Department lawsuit alleging racial discrimination in Trump's apartment buildings—hired an extremely aggressive win–lose mad-dog litigator.

Cohn's litigation and approach to life can be summarized as "go to hell" and "when attacked, counterattack with overwhelming force."[51]

"Don't Mess with Roy Cohn," a 1978 *Esquire* magazine profile of Cohn written with his cooperation stated that he fought every case as if it were a war and, "Prospective clients who want to kill their husband, torture a business partner, break the government's legs, hire Roy Cohn….He is a legal executioner—the toughest, meanest, loyalest, vilest, and one of the most brilliant lawyers in America."[52]

Trump was quoted in *Esquire* saying, *"when people know that Roy is involved, they'd rather not get involved in the lawsuits and everything else that's involved."*[53]

Trump later hired another lawyer of the same ilk to try the NFL case when Cohn got sick, Harvey Myerson. Myerson would later spend 70 months in prison for tax evasion and other crimes in what prosecutors labeled "a one-man crime wave."[54]

Significant benefits can attach to a highly aggressive adversarial litigation approach. A win–win mindset and/or result is not one of them. It's win–lose with litigators like this.

The Jury and Appellate Court's Decisions

Trump and the USFL won the case and that final battle. And they got a ton of publicity. But they lost the war.

What happened? The jury concluded the NFL inappropriately used its power to prevent the USFL from competing with it. But they only awarded the USFL $1.00 in damages. Here's what happened in the six-person jury room, according to juror interviews:

– Two jurors felt the NFL had harmed the USFL and deserved hundreds of millions of dollars;

– Two jurors felt the USFL's lawsuit was just a desperate effort to stay alive; and

– Two jurors initially were undecided, one of whom was Patricia Sibilia—who felt that the NFL acted like a monopoly and engaged in predatory action but that the USFL had overspent and was partially responsible for its own demise, violating their TV contract by moving to the fall season.

Regarding Trump, Sibilia, who brokered the ultimate compromise, "decided she didn't like Trump, whom she'd barely heard of before the trial. *'He was extremely arrogant and I thought that he was obviously playing the game,'* Sibilia recalled. *'He wanted an NFL franchise.... The USFL was a cheap way in.'*"[55]

The U.S. Second Court of Appeals upheld this verdict, noting "what the USFL seeks is essentially a judicial restructuring of major league professional football to allow it to" merge with the NFL. The decision stated, in a passage relevant to the win–lose litigation strategy pursued by Trump and the USFL:

> The jury in the present case obviously found that patient development of a loyal following among fans and an adherence to an original plan that offered long-run gains were lacking....
> The jury found that the failure of the USFL was not the result of the NFL's television contracts but of its own decision to seek entry into the NFL on the cheap.[56]

Donald Trump described his USFL experience this way,

> I bought a losing team in a losing league on a long shot. It almost worked, through our antitrust lawsuit, but when it didn't, I had no fallback. The point is that you can't be too greedy. If you go for a home run on every pitch, you're also going to strike out a lot.... If there was a single key miscalculation I made with the USFL, it was evaluating the strength of my fellow owners. In any partnership, you're only as strong as your weakest link.[57]

Another win–lose mindset hallmark: If you win, take credit; if you lose, blame your partners.

Two final notes on Trump's win–lose mindset. *One*, George Ross, his long-time lawyer, would disagree with the conclusions here. Ross notes that "the recurring theme in Trump-style negotiation is looking for ways to satisfy both sides, to structure a deal so that everyone feels that he or she comes out a winner."[58]

In fact, Ross concludes his book by stating: "Just remember this most important element of Trump-style negotiation: You can only achieve mutual satisfaction and complete the biggest and best deals when you build a relationship of trust and rapport with those with whom you become involved."[59]

Ross' statement regarding mutual satisfaction is true. Does Trump believe this? Not according to the evidence. Does Ross himself really believe Trump brings a win–win mindset to negotiations? The example he cites in his book after this statement does not even involve Trump.

Plus, the USFL negotiation and Trump's many negotiations detailed later illustrate his dominant negotiation mindset: win–lose.

It's also important to examine what constitutes a "win" here in Trump's eyes. If Trump measures wins financially, he admittedly lost $22 million here.[60]

A better *financial* deal would have been the Cowboys. He could have bought the NFL Cowboys in 1984 for $85 million. (It sold then for $85 million.) Its owners then turned around and sold it to its current owner in 1989 for $170 million. *Forbes* in 2017 declared the Cowboys the most valuable sports franchise in the world at $4.8 billion.[61]

But Trump didn't think in purely financial terms. He said in January 1984, shortly after buying the Generals, *"I feel sorry for the poor guy who is going to buy the Dallas Cowboys. It's a no-win situation for him, because if he wins, well, so what, they've won through the years, and if he loses…he'll be known to the world as a loser."* [62]

Trump became "known to the world" and gained his first national exposure for his name and brand during this time. He also gained a reputation as the wealthy New York developer who took on the uber-powerful NFL. That's a win for him.

On the other hand, he didn't end up owning an NFL team.

Bottom line—Trump views negotiations and life with a win–lose, zero-sum mindset.

As John "Jack" O'Donnell, President of the Trump Plaza Hotel & Casino in the late 1980s recalled after working closely with Trump in Atlantic City, *"Trump had a simple mindset, winners versus losers, and…his chief motivation was winning, even when he didn't need the money."* [63]

And Trump himself stated: *"Man is the most vicious of all animals, and life is a series of battles ending in victory or defeat. You can't let people make a sucker out of you."* [64]

LESSONS LEARNED	
Trump's Strategies and Tactics	Gut-level decisions drove Trump's negotiations, not strategic planning.
	A strictly win–lose mindset impacted all Trump's negotiations.
Lessons Learned	Strategic preparation based on the experts' proven research—not guts and instincts—should drive our negotiations.
	Detailed preparation and homework behind-the-table should involve two to nine times *more* time than at-the-table negotiating.
	Preparation on the *process* of negotiation—not just learning the facts—is critical to success.

CHAPTER 2

SETTING THE BAR HIGH:
SUPER AGGRESSIVE EXPECTATIONS

When asked about his goals in a television interview, Trump once said *"'Goals?'* he repeated. *'You keep winning and you win and you win, and you win.'"*[65]

He also said, *"to get momentum, you must first focus on a specific goal"* and *"remember, there's no such thing as an unrealistic goal—just unrealistic time frames."*[66]

What has Trump actually *done* regarding goal-setting? He reaches for the sky. And he doesn't let naysayers weigh in. He goes for it, often against conventional wisdom and so-called experts.

And he should set aggressive goals. To start, though, some strategic context. Setting goals lives within my First Golden Rule: Information Is Power—So Get It! The first Golden Rule is essential to success in any negotiation and is well-supported by the research.

RESEARCH: It's critical to ask questions and get as much relevant information as you can throughout the negotiation process. You need sufficient information to set aggressive, realistic goals and to evaluate the other side's goals.[67]

This was essential to Trump's success, especially early on. His father, Fred, built a highly successful residential real-estate company with thousands of apartments and projects in several states. But he shied away from Manhattan.

Based in Queens, Fred Trump made millions building standard housing for middle-class families. And when he expanded beyond New York, he bought inexpensive tracts of land from desperate sellers in California, Nevada, Ohio, and Virginia.[68]

Donald Trump wanted more. A lot more. And he set his sights on Manhattan.

As Ned Eichler, one of his early negotiation counterparts recalled, Trump, in a walk around New York City's Central Park during a break in their negotiations, viewed the park as *"merely the lawn in front of his future properties."*[69]

During that walk, Trump pointed to the buildings on Fifth Ave and Central Park South and said, *"I'll be bigger than all of them. I'll be bigger than Helmsley [a major New York developer] in five years."*[70]

Did he get there? Yes and no. It depends on when you look at him. Three Trump eras took place in terms of his goal-setting:

1) "Over-the-top" best describes Trump in the '70s and early '80s.

2) But then he got caught up in a deal-making frenzy in the mid-1980s and took a goal-setting U-turn.

3) Trump regained his signature aggressiveness again in 1990, though, when faced with financial ruin.

How aggressive should he have set his goals the entire time? Let's evaluate his goal-setting in each "Trump era." Then we'll evaluate his goals versus the experts' proven research.

Trump's Goal-setting in New York City in the '70s and Early '80s

Three examples illustrate Trump's extremely aggressive goal-setting in the '70s and early '80s.

A Fred Trump Convention Center

One of Donald Trump's first Manhattan deals involved purchasing an option to a 34th Street property from the bankrupt Penn Central railways. After he bought the option, he hoped to build "a city-funded convention center and twenty thousand apartments, in one fell swoop creating an empire that would rival his father's."[71]

But New York City in 1978 decided to build its own convention center on that site. And it needed Trump's option. Here's how Peter Solomon, the city's negotiator, described Trump's effort to get the city to name it the Fred C. Trump Convention Center.

Trump told us he was entitled to a $4.4 million commission on the sale according to his contract with Penn Central. But he told us he'd forgo his fee if we would name the convention center after his father…. After about a month of knocking the idea around, someone finally read the terms of the original Penn Central contract with Trump. He wasn't entitled to anywhere near the money he was claiming. Based on the sales price we had negotiated, his fee was only about $500,000.

But what really got me was his bravado. I think it was fantastic. It was unbelievable. He almost got us to name the convention center after his father in return for something he never really had to give away. [Emphasis added.][72]

Trump exhibited impressive "bravado" in even shooting for this goal. The question of his truthfulness, of course, also arose here.

The Commodore Hotel Redevelopment

Trump's aggressive goal-setting also manifested itself in his first big negotiated deal—the redevelopment of the Commodore Hotel across from New York City's Grand Central Station. In that deal, Trump requested a 99-year tax abatement from the city as an economic incentive to redevelop a run-down hotel in a depressed area.

The tax benefit he requested, if approved, would amount to around $400 million over forty years.[73] It would also be unprecedented—the first ever given to a commercial property in New York.

Richard Ravitch, a state official involved, described the following negotiation session with Trump. After offering Trump an option that would allow Trump to line up sufficient financing to redevelop the hotel (the alleged rationale for the tax abatement), he said Trump wouldn't even consider it.

Ravitch said he told Trump *"it would not be fair to deprive the city of the real estate taxes if the hotel was successful, but that at least would enable you to get the mortgage."*

"That's not good enough; I don't want to pay any taxes," Trump replied, according to Ravitch.[74]

That's aggressive goal-setting.

Michael Bailkin, a key city official in those negotiations, said Trump "had the energy and vision and perhaps was hungry enough and maybe a little bit crazy enough to try to do things that were in the best interest of the city, whereas more traditional developers would never have taken on a task like this."[75]

Trump got his unprecedented tax break. How? According to *TrumpNation*, a well-researched biography by long-time investigative journalist Timothy L. O'Brien (previously an editor and writer for *The Wall Street Journal* and *The New York Times*), Trump "benefited from family connections, his own determination, an economically struggling city anxious to get new construction underway, and banks ready to ramp up real estate lending again."[76]

Trump envisioned his goal and charged ahead to accomplish it.

Trump Tower

Trump also set an extremely aggressive goal in his first negotiation move to build his signature 58-story tower on Fifth Avenue. This negotiation involved his purchase of an option to buy the lease on the property.

He achieved this "with a location that was so rich everyone else assumed it could not be bought."[77]

Learning that the department store that owned a 29-year lease on the site had recently gone bankrupt, Trump:

— Recognized the opportunity;

— Immediately flew down to Nashville to buy the option from the bankruptcy trustee; and

— Bought it for $25 million *with no money down*.[78]

An extraordinarily aggressive goal. So aggressive, in fact, several other builders offered the trustee a better price for it after they learned of Trump's deal.[79] But Trump's deal was done.

And it turned out extremely well. Trump Tower was described as "an inspired, balanced business deal" in *TrumpNation*.[80] Trump at his best in negotiations.

Trump's Goal-setting Took a U-turn in the Late 1980s

Donald Trump's blockbuster autobiography *The Art of the Deal* came out in 1987. And it coincided with the stock market crash and an unparalleled Trump buying binge of widely varying high-profile assets.

It also coincided with a new Trump attitude toward goal-setting and negotiations—buy at almost any cost. As *TrumpNation* described it,

For Donald, the post-Trump Tower years were a heady rush into celebrity and entrepreneurial candyland as he snared one business bauble after another, sometimes in industries in which he knew next to nothing. While the vision he had shown in building Trump Tower remained, the discipline he had summoned to get the skyscraper built evaporated. Emboldened by easy money and a laudatory press, Donald went on a massive and ill-considered shopping spree.[81]

Two major purchases reflect his different goal-setting and negotiation approach: *The Plaza Hotel Purchase* and *The Eastern Air Shuttle Purchase*.

The Plaza Hotel Purchase

New York City's Plaza Hotel was "one of Manhattan's truly storied properties, steeped in wealth, glamour, power, and celebrity, and Donald snapped up the hotel in 1988 for $407.5 million with $425 million in borrowed funds that he could ill afford."[82]

How do we know Trump didn't aggressively set a goal and negotiate a great deal?

First, the sellers flipped the hotel to Trump just four months after buying it—garnering at least a $50 million profit. And this occurred just months after the stock market crashed, when other real-estate developers were taking very conservative approaches to deals.[83]

Second, Donald Trump himself indicated he lost sight of a financial goal here, to say nothing of an aggressive goal. *"This isn't just a building; it's the ultimate work of art. I was in love with it...I tore myself up to get the Plaza.... The spirit of the city is in this hotel. How can you possibly put a price on that?... [It is] the ultimate trophy,"* Trump said.[84]

And he wrote in *Surviving at the Top*, "The buying and selling of world-class hotels is an emotional business. When a place like the Plaza is on the block, the toughest negotiators become soft, and logic often gets tossed out the window."[85]

He even took out a full-page ad in *New York* magazine and wrote, "I can never justify the price I paid, no matter how successful the Plaza becomes."[86]

Third, Trump paid more for the Plaza Hotel than anyone had *ever* paid for a hotel, amounting to $500,000 *per room*. He also took on $425 million in debt, $125 million more than the previous owners had—and those previous owners had been "concerned that it didn't generate enough cash to support [its] $300 million mortgage."[87]

To even pay the interest on this debt, Trump would need to substantially increase the hotel's cash flow—a difficult effort given the economy and hotel market. In 1989, its first full year of operation after its renovations, it would need to generate almost *three* times its 1988 cash flow *just to cover the debt*.[88] This would have required Trump to fully book its 814 rooms for the year at a $500-per-night room rate, *more than twice its previous rates*.[89]

Trump's purchase price was also tens of millions of dollars *more* than the next highest bidder, according to *Trump Revealed*.[90] While it's unclear if Trump knew this, his overpayment reflects a poor deal for Trump.

Fourth, those close to him described him at this time as unfocused—the opposite of someone pursuing specific, aggressive negotiation goals.

Barbara Res, a longtime Trump employee who oversaw Trump's renovation of the Plaza, said *"[Trump] was in acquisition fever and he wasn't himself. It was very hard to work with him at this time because he didn't focus and was always changing his mind."*[91]

Finally, it's hard to even evaluate the aggressiveness of a goal without due diligence. As part of the negotiations, Trump agreed to purchase the hotel "as is" to allegedly outbid another purchaser. Trump's purchase thus was not even contingent on the physical condition of the hotel. Trump's later renovations, unsurprisingly, were demanding.[92]

None of these elements reflect the strategy of an aggressive goal-setter, much less Trump's '70s and early '80s aggressiveness.

The Eastern Air Shuttle Purchase

Trump signed a contract to purchase the Eastern Air Shuttle in October 1988 for $365 million. Eastern's bankruptcy judge approved the deal in May 1989.[93]

How aggressively did he set his goals here? Not very.

First, Eastern had internally analyzed its value a year prior to Trump's purchase and assessed it at $300 million. An independent appraisal subsequent to his purchase assessed its value as between $150 million and $300 million, depending on market conditions.[94]

Second, Trump noted—like in the Plaza deal—that he really wasn't financially goal-driven here, despite it being a business deal. He said, *"I like buying Mona Lisas; the Shuttle is the finest asset in the airline industry, the best.... I like collecting works of art. This is a work of art."*[95]

Third, he stuck with his purchase price of $365 million negotiated in October 1988 despite Eastern's plummeting profits between his signing and closing on the transaction. During this time, Eastern's share of the shuttle market declined from 56 percent to 17 percent after a March labor strike. Its rival Pan Am was killing it in the market. Pan Am had bought its shuttle business three years earlier for $76 million.[96]

And while Trump did use the strike to renegotiate the deal, he only got four old planes out of his renegotiation, hardly the mark of an aggressive goal-setter given the precipitous drop in Eastern's market share.[97]

Finally, Eastern was bleeding cash partially due to its old fleet of 21 Boeing 727s. In his first year of operation, Trump spent $85 million in capital and operating costs. And Trump knew this would largely be the case, as he had predicted in bankruptcy court that he would need to spend $50 million to upgrade the aging fleet.[98]

This brought his effective purchase price to well over $400 million, which is not an aggressive goal.

Trump's Goal-Setting in his Financial Restructuring in the 1990s

Donald Trump's aggressive goal setting, however, returned in the early 1990s and appeared to continue later. Examples abound, including his off-the-cuff negotiation for 50 percent of *The Apprentice*.

His biggest negotiation in this time period occurred in early 1990, when Trump and his empire faced ruin. Independent evaluator Kenneth Leventhal & Co., hired by banks to which Trump collectively **owed** $3.2 billion (of which Trump had personally guaranteed $833.5 million), found Trump was then worth a **negative $295 million**.[99]

Trump himself commented that, *"When I was in trouble in the early '90s, I went around and—you know, a lot of people couldn't believe this because they think I have an ego—I went around and openly told people I was worth minus $900 million."*[100]

Despite being financially underwater, and perhaps because of it, Trump's aggressiveness returned. In fact, he negotiated a deal that gave him **$450,000 a month** on which to live after protracted negotiations with the banks.[101]

This was so large *The New York Times* at the time quoted a billionaire saying about this allowance, *"I would have no idea how to spend $450,000 a month. It's just phenomenal."*[102]

Trump said this negotiation *"…was the greatest deal I ever made."*[103]

What does the research say about setting aggressive goals?

Do it. As I write in *Gain the Edge!*:

Set Aggressive and Specific Goals—Don't Just "Do the Best You Can"

"I believe in always having goals and always setting them high," said Wal-Mart founder Sam Walton. Be ambitious. Adopt aggressive goals. Remember that old saying: "You can't get what you don't ask for." Your goals will set the upper limit to what you can achieve. Set aggressive-enough goals to ensure you don't mentally concede anything before you have even begun. Answer the question: How much is enough? And answer it at the beginning, before you jump into the rest of the negotiation. A direct relationship exists between individuals' goals and what they achieve. The more you expect, the more you will get. The less you expect, the less you will get...

Tie Your Goals to Realistic Standards

However, a cautionary note. It's crucial to tie your goals to realistic standards. Don't be too aggressive. Instead, be realistic. If you constantly set your goals so high you never achieve them, you will become discouraged over the long term. This attitude will negatively affect your performance and you will start to set your goals too low. No one wants to continually "fail." Likewise, if you consistently set your goals too low, you won't have sufficient motivation to achieve all you can.[104]

Does Donald Trump tie his goals to realistic standards? No. He consistently and aggressively set unrealistic goals. Unprecedented, in fact. But—and here's the rub—he has been pretty successful in achieving them, at least if we ignore his goal-setting hiatus in the mid- to late 1980s. He has *not* "become discouraged over the long term" due to unrealistic goals. And maybe they weren't so unrealistic after all.

In other words, he is one of those rare individuals in which repeated failure to achieve his long-term goals—even colossal failure like what happened to him in the early 1990s—did not appreciably impact his future goal setting.

Consider this: The overwhelming majority of his businesses and investments failed up until the early 1990s: Atlantic City casinos, the Trump Shuttle, New York City's Plaza Hotel, and the West Side Yards where he wanted to build the world's tallest building.

He and entities he controlled or was involved with went through six bankruptcies, with investors and others losing more than $1.5 billion due to his business decisions.[105]

He was even forced to take out a $10 million loan from his siblings in 1993 just to pay his monthly living and office expenses, according to *TrumpNation*.[106]

Bottom line: His businesses failed and left him and the banks that financed him holding the bag.

Yet he *still* exhibited supreme self-confidence and set aggressive goals. He was "remarkably resilient" and a person who had "gumption in spades."[107]

Trump agrees that he doesn't set reasonable goals, too. In *Trump: Think Like a Billionaire*, he approvingly writes, "In *The Natural History of the Rich,* author Richard Conniff put it this way: 'Almost all successful alpha personalities display a single-minded determination to impose their vision on the world, **an irrational belief in unreasonable goals, bordering at times on lunacy**.'" [Emphasis added.][108]

Trump has taken that irrational belief and translated it into a passionate expectation of success in all his negotiations. That's not irrational. That's effective. As he has said,

> "Passion is absolutely necessary to achieve any kind of long-lasting success. I know this from experience. If you don't have passion, everything you do will ultimately fizzle out or, at best, be mediocre."[109] And "nothing great in the world has been accomplished without passion."[110]

Donald Trump's confidence and attitude toward life—and negotiations—can be summed up by the only person other than his father he called a mentor—Rev. Norman Vincent Peale of New York's Marble Collegiate Church.

Author of the 1952 bestseller *The Power of Positive Thinking*, a bible of the self-help industry, Peale preached that a positive attitude and mindset will lead to tremendous success.[111]

Trump attended Peale's sermons with his family in the 1950s and wholeheartedly internalized Peale's message. In fact, "Trump credited Peale with teaching him to win by thinking only of the best outcomes."[112]

And Trump told a *New York Times* reporter, discussing Peale and his general attitude in 1983, "The mind can overcome any obstacle. I never think of the negative."[113]

Peale, who also had a radio show and newspaper column with millions of followers and later married Trump to his first wife, Ivana, reciprocated this admiration. In 1983, he said Trump was "kindly and courteous in certain business negotiations and has a profound streak of honest humility."[114]

Trump's can-do positive mindset has been to "accentuate the positive, eliminate the negative, latch on to the affirmative, and never mess with Mr. In-Between," according to *TrumpNation*.[115]

Trump openly touts this, writing, "Even if you haven't encountered great success yet, there is no reason you can't bluff a little and act like you have. Confidence is a magnet in the best sense of the word. It will draw people to you and make your daily life…and theirs…a lot more pleasant."[116]

How has Trump's attitude manifested itself in his negotiations?

Confidence Is Contagious

Donald Trump sells an attitude, a belief, and a persona. It underlies his aggressive goal-setting and everything he does.

It also represents a fundamental factor of his negotiation success, especially early on with the Commodore Hotel redevelopment and the building of Trump Tower. Recall, Trump was in his late 20s when he negotiated an unprecedented 99-year tax abatement for the Commodore Hotel. Barbara Res, the construction manager for that project who worked for Trump for years, said Trump "had tremendous self-confidence, which is important."[117]

And he was only in his mid-30s when he built the 58-story Trump Tower on Fifth Avenue in New York City.

Of course, his detractors would suggest it's easier to exhibit confidence when you're backed up by a highly successful real estate father. And your negotiation counterparts will be more likely to accept your bona fides when you surround yourself with experienced lawyers like Roy Cohn and George Ross and real-estate experts and contractors (and Trump wisely did).

Regardless, Trump would not have achieved such early financial and brand success without a highly confident attitude. Trump's confidence was contagious in his negotiations.

Trump Tower serves as the ultimate testament to this. How?

One, he built Trump Tower on spec, meaning he got the land, lined up the financing, built the building, and simultaneously had to sell commercial and residential space in a 58-story tower in one of the most competitive commercial and residential real-estate markets in the world.

This could easily have failed. And Trump knew it. In fact, other residential luxury buildings available at the time didn't achieve this same success.

Only a supremely confident individual would have even embarked on such an ambitious effort. Trump did. And he reaped the rewards.

Two, early successes like the Commodore Hotel and Trump Tower led to more deals and increased confidence. Success bred success. And confidence bred more confidence.

Finally, Trump Tower was his first named project. He branded it to himself. This building—and all it would represent, good and bad—would immediately reflect on Donald Trump the person and businessman. You don't name something after yourself if you're not supremely confident it will reflect well on you.

Of course, Trump critics would say naming it Trump Tower simply reflected the size of his ego. But, whether you love or hate Trump, naming the building after himself started a successful and profitable luxury real-estate brand that now spans the globe.

RESEARCH: Confidence of success aligns with the experts' proven research. And it fully supports the positive and practical impact of Trump's extreme confidence.

What should you do? ***Expect to succeed.*** A passionate, positive attitude makes a difference. Those with an optimistic, can-do attitude toward achieving their desired result will be more likely to succeed than those with a lackadaisical approach. So, consciously transform your mindset about goals from theoretical targets to genuine expectations. Goals are one thing: expectations another. Expect it. Your mindset and attitude will lead to improved results.[118]

There is a downside, though. Self-confidence might come across as arrogance. And arrogant negotiators face significant challenges, especially those involving future relationships.

There's a fine line between confidence and arrogance. How can you exhibit confidence and not project arrogance? Support your attitude with facts, reason, data, and experts. Identify objective, independent standards that underlie your beliefs.

Does Trump come across as arrogant? You be the judge.

Trump Perseveres

Donald Trump also perseveres. A lot. In 2011 he told *Forbes,*

> I've seen people that are extremely brilliant, and they don't have the staying power. They don't have that never give up quality. I've always said that other than bad ideas, which is a reason for failure, the ability to never ever quit or give up is something that is very, very important for success as an entrepreneur.[119]

Trump's right. And it's equally important to negotiation success.

> **RESEARCH:** Perseverance leads to success. Persevere but don't be stubborn.

Star sports agent Leigh Steinberg in his book *Winning with Integrity* wrote that his negotiations with the Atlanta Falcons on behalf of quarterback Jeff George lasted from 1995 through 1996 and involved "what seemed like hundreds of hours of phone calls...and seven trips to Atlanta during that time."[120]

Over the course of these types of negotiations, Steinberg said he might "have to revisit an issue over and over and over again." Some might find this upsetting. A waste of time, right? Wrong. It's an important part of the process. As Steinberg noted, effective negotiation requires "tremendous patience and persistence, as well as physical stamina, resilience and perseverance.[121]

Trump spent years putting together the Commodore Hotel deal. This required perseverance.

As noted earlier, however, Trump lost this focus and stick-to-it-iveness in the mid-1980s. His deals then came fast and furious. Perhaps too easily. As *Trump Show* noted,

> [Trump in the 1980s was] buying up airlines, department store chains like Alexander's, and majestic hotels. The Hyatt [Commodore] had taken him six tortuous years, while the campaign to acquire the Plaza Hotel was over in six quick weeks. Even Donald complained about how "easy" it had become.[122]

His lost focus came with a big price: Almost all his assets in those deals later went to pay off his creditors when his businesses failed.

LESSONS LEARNED	
Trump's Strategies and Tactics	Extremely aggressive goal-setting marked many early Trump negotiations.
	Trump lost sight of his goals in the go-go '80s and got caught up in a deal-making frenzy.
	Aggressiveness returned when Trump faced financial ruin in 1990.
	Passionate expectations of success permeated Trump's negotiations.
	Trump's confidence led to good deals and effective branding.
	Hard work and perseverance characterized early Trump negotiations.
Lessons Learned	Getting sufficient information first should underlie goal-setting efforts.
	Specific, aggressive, and realistic goals should drive strategic decisions.
	Too much aggressiveness in goal-setting can lead to failure, lost confidence, and long-term harm.
	Tying goals to realistic standards increases the likelihood of achieving them.
	Passionate expectations and confidence lead to better negotiations.
	Hard work and perseverance underlie effective negotiations.

CHAPTER 3

THE KING OF HYPERBOLE: EXAGGERATE!

"[One] key to the way I promote is bravado. I play to people's fantasies. People may not always think big themselves, but they can still get very excited by those who do. That's why a little hyperbole never hurts. People want to believe something is the biggest and the greatest and the most spectacular.... I call it truthful hyperbole. It's an innocent form of exaggeration— and a very effective form of promotion."[123]

—Donald J. Trump, *The Art of the Deal*

Wayne Barrett, the investigative reporter who started reporting on Trump in 1978 and author of *Trump Show*, said Trump "was born with bullshit capabilities beyond what you and I could possibly imagine."[124]

One typical example—the sale of Trump Tower condos—illustrates Trump's tendency to use "truthful hyperbole" in his negotiations.

The Sale of Trump Tower Condos

Donald Trump's first major independent effort to sell to people's dreams came with Trump Tower. How did he do it? *"You sell them a fantasy,"* Trump said of his strategy to sell the 266 Trump Tower luxury condos that started at $500,000 for one-bedrooms in 1982 and went up to $5 million for a triplex.[125, 126]

One preliminary note about sales versus negotiation. The terms suggest separate processes. In reality, they represent two sides of the same coin. In my sales negotiation training programs, I suggest these be viewed as parallel processes that work in close conjunction with each other.

Of course, each has a slightly different emphasis and uses different terminology. But their differences pale in comparison to their similarities.

We will use the terms "sales" and "negotiation" interchangeably, as Trump seems to view them all as "deals."

So how did Trump sell Trump Tower? He wrote, "*From day one, we set out to sell Trump Tower not just as a beautiful building in a great location but as an event. We positioned ourselves as the only place for a certain kind of wealthy person to live—the hottest ticket in town.*"[127]

And he received great publicity. TV talk show host Regis Philbin recalled the following about Trump Tower:

> I remember coming back to the city in 1983 and the Grand Hyatt had replaced the old Commodore Hotel and Trump Tower had just opened. And I went over to Trump Tower and there was this doorman with this huge fur hat on and I thought: Who's putting out a doorman like this? Well, lo and behold, it was the Trumpster! And he had a waterfall inside...! And let me tell you, he saved Fifth Avenue. It was not in good shape then.[128]

TrumpNation author O'Brien described the process this way: "Donald and [Louise] Sunshine [a politically connected lobbyist who worked with Trump on many of his early projects] pitched Trump Tower as the cushy choice for a cushy era...and the media lionized the boy builder as the new face of Manhattan."[129]

But this didn't just happen with regular salesmanship. As described in *Trump Revealed*,

> Trump spread a rumor, printed in the New York papers, that Britain's royal family—Charles, Prince of Wales, and his wife, Princess Diana—were interested in spending $5 million to buy a twenty-one-room condominium, an entire floor of Trump Tower. They never showed. Trump didn't confess to creating that rumor, which the *Times* attributed to "one real estate official," but did say later that the rumor "certainly didn't hurt us."[130]

Trump Tower and its highly successful sales and marketing effort launched the Trump brand worldwide. As leading Manhattan real-estate broker and *Shark Tank* star Barbara Corcoran said, "*People might have laughed at the image that Trump gave, but the rest of the world fell for it. It was the first recognized superluxury brand in America known outside the United States. He bullshitted about it, but by bullshitting about it, he made it sell. I don't know of anyone who is a better marketer.*"[131]

The Trump Tower Marketing Effort—Puffery or Lies?

The only problematic element in the Trump Tower sales effort related to whether Trump intentionally told a journalist that Prince Charles and Princess Diana were considering a condo there. Everything else falls within the normal bounds of puffery, at the least.

But what does puffery even mean in sales negotiations? Is it just a pseudonym for lying? No.

The "Puffery vs. Lying" Standard

Black's Law Dictionary defines "puffery" as "the use of exaggeration or hyperbole in statements made to promote or sell a product or service. The inability to verify or measure the accuracy of the statements is what distinguishes puffery from false advertising."[132]

The standard is this:

- *Statements of opinion* like "the Trump Towers condos are the best in the world at the premier location in New York City" and "we use only the best and most reliable construction materials" are generally acceptable;

- *Statements about the future* like "you will love to live here" and "you will enjoy the unparalleled views of Manhattan from your living room" are generally acceptable;

- *Misstatements of material fact reasonably relied upon by your counterparts* like "we only use U.S.-made materials in our construction"—when you don't—are generally unacceptable; and

- *Vague, general, and ambiguous* misstatements decrease the likelihood someone will reasonably rely on them. Thus, while they may still be untrue and about an important fact (a misstatement of material fact), they will more likely be considered acceptable puffery.

What does this mean for the Trump Tower effort? Trump's "bullshitting" here falls squarely within the bounds of normal puffery—even his possible statement relating to Prince Charles' and Princess Diana's alleged interest.

First, there is no *proof* the statement is true or false.

Second, even if untrue, the newspapers could only attribute it to "one real-estate official" and not directly to Trump. Possible Trump Tower purchasers reading it thus would have less reason to rely on it being true. They don't even know who said it nor whether that person had any credibility or knowledge of the actual fact.

Third, even if false *and* attributed to Trump, it's an expression of the Prince's and Princess' *possible* interest. This is vague and ambiguous. The "real-estate official" did not say he showed them a condo or the royals visited Trump Tower. Nothing specific. For a purchaser to rely on this vague and general statement to buy would be unreasonable.

Puffery? Yes. Abnormal lie in sales and marketing? No.

Just because it's puffery, though, does not mean it *should* be done. Nor does it mean the research recommends it. In fact, Trump's exaggerations may have been counterproductive in many of his negotiations.

How can you evaluate this? Here's a framework to use for Trump's statements and others. Evaluate a) its morality, b) its legality, and c) its negotiation effectiveness.

Is the statement or conduct moral?

Morality is an intensely personal issue. And the purpose here is not to judge Donald Trump's morality. Instead, it is to assess his negotiation strategies and tactics. Where does Trump's "puffing" or "bullshitting" fall on the morality scale?

It depends on what you personally consider to be moral.

Let's change the Trump Tower Prince Charles/Princess Diana example to illustrate this. Assume Trump is meeting a successful business professional considering a condo, and the following conversation took place.

Trump:	This is the most incredible spot in the city to live. You will love it. Guaranteed. There's no place in the world like this location on Fifth Avenue. Best location. Best city. Best building. Best address. Just look at those amazing views from your bedroom. Imagine waking up and seeing that skyline. Your friends will be totally jealous!
Potential buyer:	I would love to live here. I'm just worried about the area. I know it's Fifth Avenue, but the department store here before went under. And what about the homeless and vagrants? Who else is going to live here? What's your security going to be?

Trump:	I'm glad you asked. In fact, just last week I took Princess Diana on a tour of a residence that takes up an entire floor of the building. She loved it! In fact, I expect to get an offer from her shortly. Wouldn't it be incredible to share an address with Prince Charles and Princess Diana? You might even run into them on the elevator. On security, absolute best that money can buy.
Potential buyer:	How do you think this will perform as an investment?
Trump:	Just think about the impact on your investment if Prince Charles and Princess Diana live here! I should be charging you twice as much. Here's the deal—it will be an unbelievable investment. We're almost completely sold out already. And that is without anyone knowing about Diana's tour last week.

Assume Trump made up the Princess Diana tour and related facts solely to entice other buyers to choose Trump Tower. An intentional misrepresentation. Was Trump wrong?

Some of you undoubtedly believe this is an easy call. He lied. It's morally wrong to lie. Therefore, he shouldn't have done it.

Others will disagree. "He was just puffing," you might say. "People puff all the time. Here the purchaser was a sophisticated business person who chose to believe Trump. No one forced him to believe this or to buy.

Others may not see this in black-and-white terms. Here they might say it's a borderline issue that rests on practical considerations. They might feel uncomfortable doing it, but they don't morally condemn it—especially if such puffing appears to be the norm in certain settings, and most everyone knows it occurs.

Here's the "moral" deal: We all have different moral compasses. And each person will judge others' behavior based on their own perception of right and wrong.

Should you engage in similar "puffery?" If it violates your moral code, don't do it. If this does not cross your moral line, consider whether it crosses the *legal* line.

Is the statement or conduct legal?

In most negotiations, the conduct's legality revolves around whether it's fraud. Most states consider conduct fraudulent if it includes: 1) a knowing 2) misrepresentation 3) of a material 4) fact 5) reasonably relied upon by your counterpart, that 6) causes damages.[133]

Here we have 1) a knowing 2) misrepresentation, but we may not have any other element of fraud. If you don't have all these elements, it's not fraud. Let's analyze the other elements.

Is the fact that the Prince and Princess toured another Trump Tower property "material?" Interesting? Yes. Material to an objective purchaser's decision? Probably not.

Is it a "fact?" Yes. But can a sophisticated business professional reasonably rely on it to make a decision? Probably not. And if reasonably relied upon, would it cause damage? Possibly, if they bought the condo at a higher price due to this misstatement. But perhaps not.

Too many contingencies here. Fraud? Probably not.

What about the earlier Trump statements extolling the "incredible spot to live" and guaranteeing they will "love it" and it's the "best address" and saying their "friends will be jealous?" Opinion and not fact. And statements about the future. Not fraud.

Might other legal theories apply? Perhaps. Different states regulate similar conduct differently. And different states also have slightly different standards for fraud. If in doubt, check with a lawyer.

Does the statement or conduct increase negotiation effectiveness?

Finally, if you consider it moral and no legal problem exists, evaluate its effectiveness.

Does Trump's puffery work, assuming he was that "real-estate official" who spread the rumor of the royals' alleged interest?

Trump stated, "It certainly didn't hurt us." Short-term, he's almost certainly right. Long-term might be a different story.

> **RESEARCH:** A reputation as a "bullshitter" versus a "straight shooter" in your negotiations—characterized as puffery or not—will be highly problematic in many negotiation environments.

Personally, I have a moral problem with stating an untrue fact like this. And while it's probably legal, it's sleazy. Effective? Not worth the possible short-term benefit. I want a reputation as a straight shooter.

LESSONS LEARNED	
Trump's Strategies and Tactics	Trump consistently used over-the-top exaggerations in many negotiations, with few restrictions.
	Trump considered "truthful hyperbole" in many negotiation environments to be morally and legally acceptable and effective.
Lessons Learned	Too much exaggeration is counterproductive.
	Consistently engaging in unacceptable puffery will negatively impact your reputation and effectiveness.
	"Truthful hyperbole" may constitute fraud or cross other legal lines.
	A "straight-shooter" reputation will lead to greater long-term effectiveness than the opposite.

CHAPTER 4

TARGETING TRUE MOTIVATIONS: USING CARROTS TO CLOSE DEALS

"It felt good seeing my name in print [when the newspaper headline "Trump Wins Game for NYMA" appeared regarding his high school baseball game]. How many people are in print? Nobody's in print. It was the first time I was ever in the newspaper. I thought it was amazing." [134]

—Donald J. Trump

Donald Trump has enjoyed a long-standing love affair with the media (until quite recently). He admittedly loves to see his name and face in print and on television. For years he adorned his office with cover pages of magazines featuring him. [135]

And for years, the media have been very good to him and his brand. He's also been very good to the media. Stories on Trump sell and sell well. Just look to the success of *The Apprentice*.

In fact, his relationship with the media—perhaps the most critical and long-standing "negotiation" in his career—garnered him so much free press during the campaign that it likely played a significant role in his winning the presidency.

How has he developed such a profitable and successful media relationship?

Trump deeply understands the media's true needs and interests. He knows *what* they want and, crucially, *why* they want it. Knowing this, he offers them carrots that satisfy their interests.

This Trump strategy was used on reporter Wayne Barrett in 1978, as described in *Trump Revealed*.

> Barrett, one of the first reporters to take a deep look at Trump's deals, was about to become one of the first to

experience a media strategy, then in its infancy, that would become familiar to reporters around New York, then across the country…. Trump handled him with carrot and stick—attempts to ingratiate himself with the reporter, followed almost immediately with thinly veiled threats.

First, the carrot. Barrett lived in Brownsville, then one of the poorest areas of Brooklyn. "I could get you an apartment," Trump told Barrett. "That must be an awfully tough neighborhood." Barrett replied that he chose to live in Brownsville and worked as a community organizer. "We do the same thing!" Trump replied. "We're both rebuilding neighborhoods…. We're going to have to really get to know each other."

Then, the stick. "I've broken one writer," Trump told Barrett another time. "You and I've been friends and all, but if your story damages my reputation, I want you to know I'll sue."[136]

Three elements make up the carrot part of Trump's carrot-and-stick negotiation strategy:

- identify his own personal and professional interests,

- ascertain reporters' personal and professional interests, and

- explore what options (carrots) can satisfy them both. Trump used this same approach in his business negotiations.

After offering up these carrots, we will then evaluate how his approach aligns with the experts' recommendations.

Identify His Own Personal and Professional Interests

Trump knows what he wants and why he wants it in his media "negotiations." These include personal *and* professional wants and needs. These merge for his personal and business brand.

Why do we care? Because his interests drive him personally *and* business-wise and form critical components in *all* his negotiations. Here is *what* he generally wants from the media.

Professional/personal positions—*what* he wants.

- Press mentions of his name and brand—the more distribution and prominent, the better

- Positive press aligned with his brand and message

- Any press, even somewhat negative press is better than no press to Trump

Trump described *what* he wanted media-wise in his bestseller *The Art of the Deal,*

> I'm not saying that [journalists] necessarily like me. Sometimes they write positively, and sometimes they write negatively. But from a pure business point of view, the benefits of being written about have far outweighed the drawbacks. It's really quite simple. If I take a full-page ad in *The New York Times* to publicize a project, it might cost $40,000, and in any case, people tend to be skeptical about advertising. But if *The New York Times* writes even a moderately positive one-column story about one of my deals, it doesn't cost me anything, and it's worth a lot more than $40,000.
>
> The funny thing is that even a critical story, which may be hurtful personally, can be very valuable to your business. Television City is a perfect example. When I bought the land in 1985, many people, even those on the West Side, didn't realize that those one hundred acres existed. Then I announced I was going to build the world's tallest building on the site. Instantly, it became a media event: *The New York Times* put it on the front page, Dan Rather announced it on the evening news, and George Will wrote a column about it in *Newsweek*. Every architecture critic had an opinion, and so did a lot of editorial writers. Not all of them liked the idea of the world's tallest building. But the point is that we got a lot of attention, and that alone creates value.[137]

Why does Trump want this? It's not just about the money.

Personal/professional interests—*why* he wants this.

- Ego satisfaction, recognition, and treatment as a celebrity
- Reputational interest as a "winner" and not a "loser"
- Reputational interest as a hugely successful businessman
- Reputational interest as a master dealmaker/negotiator
- Reputational interest as a top international real-estate developer
- Customer and potential customer perception of brand and of Trump (the person)
- Perception of financial and monetary success

– Actual financial and monetary success

– Sufficient financial success to enjoy the trappings of the uber-
wealthy

Trump's editor Peter Osnos at Random House, publisher of *The Art of
the Deal,* worked closely with Trump on the book and its marketing. He
insightfully noted Trump's core interests in these comments about their book
marketing campaign:

> It was all about being high-visibility. Trump had this urge to
> be a really big name, so he cultivated celebrity. But his lifestyle
> was surprisingly unglamorous. He's quite disciplined in some
> ways. Doesn't smoke, doesn't drink, lives above the store. He
> was not a big New York socialite, never was. He basically
> enjoyed going upstairs and watching the tube. What he was
> interested in was celebrity and his businesses—construction,
> real estate, gambling, wrestling, boxing.[138]

Priority-wise, the celebrity/reputational interest appeared to matter
even more than his interest in substantive success. Jeffrey Breslow invented
a Monopoly-like board game called *Trump: The Game* in 1988. Here was his
pitch to Trump:

> Breslow was prepared to get down on the floor and pit his
> strategic wiles against the guy whose picture would be on the
> box.... But Trump had no interest in playing or even hearing
> details of the game. He took a quick glance at the mock-up of
> the box's cover and said, "I like it—what's next?"
>
> What came next was a lightning-fast negotiation, a
> promotional blitz, and the sale of about a million units.[139]

Reporters also recognized his interest in celebrity. Former *New York*
magazine writer John Taylor covered Trump in New York and said of him:

> He was literally addicted to publicity and recognition. He
> would get this, like, dopamine surge in his brain. I would walk
> with him into some building or room, and Trump would kind
> of hang back and watch the room, and wait until the room
> had filled, and he would have that moment of recognition,
> when you'd see waves of people turn and realize it was him....
> He would live for those moments.[140]

Trump himself recognized this, as his morning routine for decades
included a review of press clippings about him from the previous day.[141]

A quick note on this celebrity, ego-related interest. Many celebrities and famous individuals crave attention. This draws them to these careers. Other similarly famous individuals shun the attention and view the celebrity as a curse. They get personal satisfaction in other ways. Some love *and* hate it.

The point here is not to judge this interest as good or bad. Instead, it is to highlight an important Trump interest that drives much of his negotiation behavior.

Ascertain Reporters' Personal and Professional Interests

So, knowing his interests, Trump's next step relates to the reporters' personal and professional interests. Trump learned these early in his career. As he wrote:

> One thing I've learned about the press is that they're always hungry for a good story, and the more sensational the better. It's in the nature of the job, and I understand that. The point is that if you are a little different, or a little outrageous, or if you do things that are bold or controversial, the press is going to write about you. I've always done things a little differently, I don't mind controversy, and my deals tend to be somewhat ambitious. Also, I achieved a lot when I was very young, and I chose to live in a certain style. The result is that the press has always wanted to write about me.
>
> Most reporters, I find, have very little interest in exploring the substance of a detailed proposal for a development. They look instead for the sensational angle.[142]

Trump also knew that reporters worked on deadlines and had a huge interest in timeliness and responsiveness.

Trump also understood perhaps the most fundamental media interest of all in an increasingly for-profit media world—readership and revenue. Anything that sells papers, increases readership, or bumps up viewers satisfies this interest.

In Trump's early New York media world, dominated by tabloids and gossip columnists, this interest prevailed.

Of course, many in the media would add truth, accuracy, and unbiased reporting as crucial interests, especially on the hard news and investigative reporting side. But Trump never seemed to recognize this as important to the media. After all, they appeared to cover everything he said and did regardless of its truth and accuracy.

As Barbara Res, Trump's longtime employee, said:

> Donald had a way of getting into print whatever he would say,
> even if it weren't necessarily the whole and honest truth.... He
> managed to say what he would say, and people would write it
> and then it would be the truth. That was the thing with him
> that they call the big lie. You say something enough times, it
> becomes the truth. And he is the master of that.[143]

So, what does Trump do—knowing his and his counterparts' personal
and professional interests? Offers carrots that satisfy their common interests.

Explore Ways to Satisfy Common Interests (The Carrots)

Trump has offered reporters many carrots over the years. And he does it in an
extremely timely fashion, understanding their interest in responsiveness. As
noted in *Trump Revealed*, "While other developers might refuse interviews
or issue carefully worded statements through publicists, Trump was almost
never unavailable to talk for a few minutes or a few hours.... Trump [also]
usually returned calls personally, within hours if not minutes."[144]

What carrots did Trump give reporters (other than offering to get Barrett
an apartment in a nicer part of New York)? "Sensational" and "bold" and
"controversial" quotes and stories and access about his business and personal
life. Everything "Trump" was newsworthy, and he knew and promoted this.

Even his divorces became tabloid fodder, which Trump managed.
He himself said, *"[a] divorce is never a pleasant thing, but from a business
standpoint, it's had a very positive effect."*[145] And business occupied the central
part of his life.

Trump employed these same strategies in his business negotiations. *First*,
he understood his personal and business needs and interests. *Second*, he
ascertained his counterparts' personal and business needs and interests. And
finally, he found ways to satisfy their common interests and offered carrots.

Two business negotiations illustrate this: the Commodore Hotel
Redevelopment and Trump Tower.

The Commodore Hotel Redevelopment

Trump needed a first project in Manhattan to demonstrate his development
abilities, prove his financial acumen independent of his dad, and establish
himself in a highly competitive real-estate environment (collectively,
his interests). To do this, he picked the redevelopment of the run-down
Commodore Hotel next to Grand Central Station.

What did he need to get this done?

- Control the Commodore site.
- Obtain a tax abatement from New York City so the redeveloped hotel could cover its mortgage and be profitable.
- Receive a loan of about $70 million from financial institutions for the redevelopment.
- Find a hotel operator to run it after redevelopment.

His counterparts? The Penn Central railways bankruptcy trustee (the landowner). New York City. Financial institutions. And Hyatt Hotels, which then had no New York City hotel.

Trump did four things in this negotiation that would tap into his counterparts' personal and business interests. These became hallmarks of his negotiation approach.

1. Trump's Carrots to Get the Site—Political Connections and Partner Relationships

Trump knew Penn Central needed a hard-driven, hungry, financially solid developer with access to capital and political clout at city hall to take on this risky redevelopment project.

So, he initially spent time with the Penn Central representative showing him various large Fred Trump-developed properties. This was meant to satisfy Penn Central's fundamental interest in a proven developer with the experience and expertise to reliably get the job done.[146]

Trump even sent the Penn Central representative a television set as a Christmas present, appealing to the representative's *personal* self-interest. The Penn Central rep returned it.[147]

To satisfy Penn Central's interest in a politically connected developer (a likely requirement to get a big tax break and other zoning benefits), Trump arranged a meeting with New York City's newly elected Mayor Abe Beame. Beame was a longtime friend of Fred Trump's and a candidate to whom the Trumps had made significant financial contributions.

At that meeting, organized within a day—illustrating Fred Trump's political clout—Beame put his arms around both Trumps and said to the Penn Central representative, "Whatever Donald and Fred want, they have my complete backing."[148]

Donald Trump appreciated the political interests involved and how to satisfy them. In fact, many would view politicians' primary interest as getting re-elected. How could Trump satisfy their interests? Financial contributions. Trump told his Penn Central counterpart, according to *Trump Show*:

> As they walked down Lexington Avenue together, Trump saw a newspaper headline announcing the arrest of a New Jersey mayor for allegedly taking an $800,000 bribe from a developer. "There's no goddamn mayor in America worth $800,000," Trump bellowed. "I can buy a U.S. Senator for $200,000."[149]

But Trump ran into problems getting Penn Central to sell him the option rights to the site, as the bankruptcy judge needed to approve the deal. The court could only accept an offer that satisfied what it perceived to be in Penn Central's best financial interest.

And a competing offer came in from a developer named Starrett that was "a lot higher than mine," according to Trump.[150]

At the same time, though, Starrett was partnering with Fred Trump in developing Starrett City, a large government-subsidized 5,000-unit residential construction project.

Upon hearing of Starrett's bid for the Commodore site, Trump met with Starrett's chairman Robert Olnick. As Trump later testified about this meeting: "Starrett and Trump are partners in Starrett City, of which we own 25 percent and they own 5 percent. Frankly, if we hadn't put in the $7 million equity, the project wouldn't have been built. We have a big relationship with Starrett."

Starrett abruptly withdrew its offer after meeting with Trump, before the court could even evaluate its competing bid.[151]

Trump appreciated Starrett's more important *interests* here—continuing its "big relationship" with the Trumps.

2. Trump's Carrot for a Competing Bidder—Join His Lawsuit

The *second* counterpart interest Trump understood involved a second competing bid supported by Penn Central's shareholders. Here's how Trump's strategy addressing this challenge unfolded, according to *Trump Revealed*.

> Trump was a construction neophyte, but he was already adept at turning around the opposition. David Berger, a lawyer who represented the railroad's shareholders, initially opposed

selling Trump the Commodore, but at a crucial moment in the negotiations, Berger flipped to support a deal with Trump.

A few years later, federal prosecutors investigated whether Berger's sudden change of heart was connected to Trump's decision to help Berger out and join his unrelated, $100 million suit by New York landlords against nine major oil companies for fixing the price of heating oil. The federal probe ended without any indictments. Both Trump and Berger denied there was any quid pro quo.[152]

But Trump joining Berger's lawsuit brought a significant financial benefit to Berger. While Berger's switch adversely impacted the interests of Berger's Penn Central shareholder clients, it more fully satisfied Berger's *personal* self-interest financially. Trump almost certainly knew this, as described in *Trump Show*.

Berger had a powerful financial stake in Trump's signing on for the lawsuit: His firm would get a third of any settlement, and the size of the award would be determined by the number of apartment units owned by landlords who became plaintiffs…. When Trump ultimately became a plaintiff, he brought more apartments into the case than any of the other eight plaintiff groups….

[This became] a pattern of Donald's business life before and since: The repeated wooing or retention of critical public or legal opponents would become a lifelong hallmark of the Trump style. [Emphasis added.][153]

Trump focused on Berger's *personal* financial self-interest—and likely offered up a powerful carrot that satisfied this interest.

3. Trump's Carrot for the Critical City Official—a Great New Job

The *third* major carrot illustrating Trump's strategy? To get the Commodore deal done, Trump needed to navigate multiple city bureaucracies and satisfy their interests and the city's overall interest in redeveloping a rundown section of the city. How did he accomplish this seemingly herculean task for a young developer in his first Manhattan project?

Enter Deputy New York City Mayor Stanley Friedman. Friedman ended up with an extremely powerful personal self-interest in getting this deal done, according to *Trump Show*.

The inducement was the job Roy Cohn [Trump's lawyer] had already promised him. Friedman was even to get Roy's fifth-floor office in Cohn's townhouse, complete with cathedral ceiling, bar, outdoor patio, a greenhouse where Friedman's secretary would work, and an adjoining apartment with kitchen, living room, fireplace, and loft bedroom. Friedman was guaranteed a six-figure salary for the first time in his life and, unless he stumbled, the rest of it.[154]

Friedman got the city's bureaucracies on board for Trump and Cohn. They reciprocated. "One of Friedman's best paying clients over the years was Donald Trump," according to *Trump Show*.[155]

4. Trump's Carrot for the Banks—His Dad's Personal Guarantee

The final counterpart interest that proved crucial to many future Trump negotiations involved the banks' security interest for their $70 million construction loan. Since Donald Trump himself had little financial creditworthiness at this time, his father Fred and Hyatt Hotels jointly guaranteed the loan.

Hyatt negotiated in return a promotion to jointly own the hotel and not just operate it. "[Trump] could not have made it happen without Fred's—and Hyatt's signatures. Hyatt chairman Jay Pritzker said later that Donald simply 'couldn't get the financing' and 'we were able to help.'"[156]

Trump knew the banks would never loan him $70 million based solely on his personal qualities and the project's strength. Their financial interest would not allow it. But Trump's carrot was his ace in the hole—Dad's guarantee.

He would use this carrot and later his trust fund to satisfy his counterpart's interests several more times in future negotiations.

Trump Tower

Donald Trump needed to build Trump Tower fast. Delays would be disastrous. The main reason he needed to move fast related to the concrete for its construction. The other reason? Time is money in development. The sooner you complete the build, the sooner revenue starts flowing.

The "concrete" problem for New York developers at the time? John Cody, who ran the union controlling the cement truckers and who would be called "the most significant labor racketeer preying on the construction industry in

New York" in 1989 by documents cited by the U.S. House Subcommittee on Criminal Justice.[157]

Trump himself would call Cody—after Cody died in 2001—"one psychopathic crazy bastard" and "real scum."[158]

Trump's interest? Timing. Get Trump Tower built fast with no construction delays.

Cody's interest? He wanted a Trump Tower luxury apartment for his girlfriend Verina Hixon.

Trump got his concrete on time with no delays. "In 1982, when union strikes froze developments across the city, construction at Trump Tower didn't miss a beat."[159]

And Cody got his girlfriend three large duplexes on two Trump Tower floors, just under Trump's penthouse, including Trump Tower's only indoor swimming pool. She wanted upgrades, too. "When Trump resisted one of Hixon's [many upgrade] requests, she called Cody, and construction deliveries to the building stopped until work at her apartment resumed," according to Hixon's sworn testimony in a related case.[160]

While Trump denied this under oath, having been subpoenaed about it by federal investigators in 1982, Cody said he "knew Trump quite well" and "Donald liked to deal with me through Roy Cohn."[161]

Barbara Res, who oversaw the Trump Tower construction, confirmed that "Donald and his wife Ivana were very friendly with a woman whom everyone associated with the project understood to be Cody's girlfriend."[162]

Pulitzer Prize–winning author David Cay Johnston in *The Making of Donald Trump* (*Making Trump*) also confirmed much of this, stating:

> Cody's son, Michael, told me that his father was both a loving dad and every bit the notorious racketeer people believed him to be. He said that, as a boy, he listened in when Trump called his father, imploring Cody to make sure concrete flowed steadily at Trump Tower so he would not go broke before it was finished....
>
> [And] John Cody invested $100,000 in [Hixon's] apartments and stayed there often. Trump helped the woman get a $3 million mortgage to pay for the three apartments.... She said she got the mortgage from a bank that Trump recommended she use, without filling out a loan application or showing financials.[163]

Much of this information came to light when Trump sued Hixon for $250,000 in unpaid upgrades. She sued him back for $20 million, accusing Trump of "taking kickbacks from contractors." Trump paid Hixon $500,000 to settle.[164]

Trump understood his own and Cody's interests. And he appeared to satisfy both.

Trump's Understanding of Interests Aligns with the Research

Finding out what the parties want and need and offering up carrots satisfying them represent a tried and true method for getting what you want in negotiations.

> **RESEARCH:** Focusing on the parties' fundamental interests, not just their positions, has been consistently taught by negotiation professors ever since Roger Fisher and William Ury first made this interests/positions distinction in *Getting to Yes* (later revised with Bruce Patton as co-author).[165]

What should all negotiators do? Uncover fundamental interests underlying positions. Interests, according to Fisher, Ury, and Patton, are parties' needs, desires, concerns, and fears. They're the fundamental driving forces that motivate parties. For some it's ego. They want everyone to know they "won." For others it may be security or economic well-being. Still others crave recognition, a sense of belonging, or control over one's life. The number and type of interests at issue in negotiations are many and varied.

Positions, by contrast, are what each side believes will satisfy their interests. Positions are **what** you want. Interests are **why** you want it.[166]

Why do you care? Fundamental interests determine success or failure. Negotiation success or failure is directly tied to the extent that the parties involved satisfy their true interests. If you haven't fully explored your interests, you can't really know whether you have succeeded or failed.[167]

On the Commodore and Trump Tower deals, Trump knew his interests, ascertained his counterparts' interests, and found ways to satisfy them. Trump in his later deals, however, stopped doing his due diligence. This later proved fatal to satisfying his and his counterparts' fundamental interests.

Uncovering interests takes time and effort.

Bribery and Conflicts of Interests

One final note on interests. Parties cannot simply negotiate based on satisfying mutual interests. Bribery, conflict of interest, and other laws prevent this. Society has determined fairness requires that business deals largely revolve around *business* interests—not the *personal* self-interests of those involved in negotiations.

You can't personally pay Employee A of Business ABC to award you a big contract with Business ABC. Nor can you pay Politician A of State A to pass legislation favorable to you or zone some property that financially benefits you. These represent illegal acts.

The key in these types of criminal matters relates to whether a quid pro quo exists. You do this *because* I paid you this. If payment A does not *cause* or is not related to the deal or a benefit, no problem. The timing, then, was just a coincidence.

Trump has been investigated several times by federal authorities regarding whether he has crossed the line into criminal behavior. At no time has he been indicted or prosecuted. And he has consistently denied being involved in any criminal behavior.

He has, however, said *"I'll do nearly anything within legal bounds to win."*[168] Keep in mind: Just because he hasn't been indicted, prosecuted, nor convicted doesn't mean he didn't do it.

It just means the prosecutors decided they didn't then have sufficient evidence to prove "beyond a reasonable doubt" that he engaged in the criminal conduct.

LESSONS LEARNED	
Trump's Strategies and Tactics	Trump understands and seeks to fulfill his personal and professional interests in negotiations.
	Trump's greatest interest is in the perception of "winning."
	Trump ascertains his counterparts' personal and professional interests.
	Trump explores ways to satisfy his counterparts' personal interests, the carrots.
	Trump deeply understands media and political interests.
Lessons Learned	Uncovering parties' true personal and professional interests and needs—not just positions—represents a crucial negotiation strategy.
	Satisfying parties' fundamental interests determines success or failure.
	Exploring underlying interests takes time and effort.
	Bribery and other legal restrictions prevent negotiations from solely revolving around interests.

CHAPTER 5

THE ART OF THE BLUFF:
WHEN HE HOLDS... AND WHEN HE FOLDS

"The worst thing you can possibly do in a deal is seem desperate to make it. That makes the other guy smell blood, and then you're dead. The best thing you can do is deal from strength, and leverage is the biggest strength you can have... Unfortunately, that isn't always the case, which is why leverage often requires imagination, and salesmanship."[169]

—Donald J. Trump

Donald Trump knows leverage. In fact, leverage has driven almost all his deals.

How? To answer this, we must define leverage. Many consider negotiation power and leverage the same. Not true. Leverage is one type of power in negotiations. But other negotiation power exists, too.

What is negotiation leverage and how does it provide power?

RESEARCH: Leverage consists of two elements:
- How much each party needs or wants an agreement relative to the other
- The consequences to each side if no agreement is reached—that is, each side's alternative to a negotiated agreement [each side's Plan B if Plan A is their deal].[170]

Overall, leverage fundamentally relates to how easy it is for you to walk away, relative to how easy it is for the other side to walk away. The easier it is for you to walk away and the harder for the other side, the stronger your leverage.[171]

Trump knows the first "level of need" element well, writing, *"Leverage is having something the other guy wants. Or, better yet, needs. Or, best of all, simply cannot do without."*[172]

He also knows the second "Plan B/alternative" element well, stating, *"Part of being a winner is knowing when enough is enough. Sometimes you have to give up the fight and walk away, and move on to something more productive."*[173] That "something more productive" would be his Plan B.

RESEARCH: Leverage also is relative and based on perception. Leverage is only strong or weak in comparison to the other side's needs and wants.

Most of us naturally focus on how much we need or want what the other side has to offer. Don't. Focus instead on the ***relative*** needs of ***all*** the parties. In leverage terms, your needs and wants don't mean much independently. They only gain relevance when analyzed relative to the other parties' needs and wants. It's natural to focus on what we need. Ignore the urge. Focus instead on the parties' ***relative*** needs.[174]

Parties' perceptions of the other side's needs and wants also impact the negotiation, not some "true" level of desperation. Perception trumps reality here. It especially impacts leverage.[175]

Leverage is also *fluid*, meaning each party can change their leverage. The most effective negotiators also know that everyone has the ability to change their leverage. Leverage is not static. Everyone's level of need likely will change during the negotiation. At the least, a party's perception of its level of need may change. This changes its leverage.

Likewise, you may be able to improve your Plan B. Or you might be able to make your counterpart's alternative (their Plan B) less attractive. In short, you can change your leverage and improve your ability to get what you want even when it appears you have weak leverage.[176]

The lesson: Analyze your leverage—then strategize ways to strengthen it. Take charge of your leverage.[177]

Trump understands this. As he has written, *"Leverage: don't make deals without it."*[178]

Trump has taken charge of his leverage in many business negotiations. Let's analyze three:

- his first Atlantic City casino lease purchases,
- his casino license negotiations, and
- his casino partnership with Harrah's.

For each, we will focus on *Trump's* level of need, *his* Plan B, and how he strengthened his leverage. We will address leverage in terms of his *counterparts'* alternative plans in Chapters 6 and 7.

Trump's First Casino Deal—Creating a Strong Plan B

Donald Trump wanted in on gaming before he ever did a New York City real-estate deal. "As far back as 1976, he was telling reporters he would build the world's largest casino in Las Vegas and name it Xanadu."[179] But when New Jersey approved casino gambling in 1977, Trump started eyeing Atlantic City seriously.

His first step—just like in real estate—obtain the rights to the land on which to build a casino. He decided to lease and not buy. Why was this a smart negotiation move? Leases better satisfied his *interests* (as opposed to buying), as Trump could lock down a key casino property but still walk away with little lost if the deal didn't happen. "Preserving his options [with this move] was precisely what Donald wanted."[180]

As Trump wrote, "I never get too attached to one deal or one approach. I keep a lot of balls in the air, because most deals fall out, no matter how promising they seem at first."[181]

Trump wanted to develop a good Plan B, too. The better his Plan B/ alternative, the stronger his leverage.

His best Plan B versus an Atlantic City casino? A New York City casino in his newly redeveloped Grand Hyatt Hotel (the old Commodore). But New York had not legalized casino gambling. Trump sought to change this— taking practical, concrete steps to strengthen his leverage vis-à-vis a New Jersey opportunity. This is a crucial and often overlooked leverage-enhancing strategy.

Here was Trump's effective research-based strategy.

> In 1979, when the campaign for gambling heated up in New York, Donald became a prominent public spokesman for it. Declaring in a multipart *Daily News* series on gambling that the still-in-construction Hyatt was designed for casino use,

Trump said: "We designed the building so it can easily be converted to one larger than the MGM Grand in Las Vegas.

[Trump later said in a July *New York Times* feature that] "We are missing the boat every day casinos are not approved."[182]

New York did not approve casino gambling. But Trump's strategy provided leverage for his Atlantic City negotiations.

He also intimately involved himself in the substance of those negotiations, using his leverage to get a great deal on the leases where he would build his first casino. Here's how his interactions were described in *Trump Show*.

The [negotiations] took place on a hot March day in an un-air-conditioned Resorts suite, and as the hard bargaining wore on, [Trump's broker and lawyers] who'd come down from New York with Donald, and many of the rest of the group got down to their shirtsleeves. Donald's only concession to the heat, however, was his unbuttoned suitcoat. He chatted and sparred with [his counterparts] and, **after threatening at various points to "just forget about it,"** he finally arrived at the basic terms of the deal. [Emphasis added.][183]

Two elements to highlight. *One*, Trump fully engaged in the substantive details. This later changed. And *two*, Trump's comment several times to "just forget about it" reflects his ability to walk and go with his Plan B—a powerful leverage move.

And while we don't know if Trump would have walked (he could have been bluffing—creating the *mis*perception he would walk), his creation of a New York Plan B and the existence of other deals at the time made this statement credible.

Did Trump negotiate a good deal? Yes. He got the lease and only paid out "an unescrowed $1.5 million, and his counterparts gave him promissory notes that would require the repayment of even these sums if certain conditions weren't met."[184]

Trump's leverage was key.

New Jersey Gaming Approval—They Are Desperate, and Trump's Not

Donald Trump wanted an Atlantic City casino. But he didn't *need* it.

New Jersey needed Donald Trump—*desperately*. This gave Trump leverage. And he knew it.

> On March 14, 1982, the [New Jersey] Casino Control
> Commission took up Trump's application for a casino
> license.... **Atlantic City officials all but bowed before him.**
> It didn't matter that he had no experience running a casino,
> had not assembled financing, and had been investigated for
> dealings with organized crime figures. To the officials, Trump's
> presence showed the city was on its way back....
>
> The license was approved in less than two hours. [Emphasis
> added.][185]

The timing worked out well for Trump, too. Atlantic City was desperate
for Trump. He wasn't. Strong leverage for Trump.

This also illustrates another important leverage element: **timing**.

RESEARCH: Given the fluid nature of leverage, you will always want
to complete your agreements when your leverage reaches its peak.
Strike while your leverage is hot.

How? **Constantly** strive to maximize your leverage. Don't assume it
will stay the same. In fact, time alone often strengthens one of the parties'
leverage. Time may work for you or against you. When you have strong
leverage, exercise it and get the deal done.[186]

When you sign the deal may determine **if** you even have one.[187]

Trump knew his strong leverage might not last.

So what negotiation strategy did he execute to seize this window of
opportunity, described in *Making Trump* as "perhaps the most lucrative
negotiation of Trump's life"?[188]

Two things. *One*, he pushed hard to get a license in six months instead
of the usual 18 months.

> New Jersey required all license applicants to complete a highly
> detailed personal history under a system designed to fulfill the
> promise to New Jersey voters that Atlantic City would not
> become a mob-run Las Vegas East.... The state was so diligent
> in vetting would-be casino owners that it sent detectives
> overseas to interview people and inspect documents.[189]

What was Trump's hurry? His leverage could change. And Trump was "unwilling to endure such a lengthy inquiry, [so he] set about arranging special terms to prevent scrutiny of his past, a practice he has continued to this day," according to *Making Trump*.[190]

In other words, an expedited process might not allow New Jersey to complete its due diligence. If New Jersey fully vetted Trump, noted *Making Trump*, it would have found several usually disqualifying elements *he did not include in his application*, including:

- A 1979 federal grand jury inquiry into how he had acquired the Penn Central railroad yards on the West Side of Manhattan (federal agents had interviewed Trump twice on this);

- The 1980 U.S. Attorney's investigation into whether Trump and Berger had illegally cheated Penn Central in the bankruptcy case;

- The FBI's questioning of Trump relating to the Trump Tower apartment he allegedly arranged for Cody's girlfriend;

- Trump's hiring a mob-connected construction firm in 1978 to work on Trump Tower; and

- A 1973 U.S. Justice Department racial discrimination case against him. (Trump checked "no" on the application asking whether he had ever been accused of civil misconduct.)

Trump was never indicted nor convicted of anything. But the application required he list these investigations regardless of result. And the cover of the application, in capital letters, stated: FAILURE TO ANSWER ANY QUESTION COMPLETELY AND TRUTHFULLY WILL RESULT IN DENIAL OF YOUR LICENSE APPLICATION.[191]

New Jersey also meant this, as "this standard had been strictly enforced for other people."[192]

Why did the Division of Gaming Enforcement report, which completed its investigation in five months, ignore Trump's failure to list these items? And why give him a free pass on the two it found that Trump subsequently added to his application?

New Jersey desperately wanted Trump. In a word, leverage.

The second strategy Trump used to get an expedited review involved politics, also related to his leverage. "Instead of going to state government offices in Trenton, Trump asked John Degnan, the New Jersey attorney general, to come to him. [Degnan did and brought with him] G. Michael Brown, the head of the Division of Gaming Enforcement."[193]

The first hint of Trump's leverage? They came to him, not the other way around. What happened? According to *Making Trump*,

> Trump assured Degnan there was no need for a long inquiry into his conduct and business dealings; he was "clean as a whistle"—too young at age thirty-five to have become enmeshed in any sort of trouble.
>
> Trump then told him that **unless the attorney general expedited approval, he would not build in Atlantic City,** where he had already acquired a prime piece of land at the center of the Boardwalk. **Finally, Trump hinted that his Grand Hyatt Hotel, next to Grand Central Terminal in midtown Manhattan, could accommodate its own casino.**
>
> ...Degnan was about to make his own run for New Jersey governor. He knew that a Trump lawsuit, a Trump campaign for casinos in New York, or denunciations from Trump about excessive government regulation would not win him any votes. He agreed to Trump's terms. He did not promise approval, but did promise that, if Trump cooperated, the investigation would be over within six months. [Emphasis added.][194]

Trump had powerful leverage and exercised it. As noted in *Trump Show*, "Donald was the white knight from New York that New Jersey *desperately needed* to lend luster and credibility to its casino industry." [Emphasis added.][195]

Trump got his license.

Trump's Harrah's Partnership—The Illusion of Need

Trump now had the land and license. But he still needed financing and an operator. Leverage again proved crucial.

For the financing, Trump was "fishing for financing everywhere," including holding detailed talks with Drexel Burnham Lambert's junk bond king Michael Milken. Milken was pushing for a $30 million equity investment from Trump. Trump, typically aggressive, wanted 100 percent financing.[196]

Trump, *at the same time*, was negotiating with Harrah's, the casino operator owned by Holiday Corp. (which also owned Holiday Inn). These negotiations were for a partnership to operate the casino. Later, after Harrah's committed to a deal as the operator, it would also include financing when Trump's promised financing failed to materialize.

Three elements of these negotiations reflect Trump's actions to maximize his leverage. *One*, Trump simultaneously engaged in negotiations with multiple parties, his Plan A (Harrah's) and B (Drexel).

Two, Trump created an illusion of great activity at his construction site when he showed it to potential partner Harrah's board members. This suggested he was well into building the casino when he had yet to get financing or do much work there.

Here is how *Trump Revealed* described his illusion. If Harrah's believed it, this would suggest Trump was interested, but not desperate.

> In June 1982, Trump hosted board members from Harrah's… at the site of his proposed casino. The Trump Organization had done little work at the construction site. To impress the Harrah's officials, Trump told a crew to dig up dirt and push the piles around the two-acre lot. Trump instructed the workers to make it look like "the most active construction site in the history of the world."
>
> On the tour, a Harrah's official asked why one of the workers was quickly filling a hole he had just dug. Trump was relieved when the questioner was not more skeptical. Trump would recall with glee his little deception: "The [Harrah's] board walked away from the site absolutely convinced that it was the perfect choice."[197]

In fact, Trump *was* desperate. But Harrah's had no idea. Had he not inked the deal with Harrah's three weeks later, "he would have literally been out of money" and would have been forced to "halt the limited construction activity then going on at the site."[198]

Trump, though, created the *perception* of not being desperate. This strengthened his leverage. Trump also understood how timing relates to leverage: he struck while the iron was hot.

Finally, Trump exercised the leverage he created to achieve what *Trump Show* noted *"might be the single best deal of [Trump's] life."*[199] What did he negotiate?

- Harrah's would pay Trump $22 million initially to cover his alleged project expenses;

- Harrah's would invest an additional $28 million in the project;
- Trump would build the casino and collect a construction fee; and
- Harrah's would operate the casino, share half the profits with Trump, and guarantee him against operating losses for five years.

Shortly thereafter, Trump's supposed financing was "lost" (Trump's term in court papers when this partnership blew up). This threw the project into crisis, effectively forcing Harrah's to "use its own corporate guarantee to secure an entirely new bank package."[200] Trump had strong leverage there, too.

Milken, when informed of the Harrah's deal in the midst of his own financing negotiations with Trump, told him, "It's a great deal."[201] He did not even attempt to compete.

Trump's knowledge, leverage and negotiation strategies here bear incredible similarity to his Commodore Hotel and Trump Tower deals. As noted in *Trump Show*,

> The parallels with the Commodore and Trump Tower deals were striking—Trump had laid claim to a prime location with a minimal early investment, parlayed political advantages and a locally downturned economy into a series of governmental concessions, and then used both the location and the concessions as a lure for an institutional partner that could help deliver the financing he otherwise could not obtain....
> [It had become] a proven formula for success.[202]

Trump created and used his leverage—his counterparts' relative desperation and his good Plan Bs—to close two financially lucrative low-risk deals and get his casino license.

Ethical Issues Related to Trump's Leverage

Three final notes on the leverage in these negotiations.

One, what about the ethics of Trump's not listing the criminal and other investigations on his casino license application? These appear to have been intentional misrepresentations of material facts. But were these material, given that he wasn't indicted or convicted of anything? Is this acceptable "bluffing?"

Or should Trump get a pass? After all, New Jersey's Division of Gaming Enforcement and its Casino Control Commission basically ignored his omissions after they investigated and found several misrepresentations. Yet they still granted him a license.

Two, was creating the perception of a busy construction site an ethically acceptable "bluff?" What about its effectiveness long-term, as he did it to a potential business partner?

And *three*, what about Trump's "bluff" to Harrah's about already having the casino financing lined up? While disputed, this fits a pattern he started with the Commodore deal. Then, he told New York City he had already bought the hotel from Penn Central when he had not (he admittedly did this and later boasted about it).[203]

These are important questions, and directly impact Trump's credibility— always a crucial issue. Each will be addressed in Chapter 12.

LESSONS LEARNED	
Trump's Strategies and Tactics	Trump enhances leverage by developing strong alternatives/Plan Bs.
	Trump takes advantage of counterparts' desperation—striking while his leverage is strong.
	Trump creates illusions of not being desperate—impacting the negotiation reality.
	Trump consistently fails to disclose information that could weaken his leverage and makes misrepresentations, threatens, and "bluffs" in others.
Lessons Learned	Leverage consists of parties' level of desperation and Plan Bs—and parties can strengthen leverage in many ways.
	Leverage is relative and based on perception. Parties can change their counterparts' perception of how much they need a deal.
	Leverage is fluid—so strike while your leverage is hot.
	Parties can strengthen their leverage by creating a better Plan B and changing the perception of their Plan B.
	Bluffing, illusions, and threats can negatively impact long-term leverage and credibility.

CHAPTER 6

THREATS AND LEVERAGE: REAL OR FAKE?

Donald Trump almost always brings a stick to his negotiations along with his carrots. He also almost always threatens to use it. Classic carrot-and-stick approach, right?

Wrong. It's one thing to have a stick in a negotiation. It's another to consistently threaten to use it. It's quite another to actually use it.

What do we mean?

Leverage, as noted earlier, consists of two elements—level of need and Plan Bs/alternatives to a deal. Since negotiations always involve more than one party and leverage is relative, each leverage element must be analyzed to the extent it involves you *and* your counterparts. For level of need, it's how much you need the deal *relative to* how much your counterparts need the deal. For Plan Bs, it's the strength of your Plan B/alternative *relative to* the strength of your counterparts' Plan Bs/alternatives.

In Chapter 5, we analyzed how Trump maximized his leverage in terms of the parties' levels of need and *his* Plan Bs.

But we did *not* evaluate the impact of *his counterparts'* Plan Bs—an equally powerful element of leverage. Nor did we consider how Trump affects his counterparts' Plan Bs, if at all. Total leverage includes these elements.

Trump exercised leverage as it relates to his counterparts' Plan Bs in three ways:

- Trump's Sticks—Find out their Plan Bs and differentiate,
- Trump's Threats—Worsen their perception of their Plan Bs, and
- Trump's Bullying—Sue them or stiff them.

Trump's Sticks—Find Out Their Plan Bs and Differentiate

Donald Trump has spent almost 50 years creating and promoting an international brand. Today that brand generates millions of dollars a year for him.

Why do people spend so much on Trump-branded housing developments, buildings, hotels, apartments, golf courses, country clubs, and the list goes on?

Those buyers perceive "Trump" as symbolizing high-end, luxury living spaces and quality goods and services and, by contrast, *that the Trump item better meets their luxury needs than their alternative, or Plan B purchase.*

In other words, Trump built his fundamental persona and brand on this element of negotiation leverage. Donald Trump knows this and has been promoting and selling it his entire life.

Here are a few of Trump's counterparts' Plan Bs from earlier-described negotiations.

- *Commodore Hotel*—New York City's Plan B: letting this part of town further deteriorate or entice another developer. Unfortunately for New York City, few others early on appeared interested. Several appeared later. But Trump's Starrett "deal" removed one and his Berger "deal" removed another. Each strengthened Trump's leverage.

- *Trump Tower lease negotiation*—Bankrupt land owner's Plan B: selling or leasing to someone other than Trump. Several offered more *after* Trump signed. Too late. Timing.

- *Plaza Hotel Deal*—Plaza's Plan B: selling to the next-highest bidder, who bid tens of millions of dollars less than Trump.[204]

But finding out your counterparts' Plan Bs is only part of evaluating and strengthening your leverage. (It's often relatively easy to find out your counterpart's Plan B if they have a good one, as it helps them to share it. If your counterpart has a bad Plan B, they will usually try to hide it. So listen deeply to what your counterparts say and *don't say*.)

Trump understands the crucial need to find out his counterparts' Plan Bs as his actions in these deals consistently reflect this.

What should you do if you find out your counterpart has a *good* Plan B, which weakens your leverage? Improve their perception of your deal (Plan A) relative to their Plan B. By making your deal appear better without any statement regarding their Plan B, it strengthens your leverage vis-à-vis your counterparts' Plan B and differentiates you.

I have trained thousands of sales professionals since I started studying and teaching negotiation in 1995. The most powerful sales-related strategy leverage-wise? Help your customers understand and evaluate how *you* (Plan A) can meet their needs and interests *better* than their alternative, or Plan B. Their Plan Bs? Your competitors.

Sales and marketing is fundamentally about this component of leverage—what differentiates you from your competitors.

Has Trump done this? Absolutely. He built and sold Trump Tower condos as an incredibly luxurious residential living space. This Plan A for his buyers, due to the features he included, was then evaluated relative to nearby luxury condos. He did this effectively.

And he didn't trash his competitors (usually an *ineffective* strategy despite Trump's comment about sometimes having to denigrate your competition). By building Trump Tower this way, he and his sales staff could act as trusted advisors and help possible buyers differentiate it from their competitors.

What else has Trump done to change his leverage? Focus on his competitors' weaknesses and inability to satisfy his counterparts' needs and interests, impacting their perception of their Plan B.

Here's how Trump has done this.

Trump's Threats: Worsen Their Perception of Their Plan Bs

Donald Trump hired New York Governor Hugh Carey's chief fundraiser Louise Sunshine in 1974 for many reasons. One, according to Sunshine, "Everybody thought Donald was this brash, hard-charging young kid.... I was the one who took Donald everyplace…no matter who it was, because they didn't really know Donald. I was Donald's credibility factor."[205]

Trump also "was not shy about using [her] political connections."[206] Donald Trump and his father had *city* connections. But Sunshine brought *state* connections, influence, and access.

Along with the Trumps' political contributions to Carey's gubernatorial campaign—$390,000 in 2016 dollars, more than anyone except Carey's brother—Donald Trump gained political influence by hiring Sunshine.[207] This brought him leverage in his real-estate deals involving political entities.

One way he attempted to exercise that influence/leverage: threats. What is a threat from a strategic perspective? A very aggressive leverage-related statement communicating, "I can make your Plan B *really, really* bad!"

The classic threat comes from *The Godfather*: an "offer you can't refuse."[208] Your Plan B? Death. Bad Plan B. You might as well accept our deal (Plan A) by comparison, right?

How consistently did Donald Trump issue business-related threats? Often and in many different negotiation contexts. Threats constituted a regular part of Trump's strategic repertoire. Here are three typical Trump threats spanning several decades of Trump's business career.

The Trump World Trade Center Threat

Trump wanted to buy the World Trade Center in the mid-1970s. But several other developers were interested (the World Trade Center's Plan Bs). Here is a classic Trump political threat, meant to make the World Trade Center's owners more likely to sell to Trump.

The following negotiation, according to *Trump Revealed*, occurred between Trump and Peter Goldmark, the executive director of the Port Authority of New York (owner of the World Trade Center). Goldmark was also a political appointee of New York Governor Hugh Carey.

> Trump's chances truly soured when he started flexing his connections. "He threatened, 'You wouldn't last in your job very long if Governor Carey decided you weren't doing the right thing on this,' Goldmark recalled [Trump saying]. "'You should know I have a lot of weight in Albany.'" Trump [then] dropped Sunshine's name. "As soon as he threatened, I made [it] clear I didn't want to talk anymore," Goldmark said. "He'd expected me to quake and shake."
>
> Trump denied Goldmark's account, saying, "I really don't talk that way."[209]

Trump's leverage-related message? My deal is your best Plan A. If you don't believe it, I can make your personal Plan B really bad as I can get Governor Carey to fire you.

The Trump NFL Threat

Here's how NFL head Pete Rozelle described another Trump threat, from his USFL-related meeting with Trump. Recall that Rozelle took notes of this and discussed it with the NFL's finance chairman. Trump, noted earlier, disputed Rozelle's characterization.

> Rozelle's version was a Trump shakedown. Trump opened the meeting, said Rozelle, with warnings [that] he was busily

developing an antitrust suit and arranging for new ownership of two floundering USFL teams....According to Rozelle, Trump then warned him that if the NFL did not agree right away to his demands, he would have to push forward on the lawsuit.[210]

Trump threatened antitrust litigation.

The Trump Reporter Threat

Trump has also consistently threatened litigation against reporters and editors when they published something unfavorable or considered doing so. Jim Brady, a gossip-page editor at *The New York Daily Post*, recounted the following, described in *Trump Revealed*.

> One summer [Brady] heard that Donald and Ivana had been granted a temporary summer membership at a club in East Hampton, where they were renting a home. The Trumps wanted to become permanent members, but Brady learned that the club's board would never approve them. Brady put that news on Page Six [the gossip page] and got a quick call from Trump. "He was cursing me with every four-letter word," Brady said. "'You SOB. You bleeping this. You bleeping that. I'm going to sue you. I'm going to sue the Post. I'm going to sue Murdoch [the Post's owner]. I'm going to sue everyone.'"
>
> A moment later, the phone rang again. It was Cohn [Trump's lawyer]. Expecting another tirade, Brady told Cohn if he was going to sue, he should call the newspaper's lawyer. "Jim, Jim, Jim" Cohn said. "There's going to be no lawsuit. It's very good for Donald to let off steam. That's just Donald. And we encourage that kind of thing, but no one's going to sue anybody. I'm just telling you that there will be no lawsuit." There was no lawsuit.[211]

Of course, Trump sued in many instances. But not every time he threatened it.

"Wait," you might say. "What's the difference between a threat and a promise to exercise your legal or other rights that negatively impact your counterparts' Plan B/alternative? Isn't it legitimate to identify the steps you might take to strengthen your leverage by increasing your counterparts' downside risk, or making their Plan B worse? Isn't that just differentiating yourself?"

Excellent questions. Here's a research-based framework in which to evaluate Trump's threats. This relates to implicit or explicit actions or statements ("threats") that can be made to impact a counterpart's perception of their Plan B.

Implicit or explicit threats, of course, can be either effective or ineffective. Just calling them threats—which has a negative connotation—doesn't strategically help determine if they work. Nor does the label address whether threats should be used in a negotiation.

RESEARCH: Initially, understand the nature of threats. Columbia Professor Adam Galinsky and Brigham Young Professor Katie Liljenquist define a threat as "a proposition that issues demands and warns of the costs of noncompliance."[212]

So, if, when, and how should you use threats? And how has Trump used them?

Threats constitute an often-unspoken element in almost all negotiations. They're simply a very aggressive effort to exercise leverage. Your ability to negatively impact their perception of their Plan B through a threat—the costs of noncompliance with your demand/offer—can strengthen your leverage.

Keep in mind, though, threats are not inherently evil. And they should be used at times, albeit in limited circumstances. As noted by Galinsky and Liljenquist, "researchers have found that people actually evaluate their counterparts more favorably when they combine promises with threats rather than extend promises alone. Whereas promises encourage exploitation, the threat of punishment motivates cooperation."[213]

Evaluating the Effectiveness of Threats

Understanding this, here are four research-based guidelines to use in evaluating the effectiveness of threats, including Trump's.

1. Strategically Planned?

"Put your bike away *now*, or no electronics for a week," Mom might threaten after she finds her 10-year-old's bike in the driveway for the umpteenth time.

Every parent has lost his or her temper. Does it help? No.

Threats based on anger, volatile emotion, and momentary pressures are almost always counterproductive. "Multiple studies have linked anger to reduced information processing, risky behaviors, and clouded judgment," according to Galinsky and Liljenquist.[214] Research also shows anger limits people's ability to identify the relative importance of issues to others, according to University of California-Hastings Law Professor Clark Freshman.[215]

Strategically planning threats *in advance*, not acting or reacting instinctively, addresses these concerns and reduces the possibility of counterthreats and retaliation, which could spiral out of control.

Crucially, the goal of a threat is to satisfy your interests. ***Effective threats thus motivate cooperation instead of punishing bad behavior.***

2. Used in Limited Circumstances?

Professor Jeanne Brett, Director of the Kellogg School's Dispute Resolution Research Center at Northwestern University, and her colleagues have identified three circumstances in which threats can be necessary and effective:

- Getting counterparts to the table when facing a seemingly intractable deadlock (like threatening aggression or sanctions to get a recalcitrant country to engage in peace talks);

- Breaking an impasse by signaling strength and fortitude (bullies sometimes only respond if you demand respect by flexing your muscles); and

- As a mechanism to ensure compliance and implementation of an agreement.

Brett and her colleagues emphasized that *the focus must be on the other parties' interests* to be effective. In other words, emphasize their interest in accepting your Plan A relative to their Plan B (your threat).[216]

The reason to only threaten in limited circumstances? Even well-crafted threats can carry significant negative consequences, including:

- Provoking resistance and anger, thus decreasing a counterparts' likelihood of granting your wishes;

- Undermining an agreement's legitimacy if a counterpart believes it resulted from coercion; and

- Inciting a desire for vengeance. "Psychologists have found that revenge has biological foundations, persisting until it is satisfied, like hunger. The more severe a threat's consequences, the more extreme the retaliation is likely to be."[217]

Threats should *not* be a regular part of a negotiator's repertoire.

3. Credible or Empty Threats?

Negotiators should never start a war they're not prepared to finish. Former President Barack Obama threatened Syria with severe consequences if it crossed a "red line" by using chemical weapons.

What did he do after the world saw unmistakable evidence it had crossed his red line? He said he didn't have congressional authority to engage militarily and negotiated a deal to stop it from happening again.[218]

Did this prevent Syria from doing it again? No. Did Obama and the United States lose credibility relating to its future promises and threats with Syria and the rest of the world? Yes.

Reputations matter, especially relating to the credibility of threats.

4. Was the Threat Appropriately Framed?

Effective threats should be framed so they can be realistically satisfied and not engender ill will. They should thus:

- be specific and detailed;
- address your counterpart's interests (This is crucial, per Brett.);
- be delivered respectfully in a measured, serious tone;
- include meaningful consequences;
- link to a timeline; and
- possibly include an escape route if circumstances change.[219]

They should also be used very sparingly in situations involving a future relationship between the parties. Threats can backfire long-term.[220]

They can also have long-term benefits. President Ronald Reagan in 1981 threatened 12,000 striking air-traffic controllers with the loss of their jobs if they did not report back to work "within 48 hours" of his statement. 11,359 did not comply. He fired them.

"Many observers view Reagan's controversial threat and follow-through as a pivotal moment in his presidency and the foundation for future political victories," according to Galinsky and Liljenquist.[221]

Has Trump Effectively Used Threats in Business?

Donald Trump has effectively used implicit and explicit threats in many business negotiations. He has also used them ineffectively, and they have backfired.

In analyzing successful and unsuccessful threats, we will do so based on two criteria. *One*, how much did they help him achieve his goals and satisfy his interests? And *two*, how much did his threats match up with our framework?

Of course, we can't know with certainty whether every threat works. It may help close a short-term deal yet induce such ill will that it eliminates a greater opportunity down the road. Even the most effective threats rarely include all the factors described earlier.

However, we know this from the research: Including these proven elements increases the likelihood the threat will work short- and long-term.

Here are two business negotiations in which Trump effectively used threats to strengthen his leverage and achieve his goals.

• *Trump's Commodore Hotel Threats*

Donald Trump, as described earlier, needed an unprecedented tax break from New York City to get his Commodore deal done. To get it, he needed New York City's land-use authority, its Board of Estimate, to approve the tax exemption.

Here's the Trump threat that got them on board, according to *Trump Revealed*. This occurred during a press conference outside the hotel called by three local lawmakers, just a day before the Board vote.

> When the politicians had finished, Trump, who had shown up to refute their argument, told reporters that if the city did not approve the assistance, he would walk, and the Commodore would rot.
>
> To dramatize how decrepit the Commodore would be without him, Trump had [earlier] directed his workers to replace the clean boards covering up the hotel windows with dirty scrap wood.[222]

Trump got his tax exemption.

Was his threat "to walk and [leave] the Commodore to rot" and the stark image of a dirty, shuttered hotel in a decrepit part of town effective? Yes.

First, it reflected strategic planning. Trump smartly understood the public impact of the image of a shuttered hotel with "dirty scrap wood" and directed it like a TV producer.

Second, was his threat to walk credible or empty? Credible. Without a significant tax exemption, no developer could make that project work. But Trump highlighted the city's risk by focusing on his control of the hotel site. And the city wanted the area improved (the city's Plan B now appeared worse).

Third, was this strategically selective? Perhaps. Trump's flair for the dramatic and the visually compelling image of the run-down hotel could have impacted a board member who might otherwise have voted against it. In that sense, his threat could have broken an impasse.

Did it undermine the legitimacy of the vote or engender ill will or resistance to implementation? Unlikely.

Fourth, was the threat appropriately framed?

- Specific and detailed? *Yes.*
- Address the Board's interests in redeveloping a rundown area? *Yes.*
- Delivered respectfully in a measured, serious tone? *Unclear.*
- Include meaningful consequences? *Yes.*
- Link to a timeline? *Yes, the Board voted the next day.*
- Include an escape route if circumstances change? *No, but that would have been counterproductive as the Board would either approve or disapprove the redevelopment.*

Overall, Trump's threat satisfied many of these elements, and he got his tax exemption two years later, after working with the city to address many other items on the negotiation table.

Thus, this particular threat didn't appear to cause long-term damage to his relationship with the city.

• *Trump's Tiffany Threat*

Trump had a grand vision for Trump Tower. To make it work, however, he needed the air rights from his soon-to-be neighbor on Fifth Ave, Tiffany. Tiffany occupied a small classic building adjacent to Trump's proposed tower. Trump was willing to pay $5 million for the air rights but didn't want to. He also was afraid Walter Hoving, who ran Tiffany, would balk, as Trump's proposed design was radically different from the architectural style in that area.

What did Trump do? Before meeting with Hoving, Trump had his architect construct two different models of his tower. One was a graceful, fifty-story building. The other was an ugly building Trump could argue would be what New York would end up with due to zoning requirements if he didn't have Tiffany's air rights. Trump showed Hoving both models, implying Hoving's Plan B would be a very ugly neighbor. Trump limited the attractiveness of Hoving's perceived Plan B.[223]

Hoving sold Trump his air rights.

Was this *implicit* threat to build an ugly tower next door effective? Yes.

First, Trump strategically planned it.

Second, was it credible or empty? Probably empty. Would Trump have built an ugly building if he didn't get it? Unlikely. He probably would have just paid more for the rights.

Third, strategically selective? Not according to our criteria. On the other hand, it would be far less likely to engender ill will and invite retaliatory measures than if it were explicit.

Fourth, did Trump appropriately frame it?
- Specific and detailed? *Yes.*
- Address Tiffany's interests in a beautiful structure next door? *Yes.*
- Delivered respectfully in a measured, serious tone? *Unclear.*
- Include meaningful consequences? *Yes.*
- Link to a timeline? *Unknown.*
- Include an escape route if circumstances change? *Unclear but unlikely.*

Overall, pretty effective.

Trump's threats, though, proved ineffective in other business negotiations.

• *Trump's NBC/Television City Threat*

Donald Trump controlled 75 acres on New York City's west side in 1986. NBC had recently informed city hall it planned on leaving Rockefeller Center and Manhattan unless it received a huge tax break. To Trump, a marriage made in heaven.

His vision? Lure NBC to the site, build the world's tallest building along with 7,600 luxury condos in six 76-story apartment buildings, two office buildings, a retail mall, a massive parking garage, and a vast amount of open space and parkland. Trump hoped to vault to the top of New York City developers in one single bound.

The problem? He needed a huge tax break to make these nuptials happen. NBC wasn't yet committed. Neither was New York City. So Trump applied for a $700 million tax abatement from New York City to underwrite the development's construction, hoping to use it to entice NBC. Trump called this development-in-waiting "Television City."[224]

Here's a description of Trump's negotiations with New York City and Mayor Ed Koch and the threats associated with them. Keep in mind that Trump's relationship with Koch and New York City had already been strained due to problems related to the Commodore Hotel.

The following meeting took place on September 11, 1986 and included Koch's top economic development officials, including Deputy Mayor Alair Townsend. It was described in *Trump Show*.

> A cocksure Trump told the assembled bureaucrats that unless the city acted, a cramped NBC might move to New Jersey or to Burbank, where the network had a great deal of extra acreage....
>
> Trump argued that he had the only site in the city suitable for major new television studios and that he had worked out a deal with the network giving it a third of his site. "NBC is in love with it," he said, claiming that the network had been designing its own facility for the property over the past three months. Asked by Townsend how strong a commitment Trump had from NBC, Donald replied: "We're negotiating the terms of a lease."
>
> Donald's strategy was to act as if he were NBC's exclusive agent, knowing that the city desperately wanted to retain

the network's thousands of jobs, and then to convince the administration to grant him zoning bonuses and tax abatements for the whole site so he could afford to offer the network a sweetheart deal on its portion of it. "I don't want the mayor to confuse the issue by bringing up other sites [NBC's and New York City's Plan Bs]," said Trump. "Nothing else in Manhattan does it."

To underline the seriousness of NBC's threatened departure, Trump then sent [Deputy Mayor] Townsend a confidential copy of the network's request for proposals for a competitive site in New Jersey's Meadowlands.[225]

Trump sought to step in the shoes of NBC—which had the leverage with New York City—and use its leverage, in the form of threats to leave New York City, to get his full tax abatement.

There are two problems here. Trump bluffed on his authority to represent NBC, which was simultaneously negotiating with New York City over a possible tax package incentivizing it to *stay* at Rockefeller Center. And Mayor Ed Koch, a huge personality, was not prone to give in to threats.

Trump's strategy backfired. Here are sections of two letters Trump and Koch exchanged after New York City rejected Trump's requested tax benefit.

Trump letter to New York City Mayor Ed Koch, May 26, 1987:

Dear Ed,

Your attitude on keeping NBC in New York City is unbelievable. For you to be playing "Russian Roulette" with perhaps the most important corporation in New York over the relatively small amounts of money involved because you and your staff are afraid that Donald Trump may actually make more than a dollar of profit, is both ludicrous and disgraceful.... I am tired of sitting back quietly and watching New Jersey and other states drain the lifeblood out of New York—and consistently get away with it for reasons that are all too obvious.[226]

Mayor Ed Koch letter to Trump, May 28, 1987:

Dear Donald,

I have received your letter of May 26. I was disappointed that you continue to believe that you can force the City's hand

to your advantage through intimidation. It will not work....
I also refuse to place hundreds of millions of dollars in future
taxes at risk so that you can more easily build a 15-million-
square-foot luxury condominium and retail development....
If NBC chooses your site and you make a profit, that's fine
and the American way, but it will not be on the backs of the
New York City taxpayer.... I urge you to refrain from further
attempts to influence the process through intimidation.
It should already be clear to you that this tactic is counterproductive.[227]

This wasn't just a personal feud between Trump and Koch. The city
officials' attitude toward Trump was summed up by NBC's representative,
Michael Bailkin, a former city official who had worked *with* Trump on the
Commodore deal.

Bailkin indicated "the city did not like or trust Trump and was being
forced to do business with him."[228]

But Donald Trump wasn't prepared to give up on Television City even
without NBC. How could he proceed? Threaten to support a new mayor in
the 1989 elections.

He met in Trump Tower with Lee Atwater, head of the
Republican National Committee, and Roger Stone, the GOP
consultant who was Donald's lobbyist, and discussed ways he
could put a fortune on the line against Koch without violating
campaign finance limits. The strategy they came up with,
leaked to the newspapers, was that he would spend up to
$2 million on commercials that assailed Koch yet endorsed
no one.[229]

Later, after several political developments, and with Koch looking better
in the polls, Trump dropped this effort.

We know Trump's advertising threat was empty. How? Trump and Koch
ran into each other at Cardinal John O'Connor's residence on Christmas
eve 1988, shortly after Trump made this threat. According to *Trump Show*,
"Donald [there] confided [to Koch] that he wasn't really going to buy the
commercials attacking Koch that he'd announced only days before."[230]

Koch lost that election. But before he left, he put another nail in the coffin for Trump's Television City. It was yet another example of how Trump's threats backfired. According to *Trump Show*,

> In the final months of the mayor's twelve-year reign, top Koch officials moved to push the administration's favorite projects to the top of the certification list.... [Trump's Television City was placed] on the bottom. It was the first time that City Hall had ever dictated the priority list for certification.[231]

A footnote. NBC and New York City negotiated a deal directly in which New York City gave NBC and Rockefeller Center a "thirty-five-year property tax abatement, $800 million in partially tax exempt bond financing, and a fifteen-year sales tax write-off on most of an estimated billion in machinery and equipment purchases.... [This was] the richest package of public benefits ever given [to] a city business."[232]

Its value to NBC? $98 million.[233]

Trump's reaction? Threaten to sue. He also claimed the city deal gave NBC "substantially more tax abatements" than had ever been offered for Television City and that it created a "horrible precedent." NBC's representative Bailkin conceded this, noting that NBC received a *better* package than anything it had offered Trump.[234]

This seems strange. Why would the city give up a financially better deal with Trump to go with NBC? Only one reason—the city distrusted Trump. This had value.

One final comment on this deal, this one from Trump.

> There were some who told me that I was hurting my chances for zoning approval by taking on Koch in the media. They may well have been right. I've waited a long time to build on the West Side, and I can wait a little longer to get the zoning I feel is necessary. In the end, I will build Television City with or without NBC and with or without the current administration.[235]

He did not achieve this goal.

Were Trump's threats and intimidation tactics effective? No. These were classic *ineffective* threats, failing on almost all the criteria. And they poisoned the relationship between Trump and Koch *and* other city officials.

- *Trump's Gossip Reporter and World Trade Center Threats*

Trump's Page Six gossip reporter and World Trade Center threats also proved ineffective—each was an empty threat and not credible *from the start*. Each also violated virtually all the criteria.

Are Trump's Overall Threats Effective?

Trump effectively delivered on some threats and not others. He could continue in a similar vein and achieve some success, right? Wrong.

The *cumulative, public,* and *consistent* nature of his threats makes them ineffective. Each threat, effective or ineffective, impacts his reputation.

The result? A public reputation as someone who consistently makes business-related threats, *many of which have limited credibility.*

As stated in University of Pennsylvania-Wharton Business School Negotiation Professor G. Richard Shell's *Bargaining for Advantage: Negotiation Strategies for Reasonable People,* originally published in 1999, "Donald Trump walks out of deals so often that the 'Trump Walkout' has become a trademark of his style."[236]

This lack of credibility and follow-through on threats is toxic to the impact of *future* Trump threats. If I'm negotiating with Trump and conclude after due diligence that he often makes empty threats, I will assess a Trump threat differently.

I will either a) decide not to deal with Trump, given his reputation (Who wants to partner with someone who behaves this way?); or, if I have a really bad Plan B and must deal with him, I might b) ignore his threat, figuring it's just another empty Trump threat.

One thing I would *not* do is react as if he will likely follow through—the optimal reaction that would result from a truly effective threat.

"Hold on," Trump might respond. "These reactions ignore the fact that I follow through on many of my threats. The unpredictability of whether I follow through is an *effective* negotiation strategy. My counterparts thus ignore my threats *at their peril.*"

Trump's unpredictability does lead to a greater assessment of the risk involved. He might follow through. This must be evaluated.

But Trump's credibility related to his threats causes significant negotiation problems, especially if the deal involves a future relationship between the parties and not just a one-shot transaction.

Trump's unpredictability also poses similar challenges, as effective threats should be *predictable* and *credible*. Trump's unpredictability thus undermines his threat's effectiveness, not the other way around.

LESSONS LEARNED	
Trump's Strategies and Tactics	Finds out their alternative/Plan B and illustrates how his deal is better.
	Consistently threatens to worsen his counterparts' perception of their Plan Bs.
	Sometimes follows through on his threats. Other times not.
	Sometimes effectively uses threats. Other times not.
Lessons Learned	Differentiating your deal from your counterpart's Plan B strengthens your leverage.
	Threats underlie almost all negotiations.
	Effective threats should be sparingly used, strategically planned, used in limited circumstances, credible, and appropriately framed.
	Effective threats should be predictable.
	Long-term effectiveness of threats goes down if you get a reputation as often issuing empty threats.

CHAPTER 7

BUSINESS BULLYING

It's one thing to *differentiate* between your counterpart's Plan A and B by making their Plan A with you appear better—Trump did this by building the luxurious Trump Tower—but it's another to *threaten* to make your counterpart's Plan B worse. Trump did this with his threats involving the World Trade Center, the NFL, the gossip reporter, the Commodore Hotel, Tiffany, and NBC.

It's yet another to take concrete, practical steps that *change* your counterpart's Plan B and *make it worse.*

Bullies don't just threaten. They act. And their actions carry direct, negative consequences. They also design their actions for this purpose, signaling to their counterpart *and* future counterparts to accept their Plan A or they will make your Plan B really, really bad.

What about *business* bullies? How do they bully in negotiations? They often use the legal system as their fists and the proverbial sword. Litigation—for business bullies—represents an integral part of their negotiation strategy. They sue or threaten to sue to make their business counterparts' Plan Bs worse. Or they just stiff them, knowing their counterparts won't do anything to collect.

Before we analyze *how* business bullies operate and whether Trump fits within this mold, it's important to specify:

- the circumstances in which they choose to bully;

- what they expect to achieve by bullying; and

- what they do not expect to accomplish.

To Bully or Not to Bully

Bullies pick on those less powerful than them. They rarely pick on bigger, more powerful foes. Why pick a fight they will likely lose? This proposition sounds straightforward. It's not. The reason revolves around the notion of leverage and power in negotiations.

To explain, consider that many believe negotiation leverage revolves around conventional notions of power, like a company's size, number of employees, financial strength, market share, and so forth. Looking solely at these elements, however, misses the boat.

Instead, as noted earlier, negotiation leverage depends on two interrelated elements based on perception: a) how much you need a deal relative to the other side, and b) the strength of your alternative/Plan B relative to your counterpart's alternative/Plan B.

While leverage may be related to conventional notions of power like a company's size, as these factors can impact a company's need level and their Plan B, *they do not fundamentally define negotiation leverage and power*.

Here's an example involving the most powerful entity in the world based on conventional notions of power, the U.S. government (with millions of employees, the ability to destroy the world many times over with nuclear weapons, the most powerful conventional military of any country, a very strong economy health-wise relative to other countries, and the ability to print money!).

On the other side—relatively tiny housing contractors in the New Orleans area just after Hurricane Katrina hit. By any measure of conventional strength—financial, economic, military—there is no more powerful entity in the world than the U.S. government. And yet, just after Katrina, the government also was desperate for housing for those displaced. Housing contractors, in contrast, were not nearly as desperate. Most were doing fine at the time.

The government was also getting publicly beaten up each day it failed to provide housing for those displaced. In other words, it had a weak Plan B to deals with those contractors—and it was getting worse each day. But the contractors already had regular customers—decent alternatives to doing deals with the government (the contractors' Plan Bs). The result? The contractors had pretty strong leverage vis-a-vis the U.S. government.

So, don't assume a party has more power just because it is big. Of course, size can have a significant impact. A company's size may lessen its level of need for any one deal and may allow it to develop better alternatives to a deal with the smaller company.[237]

How does this impact when, where, and under what circumstances business bullies bully? Sophisticated business bullies understand negotiation power. So they usually only pick on entities with relatively weak alternatives, or Plan Bs. By doing so, business bullies can make their counterpart's Plan Bs *worse* without much risk of reciprocal harm.

Of course, they might try to bully someone with seemingly stronger leverage. If their counterparts push back, bullies almost always back off.

Business bullies understand and respect this situational element of leverage power.

Business Bullies Do It Because They Can

Why do business bullies bully in negotiations? Two reasons. One practical, one psychological.

Practically, business bullies consider almost all negotiation strategies and tactics within bounds as long as they believe the strategies will likely be effective and legally acceptable.

On the effectiveness front, business bullying can work as it can change leverage. Many find it distasteful and ineffective, especially long-term. But bullies don't view this long-term. They changed your Plan B. They accomplished their goal. They saved money. They forced you to make a concession. End of story.

They often *can* do it legally, too. No law specifically prohibits bullying in business, although some laws prohibit related conduct like harassment, interference with contractual relations, predatory pricing, and so on.

To bullies, it would be stupid *not* to use this powerful weapon in their negotiation arsenal.

Psychologically, bullies also crave power and the perception of power. It's not nice or pretty. And society frowns on it. But bullies get it—and some get away with it. So, they do it.

Bullies Rarely Care About Right or Wrong or Morality or Ethics

I recently told my 12-year-old son and eight-year-old daughter "just because it works doesn't mean you *should* do it. It doesn't make it right."

Most bullies probably never heard this from their parents. Or if they did, they ignored it. And business bullies probably never heard it from their mentors, bosses, partners, or colleagues.

Here's the deal. Business bullying in the U.S. and in many other countries exists *outside* the norms of morally or ethically acceptable negotiation strategies and tactics.

The Golden Rule applies: Do unto others as you would have them do unto you. Since we wouldn't want to be bullied, we shouldn't bully others.

Unfortunately, business bullies don't care. Instead, they care almost exclusively about their own bottom line goals.

But It's Not Fair to Tie My Hands Behind My Back

"Hold on," you say. "I understand the morality and ethics. But it wouldn't be fair to tie my hands behind my back if others are doing it. Especially if it works and it's legal. I'm being evaluated on my contribution to our revenues. I can't afford to be Pollyanna-ish about negotiation strategies."

I understand. We all have a strong personal interest in increasing our negotiation effectiveness. No one wants to unilaterally disarm. But business bullying is often *counter-productive*.

First, our *long-term* effectiveness *increases* by operating within ethically acceptable norms of negotiation behavior. Your negotiation reputation matters and impacts your effectiveness. A lot.

Second, bullying is often ineffective short-term, too. Business professionals often react negatively to bullies, deciding to walk away even though their Plan B will likely get worse from the bullying.

This seems counter-strategic. You should go with your Plan A if it's better than your Plan B. But I might incorporate the ethical element in determining the value of my Plan B. In other words, my Plan B may appear bad—but it actually is better if in choosing it I remain true to my personal ethics.

And *third*, while some business bullying exists, it does not permeate our business environment. Many corporations spend significant resources infusing business ethics and values that, ideally, govern their employees' behavior.

I conduct negotiation training programs throughout North America for a broad cross-section of business professionals and lawyers, plus some training overseas. And I have trained over 100,000 individuals since I started.

My overwhelming experience has been that my clients adhere to a fairly rigid set of moral and ethical standards for their employees in terms of their negotiation behavior. Their standards prohibit behavior such as business bullying.

Is this scientific? No. But it's a broad and diverse anecdotal evaluation.

So how do business bullies try to achieve their goals?

Business bullying often takes one of two legal forms:

- *Sue Them*: Sue a weaker party regardless of the legal merits in order to cause "litigation pain," thus worsening their Plan B (which is litigation); or

- *Stiff Them*: Intentionally breach a contract or deal or violate a law, knowing their counterpart will be unwilling or unable to pursue their Plan B and enforce their legal rights through litigation.

In both circumstances, the business bully abuses our legal system to gain a perceived strategic negotiation advantage. Let me explain.

Almost every litigation participant in our legal system invariably knows a few truths about it—it's expensive, time-consuming, risky, unpredictable, psychologically draining, and can consume copious energy and effort that could be more productively directed elsewhere.

And certain litigators can, with a highly aggressive and adversarial strategy and style, make the process even *more* expensive, time-consuming, psychologically draining, and so on. I know this, as I was a litigation lawyer before entering the negotiation field.

Business bullies take advantage of this.

Trump's Business Bullying—True or Not True?

Has Donald Trump bullied his business counterparts over the years?

We know some things for certain. Trump has been involved in over 4,000 litigation matters, initiating suits in more than 1,900 cases.

It's important to analyze a few typical matters where he sued and where he was sued. These will give us some evidence on which to evaluate if he has engaged in business bullying.

Understand that—given the size, number, and type of his deals and companies over the past 40-plus years and the litigious nature of many in business today—some of these lawsuits were undoubtedly legitimate, non-frivolous, and not filed to harass.

Plus, our analysis is made more difficult because the vast majority of cases settle and include confidentiality clauses preventing the parties from discussing it. But it's not impossible, given the public nature of many of Trump's lawsuits over the years. We also benefit from Trump's sworn testimony in some of these matters along with his counterparts and the extensive investigative reporting done in this area.

Our challenge is then to analyze typical lawsuits and disputes involving Trump's deals to find evidence and patterns, if any, of business bullying.

Trump's "Sue Them" Lawsuits

Trump's Revenge on O'Brien

Donald Trump sued *TrumpNation* author Timothy O'Brien and his publisher in 2006 over the book's estimate of Trump's net worth. Here is how Pulitzer Prize–winning journalist David Cay Johnston described the suit:

> After a court dismissed the case, Trump made it clear that he merely wanted to harass O'Brien, not necessarily win damages. "I spent a couple of bucks on legal fees and they spent a whole lot more. **I did it to make his life miserable, which I'm happy about,**" Trump bragged. It was a comment that fit cozily within his philosophy of revenge. [Emphasis added.][238]

Was the lawsuit about Trump's net worth—or was it about revenge against O'Brien for writing something Trump didn't like? And was the lawsuit also meant to send a message to future reporters and authors considering writing something negative about Trump?

This same lawsuit was described in *Trump Revealed*, which interviewed Trump about it. Here is its description, including another remarkably candid response from Trump regarding why he sued.

> Trump believed he should have won [the lawsuit], but he said later that wasn't the point. In an interview for this book, he said he wanted to strike back at O'Brien, whom he called a "low-life sleazebag....**I liked it because it cost him a lot of time and a lot of energy and a lot of money.** I didn't read [O'Brien's book], to be honest with you....I never read it. I saw some of the things they said. I said, 'Go sue him, it will cost him a lot of money.'" [Emphasis added.][239]

How did Trump's suit create leverage? Plan A for Trump was getting O'Brien to publish his preferred net worth. He didn't. So Trump made O'Brien's Plan B really bad.

Remember, Trump lost the lawsuit. But he still "won" based on his own candid statements. It's the business equivalent of beating up your counterpart after they refuse to give you what you want.

Classic business bully move.

Trump's New Leverage against His Law Firm Tenant

In 1995, Trump negotiated a great deal to buy a 72-story office building in lower Manhattan called 40 Wall Street. He smartly took advantage of depressed market conditions at the time to purchase the building for less than $8 million, according to *Bloomberg Business News*.[240] Before the sale, it was reported to be 89 percent vacant and in need of about $100 million in renovations.

Trump made a killing on that deal as "a classic example of Trump tactics and tenacity.... Long after, Trump pointed proudly to the purchase; by then, the building's value had risen by an estimate of $500 million: 'Some people think that's the best deal made in New York in many, many years.'"[241]

The following event occurred shortly after he bought 40 Wall Street, involving litigation over its rental amount with a law firm tenant that occupied the building's upper floors. Trump needed to temporarily move them to renovate. What happened in that negotiation?

- Over a hundred lawyers one day showed up at work and found the building's heat off and elevators inoperable;

- At the time, Trump was in the building, went to the lobby, and told them they would have to walk up sixty floors to get to their offices.

Trump, in an interview with *Trump Revealed*, later "recalled the day with an impish smile: 'There are those that say that I turned down the heat and that I turned off the elevator.... I was in the building, I came down...[and] I was lucky I was with some very tough construction guys because it was brutal. And I said, "Fellas, you got to walk upstairs because the elevators are under repair." And so, there is that story. So, who knows?'"[242]

A creative and extremely aggressive way to strengthen his leverage? Yes. He needed leverage with the law firm as they could litigate at a low cost (the litigation was their Plan B). Trump changed it. By turning off the heat and elevators, he made their Plan B litigating *and* not accessing their offices.

Did Trump's tactics violate standard norms of negotiation behavior? Yes. Were his tactics ethical or legal? Probably not. Our legal system is designed to resolve disputes like this (and I suspect those lawyers marched right over to the courthouse seeking a court order restoring access). But that still took time. And time is money, especially for lawyers.

Some might suggest this was simply a very aggressive way to strengthen his leverage. And he didn't use the legal system here to bully the lawyers. I agree. And it definitely illustrates Trump's insightful and deep understanding of negotiation leverage. No doubt about it.

But just because it strengthened his leverage doesn't make it right, moral, or ethical. Did Trump care about these norms or ethics or the legality of his actions? Apparently not.

Of course, Trump legitimately used the legal system, too. He and his fellow USFL owners won the USFL v. NFL antitrust suit. In fact, he came within one juror of getting a ton in damages.

Interestingly, though, the swing juror viewed Trump's litigation as an illegitimate mechanism to try to get what he couldn't get in business. The pattern here is using litigation as a business strategy to gain leverage. Not to redress legal rights and wrongs.

Trump regularly used this tactic, according to *Trump Revealed*.

> Legal threats [and litigation] were as much a part of Trump's business tactics as brash talk, publicity stunts, and the renegotiation of deals. "I'll sue" became the watchwords of his business, just as "You're fired" became the mantra of his television image....
>
> Over three decades, Trump and his companies filed more than 1,900 lawsuits and were named as defendants in 1,450 others, according to a *USA Today* analysis.... He once filed a $500 million defamation complaint against a *Chicago Tribune* critic who described Trump Tower's main hall as "a kitschy shopping atrium of blinding flamboyance." A judge dismissed the complaint. *Fortune* claimed in an article that Trump had once threatened "to sue the ass off" the magazine if one of its writers wrote anything negative about Trump's cash flow.[243]

The consistent theme? Anything that made Trump look bad—sue. Punish counterparts through litigation. Make their Plan B really bad regardless of whether their "offending" conduct was right, wrong, accurate, or inaccurate. Use the legal system for revenge. And signal future counterparts contemplating any negative Trump element—beware.

Classic business bullying behavior.

"Hold on," you might ask. "If business bullying is so bad, shouldn't it be legally prohibited? And doesn't the legal system prohibit this misuse of the court system?"

Yes, and it sort of does. Unfortunately, it's hard to govern this, practically-speaking. So, the courts and our lawmakers have basically punted.

How?

Society governs appropriate negotiation behavior through our legal system, which sets up acceptable rules of the road. In part because state or federal law generally does not specifically prohibit this type of business bullying, business bullies can and do use and abuse the legal system to worsen their counterparts' Plan Bs and achieve their goals.

The most significant way to legally prevent this type of behavior involves a legal rule requiring lawyers to swear under oath to the court ensuring their litigation is neither "frivolous" nor meant to "harass."

If a violation occurs, courts can hit those lawyers and the parties with big penalties.

Practically speaking, however, courts very reluctantly impose these sanctions due to their severity and the difficulty of proving the improper conduct. It's really tough to determine what's frivolous or harassment in business cases, especially with individuals willing to lie, obfuscate, and engage in unethical behavior. It's also expensive to try to prove it.

The result? Business bullying occurs. And these bullies take advantage of a flaw in the legal process. Legally, little can be done to prevent it.

Stiff Them—Make Them Sue You If They Can

"If [the vendor's work is] ok, then sometimes I'll cut them." [244]

-Donald J. Trump

Wow. The candor, once again, is remarkable. Trump admits that he stiffs vendors and others who have done "okay" work for him and his companies.

Trump's General "Stiff Them" Attitude

According to the *Wall Street Journal (WSJ)* article that quoted him, entitled *"Donald Trump's Business Plan Left a Trail of Unpaid Bills,"* Trump told them "he occasionally won't pay fully when work is simply satisfactory or 'an okay to bad job.'" [245]

Simply satisfactory. Okay job.

A pattern? According to Trump, no. He told the *WSJ* reporters, "If they do a good job, I won't cut them at all.... It's probably 1,000 to one where I pay." [246]

Is this true? Not according to this *WSJ* article, which concluded *"[a] review of court filings from jurisdictions in 33 states, along with interviews with business people, real-estate executives and others, shows a pattern over Mr. Trump's 40-year career of his sometimes refusing to pay what some business owners said Trump companies owed them."* [247]

A *USA Today* article reached this same conclusion: *"Hundreds allege Donald Trump doesn't pay his bills."* *USA Today* concluded *"a large number of those [lawsuits] involve ordinary Americans...who say Trump or his companies have refused to pay them."*

Specifically, *USA Today's* research found:

> At least 60 lawsuits, along with hundreds of liens, judgments, and other government filings reviewed by USA TODAY NETWORK, document people who have accused Trump and his businesses of failing to pay them for their work...

> In addition to the lawsuits, the review found more than 200 mechanic's liens—filed by contractors and employees against Trump, his companies or his properties claiming they were owed money for the work—since the 1980s. The liens range from a $75,000 claim by a Plainview, N.Y., air conditioning and heating company to a $1 million claim from the president of a New York City real estate banking firm...

The actions in total paint a portrait of Trump's sprawling organization frequently failing to pay small businesses and individuals, then sometimes tying them up in court and other negotiations for years. In some cases, the Trump teams financially overpower and outlast much smaller opponents, draining their resources. Some just give up the fight, or settle for less; some have ended up in bankruptcy or out of business altogether. [Emphasis added.][248]

Trump and his daughter Ivanka's response in *USA Today*? "*If a company or worker he hires isn't paid fully, the Trumps said, it's because The Trump Organization was unhappy with the work.*"[249]

Donald Trump responded, "*Let's say that they do a job that's not good, or a job that they didn't finish, or a job that was way late. I'll deduct from their contract, absolutely.*"[250]

Trump and his daughter are right, at least in some of these cases. Trump has won some of these suits. And some contractors certainly did substandard work and delivered late goods and services.

But the scope, breadth, and details of these claims, research, court cases, New Jersey Casino Control Commission audit report, U.S. Department of Labor records, investigative reports and interviews with Trump's vendors, contractors, employees and others—from the *WSJ* and *USA Today* and later similar reports from *Fox News, Reuters, NBC News*, and *New York Magazine*—represent an astounding and seemingly long-standing practice by Trump.

As noted in *USA Today*, "Legal records, New Jersey Casino Control Commission records and contemporaneous local newspaper stories recounted time and again tales of the Trumps paying late or renegotiating deals for dimes on the dollar."[251]

Let's break down the details to analyze Trump's behavior. Then we will address Trump's explanations.

One final note before we analyze the details: Diehard Trump supporters will undoubtedly claim the "liberal mainstream media" made this up. "Fake news," right?

Wrong. *Objective* evidence supports these conclusions, including:

- *Trump's own words* admitting he "cut" vendors' pay even when he deemed their work "okay" and "satisfactory." Trump admits here *intentionally* violating his agreements.

- *Evidence and conclusions by **conservative** publications like the WSJ and Fox News*, which Trump's friend and conservative fellow billionaire Rupert Murdoch owns.

- *Evidence and conclusions by USA Today*, owned by Gannett—a media organization that owns a wide variety of publications, its biggest including such large newspapers as *The Indianapolis Star* and *The Arizona Republic*, historically conservative papers and the dominant media in two red states that reliably vote Republican up and down the ballot.

- *Evidence and conclusions from **non-media sources** like court cases and New Jersey's Casino Control Commission.*

- *Consistent evidence from Trump biographies.*

What specific objective evidence exists of Trump stiffing these vendors, employees, and contractors?

Trump's stiffed negotiation counterparts fall into three general categories, from the weakest to the strongest:

- weaker counterparts who didn't fight or sue; (Many couldn't.)

- weaker counterparts who fought but settled for less than the amount owed; and

- stronger counterparts who won lawsuits or settled—but never recovered for their lost time and effort or settled for less than the amount owed.

Weaker counterparts who didn't fight or sue

The most vulnerable tend to be the most bullied. Why? They can't do much about it.

The Edward Friel Family Cabinet Company

Case in point: Philadelphia cabinet-builder Edward Friel, Jr., a family business around since the 1940s that contracted with Trump to build cabinets for Harrah's at Trump Plaza in the early 1980s. After finishing its work—*and Trump's general contractor accepting it as satisfactory*—Friel submitted its final invoice in 1984 to Trump for $83,600 (out of a $400,000 job).

Edward Friel's son Paul, the family company's accountant, described in *USA Today* what happened next.

Paul Friel said he got a call asking that his father, Edward, come to the Trump family's offices at the casino for a meeting. There Edward, and some other contractors, were called in one by one to meet with Donald Trump and his brother, Robert Trump.

"He sat in a room with nine guys," Paul Friel said. "We found out some of them were carpet guys. Some of them were glass guys. Plumbers. You name it."

In the meeting, Donald Trump told his father that the company's work was inferior, Friel said, even though the general contractor on the casino had approved it. The bottom line, Trump told Edward Friel, was the company wouldn't get the final payment. Then, Friel said something that struck the family as bizarre. Trump told his dad that he could work on other Trump projects in the future.[252]

When *USA Today* asked Trump to comment on this in June 2016, he responded, *"'was the work bad? Was it bad work?'* And, then, after being told the general contractor had approved it, Trump added, *'Well, see here's the thing. You're talking about, what, 30 years ago?'"*[253]

Two crucial elements here. *One*, Trump's offer to hire Friel for more work undermines his claim that he only cut contractors' work if they did an inferior job or delivered late. No one voluntarily hires bad contractors.

And *two*, Paul Friel said his dad hired a lawyer to sue Trump for the outstanding invoice. The lawyer's advice? *"The Trumps would drag the case out in court and legal fees would exceed what they'd recover,"* recounted Paul Friel.[254]

The Friels never recovered the $83,600, a "huge chunk out of the bottom line" of their business. After standing up to Trump, Paul Friel said, they "struggled to get other casino work in Atlantic City." The Friel family business filed for bankruptcy five years later.[255]

Trump's Plaza Casino President Confirms His Approach

Trump's negotiation attitude toward his vendors and contractors permeated his organization and also carried through in many other negotiations, according to the *WSJ's* article.

Here's how John "Jack" O'Donnell, president of Trump's Atlantic City Plaza Hotel in the late 1980s, described Trump's mindset.

"Part of how he did business as a philosophy was to negotiate the best price he could. And then when it came time to pay the bills," he said, Mr. Trump would say that "'I'm going to pay you but I'm going to pay you 75 percent of what we agreed to.'"...

Executives at the casino paid vendors fully despite Mr. Trump's directives, he said, and "it used to infuriate him."[256]

Notice the math on O'Donnell's 75 percent figure for Friel—it comes to "cutting" him $100,000. Friel got paid 79 percent of the total amount due, four percent off O'Donnell's estimate of Trump's modus operandi.

Weaker counterparts who sued but settled for less than what was contractually owed

Trump's Taj Mahal Cram Down

Trump's Taj Mahal Casino in Atlantic City opened in early April 1990 and included 1,250 hotel rooms in a 42-story tower, a 120,000-square-foot casino with 167 gaming tables, 2,900 slot machines, and employed 5,800. It cost Trump about $1 billion to build.[257]

At the opening, Donald Trump was quoted in *The New York Times* saying he was making so much money *"we couldn't count it fast enough."*[258]

According to media reports and Trump, the opening was spectacular:

- Trump said its opening week had exceeded his "wildest expectations,"

- Trump's former rival Merv Griffin predicted it would revitalize Atlantic City, and

- The television show *Lifestyles of the Rich and Famous* indicated *"Donald's biggest gamble is turning up aces."*[259]

But behind closed doors—just before the Taj opened and Trump started raking in the cash—Trump presented another story to 253 subcontractors on the Taj Mahal project. Owed a total of $69.5 million, according to a later New Jersey Casino Control Commission audit, they were getting stiffed.

Here's how *USA Today* described it.

> Some [contractors] had already sued Trump, the state audit said; others were negotiating with Trump to try to recover what they could. The companies and their hundreds of workers had installed walls, chandeliers, plumbing, lighting and even the casino's trademark minarets.

> One of the builders was Marty Rosenberg, vice president of Atlantic Plate Glass Co., who said he was owed about $1.5 million for work at the Taj Mahal. When it became clear Trump was not going to pay in full, Rosenberg took on an informal leadership role, representing about 100 to 150 contractors in negotiations with Trump.

> Rosenberg's mission: with Trump offering as little as 30 cents on the dollar to some of the contractors, Rosenberg wanted to get as much as he could for the small businesses, most staffed by younger tradesmen with modest incomes and often families to support.

> "Yes, there were a lot of other companies," he said of those Trump left waiting to get paid. "Yes, some did not survive."

> Rosenberg said his company was among the lucky ones. He had to delay paying his own suppliers to the project. The negotiations led to him eventually getting about 70 cents on the dollar for his work, and he was able to pay all of his suppliers in full.[260]

Trump's response when asked about these contractors? According to a *WSJ* interview in 2015, he responded they *"wouldn't have had jobs or contracts in the first place if it weren't for him."*[261]

He's right. They wouldn't have had jobs with Trump. But they might have had jobs with others. And they might then have been paid in full for their work.

Notice also what Trump *didn't* say. Nothing about inferior quality. Nothing about late delivery. Nothing about bad attitudes.

Trump's executives also used additional leverage in these negotiations relating to the Taj Mahal's possible bankruptcy, telling the contractors "they should agree to accept less than full payment or risk becoming unsecured creditors in bankruptcy court."[262]

This is powerful leverage, as unsecured creditors in bankruptcy court often get left holding the bag. How real was this threat? That's unclear. I doubt Trump considered bankruptcy a possibility at the time. His positive attitude and goal-setting wouldn't allow it. The Taj had just opened and was raking in the money.

On the other hand, it declared bankruptcy that next year, in 1991.

The Catalina Draperies Dispute

More recently in 2008, Trump shorted Larry Walters' Las Vegas drapery company, Catalina Draperies, by about $380,000 Walters claimed that he was owed in *additional* work he had completed beyond their original contract. Walters made curtains, bedspreads, and pillow covers for Trump International Hotel & Tower, in construction at the time.

According to the *WSJ*, the "original order in 2007 had been for $702,958....Trump Ruffin, managed by Mr. Trump, pressed Mr. Walters to hurry, repeatedly asking for extra work, Mr. Walters said in court testimony and other court records."[263]

The extra orders added up to a total of $1.2 million, and Walters told the *WSJ* he "complied with demands for extras, even without formal documentation, because he trusted the Trump company and hoped for more of his business."[264]

That sounds reasonable, especially as Walters told the *WSJ* he "never had payment problems with other casino or hotel clients," a fact confirmed by the *WSJ*.[265]

Trump paid $553,000 but rejected Walters' invoices for the extras. Walters then stopped his work and kept his fabrics as collateral. Trump sued to get the fabrics.

There are three interesting elements in this court dispute. *One*, when asked about this dispute by the *WSJ* in 2016, Trump said, "I love to hold back and negotiate when people don't do good work." He then said of Mr. Walters that they "were unhappy with his work."[266]

Yet they were happy enough with his original work to order half a million dollars *extra* work and fabric.

Two, they sued to get Walters' extra fabric—suggesting they considered it good enough quality to use anyway.

And, *three*, they ultimately settled and paid Walters an "extra" $185,000. Walters thus collected $823,000 in total of $1.2 million owed, before legal fees. Walters said he settled because "they were going to drag it on for many, many years."

Catalina Draperies closed in 2011.

Of course, Walters should have better documented the orders. But many small businesses go the extra mile for bigger clients and sometimes forget to dot the i's and cross the t's. Usually it doesn't become a legal problem.

It cost Walters here.

Stronger Counterparts Who Sued and Won—But Never Recovered Their Lost Time and Effort or Settled for Less

Some counterparts *will* sue, however. And many did when Trump "cut" their bills. But even winning wouldn't get them everything back.

Even if a court awarded them their attorneys' fees, a relatively rare occurrence, they would never recover the hassle, energy, and lost opportunity cost of their time and effort in suing Trump. Ironically, this group includes some Trump lawyers who racked up legal fees helping him in these disputes.

Some sued and then settled almost certainly for less than the amount owed. I say "almost certainly" because the settlements were confidential. It's exceedingly rare for lawsuit settlements to resolve matters 100 percent for one side or the other.

Of course, none should have been forced to sue.

The following chart details some of these, reported by the *WSJ*[267] and *USA Today*.[268]

Trump Entity	Counterpart	Dispute Facts
Trump Mortgage LLC (now defunct)	Jennifer McGovern	Commissions earned but not paid.
Trump International Realty	Real-estate broker Rana Williams	Worked for Trump for over two decades. Deposition testimony of Williams "There were instances where a sizable commission would come in and we would be waiting for payment and it wouldn't come. That was both for myself and for some of the agents." Williams also said Trump and his deputies shorted her "based on nothing more than whimsy."
Trump	Morrison Cohen LLP (New York law firm)	Legal fees
Trump	Cook, Heyward, Lee, Hopper & Feehan	Legal fees
Trump University	MGM Grand in Las Vegas	Fee due MGM for canceled event.
Trump	Barbara Corcoran (frequent panelist on *Shark Tank*)	Commission due on a $100 million investment in New York City real estate project in 1994.

Amount unpaid	Trump Excuse	Resolution
$298,274 (amount ordered by court to be paid)	Unknown	Court ordered Trump Mortgage to pay $298,274.
$735,212 in commissions from 2009 to 2012	Unknown	Confidential settlement in 2015
Nearly $500,000 in legal fees incurred representing Trump in suit v. construction contractor that allegedly overcharged Trump.	Unknown	Confidential settlement in 2009
$94,511 in legal fees and costs	Trump associates attacked lawyers' quality of work in press. Trump quoted as saying, "we thought he was charging too much." In court filings, Trump representatives said the legal bills were "too high" and it should agree to cap them or reduce them by 70 percent.	Settled
$12,359.51	Unknown	Trump Univ. eventually paid and suit dropped.
Trump made two monthly payments on three years of monthly payments owed.	Unknown	Trump lost in court.

Contracts in our legal system are not meant to be ignored. We negotiate contracts *at the start* to avoid this.

Why? In part because leverage can change during engagements. We execute binding legal contracts to prevent inefficient and unfair "renegotiations" by those whose leverage may increase, giving them the power to get better deals.

Of course, some fulfill commitments regardless of legal obligations. They value morality and ethics over dollars. These are not business bullies.

How does leverage fluctuate in typical deals between purchasers and vendors, or between developers and contractors? At the start, developers often enjoy strong leverage, with multiple contractors bidding for their work. (The developer has a good Plan B and C and D.)

Amid the engagement, leverage changes. Now the contractors or suppliers often enjoy strong leverage, as developers can't easily switch contractors in the middle of a job. (The developers now have bad Plan Bs.)

But then leverage changes again, after the work has been completed. Now, often with the final payment due, developers often have strong leverage again. (Contractors now have a bad Plan B—litigating to get the moneys owed.)

This shifting leverage gives rise to some renegotiations at the end.

Of course, this assumes the parties don't want a future relationship. Parties generally don't want to do business with serial re-negotiators or business bullies.

Business Bullies' Common Responses

Business bullies respond in many ways. Not only do they suggest the contractors "did inferior or late work" or similar variations of "it's their fault" regardless of its truth, they also make other excuses. Trump has used variations of three excuses:

- *1,000 Contractors Get Paid for Every One Whose Bill is Cut*
- *Everybody Does It*
- *It's Legal*

1,000 Contractors Get Paid for Every One Whose Bill Is Cut

The rarity of an entity's business bullying does not excuse it morally or ethically. And it doesn't make those who get stiffed feel better. A deal is a deal.

A binding agreement is a binding agreement. Contracts cannot be simply suggestions or recommendations.

Our legal system and free market business environment fundamentally depend on parties' ability to reach binding, legal agreements with compliance by the parties. Without this, our economic system would operate inefficiently and ineffectively and break down.

Trump and like-minded business professionals know this, so they don't bully everybody. The *WSJ* and *USA Today* articles included many examples of Trump vendors paid in full and on time. No one disputes this. Those vendors may even constitute the overwhelming majority of Trump's business relationships, as he suggests.

But even highly selective business bullying has a disproportionate impact on a parties' reputation. And a reputation as a business bully carries a major negative cost, often proving disastrous to businesses dependent on customers' goodwill for success.

This especially holds true in our digital age, with online social media and business networks exploding in popularity and usage.

Everybody Does It—Standard Operating Practice

"Give me a break," my New Jersey-based business colleague responded when I recently described Trump's litigious nature and business bullying behavior. "All New York and New Jersey real-estate developers practically keep lawyers on retainer. Someone sues someone else on almost every development. I should know—my family has been developing real estate there for years."[269]

Is Trump's behavior standard operating practice amongst New York and New Jersey real estate developers?

No. They may be more litigious, but business bullying is not standard practice in that industry nor in New York and New Jersey. Colette Nelson, chief advocacy officer of the American Subcontractors Association, shared with *USA Today* that "developers with histories of not paying contractors are a very small minority of the industry."

She was quoted saying, "Real estate is a tough and aggressive business, but most business people don't set out to make their money by breaking the companies that they do business with," she said, stressing she couldn't speak directly to the specifics of cases in Trump's record. "But there are a few."[270]

This was confirmed by Wayne Rivers, an independent small-business construction consultant quoted in the *WSJ*. While the *WSJ* noted that:

> Payment disputes aren't unusual in the construction industry, where aggressive developers sometimes leave behind dissatisfied vendors and contractors.... **Yet, Mr. Trump's withholding of payments stood out as particularly aggressive in the industry and in the broader business world, said some vendors who had trouble getting paid....**
>
> It is "a strong-arm tactic that is frowned on," said Wayne Rivers.... The tactic is more common in Northeast construction than in other regions, he said, and is abnormal in much of American business. [Emphasis added.][271]

Attorney Richard Selzer also confirmed this, a former chair of the real-estate litigation section at New York–based international law firm Kaye Scholer LLP (now Arnold & Porter Kaye Scholer). Selzer should know. He represented Barbara Corcoran, the real estate contributor of NBC's *Today Show* and of *Shark Tank* fame, in her suit to get her commissions from Trump. (Disclosure: I have done negotiation training programs for these law firms).

Selzer, who admittedly represented a stiffed Trump party but also represented developers and others in real-estate litigation in that business environment, noted, "[Trump] took advantage of the legal system to try to avoid debts. [He] said Mr. Trump's approach to business agreements is common only among a small subset of privately held New York development companies he has encountered but rare in the broader world of real estate and business.[272]

Just because others do it does not make it right, either.

It's Legal—So It Must Be Okay

In the September 2016 presidential debate, Donald Trump confronted business bullying head-on. Asked about an architect who had designed a Trump golf course clubhouse and who got stiffed despite the clubhouse using his design, Trump replied in the following way, as reported in a *Fortune* magazine commentary by Editor-at-Large Roger Parloff entitled *"Why U.S. Law Makes It Easy for Donald Trump to Stiff Contractors"*:

> One of the more startling moments in Monday night's debate was the one where Donald Trump appeared to admit that

one of his business secrets is an unsavory one: He stiffs his contractors.

What many Americans may not realize is that the prospect of a businessman systematically reneging on his promises as a negotiating strategy—known as "selling out one's goodwill"—is a recognized danger of the way our contract law works. Fortunately, it's one that few business people actually exploit....

[Trump's defense at the debate was] "Maybe he didn't do a good job and I was unsatisfied with his work."

But at the debate he went on to make another point. "First of all, they did get paid a lot," he said. "But I take advantage of the laws of the nation because I'm running a company. My obligation right now is to do well for myself, my family, my employees, for my companies. And that's what I do."[273]

Trump's goal? To do well for himself. And the contractors? Not so important. If it's legal, it's okay. But just because it's legal doesn't make it right.

But is it effective? Does it work? Donald Trump would almost certainly answer "yes."

What has the negotiation research concluded? Is business bullying effective? Here's a great legal answer—it depends. On what? Your goals. If you care about morals, ethics, trustworthiness, and your credibility—business bullying will never work for you. It violates your goals.

On the other hand, you might respond differently if you *don't* care about these and if *all* the following apply:

- you only want a one-shot, short-term "win" over your counterpart;
- the issue is zero-sum (meaning one dollar more for one side is necessarily one dollar less for the other, and no opportunities exist to create value in the negotiation);
- one (or, at most, two) zero-sum issues are on the table;
- you will never do business with this counterpart again; *and*
- you will never do business with anyone this counterpart will ever contact or be in contact with through others concerning your behavior.

Then, and only then, might business bullying work on one deal.

As Parloff noted, business bullying works with "one-off contracts, where the parties are never going to deal with each other again. If a hotel owner builds one hotel in Rhode Island, for instance, and contracts with a local carpet supplier there, and then builds another in Abu Dhabi, and contracts with another local supplier there, and then builds another in Las Vegas, and so on, he may be able to get away with serially stiffing local suppliers."[274]

I agree, with two caveats. *One*, in our increasingly interconnected social media world, business bullies may become known even in different countries. This will impact whether even local suppliers will work with them.

And, *two*, this depends on local suppliers' business sophistication and the extent to which they do their strategic due diligence on their counterparts. If they don't check out the negotiation reputation of their counterparts *before* negotiating their deals, they may suffer the consequences anyway.

"Come on," you might say. "Get off your high moral horse. This is ridiculous. Donald Trump appears to have been doing this to contractors for years *and saving a lot of money as a result*. It hasn't hurt him much. He still finds vendors and contractors and law firms to work for him and his companies. And he finds them all over the world.

"He's also a multi-billionaire. And he got elected President of the United States and received millions of votes. His alleged reputation for stiffing contractors apparently didn't hurt him in the election. He must be doing something right, right?"

Of course he has done a lot right negotiation-wise. We've already identified many Trump negotiation strategies supported by the experts' proven research. He has also, though, utilized some highly *counterproductive* strategies and tactics. These facts don't change the conclusion.

What about the election, Trump's financial success, and his continuing ability to find new vendors?

First, I am not qualified to strategically assess what happened in the election. I do know, however, that many factors were at play in addition to Trump's business reputation and what the American public believed about him. Just because he got elected does not impact whether business bullying works.

Second, Trump's financial success over the years may be related to his negotiation skills, but not necessarily. He might have timed his real-estate and other business transactions particularly well.

Trump bought 40 Wall Street for $8 million and it ballooned in value to around $500 million. Its exponential increase had more to do with Trump's timing than with his negotiation skills. He could have "overpaid" by five times as much—paying $40 million—and still made hundreds of millions.

And, yes, his negotiation skills had an impact. The seller sold to Trump, presumably, because he was the high bidder. They would have sold to someone like him whether or not that individual had a reputation as a business bully.

Trump's financial and brand success and reputation from *The Apprentice* also had nothing to do with business bullying. Personal and business brand promotion and aggressive goal-setting drove that deal. Are these important, proven negotiation skills? Of course. Still, they wouldn't undermine the negative negotiation impact of business bullying.

Trump started with a significant family fortune, too.

But why do vendors and contractors still do business with Trump and other business bullies? Doesn't their reputation matter?

Yes. Reputations matter. A lot. But other factors also impact their decisions.

Why Do Parties Do Business with Business Bullies?

Here are five reasons business bullies still find vendors and contractors to do their work. Others may also exist.

1. Vendors don't do their strategic due diligence and aren't aware of others' business bullying reputation.

"I didn't know. I never would have risked it had I known. I will certainly do my homework better next time. I will just use my business network more effectively before I bid again."

What should you do? Investigate your counterpart's reputation and past tactics. Knowing your counterpart has acted irrationally in the past as a tactic will help you immeasurably. Same for business bullies. Find out their reputation for paying and paying on time. It will save you.

And if you work for an organization, track this intelligence in a "Counterpart Intelligence Bank." Then you *and your company and colleagues* will benefit if that business bully's name crops up again.

2. *Vendors believe business bullies' excuses for their past behavior.*

Bullies rarely own up to their bullying. They make excuses, like:

"The vendor did inferior work."

"He installed it incorrectly."

"They used the wrong materials."

The list goes on. None are true, but new vendors have a limited ability to find out the truth. Plus, new contractors really want to believe the bullies. It may be substantial new work and more revenue.

3. *Desperate vendors might accept the risk of getting stiffed.*

What about contractors and vendors that *do* their homework? They know these companies' reputations, yet some *still* do business with them. Why?

Desperate folks do desperate things. If that vendor has no other business on the horizon, they might take the risk of getting stiffed.

4. *Internationally different norms and standards may view the conduct differently.*

Americans frown on business bullying and abrogating written, binding agreements. We should. It's morally and ethically wrong in our culture.

How do other cultures and companies feel about agreeing to pay and then only paying a portion of the amount owed? It differs based on the culture, legal system, and company.

I've done negotiation training around the world. Different cultures view contractual commitments—even written ones seemingly binding on the parties—through different moral and ethical lenses.

In some countries and cultures, parties consider handshakes more binding than written contracts. In other countries and cultures, parties view handshakes and written contracts as pretty worthless—it's all about who has the leverage in the deal at the time.

Let me be clear: I am not making a moral judgment regarding where or with whom to do business. Just make sure you enter into agreements with your eyes open.

5. Business Bullies Change Their Names

"I did my homework and the developer came up clean as a whistle. Yet I still got stiffed. What did I do wrong?"

Perhaps nothing. Companies and individuals do change their names to protect the guilty.

Bottom line: business bullies exist and will continue their bullying behavior if they believe it benefits them.

Donald Trump has been doing this for a long time. Objective evidence proves it. As do his own words and the words of his counterparts.

LESSONS LEARNED	
Trump's Strategies and Tactics	Trump regularly sues and threatens to sue counterparts to strengthen leverage and worsen their perception of their Plan Bs.
	Trump has created leverage where little appears to exist with bullying-like tactics.
	Trump has stiffed contractors for many reasons, sometimes just to save money.
	Trump does not appear to distinguish in his bullying-like behavior between strong and weak counterparts.
	Trump sometimes forces his counterparts to sue him to recover what he owes, then often confidentially settles.
	Trump excuses his bullying-like behavior with legitimate-sounding excuses, some true—others not.
Lessons Learned	Leverage is not based on conventional notions of power like size and financial strength.
	Business bullies usually pick on those with weaker leverage and don't care about morality or ethics.
	Business bullies sue or threaten to sue solely to strengthen their leverage, sometimes effectively.
	Business bullies refuse to pay solely to strengthen their leverage, sometimes effectively.
	The U.S. legal system does not prevent business bullying.
	Business bullying can work short-term in extremely limited circumstances, if you don't care about morality and ethics.
	Various measures can be taken to prevent business bullying.

CHAPTER 8

HELPFUL STANDARDS ONLY NEED APPLY

"You are fake news."[275]

—Donald J. Trump, talking about the media

Donald Trump has enjoyed a love–hate relationship with the media for over 40 years. He admittedly loves the attention, free publicity, and credibility he derives every time they print his name, interview him, or show his properties. It's been invaluable to his brand.

And he loved playing the rich, tough, *"You're Fired"* business titan portrayed in *The Apprentice*, the ultimate in positive media attention. A weekly hour of produced and edited television promoting his brand to millions. NBC paid him a fortune for it, too. Invaluable.

But Trump also hates the media. Despite his best efforts, he can't control what they say, write, or broadcast. And he hates media portraying him negatively.

Of course, he says any media attention helps. Still, his actions speak louder than his words. He has consistently used threats and litigation to attempt to bend reporters and publications to include favorable and exclude unfavorable information.

Why does he care so much? Because media reports disproportionately impact him and his brand.

Where does the media get its power to impact our perceptions of him? From its perceived credibility, objectivity, and independence.

> **RESEARCH:** Credible, objective, and independent criteria—like the media—provide power and play a crucial role in almost all negotiations. It also underlies my Third Golden Rule of Negotiation: Employ "Fair" Objective Criteria.

How many times have you heard or used the terms "fair" or "reasonable" or "unfair" or "unreasonable" in a negotiation? A ton. What do they mean? Virtually nothing. Each is a conclusion.

Effective negotiators need to ascertain *why* it's "fair" or "reasonable" or "unfair" or "unreasonable?" Find out the objective criteria, or underlying independent standard, justifying that conclusion.

Many forms of powerful objective criteria exist in negotiations, including market-value, precedent, tradition, expert- and scientific-judgment, efficiency, costs and profit margins, policy, reciprocity, status power, and professional or industry standards.

Why does it help to use objective criteria to support your position? Because we derive power and legitimacy from the perception that standards and criteria are based on objective, independent factors. Standards and criteria are usually not simply tied to what any individual wants. As a result, since our position appears to be based on objective, independent factors, our counterparts will more likely conclude our position is truly "fair and reasonable."[276]

Donald Trump fully appreciates the roles objective criteria and independent standards play in negotiations. And he aggressively fights to use, shape, change, overcome, impact, and sometimes undermine the influence of these criteria and standards.

How?

- He highlights helpful objective standards.

- He hides and ignores harmful objective standards.

- And if objective standards hurt him, especially publicly, he fights like the devil to undermine their perceived independence, credibility, and legitimacy.

Let's analyze his actions in various negotiation environments, including: his negotiation with his customers, the public, in creating the perception of stupendous financial success as measured by his net worth; his negotiations with the financial institutions that bankrolled his deals over the years; and his numerous real-estate and other deals.

Trump's Standards Fight Over His Net Worth

No Trump negotiation illustrates his objective-criteria-related strategies better than his ongoing effort to impact the public's perception of his net worth. This negotiation strikes at the heart of his brand—his business and financial success. Without a public perception of stupendous success, his brand loses its luster. That would be disastrous for Trump in *all* his negotiations.

Why? Because it is "central to his public persona as a kind of modern Midas...[and underlies] the careful image of his ability to make money through deal artistry," according to *Making Trump*.[277]

Trump's finely-honed image as an incredibly successful dealmaker and negotiator—and his ability to profit from that brand in licensing and other deals—depend on the accuracy of his uber-high net worth.

"I'm really rich," he said in his presidential announcement address. He then trumpeted loudly the central premise of his candidacy—that building an incredibly profitable business and achieving extraordinary wealth qualified him to be president. "I'm proud of my net worth," he said. "I've done an amazing job."[278]

Trump's net worth also cuts to the core of his win–lose mindset, essentially serving as a scorecard of his financial wins and losses. He wrote "Money was never a big motivation for me, except as a way to keep score."[279]

This highly public negotiation started in 1982, when Trump Tower's success led to significant profits for Trump, international branding in the luxury real-estate space, and inclusion in the inaugural *Forbes* list of the top 400 wealthiest people in America. (*Forbes* estimated his and his father's combined wealth then at $200 million.)[280]

Since then, Trump's wealth, financial success, and net worth have been an almost continuous subject of speculation, lawsuits, Trump's and others' statements, and just general wonderment by people around the world.

What objective-criteria-related strategies has Trump used to promote and defend his public "I'm a super wealthy and successful businessman" persona?

Highlight Helpful Standards

Trump's Public Statements through the Independent, Credible Media

Donald Trump has consistently, loudly and publicly proclaimed his success, wealth, and net worth for years. But he has *not* traditionally communicated it directly to the public in speeches, statements, and through business marketing and advertisements (although he does this a bit).

Instead, he has smartly used the media and journalists as the conduit through which he has communicated this message to his customers, the public.

Getting the media to publish stories about his success, wealth, and net worth ensures the facts in those stories will be viewed with more legitimacy, having been filtered through an independent, credible, objective source.

How has Trump accomplished this?

The ranking of the wealthiest Americans appears annually in *Forbes* magazine. Here is the context of how *Forbes* estimates net worth and how Trump's strategy played out regarding its inaugural ranking of America's 400 richest people in 1982.

- *Forbes'* staffers had limited time to produce the list and couldn't determine many individuals' true net worth with a substantial degree of certainty given the financial impenetrability of many private companies;

- Trump told *Forbes* he was worth about $500 million, but he ran a private company and only offered *Forbes* limited financial documentation to support his estimate;

- Harold Seneker, a *Forbes* senior editor in charge of the rich list, said it was especially difficult to evaluate Trump's net worth given his limited disclosures; and

- *Forbes* thus had to mostly guess at what Trump properties might sell for and subtract the publicly known debt related to it.

Given these factors, *Forbes* made a combined net worth estimate for Fred and Donald Trump of $200 million in 1982. As Seneker said, "*Our rule of thumb was to divide whatever [Trump] said by three.*"[281]

Interestingly, Trump's strategy differed from other really wealthy individuals. Many loathed their inclusion in the list as it prompted an "avalanche of phone calls from charities or scamsters." According to *TrumpNation*,

> *Forbes,* "if not entirely skeptical of Donald, had, of course, grown accustomed to his intense lobbying.
>
> 'There are a couple of guys who call and say you're low on other guys, but Trump is one of the most glaring examples of someone who constantly calls about himself and says we're not only low, but low by a multiple,' said Peter Newcomb, a veteran editor of *Forbes's* richlist."[282]

Trump understood the value to his brand-based business of inclusion on this "richlist." He thus intensely lobbied for it.

Trump also consistently brought up his net worth in conversations with journalists, despite their topics often being unrelated to his net worth. Here's how *TrumpNation* author Timothy L. O'Brien described it: "Donald's verbal billions were always a topic of conversation whenever we visited. In my first conversation with him, in 1996, he brought up his billions.... When Donald and I spent time together one weekend in early 2005, the subject of his verbal billions inevitably came up."[283]

The topic even came up in a *Playboy* profile, as noted in *TrumpNation*.

> The all-time howler award for a publication taking [Trump's] verbal billions at face value belonged to *Playboy*. In early 1990, just a month before the Taj Mahal opened in Atlantic City and began a slide that would take Donald's empire with it, the magazine profiled the developer and said he had amassed 'a fortune his father never dreamed possible,' including 'a cash hoard of $900,000,000,' and a 'geyser of $50,000,000 a week from his hotel casinos.'[284]

Trump promoted this perception with the media. He used them to bolster his brand around the world.

Trump's Lifestyle as Reported by the Independent, Credible Media

Trump's public and well-known business purchases and over-the-top luxurious lifestyle—starting with his gold-dominated Trump Tower apartment and continuing with his purchase of high-profile assets—cemented his public perception as one of the world's wealthiest individuals.

He understood the value of this branding and promoted it tirelessly to the media. The more they covered his wealth, the more valuable his brand.

And the more valuable his brand and the perception that everything he touched turned to gold, the more he believed the public would flock to his casinos, hotels and other businesses.

All of this rested in part on how the media reported his net worth and success.

The Trump Princess Purchase

Perhaps Trump's most visually impactful transaction involved his $29-million purchase of one of the world's largest yachts, previously owned by Saudi arms dealer Adnan Khashoggi. Upon buying the yacht, which Trump named *The Trump Princess*, he spent $8 million to refurbish the 282-foot-long yacht, despite it already coming with a helipad, swimming pool, disco, movie-screening room, 200 telephones, and accommodations for a 52-member crew. He even gold-plated the sinks and the screws.

As described in *Trump Revealed*, he "kept buying 'trophy' properties that fed the image that he had money to burn…. He didn't care much about sailing. The *Princess* was to be a docked spectacle to enhance the Trump brand."[285]

Trump's media profiles and appearances in the late 1980s, from *Lifestyles of the Rich and Famous* to *Donahue* to numerous magazine covers, were also ubiquitous.

He didn't just say it. He didn't just show it. He got the media to report it. This greatly increased the impact of this crucial message on the public—his negotiation counterparts and customers.

Aggressively Use Favorable Market Comps, Precedent, Cost, Experts' Appraisals, and Status Standards in Real Estate and Related Transactions

Trump didn't only use the media as a helpful independent standard in his negotiations, however. He and other real-estate professionals also use objective standards in almost all their negotiations. As does anyone who has ever bought or sold a house or a car. How? By pointing to the "market" or "comparables/comps" to justify an offer or a price.

Here's the most commonly used standard—**market value power**.

RESEARCH: Because market value is generally understood to reflect an objective value assigned by the laws of free market economics and supply and demand, it is perhaps the most common and powerful independent standard. In lay terms, we commonly understand "market value" to be shorthand for what all buyers and sellers through their collective buying and selling behavior have determined to be a particular value for an item at a certain time.

Why is this important in a negotiation? If every other interested person (collectively, the market) will pay or accept X dollars for an item, X must then by definition be "fair and reasonable," right? If you disagree, the rationale continues, you're rejecting the collective standard and want more than what everyone else will accept. Since most consider this greedy and somehow "unfair," you should thus accept "market value."[286]

Trump has commonly used market value to justify what he paid for something and to support his contention that he's a great negotiator. Recall his purchase of 40 Wall Street and its change in market value from his purchase price of $8 million to around $500 million later.[287] How can you determine its value without selling it? The market.

While Trump uses market analyses to buttress his claims of really "fair" deals, perhaps the standard that most aptly describes Trump is precedent— another standard. Or more accurately, unprecedented.

How do parties use "precedent" and "unprecedented" in their negotiations? **Precedent power**.

Historians suggest that the past represents the best evidence of what might occur in the future. In the negotiation world, past negotiations history represents powerful independent evidence of what may happen in future negotiations.

RESEARCH: Precedent—what has happened in the past in similar negotiations—forms another powerful independent standard for determining what now might be "fair and reasonable."[288]

Trump knows unprecedented. He received an "unprecedented" New York City tax break on his Commodore Hotel redevelopment.[289] He also used it offensively later, calling the tax break New York City gave NBC to stay at Rockefeller Center "unprecedented" and much bigger than he would have received had New York City gone with Television City.[290]

Another common Trump-used standard relates to an item's cost and a deal's profitability: **costs and profits power**.

Almost every negotiation involving the transfer of business or consumer goods or services involves costs and profit power. It doesn't matter if you want to purchase or sell a car, refrigerator, television, business, restaurant meal, software program, building, furniture, or business suit.

> **RESEARCH:** In each of these negotiations, both the seller and the buyer will benefit from knowing the item or service's cost and/or profit margin. Why? The item's cost provides you with a benchmark idea of what profit might be "fair and reasonable" on the transaction."[291]

Trump knows this standard well. In *The Art of the Deal*, he described his negotiation to purchase the historic Palm Beach Mar-a-Lago estate originally built in 1927 by Marjorie Merriweather Post, one of the world's richest women. Trump, in a masterful negotiation, used the costs and profits standard in part to illustrate his negotiations skills. How did he do it?

He first offered $28 million, which the Post Foundation rejected. Then, according to *Trump Revealed*, he "didn't raise his offer; he lowered it. He decided to play hardball. Through a third party, he bought the beachfront property directly in front of Mar-a-Lago and threatened to erect a hideous home to block the Post estate's ocean view. 'That drove everyone nuts,' Trump said. 'They couldn't sell the big house because I owned the beach, so the price kept going down and down.'"[292]

In doing this, Trump smartly strengthened his leverage by buying the beachfront property—making the Post's Plan B, relative to selling to him, much worse.

This worked, and Trump ultimately bought the house for only $5 million plus an additional $3 million for its antiques and valuable furnishings.

Trump wrote that this deal showcased his negotiating skills, noting, "I've been told the furnishings in Mar-a-Lago alone are worth more than what I paid for the house."[293]

How much cash did Trump outlay for the property? Another standard—his cash cost—also highlights his negotiating skills. Trump wrote, "I put in a cash offer of five million, plus another three million for the furnishings in the house."[294]

According to Trump's later court testimony, this wasn't true.

> In testimony five years later, Trump confirmed that his primary bank, Chase Manhattan, had loaned him the entire purchase price.
>
> "They put up the eight million dollars. I believe it was [an] eight million purchase price," Trump testified.
>
> "Was there any security given to Chase Manhattan for that?" the lawyer asked, inquiring as to whether a mortgage had been taken out to finance the purchase and secure the bank's interest.
>
> "It's a mortgage, a non-recorded mortgage," said Trump. "And because it's non-recorded, I personally guaranteed it." …The bank loaned Trump $2 million more than the purchase price, a total of $10 million, on his personal guarantee. **Trump put up only $2,800 cash.** [Emphasis added.][295]

Based on Trump's actual cash outlay, $2,800, a truly great deal.

Importantly, Trump cherry-picked a *different* cost standard to justify a much *lower* value for Mar-a-Lago shortly thereafter.

Trump used this new cost standard in negotiating with the local property tax authorities—where Trump sought to justify a lower value for the estate (which would lower his property taxes).

The local property tax authorities initially "put a value of $11.5 million on the land and buildings. Trump countered, saying that was far too much. Keeping up the estate would **cost** him $2 million or $2.5 million a year, he said." [Emphasis added.][296]

Yet another standard Trump used, when it benefited him, underlies the thousands of financial transactions that take place every day in our economy.

That standard? **Expert opinion power** in the form of appraisals and independent expert reports. How do skilled negotiators use this power to justify "fair and reasonable" transactions?

> **RESEARCH:** Experts' power derives from both their actual expertise and knowledge, and their perceived knowledge. If your counterpart considers you a trustworthy expert, your opinion will be valued and your persuasive power substantial regardless of your actual expertise. Of course, the more you know, the better you will be able to use this knowledge to your advantage.[297]

In fact, experts provide power to parties in negotiations in almost every field. Businesses use the opinions of stock market experts to help predict companies' stock prices in merger-and-acquisition negotiations. Banks use real estate appraisers to provide independent opinions supporting home and commercial real estate loans, which they use in negotiating rates and loan amounts with customers.

Financial institutions normally require expert evaluations justifying purchase or sale prices of property, as to go without evaluations would be too risky. Rarely will financial institutions just rely on the parties' opinions of the value of the subject property or business. Too much self-interest.

Parties have neither the credibility, expertise, nor the independence that underlies this standard's true power.

Trump fully understands the power of independent, credible experts. And he uses it *where it helps him*. Here are three examples:

- The Resorts Expert
- The Wallach Financial Expert
- The Trump University Status Play

Expert Standard Power Where It Helps: The Resorts Expert

Donald Trump bet much of his business career on his purchase and control of Resorts, a public company that, in late 1986, was the largest Atlantic City landowner in the midst of building the delayed and overbudgeted Taj Mahal Casino. The Taj was then projected to be the world's largest casino and had already cost Resorts almost half a billion dollars. After negotiating a deal with Resorts' management, Trump brought in experts to help convince several independent Resorts' board members to approve his deal.

Notice Trump's use of two experts and the unprecedented nature of the service and management fees Trump would receive (a standard Trump wisely ignored), as described by *Trump Show*.

To answer his critics, Donald brought in a supposedly independent consultant to evaluate the agreement, Laventhol & Horwath. He did not divulge that L&H had been the Grand Hyatt's accountant since the hotel opened and had done other work for him as well. Predictably, L&H endorsed every aspect of the comprehensive Resorts agreement in a lengthy report....

Trump and [Resorts' President Jack] Davis also brought in Bear Stearns's Ace Greenberg [whom Trump and Resorts had previously used as an investment banker], who ringingly endorsed the service fees [that Trump stood to earn from the agreement], calling them "the price of Trump coming to the party." Without Trump, Greenberg argued, there would be no bond financing, no Taj, and conceivably, no company. And without the management contract, there would be no real Trump involvement, said Greenberg, who stood to earn millions in fees on future Taj bonds [so he wasn't independent either].[298]

Two things about Trump's use of the experts stand out. *One*, neither could claim true independence from Trump, although Trump appeared to present them as such. This devalued the impact of their opinions, but only insofar as the directors knew or found out about their bias. Their impact power on the directors came from their *perceived* independence.

And, *two*, they had substantive expertise, which carried power.

Trump's strategy here did not get him everything he wanted, perhaps due to his experts' lack of independence, but he still got a great deal. His counterparts' response? Again, *Trump Show*,

They insisted on an incentive provision in the management agreement, cutting Donald's percent of gross revenue in half (1.75 percent) while adding a 15 percent share of corporate profits for Trump. Leaving the rest of the agreement largely intact, [one of Trump's counterparts] estimated Donald's fees at $108 million for the first five years of a ten-year agreement. [Trump's counterpart] recognized that even these sharply reduced terms were still a bonanza for Trump, but he and the independent directors and advisers were fearful that if they pushed any further, Donald would walk away from the company [Trump's leverage]....

Donald instantly accepted.[299]

Expert Standard Power Where It Helps: The Wallach Financial Expert

Another Trump use of an expert involved Abe Wallach, a senior vice president at a New York real-estate firm who had been featured as a financial and real-estate expert on the national public television news show *MacNeil/ Lehrer NewsHour.*

After Wallach's *NewsHour* appearance, Trump hired him as an internal financial and real-estate expert.

Trump then used Wallach's credibility to help convince a reporter of his uber-high net worth. How? After telling a reporter he was worth $1 billion, Wallach recalled that Trump asked him to generate a financial statement to back up the claim.[300]

Why? Because a financial statement—even if prepared by an internal financial expert like Wallach—carried more credibility than Trump's statement alone.

Trump used experts. But he didn't rely on them. As he noted in *The Art of the Deal* in a section entitled "Know Your Market," "Some people have a sense of the market and some people don't.... I like to think that I have that instinct. That's why I don't hire a lot of number-crunchers, and I don't trust fancy marketing surveys. I do my own surveys and draw my own conclusions."[301]

Trump trusts his instincts more than independent experts. But he knows others, especially the public, trust seemingly independent experts more.

That's a major reason his brand has value—due to the public's perception that Trump succeeded from his real-estate and business expertise.

Expert Standard Power Where It Helps: The Trump University Status Play

In fact, Trump used his public perception as a successful real-estate expert as the fundamental value proposition underlying his foray into for-profit education, Trump University. The idea? Sell his expertise and knowledge to students willing to pay for it—another negotiation.

Trump played on another standard in this negotiation: **status power**. Webster's defines "status" as a "position or rank in relation to others."[302]

Trump unveiled Trump University in 2005 to "teach success. That's what it's all about—success," as he put it in a promotional video.[303]

> **RESEARCH:** In the negotiation context, the higher you sit on the status totem pole, the greater your credibility, or at least the appearance of credibility. Many people use another's perceived status as shorthand in determining how much influence and credibility to afford the holder. That, in turn, can increase your ability to influence the parties' belief of what is "fair and reasonable."

Trump University's market? Those interested in successfully investing in real estate.

Its unique sales credibility? Trump's real-estate background and expertise—the one on which his status as an extremely successful businessman rested.

And, after the 2008 crisis, its pitch? Empower people with Trump's secret real-estate investing sauce so they can make a ton of money—just like Trump—in a depressed market.[304]

Three crucial elements of the Trump University sales/negotiation pitch with the public fundamentally relied on Trump's status power. *One*, Trump alone knew the secret sauce that would lead to their riches. He would thus develop the curriculum and share that secret sauce with them.[305]

Two, Trump would handpick the professors and teachers of his curriculum.[306] His status as a successful businessman who had hired many employees gave him legitimacy and credibility.

And, *three*, Trump would donate Trump University's profits to charity.[307] Trump would thus appear independent, like the other standards, and not have a vested financial interest in getting the students' money.

As a Trump University ad in a San Antonio newspaper in 2009 stated, "Learn from Donald Trump's handpicked experts how you can profit from the largest real estate liquidation in history."[308]

Many ponied up, paying $1,495 for a three-day workshop. Almost 600 paid $34,995 for classes with a mentor.[309]

Unfortunately for these students, Trump's promises were false. The following facts came to light in two class-action fraud lawsuits filed by disaffected former students:

- Trump University President Michael Sexton indicated Trump did *not* pick the instructors;

- Sexton could not recall any special Trump methods being taught, other than that foreclosures presented investment opportunities (a well-known real-estate fact);

- Trump lawyer Alan Garten said Trump had not donated any profits to charity, spending the money instead to defend the lawsuits; and

- Trump noted that he had simply lent his name to the courses but had little connection to its operations.[310]

Trump vigorously defended these cases, with his lawyers noting that its ads describing Trump's personal involvement constituted "mere puffery."[311]

And Trump repeatedly pointed to Trump University's surveys that found the vast majority of students highly satisfied with the courses.[312] Of course, the plaintiffs pointed out that 25 percent of its students requested refunds, casting doubt on their level of satisfaction.[313]

Trump settled these cases shortly after his election as President for $25 million but did not admit liability.[314]

Donald Trump understands status power. In fact, he has consistently used celebrity endorsers—the ultimate in status power—to sell and promote his buildings, casinos, and developments.

We see celebrities in ads for a reason. People presume that their status, derived from their roles on television and in the movies, lends credibility to the products or services they endorse.

That's status power.

Hide Harmful Standards

Trump has used favorable independent standards like market value, precedent, costs and profits power, expert power, and status power for years. And they have substantially helped him build his business and a great brand, often by filtering them through the independent, credible media for a double benefit.

But he didn't just publicly promote this with positive standards relating to his brand and net worth. He also hid and failed to disclose standards casting doubt on his brand and net worth. He even manipulated those standards to benefit himself. Bottom line: He also understands the *negative* impact of independent, credible standards.

Here are three examples of how he has hidden harmful standards or manipulated those standards in negotiations.

- Hiding net worth standards from his customers, the public
- Hiding true debt level from new bank financing counterparts
- Manipulating a mortgage application to hide his true financial condition

Hiding Harmful Standards: Trump Promotes Billions in Net Worth While Ignoring Standards on his True Net Worth

The way Trump treated evidence of his financial condition in 1990 illustrates how he fights to hide harmful standards. This occurred around the time of the Taj opening and shortly after *Playboy* reported he had $900 million cash in the bank. Importantly, multiple sources of information exist relating to Trump's actual net worth in 1990.

First, what did Trump publicly promote as his net worth? According to David Johnston in *Making Trump*: "In 1990, when his business empire was on the verge of collapse, Trump told me and many other journalists that he was worth $3 billion. He told others $5 billion."[315]

Second, how did Trump treat the several independent, objective standards that reported on his net worth at the time? According to Johnston, "I got my hands on a copy of his personal net worth statement that spring [1990], which revealed a much smaller figure."[316]

This personal net worth statement substantially differed from Trump's public statements at the time. It was *not* disclosed by Trump.

We also know that Leventhal, the independent auditor expert hired by the banks to assess Trump's net worth at the time—another independent, objective standard—found Trump's net worth several months later to be "in the red by almost $300 million." This was publicly reported on August 16, 1990, by Johnston in a *Philadelphia Inquirer* article entitled *"Bankers Say Trump May Be Worth Less Than Zero."*[317]

Again, *not* disclosed by Trump.

New Jersey casino auditors—another objective, independent standard— also reached conclusions on Trump's financial condition at the time.

> New Jersey casino auditors estimated that as of September 1990, Donald was worth about $206 million—almost all of which was tied up in hotels, an airline, casinos, and other properties that were devaluing rapidly or about to be taken away from him. Donald's cash on hand was only $17 million, and that was dissolving quickly as well.[318]

Trump Revealed also described his 1990 financial condition, based on these and additional objective standards.

> By spring of 1990, Trump oversaw an empire at risk of collapse. It was in "severe financial distress as a result of cash flow shortages," a [New Jersey] Casino Commission report found. The Trump Shuttle lost $34 million during the first half of the year, and Trump was trying to sell it, along with his yacht. The opening of the Taj initially brought a windfall—which wouldn't last—but the Taj was cannibalizing business from his other Atlantic City properties.... A $63 million loan payment was due the following month on stock Trump had bought in Alexander's department store, a struggling, middlebrow retailer.[319]

Note two crucial elements about these descriptions of Trump's *true* financial condition at the time.

One, the description of Trump's actual financial condition derives from a) independent, credible analyses by New Jersey regulators in an audit conducted post-1990, b) an independent, credible analysis by an expert hired by banks that had loaned Trump money, c) a personal financial report made by Trump, d) financial analyses of some of Trump's assets, which were losing money, and e) independent reporting by investigative journalists then and later.

And, *two*, Trump alone knew his true financial condition *at the time*.

All point to one conclusion—Trump kept his true financial condition closely under wraps while he actively promoted a net worth of $3 to $5 billion, the opposite image.

Why? Because he knew the negative impact independent, objective, and credible standards and the truth about his financial condition would have had on his negotiations with the public and everyone else.

Of course, Trump was not alone in promoting an image of being incredibly successful while skirting on the edge of personal bankruptcy. Many individuals and companies promote successful images unsupported by the facts and evidence at the time.

In many cases, in fact, this is advisable. The public does not have a right to know a business person's net worth or even a private companies' financial status. (This differs for public companies.)

On the other hand, Trump put his net worth out there with his many net-worth-related public statements. Misleading, at best. But we are not addressing here the ethics or legality of Trump's statements of financial condition.

The point is to identify Trump's knowledge and strategy relating to the impact of independent, credible sources of information of his net worth—and his hiding his actual financial status—in his negotiations with his customers, the public.

Hiding Harmful Standards: Trump Hides His True Debt Level from New Financial Counterparts

Trump utilized this same "hide the harmful standards" strategy in negotiations with financial institutions leading up to his financial crisis in 1990.

During the mid- to late 1980s, numerous financial institutions financed Trump's buying binge. As Trump would later say, *"You have to understand, those were the go-go days where the banks would give you more money than you needed."*[320]

This came to a screeching halt in mid-1990, when his empire collapsed and he faced personal bankruptcy, having personally guaranteed $833.5 million of his $3.2 billion owed.

At the time, according to the independent Leventhal Report those bankers commissioned, Trump was underwater by almost $300 million.

Here's how *Trump Revealed* described his first-ever meeting with those bankers, many of whom had no idea *until then* of the scope and breadth of Trump's collective debt and personal obligations.

> Trump was used to being in charge, but on this spring 1990 morning at the law firm of Weil, Gotshal & Manges [Full disclosure—Weil, Gotshal is a training client of mine.], he was surrounded by nearly thirty bankers united by a shared goal: to prevent Trump's tottering financial empire from tumbling over the precipice—and taking their money with it....
>
> **Only now had the bankers compared notes.** Trump would later say the negotiations had been his idea. But with so much of his empire losing money—and so many loan payments coming due—bankers had their reasons for wanting to sit down with Trump. What the bankers discovered worried them. The arithmetic showed that Trump owed them, collectively, two-thirds of his $3.2 billion debt....

To avert mutual destruction, a few of the lead bankers decided that their best hope would be to negotiate jointly with Trump. They would rein Trump in but leave him at the helm of his businesses. "He was basically worth more alive than dead," said Alan Pomerantz, a Weil, Gotshal real estate attorney who represented Citibank. [Emphasis added.][321]

Several independent standard elements relate to this negotiation.

First, it's extraordinary these bankers did not previously know of each other nor of Trump's collective debt and personal guarantees. These should have been known to them through the Trump financial statements they required to provide the loans. Had they known, those loaning him the later funds presumably would never had loaned him additional money. Too risky.

What happened? *Trump hid his true financial condition and incredible debt from the banks, including standards relating to it.*

As Steve Bollenbach, the chief financial officer Trump hired at the behest of the banks, noted *"It was so complicated that I think Donald had an advantage in terms of knowing where all the pieces fit, whereas many of the creditors had a much more limited view."* [322]

In fact, *Making Trump* noted that *"Many banks complained that they were unaware other banks had loaned money to Trump on his personal guarantee **with no public record of the obligation.**"* [Emphasis added.][323]

During this time, according to *Trump Show*, "**not one bank seemed to have a real sense of the mountain of guarantees he was piling up**. Even in late 1989 Bankers Trust was willing to loan him $100 million on his signature alone, with no asset or acquisition involved. No one sorted out the crisscrossed trail of debt." [Emphasis added.][324]

One small example of Trump's "hide the harmful standards" strategy—he insisted that the Citibank loan for his Mar-a-Lago purchase *not* be publicly recorded.[325] This way, no future bank considering a new Trump loan could learn of it from a public-records search. Banks usually require such loans be publicly recorded *to avoid this very problem.*

Hiding Harmful Standards: Manipulating a Mortgage Application to Hide his True Financial Condition

Another example of this strategy: Trump artificially inflated the asset values on financial statements used to support his loan applications. These were seemingly credible standards supporting his net worth at the time.

Trump's mortgage application for the Palace apartments in New York, a 283-unit apartment building, illustrates this. This transaction also became the subject of a fraud investigation by New York Attorney General Robert Abrams. Here is how *Trump Show* described Trump's effort to get a mortgage, which was based on the value of the building and sales projections.

> Blanche Sprague, Trump's longtime condominium sales chief, wrote Trump a memo in the summer of 1990 detailing the history of Palace price lists. She claimed that the "original price list" of apartments she prepared for him in mid-1988 anticipated that the building "should realize a sell-out of $179.2 million." But this total fell far short of the $220 million mortgage Donald wanted to borrow from Citibank for the project, meaning a sold-out building would still not earn back the mortgage. "You told me to up the number to '$260 million plus,'" Sprague wrote, "even though I told you it would be impossible to realize this number."
>
> Sprague prepared a second price list, which still failed to reach Donald's magic number. Finally, in an August 18, 1988, letter to Trump's lawyer, she forwarded a third list, "showing a sell-out of $265,008,000 per Donald's instructions." She noted in her letter: "You are aware of my views on this subject so I will not rehash them."
>
> Donald got his $220 million mortgage.[326]

The Banks Bought into the Trump Image

"This appears problematic," you might respond. "But isn't it the banks' responsibility to check his numbers and evaluations?" Absolutely. They shared blame here for loaning such extraordinary sums to Trump on such bare evidence of creditworthiness. In short, they failed to do their due diligence and failed to operate—as our financial system needs—as independent, credible standards during this time period. Those banks' shareholders paid the price.

Here is the role they played in Trump's demise, described in *Trump Show*.

> The eagerness of his bankers and investment brokers had, of course, helped make [Trump] a deal addict. When he did this string of late-eighties deals, he was riding his celebrity high, astonished that he suddenly seemed to have the same mesmerizing impact in a Citibank boardroom that he'd once

had on the *Donahue* show. Debt had become his drug, and the loans routinely grew larger than the price of the purchases, leaving an excess for his organizational needs....

In the end, even the buffaloed bankers had to agree, the power of [Trump's] personality and notoriety was a magnet. Like virtually everyone else, the bankers were taking his credit rating from *Lifestyles of the Rich and Famous....* "We just wanted to be associated" with his deals, said the Citibank executive, who'd basked in the media glory of the Plaza opening and partied on the *Princess.*[327]

Ironically, in the end, the media—that independent, credible entity through which he filtered his brand image—also contributed to the banks buying into his failed businesses.

Trump's Near Bankruptcy Gave Him Strong Leverage

Another important element in these workout negotiations—in addition to Trump hiding his true net worth and manipulating the standards involved—relates to his deep appreciation of leverage. Three negotiations at the time reflect this.

- Trump's Leverage in the Workout Negotiations
- Trump's Leverage with the Banks and his Divorce Settlement
- Trump's Leverage with The Boston Safe Deposit and Trust

Trump's Leverage in the Workout Negotiations

Despite the banks seemingly holding all the cards in this negotiation, Trump and the banks were in this bed together. How? As Weil Gotshal's real-estate attorney Alan Pomerantz noted earlier, Trump was worth more to them alive and in charge of his businesses than dead. And Trump knew it.

In other words, Trump faced certain default on his bank loans, as he didn't have the money to make his payments. But here's the kicker: The banks, if he went bankrupt, would own and have to run and sell his failing businesses at a fire sale. Bankruptcy would also cost the banks huge legal fees and years of fighting, with a bad resolution in the end guaranteed. Bad Plan B relative to a deal with Trump (the banks' Plan A). Trump was too big to fail. No bank wanted this.

Trump appreciated this leverage, repeatedly reminding the bankers that "unless they gave him relief, they all would suffer together."[328] Strong leverage.

How well did he exercise it? Trump described it as *"The greatest deal I ever made because I saw the world collapsing, and instead of waiting a year, I took my pride and I said the hell with it. I'm telling you, six months later the banks were in such trouble they couldn't have given you ten cents."* [329]

Trump negotiated the following deal with the banks:

- Trump would get a $65-million line of credit and deferred interest payments on about $1 billion in loans for up to five years;

- the banks would get control of most of Trump's empire and put liens on his three casinos, his yacht, his personal plane and other of his prized assets;

- Trump would be forced to sell much of what he owned; and

- Trump would go on a $450,000/month budget at first, dropping to $300,000 within two years—a substantial restriction on Trump's habits. [330]

Did Trump foresee the demise of the banks and himself in 1990 and call the meeting with his bankers, as he later contended? Highly doubtful. Trump would never set up an initial meeting with his negotiation counterparts *at the offices of the attorneys for one of his main adversaries, Citibank.*

His offices at Trump Tower—his turf—is far more likely. And if not Trump Tower, he would have set it at *his attorneys'* offices, not his counterparts'.

Trump's Leverage with the Banks and his Divorce Settlement

Trump also exercised his strong leverage with the banks about eight months after finalizing his workout deal. Trump then intentionally violated this deal and spent $10 million of the banks' money *without authorization. And they did nothing about it.* How did he get away with it? Leverage.

What happened? Trump—without permission from the banks and in breach of his agreement with them—gave his soon-to-be-ex-wife Ivana a certified check for $10 million as part of their divorce settlement. He took it from the $65 million the banks had advanced him to keep his businesses afloat. [331]

His chief financial officer at the time learned about this after the fact and told him it was a mistake. Trump replied, "What are they going to do?" [332]

The banks' Plan B even after their deal—forcing Trump into personal bankruptcy—was worse than just letting him breach, seemingly at will.

Even to the tune of $10 million. Trump knew this. So, he kept taking them to the cleaners.

Trump's Leverage with Boston Safe Deposit and Trust

One final example of Trump exercising strong leverage with the banks. This negotiation also occurred in early 1991. It seemed like his divorce payment might come back to haunt him, but it didn't, as his leverage—not his cash situation—was still strong.

This negotiation involved the insurance payment Trump owed on *The Trump Princess*, his yacht the banks were forcing him to sell. Here's how that negotiation played out.

- Boston Safe Deposit and Trust held the $29-million loan Trump had used to buy *The Trump Princess*.

- Under the loan, Trump owed the $500,000 annual insurance payment on the yacht.

- Trump didn't have the cash to pay it and had already depleted his $65 million line of credit with his divorce settlement.

- If the bank called the loan due to Trump's defaulting on the insurance payment, all the other banks could call their loans and trigger the collapse of Trump's financial world.

- Trump and his chief financial officer Stephen Bollenbach gambled and told the bank they wouldn't make the insurance payment. "'We told them, you got the mortgage payment on it and there's an insurance payment due so you should make it,' Bollenbach told [*TrumpNation* author Timothy L. O'Brien]. 'And they did. I think that's when we knew that we had some room to maneuver and negotiate.'"

- According to *TrumpNation*, "We said, *'You pay the fuckin' insurance. We're not paying it.'* Half a million dollars' worth of insurance annually," Donald recalled. *"They said, 'We're not going to pay it, you have an obligation. We're going to foreclose it and blah, blah, blah. I said, 'I don't give a fuck: You pay it.' And we waited, and the deadline came. And they paid it."* [333]

Again, Trump had strong leverage and aggressively exercised it.

Trump Fights to Undermine Harmful Standards Regardless of the Truth

Trump knows the power of sharing independent, credible standards when they help in negotiations. He did this in his negotiations involving his net worth, NBC/Television City, Commodore Hotel, Mar-a-Lago purchase, Mar-a-Lago property tax, banks loaning his money, the Resorts' deal, and Trump University.

He also knows the power of hiding independent, credible standards when they can hurt him if they become known. He did this in his negotiations involving his net worth, financial institutions, and asset values.

But what can he do if those independent, credible standards become publicly known despite his best efforts? Fight to undermine their perceived independence, legitimacy, and credibility. He's done this, too. Numerous times.

Here are two examples.

- Trump Fights to Undermine O'Brien's Net-Worth Estimate
- Trump Undermines a Gaming Analyst and Gets Him Fired

Notice how the merits of each fight play second fiddle to the public nature of the fight itself. It's the publicity of the fight that plays a bigger role in undermining the credibility and independence of the standards—not who won or lost in the end.

Trump's Fight to Undermine O'Brien's Public Net-Worth Estimate

Trump's most high-profile business fight to delegitimize an independent, credible standard involved *TrumpNation* author and former *New York Times* award-winning journalist Timothy L. O'Brien. What did O'Brien do? He published a book publicly questioning Trump's claims of stupendous net worth.

What did Trump do? Sued him and his publisher in early 2006 for $5 billion, alleging that O'Brien's estimate of Trump's 2005 net worth was false. O'Brien estimated Trump's net worth was $150 million to $250 million. Trump's lawsuit claimed his net worth was $5 billion to $6 billion.[334]

Why did Trump sue? Three reasons. *One*, send a bullying message to O'Brien. *Two*, undermine the credibility and independence of journalist O'Brien in the public's eyes. And, *three*, attempt to preserve his public image as a super-rich multi-billionaire and successful businessman.

Importantly, Trump largely accomplished his goals by aggressively engaging in this public fight—*regardless of who ultimately won the lawsuit.* Of course, Trump wanted to win. It's in his DNA. But he wins the public relations battle undermining O'Brien, whether he prevails in the suit or not.

How? The publicity regarding the suit will play out over many years. The publicity will inevitably create the narrative of two fighters duking it out—Trump v. O'Brien. The public will then likely perceive the issue—Trump's net worth—as controversial, with neither party wholly in the right. This largely benefits Trump, even if O'Brien's estimate is accurate.

Plus, the result will be a one-day story. Few will remember who won. But they will remember the big fight over billionaire Donald Trump's net worth. More PR for the Trump brand. And a successful undermining of a potentially impactful independent, credible standard.

Of course, Trump claimed O'Brien falsely understated Trump's net worth to sell more books and that it caused irreparable damage to his reputation. O'Brien, by contrast, countered that his evaluation was based on documents shown to him by Trump and statements from three unnamed sources.

Importantly, Trump testified under oath about it. Here is his testimony when questioned by O'Brien's attorney Andrew Ceresney.

Note the unusual way Trump assesses his net worth and the value of his assets. The substantive case revolved around Trump's and O'Brien's assessments of Trump's net worth. Here, Trump does *not* base his opinion on objective, credible, independent standards like market value, experts' opinions, and so on. O'Brien based his on such standards.

> Ceresney: Mr. Trump, have you always been completely truthful in your public statements about your net worth of properties?
>
> Trump: I try.
>
> Ceresney: Have you ever not been truthful?
>
> Trump: My net worth fluctuates, and it goes up and down with markets and with attitudes and with feelings, even my own feelings, but I try.
>
> Ceresney: Let me just understand that a little bit. Let's talk about net worth for a second. You said that the net worth goes up and down based upon your own feelings?

Trump:	Yes. Even my own feelings, as to where the world is, where the world is going, and that can change rapidly from day to day. Then you have a September 11th, and you don't feel so good about yourself and you don't feel so good about the world and you don't feel so good about New York City. Then you have a year later, and the city is as hot as a pistol. Even months after that it was a different feeling. So yeah, even my own feelings affect my value to myself.
Ceresney:	When you publicly state what you're worth, what do you base that number on?
Trump:	I would say it's my general attitude at the time that the question may be asked. And as I say, it varies.[335]

Trump correctly indicated that real-estate and other property values fluctuate due to many factors. But those factors, according to real estate and financial experts, do *not* include the owner's general feelings of value. Instead, they include values based on objective, independent, credible standards—like comparable properties, recent sales of similar properties, expert opinions of value/appraisals, and costs.

Plus, a variation of value from $250 million based on independent, credible standards to $5 billion based on Trump's "general attitude" and "feelings?"

The judge also noted several other discrepancies making it impossible to accurately determine that O'Brien's estimate of Trump's net worth was not true, including:

- Trump not disclosing the value of his closely held businesses in terms of assets or net of liabilities (This would be an objective credible standard.);

- Trump not disclosing the ownership percentages of his closely held businesses;

- Trump not disclosing the tax consequences of his holdings (This would be another objective, credible standard.); and

- A huge property that Trump claimed he owned was actually a partnership in which Trump had a stake to future profits only *after* the general partners had recovered their entire investment—which may never occur.[336]

Interestingly, despite Trump's loss at the trial court level, he appealed. This lengthened the proceeding, along with its publicity. The New Jersey state appeals court in 2011—six years after Trump filed suit—dismissed it, stating that Trump's testimony "failed to provide a reliable measure" of his net worth sufficient to support his claim of defamation.[337]

The court (another independent standard), effectively substantiated O'Brien's conclusions, finding:

> The largest portion of Mr. Trump's fortune, according to three people who had had direct knowledge of his holdings, apparently comes from his lucrative [family] inheritance. These people estimated that Mr. Trump's wealth, presuming that it is not encumbered by heavy debt, may amount to about $200 million to $300 million. That is an enviably large sum of money by most people's standards but far short of the billionaire's club.[338, 339]

In other words, two judges—themselves independent standards—found that Trump had not relied on any credible, independent standards to support his net worth contention of $5–6 billion. He lost. His case, which cost him a ton in legal fees, was found to be largely meritless.

But Trump didn't need to get the truth out about his net worth nor to prove defamation by O'Brien. He accomplished his goal of undermining O'Brien and his independent standards simply by bringing the suit and duking it out in the public sphere.

Trump Undermines a Gaming Analyst and Gets Him Fired

Trump also undermined independent gaming securities analyst Marvin Roffman, vice president of research with the Philadelphia-based Janney Montgomery Scott firm, in early 1990. In fact, he got him fired.

How did this happen? Roffman had a stellar and highly credible reputation as an expert specializing in Atlantic City's gaming industry, at least until he crossed swords with Trump. And he wasn't shy, as he regularly opined on the risks and rewards of the gaming business to reporters, casino operators, and investors, including Trump and his team. In fact, he presciently said in June 1987 that the Taj opening would put pressure on all of Atlantic City's profits and that leaner years might lie ahead.[340]

Trump ignored him, taking over Resorts (the public company then building the Taj) that next month. Trump subsequently sunk hundreds of millions of dollars more into completing the Taj.

But Trump couldn't ignore Roffman shortly before the Taj opened. Here's what happened and how Trump undermined the independent, credible expert Roffman for stating an opinion Trump didn't like, according to *Trump Revealed.*[341]

- Two weeks before the Taj opening, on March 20, 1990, Roffman was quoted in a *WSJ* story as stating "When this property [the Taj] opens, he [Trump] will break every record in the books in April, June, and July. But once the cold winds blow from October to February, it won't make it. The market just isn't there…. Atlantic City is an ugly and dreary kind of place. Even its hard-core customers aren't coming down as much."[342]

- That morning, Donald Trump faxed a letter to Roffman's firm stating, "You will be hearing shortly from my lawyers unless Mr. Roffman is immediately dismissed or apologizes."

- Trump also called Roffman and suggested he "write me a letter stating that the Taj is going to be one of the greatest successes ever, and I'm going to have it published."

- Janney Montgomery Scott's Chairman called in Roffman, who told him that he believed the junk bonds that Trump had used to finance the Taj "would fail"—leaving its bondholders with huge losses.

- The Chairman also called Trump, who demanded that the firm contact the *WSJ* and indicate that Roffman had been misquoted and that he believed that "the Taj Mahal is going to be the greatest success story ever."

- Roffman's boss subsequently drafted a letter of retraction for Roffman to sign, and he did, although he said later he felt he had no choice but to sign.

- The next morning, Roffman told his bosses he wanted to recommend that Taj bonds be "sold immediately" as he believed they would drop in value.

- The firm refused to allow him to issue that opinion publicly.

- Roffman then wrote a letter in which he "basically canceled" his previous day's retraction.

- With the threat of a Trump lawsuit hanging over their head, the firm then fired Roffman.

- Roffman subsequently took the company to arbitration over his firing and received a $750,000 settlement and sued Trump, ultimately agreeing to a confidential settlement.

- In a deposition, Trump said that he had not intended to get Roffman fired.

Trump again accomplished his goal. He undermined the credibility of the independent expert Roffman at a crucial time for the Trump Taj. He got his retraction. He got his scalp. He sent a "watch out or else" message to other independent credible analysts looking at his businesses.

It didn't even cost Trump much, at least financially. Of course, Trump would have been better off financially had he taken Roffman's advice in the first place and not bought Resorts. The Taj and Trump's Atlantic City casinos all experienced very hard times, just like Roffman predicted in 1987. As did Trump.

So, we know Donald Trump aggressively highlights helpful objective standards, hides and ignores harmful ones, and—if harmful ones get into the public realm—fights hard to undermine their perceived independence, credibility, and legitimacy.

How do these strategies—one of which Trump applies in almost all his negotiations—stack up with the research?

Pretty well, in highly competitive negotiation environments, but pretty poorly in more collaborative and problem-solving situations.

The Competitive Trump Standards Dance

Trump's aggressive standards-related strategies work effectively in highly competitive, zero-sum negotiation environments where neither party wants a future relationship. Many of Trump's negotiations fit this model, but not all. Importantly, though, he appears to use these strategies regardless of his potential future relationship with his counterparts. Sometimes it worked. Other times—counterproductive.

Here's the classic use of this "standards dance" in many negotiations.

In many sophisticated negotiations, everyone will have found the standards that favor their side and will use their most favorable standards to independently justify the 'fairness' of their positions. But what next? What happens when one side suggests "market value" to justify their position and the other suggests "precedent" and "cost" as more powerful justifications for their position? We get the "standards dance." The parties negotiate over which standard represents the more fair and applicable justification.[343]

Donald Trump does this dance well.

Leverage Trumps Standards

Trump also knows, however, that these standards-related moves often take a back seat to leverage. And they take a rear back seat in competitive negotiation environments—which is how Trump's win–lose mindset perceives all his deals.

Trump's appreciation of this leverage-trumps-standards element explains many facets of his typically aggressive approach. Here is an example.

"We're selling our company and trying really hard to be fair and reasonable, but the buyer with the most synergy is now being stubborn and taking a hard line on the tough financial issues. We've narrowed it down to them and have made excellent progress by exploring our mutual interests and generating creative options that add value for everyone.

"But when we request more money based on an independent, credible market value appraisal of our company and highlight how much they will profit from our technology and their distribution network—pointing to the fairness of a higher sales price—they just refuse to move. What should we do?"

This situation reflects a classic negotiation battle between leverage and standards. The buyer appears to have strong leverage (probably a really good Plan B to the Plan A with the seller). And the seller has strong independent, objective standards—powerful justifications for a higher sale price.

What would I recommend? At the end of the day, I would rather be in the buyer's situation. Why?

> **RESEARCH:** Leverage and a good Plan B in the end will almost always beat fair and reasonable standards. In other words, if I'm a seller I would rather have three buyers bidding against each other than that expert appraisal. And if I'm a buyer, I would rather have three good targets than a cost-benefit analysis explaining the synergy with one.[344]

Because Trump understands this well, he almost always *relies* on leverage and discounts any standards—even truly independent, credible ones. In fact, he relies on leverage *and* disbelieves, delegitimizes, and manipulates seemingly independent credible standards. By doing this, he brings the crux of the negotiation back to leverage, where he often believes he enjoys a power advantage.

This works in many competitive zero-sum environments, but it fails in others, especially where parties want future relationships. There, Trump's moves have been highly problematic. Here's an cxample.

Trump's Negotiations to Regain his Wealth

After Trump's near personal bankruptcy in 1990 and the long workout negotiation that followed in which the banks forced him to sell or give up control of almost all his assets, those financial institutions were certainly wary about loaning him more money without rock-solid security. Maybe not even then. They got burned big-time.

With Trump's business and financial failures then publicly known, other banks would also seemingly be reluctant to loan him much either.

How did Trump get sufficient wealth to regain his listing on the *Forbes* 400 in 1996, his first since his financial freefall started in 1990? And how did he do this despite having burned business relationships with financial institutions around the world?

Initially, understand the depth of his financial problems. From 1990 to 1993, Trump's financial world had been effectively destroyed, with:

- Four corporate bankruptcies.

- A repossessed airline.

- Millions of dollars of his Alexander's department store stock held by his banks.

- His yacht's sailing around the world in search of a buyer, finally finding a Saudi prince willing to purchase it for one-third less than what Trump had paid.

And, despite all this, he still faced massive debts.

How did Trump turn it around? And how did it involve his standards-related negotiation strategies?

Three factors appeared to play significant roles in the Trump turnaround—none of which involved Trump going back to financial institutions for more loans.

One, the economy started improving in the mid-1990s and more and more gamblers were hitting Trump's Atlantic City properties.

Two, and most importantly, Trump cashed in on his tarnished but still valuable public brand and went directly to the public for funds. He did this by creating a publicly traded company—DJT—that owned the Trump Plaza Hotel & Casino and would serve as his vehicle to operate his new ventures. The public could now buy into the Trump brand—and he sold it at a hefty price.

He initially raised $140 million at $14 per share and then raised an additional $155 million by having DJT sell new casino junk bonds. And when DJT shares jumped to $36 in 1996, Trump's shares were worth about $290 million. That was enough to put him back on the *Forbes* 400 list, the first time in seven years.[345]

Trump smartly recognized the value his brand still held with the American public. And he sold it to his best and most loyal negotiation counterparts, the public who had followed him for years. Crucial to this successful stock offering? The media's years-long independent, credible coverage of Trump. It's a powerful independent standard—and the public believed them.

Was this a traditional business negotiation between two professionals? No. But did it involve Trump communicating with many parties seeking to satisfy mutual interests—the classic definition of negotiation? Yes.

The *third* strategy Trump used to regain his wealth: a) saddle up his new public company with his personal debt; b) use the new capital from its public investors to buy up his other debt-laden assets at inflated prices; and c) put a big salary and bonuses from the company in his pocket.

Here is what happened in his foray into the public company world (Public companies must legally disclose a lot of this information.), according to *Trump Revealed*.

- Trump initially took some of the money raised from the public and the junk bonds to pay off $88 million of **his** debts.

- After a year, DJT the public company paid inflated values for Trump's two *personally* owned but deeply indebted casinos, the Trump Taj Mahal and Trump Castle. *Amazingly, Trump here was both the buyer (DJT CEO) and the seller (personal Trump). He thus effectively set his own price—a great negotiation situation.*[346]

- DJT bought Trump Castle for $100 million more than independent experts indicated it was objectively worth. Trump also received $880,000 in cash for arranging the deal.

- DJT shareholders at the end of 1996 found themselves on the hook for $1.7 billion of Trump's debt, with much of its cash going to interest payments on that new debt.

- DJT share prices plummeted in 1996 to $12, while Trump received $7 million in compensation that year (including a $5 million bonus).[347]

How well did public casino company CEO Trump negotiate on behalf of his *public* shareholders, to whom he owed a fiduciary duty? Not well.

CEO Donald Trump negotiated against personal Donald Trump in buying the Trump Castle and Trump Taj—and personal Donald Trump won that win–lose negotiation. Independent, credible analysts indicated CEO Trump *overpaid* $100 million for the Castle. This was borne out later by another independent, credible standard—the cost standard—as CEO Trump bought the Castle in 1996 from himself for $525 million but sold it for only $38 million in 2011.[348]

Trump again ignored harmful standards—the independent analysts who said he overpaid. Instead, he seemingly only cared about his leverage—his power as CEO to buy the assets and as owner to sell them.

How well did personal Trump benefit from these "negotiations?" Extremely well, according to *Trump Revealed*.

- While Trump was Chairman of DJT, it lost over $1 billion and was *never* in the black between 1995 and 2005.

- DJT's share prices went from a $35 high to a low of 17 cents during that time.

- If you had bought $100 of DJT shares in 1995, you could sell them for around $4 in 2005.

- If you had bought $100 in MGM Resorts shares in 1995 (another casino company), you could sell them for around $600 in 2005.

- DJT stock and bondholders lost over $1.5 billion under Trump's management.

- Stock exchange officials froze DJT trading in 2004 as rumors spread of its filing for bankruptcy—Trump's fifth corporate bankruptcy action.

- Trump as DJT Chairman from 1995 to 2009 received more than $44 million from DJT.[349]

DJT's public shareholders paid the price, just like their banking predecessors. Trump himself acknowledged how *his* tenure as a public company head benefited *him* more than his shareholders. He said later, *"Entrepreneurially speaking, not necessarily from the standpoint of running a company but from an entrepreneur's standpoint, [the stock offering] was one of the great deals."*[350]

Great for whom? Trump the personal entrepreneur. By all objective and credible standards, he was 100 percent correct—he made out like a bandit.

The media—that consistent standard throughout Trump's career—would likely agree. *Forbes* in 2004 assessed Trump's wealth at a minimum $2.6 billion.[351]

LESSONS LEARNED	
Trump's Strategies and Tactics	Trump highlights objective standards that help him.
	Trump hides harmful standards that hurt him.
	Trump fights to undermine harmful standards regardless of their truth.
	Trump regained his wealth in part by using his media-created image to sell public company stock.
	Trump ignored all standards in negotiating as buyer and seller while CEO of DJT.
Lessons Learned	Credible, objective, and independent standards underlie "fair and reasonable" conclusions in negotiations.
	Independent standards like market value, precedent, costs and profits power, experts, and status play powerful negotiation roles.
	Parties often negotiate over the most "fair and reasonable" standard—the standards dance.
	Trump delegitimizes standards, making them less relevant and helpful in negotiations.
	Leverage trumps standards.

CHAPTER 9

OUTRAGEOUS MOVES AND COUNTERMOVES

D onald Trump asked NBC to pay him *$18 million per episode* before Season Two of *The Apprentice*—up from $50,000 per episode in Season One.[352] Quite a raise! And this in addition to his 50-percent ownership in the show.

NBC turned him down. But it started his negotiation for a raise. (Full disclosure—NBCUniversal is a training client of mine but has not shared any information with me relating to Trump.)

Trump described his typical offer-concession strategy, saying, "My style of deal-making is quite simple and straightforward. I aim very high, and then I just keep pushing and pushing and pushing to get what I'm after. Sometimes I settle for less than I sought, but in most cases I still end up with what I want."[353]

TrumpNation also described Trump's back-and-forth process that inevitably occurred in his deals. "Zoom in for the jackpot. Be outrageous in your demands. Keep a straight face. See what happens. Make a buck as fast as possible. Keep a straight face. Pretend you knew exactly what would happen all along.... The least you can do is ask if the opportunity presented itself. So Donald asked."[354]

Yes, we teach in the negotiation world that you will never get what you don't ask for. But *$18 million* per episode?

Donald Trump moves extremely aggressively in the offer-concession stage of the process. Everyone knows this.

But does he, as suggested by the research:

- start appropriately aggressively with his initial moves?

- start with an end goal in mind and map his moves so he ends up where he wants?

- know the offer-concession patterns that exist in his negotiation environments?

- evaluate the advantages and disadvantages of making first offers?

- support his moves with powerful independent standards?

- understand the psychology underlying this back-and-forth part of the process?

Let's start by evaluating just how aggressively he moves overall.

Trump's Extremely Aggressive Moves Overall

The Apprentice Fee Negotiation

The Apprentice fee negotiation reflects Trump's vintage aggressiveness in the offer-concession stage of the process.

> Donald reveled in his new star status [at NBC], asserting to me [*TrumpNation* author Timothy L. O'Brien] in early 2004 in an interview for *The New York Times* that, "In prime-time television, I'm the highest-paid person."
>
> "You get more than Oprah?" I asked.
>
> "Oprah's not prime time," he retorted.
>
> "You get more than Larry King?"
>
> "Yeah, and Larry King is cable."
>
> "More than even the cast of *Friends*?"
>
> "Well, collectively, no," he acknowledged. "But individually, yes."
>
> In fact, Donald's $50,000-per-show fee for *The Apprentice's* debut season did not make him the highest-paid person in prime time. Nor was he anywhere near to clearing the kind of lucre that each *Friends* star took home. But Donald knew what they were making, and he shook the money tree. Before the second season of *The Apprentice* got under way, he told NBC that he wanted $18 million an episode for his future participation. Donald's logic was simple. He was filling very big shoes on Thursday nights: the slot vacated by the six

members of the *Friends* cast. The *Friends* stars each made $1.5 million per episode, for a total haul of $9 million per thirty-minute show. As the solo attraction of *The Apprentice*, Donald said, he should be paid $9 million every thirty minutes. Since his show was an hour long, he deserved $18 million a pop.

"That seemed fair," he told the *WSJ*. "I'm not being facetious."[355]

First, notice the role that standards played in this negotiation. Trump appreciated the power of the market value standard for his appearances, referencing the amounts paid to Larry King, Oprah, and the *Friends* stars (the standard he used as it most favored him).

He also ignored the precedent standard—his $50,000-per-show fee for the initial season—and instead falsely said it made him the "highest-paid" (another standard). Why lie about the precedent? It disfavored him.

Trump also knew several other standards supported his incredible demand, as he knew the show only cost about $2 million per episode to make (the cost standard), and it grossed multi-millions in ad revenue (the profits standard). According to *TrumpNation's* O'Brien, he ended up negotiating "'substantially more' than $1.25 million per episode, he told me, but he couldn't be more specific because the deal was confidential."[356]

Interestingly, Trump's NBC counterpart Jeff Zucker said NBC paid Trump $60,000 per episode.[357] How profitable did *The Apprentice* turn out for Trump? Trump said he made *"as much as $214 million over fourteen seasons."*[358] Part of this was undoubtedly due to his "outrageous" asks.

The Jimmy Carter Aggressive Ask

Here's another example of how Trump views the aggressiveness element during the offer-concession stage of negotiations. He found the following request admirable about former President Jimmy Carter, recounted in *Art of the Deal*:

> After he lost the election to Ronald Reagan, Carter came to see me in my office. He told me he was seeking contributions to the Jimmy Carter Library. I asked how much he had in mind. And he said, "Donald, I would be very appreciative if you contributed five million dollars."
>
> I was dumbfounded. I didn't even answer him.
>
> But that experience also taught me something. Until then, I'd never understood how Jimmy Carter became president.

The answer is that as poorly qualified as he was for the job,
**Jimmy Carter had the nerve, the guts, the balls, to ask for
something extraordinary.** That ability above all helped him
get elected president. [Emphasis added.][359]

Trump acts the same way in his negotiations, exhibiting extreme
aggressiveness in his asks, demands, moves, and countermoves.

Here is one final example illustrating Trump's overall aggressiveness in
the offer-concession stage. Then we will analyze how his strategies align with
the experts' research.

The Barbizon Hotel and 100 Central Park South "Sale"

In 1981, Donald Trump had a grand vision for two old buildings on the
south side of New York's Central Park—The Barbizon Plaza Hotel and a
15-story building housing rent-controlled apartments at 100 Central Park
South. Trump wanted to demolish the buildings and build luxury apartments
there.[360]

But Trump could not legally boot the tenants, and some refused to
leave as they were paying rock-bottom prices for apartments with a prime
location. Some even had spectacular Central Park views. What did Trump
do? He started with a little bullying—trying to change their Plan Bs (their
Plan A being a deal with Trump whereby they agreed to leave). According to
Trump Show, the tenants said Trump:

> ...tried to force them out by annoying them. He proposed
> to move homeless people into at least ten vacant apartments;
> the city declined the generous offer. Maintenance workers
> ignored leaky faucets and broken appliances and covered up
> windows of empty apartments with ratty tinfoil. A tenants'
> group accused Trump of harassment, but he denied it all.[361]

They reached an impasse in their negotiations, and litigation ensued. In
1985, the New York Department of Housing and Community Renewal, after
eight months of reviewing tenants' complaints detailing alleged harassment
by Trump, issued an order "requiring full hearings and charging Trump with
'an unrelenting, systematic and illegal campaign' whose 'singleminded intent'
was to 'force the tenants from their housing accommodations at the earliest
possible time.'"[362]

Trump had, according to the Department's Housing enforcement
division hearing notice,

...tried to force the tenants out by 'verbally intimidating' them with claims that the demolition [of their building] was 'certain and imminent,' by instituting 'unwarranted litigation' against a variety of individual tenants, by permitting 'breaches in the security of the building,' and by 'interfering with or decreasing a broad panorama of basic and essential services.'[363]

After negotiations with the tenants and millions in Trump legal fees, the standoff ended with Trump dropping his demolition demands, letting the tenants stay, and renovating the building into 26 luxury apartments. He also closed the Barbizon and renovated it into 400 luxury apartments.[364]

How aggressively did Trump engage with the tenants in terms of his moves? Extremely aggressively.

So, how does Trump's overall aggressiveness in the offer-concession stage stack up with the research? Mixed. His extreme aggressiveness includes a downside risk to his credibility and trust and may lead to significant long-term costs.

What about the extent that Trump's specific offer-concession moves align with the research? Let's evaluate this in connection with his potential sale of these buildings during his negotiations with the tenants in 1983.

At the time, Trump reached out to commercial real-estate broker Stephen N. Ifshin and informed him he might sell these buildings. Ifshin thought he could find a buyer. What occurred next, according to Ifshin, illustrates signature Trump offer-concession strategies.

I want $100 million for the two buildings packaged together, Trump said [which he had bought two years prior for $13 million, the cost standard]. **It's a lot of money, Ifshin said, astounded by such a huge ask. Such a price was unheard of in Manhattan's real-estate scene at the time, even as an unofficial high number to be floated to favored buyers, called a "whisper number."** But brokering such a sale could earn Ifshin several million dollars in commissions, and he put out the word that the buildings could be had. Sherman Cohen, a tough negotiator in the Manhattan properties market, expressed interest, and Ifshin set up a meeting in Trump's office....

They got down to business, and Trump announced that the buildings were for sale, for $100 million, firm. When I give out a price, that's the price, he said. Cohen replied that he didn't have $100 million to offer, but he could see his way to $90 million.

They were close, so close, Ifshin thought. Now a serious negotiation could begin. But Trump merely thanked Cohen and repeated the price, $100 million, nothing less. Cohen said no more. Trump said no more. It was a stare-down, an impasse. The meeting ended in less than half an hour. Cohen left, but Ifshin stayed behind, flabbergasted. Why? he asked Trump. Why turn such an offer down? You were close.

It wasn't what I was asking, Trump said. I never sell for less than I'm asking.

Preposterous, Ifshin thought. There's always a negotiation. And then it dawned on Ifshin that he had been used. Donald, he said, this was your way of getting an informal appraisal, to see if someone would bite, and for how much. Trump denied it, but Ifshin pushed back: This was just a ruse to see what the buildings might be worth in the marketplace, and now Trump knew, at least $90 million. You owe me a commission for getting you an informal appraisal from my buyer, Ifshin said. You owe me $10,000.

Trump looked at him like he was insane, but said he'd pay him back with a favor in the future. That never happened. Ifshin never dealt with Trump again and Trump didn't sell the buildings. "He wasn't upfront," Ifshin said. "He sort of hid his intentions. And that's the part that bothered me—very clever but not straight." Trump, Ifshin concluded, was someone who was unreliable, didn't care about long-term relationships, and burned through people. [Emphasis added.][365]

In addition to his overall offer-concession aggressiveness, five specific Trump elements bear analysis relative to how they match up with the research.

- Trump once again demonstrated extreme aggressiveness in his initial demand.

- Trump understood the pattern of moves in this commercial real-estate negotiation, with a highly unusual "take-it-or-leave-it" first offer.

- Trump knew to make the first offer, even as a "whisper number," and likely intuited its advantages.

- Trump used Ifshin to create an independent, credible standard for the buildings' market value—and could then use it in a later negotiation as a standard supporting a future sale price.

- Trump appreciated the principle of reciprocity—recognizing the value Ifshin gave him and offering to pay him back with a "favor in the future."

1. Trump's Outrageously Aggressive First Demands

"Astounded" and "unheard of in Manhattan's real estate scene at the time," were Ifshin's thoughts describing Trump's initial demand. While this ultimately was a "fake" sale, Ifshin initially took it seriously, as did potential buyer Sherman Cohen.

This level of aggressiveness is consistent with how long-time Trump lawyer George Ross describes Trump's strategy in this offer-concession arena. He writes:

> Good negotiation is a continual exploration of the realm of possibilities. In many cases, your success is going to depend on your ability to think in reverse, something Trump is a master of. **Thinking in reverse comes into play when you make a proposal that is so outrageous that you know it has no chance of acceptance in its raw form** and then reversing your course and agreeing to modify your proposal to make it more palatable for the other side. [Emphasis added.][366]

What does the research suggest in terms of aggressiveness in making a first move or counter? This can be difficult. You don't want to risk leaving a lot on the table. Yet, you don't want to poison the atmosphere by appearing unrealistic. You also need to give yourself enough room to move, so everyone ultimately feels comfortable they reached a "fair" result.

How can you strike the right balance?

RESEARCH: Four main factors should be evaluated in making this decision, some of which Trump appears to have considered (although not necessarily followed).
- First-offer expectations peculiar to your industry or context
- Your original goal
- Your most aggressive yet reasonable independent standard
- The "room to move" psychological gamesmanship dynamic[367]

What first-offer expectations existed for Trump in his possible sale of the Barbizon buildings in New York City's commercial real-estate environment? Trump knew that sellers in that environment traditionally make the first move, even as a "whisper number." And Ifshin, as a commercial real-estate broker, lived and breathed this every day. Trump's first move here? Consistent with the following research relating to first-offer expectations.

First-Offer Expectations Peculiar to Your Industry or Context

Here's the deal. Expectations exist in various industries and contexts as to who makes the first offer. Similar expectations often exist regarding the nature of the offer or first counter. What should you do? Find out what first offer, or first counter expectation, exists in your industry. If you don't, you risk sending the wrong signal concerning what you ultimately will find acceptable. The messages you send at the start have a disproportionate impact, just like first impressions when you meet someone. Make this move count.[368]

Donald Trump made his $18-million-per-episode and $100-million first moves count. And he clearly knew the first-offer expectations in those industries. He intuitively shoots for the moon and largely benefits as a result.

How did Trump's moves match up with his original goals? Unclear. Let's analyze his moves relative to the research.

Your Original Goal

At the onset of the offer-concession stage, you should have an excellent idea of your leverage and your most favorable independent standards. Based on these, reassess your goals and, if necessary, reset them. Make these goals your touchstone. In other words, where you start and how far you move each time should be evaluated relative to your goals. Your goals should drive your offer-concession strategy.[369]

Trump appeared to do this pretty well in his *Apprentice* negotiations, at least according to Trump's account. But his intuition—not strategically set goals—almost certainly drove his offer-concession moves. This is typical for most negotiators, even extremely skilled ones. Ideally, your end goal will drive your offer-concession decisions and occupy front-and-center in your strategic plan. This includes where you start.

Your Most Aggressive yet Reasonable Independent Standard

Trump did not do as well, however, in incorporating his most aggressive yet reasonable standard. At least in *The Apprentice* fee negotiations. As noted earlier, he used a variety of standards to support his $18-million-per-episode demand.

But NBC could easily differentiate and undermine them. Trump's standards, while independent, didn't pass the straight-face test. And his true value, their final deal, ended up football fields less than those standards. End of day: His standards weren't in any way "reasonable."

His extreme aggressiveness there was almost certainly counterproductive.

> **RESEARCH:** In making an initial offer, parties should usually start with their most aggressive realistic expectation that can be justified in some objective way with an independent standard.[370]

Here's the problem with Trump's $18-million-per-episode starting move. Despite the standards he identified, $18 million still feels completely unrealistic relative to what any one other actor or star receives for a one-hour television episode. And that's the most applicable, objective standard. While Trump can argue for $18 million based on cherry-picked standards, it just doesn't seem remotely realistic. He thus loses credibility by even floating that number.

Trump's $100 million sale price demand for the Barbizon buildings, however, appears spot-on, standard-wise. While Ifshin found it astounding relative to other standards, potential buyer Cohen responded at *$90 million*— proof that Trump's $100 million first move was appropriately aggressive. And Cohen certainly would have gone higher, based on the patterns in similar negotiations (analyzed next). But Cohen wouldn't have even started at $90 million had Trump been less aggressive in his first move.

The "Room to Move" Psychological Gamesmanship Dynamic

What about the "room to move" psychological gamesmanship dynamic?

Does he make sure, as the research suggests, that he builds into his starting point sufficient "room to move," so his counterparts *feel* that they psychologically achieved success.[371]

Trump gets this and understands the "room to move" psychology of the offer-concession stage well. In fact, his aggressiveness in this stage virtually guarantees that he will make substantial moves off his starting point before landing on a mutually acceptable result. This means his counterparts will almost always see him move, a lot, thus feeling better about the endpoint.

Ironically, the absence of this "room to move" element in Trump's take-it-or-leave-it offer in the Barbizon negotiation predictably caused the breakdown. Trump intended this, according to Ifshin. If true, this underscores his understanding of this psychological part of the process.

2. Trump Understands General Offer-Concession Patterns

Just as Trump likely understands who traditionally makes the first offer in his industry contexts—first-offer expectations—he also likely understands the patterns underlying the subsequent back-and-forth process that occurs in most negotiations. As Ifshin noted, it's *"preposterous"* to just stop after the first offer in commercial real estate. *"There's always a negotiation."*

Trump lawyer Ross agrees, noting that "thinking in reverse"—a Trump specialty—means making an *"outrageous"* proposal/first move "and then reversing your course and agreeing to modify your proposal to make it more palatable for the other side."[372] Those modifications represent subsequent Trump moves, and his counterparts' moves, until they reach agreement.

Many consider these back-and-forth moves the "real" negotiation. Negotiation experts, though, understand these moves only represent one of the final stages in the process.

What does the research indicate regarding these different patterns in different negotiation contexts?

> **RESEARCH:** Find out and know these offer-concession patterns. The best way to predict future offer-concession behavior is to research the offer-concession patterns that exist in similar situations in the past.[373]

By identifying these patterns of acting and reacting in general negotiation circumstances, you will increase your ability to predict what similarly situated negotiators will do in the future. These patterns shape your expectations.

Knowing these patterns, you can then more logically determine what offer to make, when and how to make it, how much to concede, if at all, and whether (and how much of) a response is to be expected from your counterparts. Understanding offer-concession patterns forms a crucial element in the negotiation process.

Keep in mind, though, two caveats. *First,* patterns represent general conclusions that do not apply in every instance. But in terms of your ability to predict future actions, relying on patterns of past behavior is a good general rule of thumb.

Second, different patterns may exist in your industry or in your own typical negotiation context. Patterns in negotiations in the Middle East are different from those in negotiations in the Far East. Find the patterns that apply in your industry or your context. The more specific the context in which the pattern appears, the more it will help you determine what to expect and how to act and react with your own offers and concessions.

So, what general offer-concession patterns generally exist in American culture?

- Most negotiators enter the offer-concession stage too soon—so beware of the premature offer.

- The longer you wait, the less eager you appear, and vice versa—the timing pattern.

- Early concessions include relatively larger moves—the size pattern.[3/4]

How well does Trump find out or know the patterns in the industries in which he has negotiated? It depends. He has a wide breadth of knowledge regarding the patterns in commercial real-estate negotiations in New York City. These include different patterns with city officials, subcontractors, apartment buyers, and so on.

He also likely understands the patterns in the gaming industry, particularly in Atlantic City.

But in the 1980s, Trump branched into various businesses unrelated to his core residential and commercial real-estate development experiences— like operating hotels, owning a professional football team, and managing an airline. Based on his intuitive approach and his style of doing deals at that time, it's unlikely he researched the negotiation patterns prior to jumping into his negotiations in those industries.

Of course, this evaluation involves some speculation. We don't have much evidence of the back-and-forth moves in many of his negotiations then.

Trump may also have hired brokers and others with extensive experience in those industries. They would have known these patterns and, if asked, advised Trump of them. We know he did this when he started in Manhattan real estate in his late 20s.

We also know, however, that he often just went with his gut, like when he started buying stock in Bally's, and when he overpaid for New York's Plaza Hotel.

Plus, Trump, like many good business negotiators, may have mixed things up to avoid developing a reputation as predictable. In business negotiations, you generally don't want to be perceived as particularly predictable. Too much predictability empowers your counterparts to pretty much know your moves in advance. That's counterproductive.

On the other hand, you want to follow general offer-concession patterns in your industry. Otherwise you risk a reputation as someone who negotiates in bad faith. Good-faith negotiating in this context basically means that you do what most expect you to do based on industry-established patterns. (Often this means A traditionally starts. Then B moves. Then A goes again—with A moving closer to B's first move. Then B moves again—now getting closer to A's last move, and so on.) There's a balance between predictability of moves and good-faith negotiating. Finding it can be tough.

Trump's challenge—and the extent that his offer-concession moves will be effective based on the research—relate to how much his offer-concession aggressiveness differs from the general patterns. His effectiveness also relates to how his counterparts perceive his moves.

Based on Trump's typically incredibly aggressive first moves, I suspect his later moves adhere to this same level of aggressiveness. If so, they may very well have limited or negative impact on his counterparts and *their* counters. That would largely defeat the purpose of his counters and undermine their effectiveness.

Trump's Mar-a-Lago Counter-Pattern

Perhaps the singular example providing insight into Trump's offer-concession knowledge and patterns comes from his Mar-a-Lago negotiation. Here, he deliberately ignored the traditional pattern in the residential real-estate world—where buyers start low and go higher and sellers start high and go lower and you almost always land somewhere in between.

In purchasing Mar-a-Lago, Trump did the opposite—an even *more* aggressive strategy than starting super low and moving up. Here's how he described his strategy.

> "[The Post Foundation owner] put it up for sale at an asking price of $25 million. I first looked at Mar-a-Lago while vacationing in Palm Beach in 1982. Almost immediately I put in a bid of $15 million, and it was promptly rejected. Over the next few years, the foundation signed contracts with several other buyers at higher prices than I'd offered, only to have them fall through before closing. Each time that happened, I put in another bid, but always at a lower sum than before. Finally, in late 1985, I put in a cash offer of $5 million, plus another $3 million for the furnishings in the house. Apparently, the foundation was tired of broken deals. They accepted my offer, and we closed one month later.... It just goes to show that it pays to move quickly and decisively when the time is right.[375]

Notice five elements here relating to Trump's offer-concession strategy.

- His first move was $15 million versus a $25 million asking price. I don't know the residential real-estate patterns in Palm Beach for multi-million-dollar properties at the time, but I strongly suspect a $15 million offer on a $25 million listed property could reasonably be termed a lowball offer.

- Trump's initial offer being "promptly rejected" suggests—due to the timing pattern noted earlier—it was an aggressive lowball offer. In other words, the Post Foundation seller in "promptly" rejecting the offer sent the message to Trump, through its timing of the rejection, that it considered $15 million super low and unacceptable.

- Trump failed to mention his leverage-enhancing tactic in which he had bought the beachfront property in front of Mar-a-Lago after his initial offers. His strengthened leverage thus fully justified his subsequently lower offers. Offer-concession patterns change when leverage changes. It did here, too. Trump took advantage of it.

- This negotiation took place over several years. The length of this negotiation—part of the timing pattern—impacts the parties' leverage. The longer the property remained listed and unsold, the more potential buyers will have perceived the seller as desperate. After all, it means no one was willing to cough up sufficient funds to buy it over several years. This means the seller saw few, if any, good Plan Bs. (Its Plan B would be selling to someone other than Trump.) This translates to weaker leverage for sellers and stronger leverage for buyers like Trump. By waiting, Trump's leverage strengthened solely by the time elapsing—again justifying a departure from the buyer's general pattern of starting low and moving up. As Trump's leverage increased, he made offers consistent with his strengthened leverage. Smart moves.

- Trump said he made a cash offer which, as we know from his litigation testimony under oath later, was untrue. Why do we care? Because real-estate sellers value cash offers higher than non-cash offers involving bank financing. A $10 million cash offer to a seller may be functionally equivalent to a $10.5 million offer with a mortgage. The reason? Cash offers do not depend on buyers getting approved for financing—a risk for sellers. This could be a significant risk for the seller, depending on the buyer's finances and creditworthiness. It also affects the patterns involved.

What does this tell us about Trump's knowledge and practice regarding general offer-concession patterns? He understands them, at least in the real-estate world, and pretty much incorporates them into his own moves and countermoves.

3. Trump's First Offers—He Often Uses Them to Anchor Expectations and Sometimes Refuses, Too

Donald Trump regularly makes first offers. He also often waits for his counterparts to make first offers. Which reflects negotiation best practices? Both.

> **RESEARCH:** You should make first offers in certain circumstances. And you should wait for a first offer from your counterpart in other circumstances.[376]

The challenge? Deciding when and where to make it or wait. In many negotiations this can be the most critical strategic decision you make.

Early in my career I heard that you should never make the first offer. Frankly, this is unrealistic. Sometimes this decision is out of your control. If you're selling your house, tradition dictates that sellers make the first offer. If you decide not to make it, you might be waiting a long time to sell.

Tradition, of course, often plays a major role in who starts. If tradition doesn't dictate this decision, however, or if you believe you might gain by bucking the trend, analyze the advantages and disadvantages of making first offers. Here's a preview of them:

Advantages to Making First Offers

- Set expectations
- Elicit genuine reaction
- Strategic advantages: leverage timing, information, and so on

Disadvantages to Making First Offers

- Lack of information to appropriately set it
- Other side gains important information
- Bracketing[377]

How does Trump determine whether to start? Tradition largely dictates his answer, as it should. However, Trump seems to lean *toward* making a first move when the first-offer tradition is unclear, no tradition exists, or when the tradition and the precedent involved appear unfavorable to him.

Let's evaluate his first offer decisions in several negotiations, taking into account these considerations.

Donald Trump's First Offer for His Boeing 727

Donald Trump's description of how he negotiated to buy his Boeing 727 illustrates his attitude toward first offers. Here's how he described this mid-1980s negotiation, including his first move.

> I finally found a plane. I happened to be reading an article in *Business Week* in the spring of 1987 about a troubled, Texas-based company named Diamond Shamrock. The article described how top Shamrock executives were enjoying incredible perks, actually living like kings. Among the examples cited was a lavishly equipped company-owned 727, which executives flew around in at will.
>
> I sensed an opportunity. On Monday morning, I called the office of the Diamond Shamrock executive who had been pictured on the cover of the *Business Week* article. It turned out that he was no longer there and a new chairman, Charles Blackburn, had just been named. I was immediately put

through to him, we talked for a few minutes, and I wished him well. Then I said that I'd read about the company's 727, and that if he had any interest in selling, I was interested in buying. Sure enough, Blackburn said that as much as they all loved that plane, selling it was one of the first things on his agenda. He even offered to send it up to New York, so that I could take a look at it.

The next day I went out to La Guardia airport for a look. I had to smile. This plane could seat up to two hundred passengers, but it had been reconfigured for fifteen, and it included such luxuries as a bedroom, a full bath, and a separate working area. It was a little more plane than I needed, but I find it hard to resist a good deal when the opportunity presents itself.

A new 727 sells for approximately $30 million. A G-4, which is one fourth the size, goes for about $18 million. However, I knew that Diamond Shamrock was hungry to sell, and that not very many people are in the market for 727s.

I offered $5 million, which was obviously ridiculously low. They countered at $10 million, and at that point I knew I had a great deal, regardless of how the negotiation ended. Still, I haggled some more, and we finally agreed on a price of $8 million. [Emphasis added.][378]

What does this negotiation tell us about Trump's tendency to make first offers and his strategic analysis underlying them?

First, some context relating to the negotiation, based on Trump's account. Each likely contributed to Trump's decision to move first and move aggressively.

- Diamond Shamrock appeared desperate to sell its 727, given its new chairman, troubled financial condition, and bad publicity for its executives "living like kings." *"Selling [its 727] was one of the first things on its agenda,"* said its new chairman. Each of these elements gave Trump leverage.

- Diamond Shamrock offered to fly the plane to New York *the next day* so Trump could view it. This further strengthened Trump's leverage by emphasizing Diamond's desperation, based in part on the timing pattern. It's like your counterpart calls you back one minute after you leave a voice mail message expressing interest in their used car. They should have waited at least a little bit to call you back.

- Trump knew Diamond did not have any other potential buyers yet interested (no Plan Bs at the time other than not selling). In fact, the 727 wasn't even then listed for sale. And few buyers for used private 727s even existed. More leverage for Trump. This also hearkens back to Trump's deal for the Trump Tower site—he bought that from a financially troubled department store prior to other developers even knowing the site was for sale.

- Trump wanted to buy, but he wasn't desperate. More leverage for Trump. Plus, he could have found other private planes for sale or bought a new one (his Plan Bs).

- Trump appeared to have done his homework on the independent, objective standards like "market value" relating to private planes. A new 727 cost $30 million. And a new G-4 cost $18 million. And while this 727 was used, substantial costs had reconfigured it to make it extraordinarily luxurious. These independent standards gave Trump some context in which to evaluate when and what to offer for the plane.

And who traditionally makes the first move in the sale of private planes? If it's like the sale of other items, like cars, the sellers likely start. Unless it's an auction—where sellers get the buyers to start and bid against each other.

Here, though, Diamond or Trump could have made the first move. The 727 wasn't even listed. Trump jumped in first, and quite aggressively. Clever move. Why? He took advantage of his strong leverage, favorable standards, and the major advantage to making a first move—setting the parties' psychological expectations. We call this "anchoring" in the negotiation world—it anchors their expectations. It's akin to first impressions. The first time you meet someone disproportionately impacts your impression of them. Same thing for first offers.

RESEARCH: First offers disproportionately impact parties' expectations of what will occur in the offer-concession stage of negotiations. It's one advantage to making first offers. They set expectations.

Longtime Wall Street lawyer James Freund, who was involved in many of the 1980s takeover battles, says he often likes to make the first offer on price matters, because it allows him to take control of the issue. If you are a knowledgeable buyer, he writes in *Smart Negotiating: How to Make Good Deals in the Real World*, you want the seller "negotiating off your opening number, not his own. Your bid sends a message to your counterpart: If he wants to play ball, here's the ballpark where the action will occur. Or, to change (and mix) metaphors, think of this as a first-strike deterrent against the seller shooting for the moon."[379]

Freund makes an important point. Jumping out front with a first offer provides parties with the opportunity to set the initial offer-concession tone and sends an important message to the other side about your range of acceptable numbers and the value you place on the item. You set the tone, mindset, and range for concessions. This has important strategic benefits.

For this same reason you also regularly see first offers for rates in many professional areas, like lawyers, accountants, doctors, and business consultants.[380]

Making first offers also gives individuals a greater sense of control. Their decision sets the tone for the negotiation. This especially appeals to strong, dominating personalities like Trump's.

Commodore Hotel and Trump Tower Abatement First Offers

Donald Trump also made first offers on his first two big deals: the Commodore Hotel redevelopment and Trump Tower. His counterparts in those negotiations? New York City. The biggest issue on the table between them? Tax abatements.

One reason Trump successfully got them? Aggressive first moves. Had he waited for New York City to offer the incentives, they would probably have been much less.

Recall, Trump received an unprecedented Commodore Hotel abatement: 99 years with an estimated $400 million value over its first 40 years. The Trump Tower one proved extremely valuable, too.

In each instance, Trump applied for the abatement. A first offer. Why? Two reasons. It appears developers traditionally did this. But not always. Sometimes cities offer local companies tax incentives to stay—like New York City did to keep NBC at Rockefeller Center. They do the same to incentivize companies to relocate their headquarters from other cities.

For Trump and his tax abatements, more importantly, it made strategic sense as it set the parties' expectations for the negotiation.

The Apprentice $18-Million-Per-Episode First Offer

Donald Trump offered to star in Season Two of *The Apprentice* for $18 million per episode. Too aggressive a starting move? Yes. Appropriate to make the starting move? Yes.

He could have waited for NBC to offer him a raise after Season One. Since *The Apprentice* was a hit, NBC almost certainly would have offered a big jump. Instead, Trump used his first offer to set the parties' expectations, which then likely drove their perceptions of the back-and-forth process that subsequently took place.

> **RESEARCH:** First offers *initially* set parties' expectations *and* impact many parties' final perceptions of value. If I start at $10 million and we end at $2 million, I will *feel* like I got a great deal, often regardless of the standards involved.

Trump Avoids Making First Offers, Too

Donald Trump also regularly solicits first offers—knowing that making a first move in certain circumstances would be a strategic mistake. Where does he do this? In negotiations with subcontractors on his developments. Traditionally, real-estate developers send out a request for proposal (RFP) to all subcontractors interested in working on their proposed development. Subcontractors like electricians, plumbers, and concrete suppliers then bid for the business—making first offers.

Why do developers solicit bids and not just name their price in a first move? Because the solicitation process strengthens their leverage by creating Plans B and C and D (the bidders in each trade). Once subcontractors start bidding against each other, the developer has strong leverage.

Plus, the subcontractors often have greater information relating to how they can do the job, putting the developer at a strategic disadvantage if it just named a price. In fact, a major disadvantage of making a first move is a lack of information to appropriately set it.

Trump understands this disadvantage given his experience with commercial real-estate subcontractors.

> **RESEARCH:** Disadvantages exist to making first offers, too. The biggest one? Lack of information or independent standards to appropriately set a starting point. If this happens, you just may lose a great deal, and you may never even know it. If you don't have enough information, especially about your leverage and the independent standards, don't make the first offer. Rule of thumb: When in doubt, don't start out.[381]

Let's say you put your house on the market for $350,000 and get a full price offer within 30 minutes. Do you think, "Wow—what an efficient way to sell a house?" No. You think you just underpriced it due to a miscalculation based on lack of true market information.

Donald Trump, in his negotiations with subcontractors, likewise doesn't have sufficient information to start. No subcontractors have yet made any bids. He thus requests first offers. And they make them.

In the Boeing 727 negotiation, by contrast, Trump had sufficient information about his leverage and the independent standards involved. He thus made the first offer. A good move.

One final note on Trump and his effort to obtain information related to first-offer decisions. After the early 1980s, while he rarely did his own homework on negotiations, this doesn't mean he didn't understand the value of that information.

His solution at times? Hire those who worked for his counterparts. As Tony Schwartz, who ghostwrote *The Art of the Deal* and spent many hours with Trump in the process, wrote:

> Let me put it this way: when it comes to hiring people, Donald Trump, and I think he would agree with this, would not be averse to hiring a person, in part, because he felt they had knowledge they could use from a previous job they had done. It wouldn't bother him a bit.... He would try to do it within the bounds of legality, but he would go right up to the limit of what he was permitted to do in order to get the person with the most information.[382]

Imagine hiring a counterpart's employee to find out your counterpart's negotiation tendencies and patterns and how far they typically move off their starting positions. Pretty powerful move. Of course, employers often require employees to sign confidentiality agreements to protect exactly this type of strategic intelligence.

4. Trump Appears to Rarely Use Standards to Justify His Later Moves

In the Barbizon apartments negotiation, Trump didn't make any moves other than his first-and-final offer. But he set himself up, with Ifshin's "help," to use Cohen's $90 million bid in a later negotiation as a supporting standard.

He likely did this as tying aggressive, realistic standards to a future first offer bolsters its impact. But what about using standards *within* the back-and-forth offer-concession stage, *after* the first moves? Should you just trade numbers and dance on the issues? Or should you explain the rationale underlying each move? What does Trump do?

> **RESEARCH:** Trading numbers alone usually will be counterproductive. Instead, it's more effective to explain why you're making the move and connect it to standards. Better yet, explain and connect this before you share the number or move.[383]

The more you discuss your offers and concessions within the context of appropriate independent standards, the more they will appear "fair and reasonable." Explain upfront why your counterpart should accept your offer. Illustrate the "fairness and reasonableness" of your offer by tying it to a specific, independent standard or combination of standards.

Bottom line: The longer and stronger you can connect your moves to independent standards, the more likely your moves will generate a positive and principled response.[384]

Does Trump do this? Not sure. Unlikely, though. *One*, relatively few negotiators do this, even very skilled negotiators. It's easier to just bat numbers or issues back and forth, especially on the phone or in person. This particular strategy is better suited to negotiations via email or through trading documents. While Trump did this early in his career, his attention to this level of detail since the 1980s was rare.

And, *two*, it seems inefficient. After all, why explain every move and its justification if you're still going to get a counter?

Of course, this is somewhat speculative. Trump might research these standards and tie his moves to that research. But I doubt it. I expect he loves the back-and-forth dancing on the numbers and issues. The rationale underlying each move? Not so interesting.

5. Trump "Gets" Cialdini's Reciprocity Principle

I'll pay you back with a "favor in the future," Trump told Ifshin. And while this never happened, I expect Trump intended it at the time. Why?

Trump understands the psychological principle of reciprocity, or reciprocity power. How does this work?

"Fair is fair," Congresswoman A told Congressman B. "Remember six months ago when you asked me to vote for your farm aid legislation? Since my urban district includes few farmers, I didn't care much about it. But you told me then if I supported you on farm aid you would support me on one of my pet issues where your district didn't have strong feelings one way or the other. I need your support now. I strongly support campaign finance reform, and so do my constituents. You owe me." [385]

RESEARCH: The "reciprocity" standard—it is "fair and reasonable" for you to do this for me because I did something for you in the past—can be powerful. Political negotiations involving the same players again and again use it, even though it's bad form in some contexts to explicitly mention the return of a favor. Individuals also use this when involved in long-term relationships and where they depend in part on their reputations for their success.

The power of reciprocity often applies when there are ongoing negotiations between parties involving disparate issues. There's no substantive connection between farm aid and campaign finance. Instead, Congressman B will likely support campaign finance reform because of the power of reciprocity. If he doesn't support Congresswoman A here, his reputation will suffer. He will then have a more difficult time rounding up support for his pet issues in the future. Politicians have long memories—to survive and thrive, they must.

Former President Lyndon B. Johnson was a master at horse trading and using the power of reciprocity to get legislation passed. Members of Congress knew if they crossed him or broke their promises to him, they would pay a price.

In a business context, imagine that you ask your boss if you can leave early Friday, as your son is coming home from college for an extended weekend and you're taking him fishing. Your boss says fine. Three weeks later your boss asks if you can stay late two nights that week as his boss just asked him to finish the year-end report early. He needs your data for the report. Likely you will agree. This is how the power of reciprocity works. Two separate negotiations, but one independent standard determining a "fair and reasonable" result. Fair is fair.[386]

Donald Trump has relied on reciprocity power his entire business career. In fact, he has spent millions of dollars related to negotiations solely for the benefit he derives from this power. Fred Trump also masterfully used reciprocity power to help build the family real-estate business. How?

Political contributions. Trump contributes to Politician A. Politician A returns the favor, granting Trump access, a friendly ear, influence, and possibly a benefit. Let me be clear: I am not suggesting Trump illegally bribed anyone. Nor am I suggesting any *quid pro quo* or illegality existed between Trump and the politicians he financially supported.

I am suggesting that Trump and many others contribute time and money and effort for a practical, bottom-line reason. They seek and often get something in return, if only an "I owe you" feeling from the politician due to the reciprocity principle.

Examples abound of Trump's political contributions helping him in many negotiations. And, even if his contributions didn't seem to help, Trump perceived they would, as evidenced by his statements about his political influence.

Again, I am not suggesting anything illegal or unethical. I am simply identifying an environment in which Trump regularly, consistently, and in large sums contributed to politicians who held great sway over negotiations involving Trump's business interests. The principle of reciprocity played a psychological role in each one.

I hope this section will not be perceived as denigrating politicians, political contributors, or criticizing Trump for financially supporting various political candidates. This is our system. Trump has admittedly played this political contribution game to the fullest. Our campaign finance system does, however, depend in large part on the principle of reciprocity. Politicians inevitably feel somewhat beholden to their biggest contributors, and their contributors often expect—and get—something in return.

Here is a description from *Trump Revealed* of Trump's business-related political activity—and the reciprocity he expected from it.

> Trump was no political naif. He and his father had thrived in New York City's pay-to-play culture for years, in part by cultivating local elected officials. Trump almost always answered political operatives' calls for money. His criterion was simple: he wanted a winner, **someone who would be an ally once in office.** Sometimes he contributed to opposing

candidates in the same local race. He showed no concern about a candidate's views or political party. "He wanted someone who was going to continue to climb…and someone he was going to have a relationship [with] over that time," said longtime New York Democratic consultant George Arzt, who over the years asked Trump to support several candidates.

In the late 1980s, Trump's largesse caught the attention of a New York State commission examining possible political corruption. Armed with subpoena power, the commission called Trump to testify in March 1988. Under oath, Trump acknowledged that political donations had been a routine part of his business for nearly two decades. He gave so generously that he sometimes lost track of the amounts. When an attorney for the commission asked him to verify that he had given $150,000 to local candidates in 1985 alone, Trump responded, "I really don't know. I assume that is correct, yes." [Emphasis added.][387]

This reciprocity principle also underlies much of the offer-concession dynamic. Social psychologist Robert Cialdini introduced this in his classic book on persuasion, *Influence: Science and Practice*.[388]

"I just moved. It's your turn, right?" You should repay my offer, in kind, with a counteroffer. That's the psychology underpinning our back-and-forth process in most negotiations. Most negotiators intuitively understand this. So does Trump. After all, he still owes Ifshin.

Trump's Offer-Concession Aggressiveness Comes with a Cost

Let's say you represent NBC in its initial per-episode-fee negotiations with Trump *prior* to Season One. No hit yet. And the last issue on the table is Trump's per-episode fee. What does Trump do? Hits you with a $1.5 million demand. Preposterous, you think. And it is, based on independent, objective standards. In fact, your *Friends'* stars—professional actors in a long-time proven hit series—get $1.5 million per episode.

Trump says he's unique. He's got "it." He supports his $1.5 million demand by noting that NBC collectively pays $9 million to its *Friends* stars for a 30-minute episode. And *The Apprentice* will be 60 minutes. This guy has been interviewed a ton, but he's a totally unproven network TV neophyte. He could crash and burn.

How do you react to Trump's $1.5 million demand?

One of four reactions is likely:

a) you laugh, treat it as a joke, and lowball him with an equally unreasonable counteroffer;

b) you figure he doesn't know what he's doing, and refuse to respond until he brings in someone with expertise in this negotiation environment;

c) you believe his demand reflects an out-of-control ego, shows he doesn't do his homework, and conclude that he would be bad for the role—so you walk; or

d) some combination of the above.

None of these possible reactions include treating the $1.5 million move as a credible demand. None would elicit a serious counteroffer—a main goal of a first move. Each also includes diminished levels of credibility and trust in Trump.

Importantly, none of the reactions support that this is a message from a person interested in a future working relationship with NBC. In fact, the opposite message may very well be received—the demand is so outrageous that he's signaling NBC that he really *doesn't* want to do the deal anyway.

Trump might respond by noting that he can mitigate these disadvantages with his charisma. Perhaps. But he will be fighting an uphill battle. That NBC representative has already formed an opinion of Trump from his outrageous aggressiveness.

First impressions can be tough to change.

LESSONS LEARNED	
Trump's Strategies and Tactics	Trump engages extremely aggressively throughout the offer-concession stage.
	Trump regularly makes outrageously aggressive first moves.
	Trump intuitively shoots for the moon, goal-wise.
	Trump understands and accounts for the psychology involved when moving.
	Trump generally knows the patterns and traditions in his negotiation contexts.
	Trump often makes first moves to anchor his counterparts' expectations.
	Trump often makes the second move where it's strategically beneficial.
	Trump rarely uses standards to justify later moves.
	Trump understands reciprocity—especially regarding political interests.
	Trump's consistently super aggressive moves cost him credibility long-term.
Lessons Learned	Initial moves should be sufficiently aggressive to ensure you don't leave value on the table.
	Parties should start with an end goal and make their moves so they end up there.
	Parties should include "room to move" to ensure their counterparts feel good in the end.
	Offer-concession patterns impact parties' expectations and behavior in all industries.
	Advantages and disadvantages of first offers exist.
	Parties should base their moves on powerful independent standards.
	The reciprocity principle largely underlies the offer-concession stage.

CHAPTER 10

A TOWERING HOME-FIELD AGENDA

New York Giants' Hall of Fame linebacker Lawrence Taylor controlled many NFL games during his career. But, in 1983, Donald Trump took control of his negotiation with Taylor when he attempted to lure Taylor to play for his USFL Generals, as described in *Trump Revealed*.

> That day, the Giants star got an unexpected phone call: "Mr. Taylor, please hold for Mr. Trump." A few hours later, one of the greatest players in football history arrived at Trump Tower, in a car Trump had sent. [Jim] Gould [President of Trump's USFL's Generals] greeted Taylor and told him Trump had insisted he first watch praise on Trump Tower and its "visionary builder": "This is Manhattan through a golden eye, and only for the select few.... Any wish, no matter how opulent or unusual, may come true." Taylor was still uncertain why he was there. He wasn't interested in a condo. He was, however, very interested in what Trump had to say a few minutes later.

> Trump offered Taylor a $1-million bonus to sign a contract guaranteeing he'd play for the Generals after his deal with the NFL's Giants expired. If Taylor signed that day, Trump offered to wire him the $1 million immediately. "He had me call my bank, and sure as shit, thirty minutes later he wired a million dollars into my account," Taylor recalled. "I was like, 'Thanks, Don.' I respected that he put his money where his mouth was." Before Taylor even got back home that night, word leaked to the press about the deal, and there was little mystery about who had leaked it. Trump dealt coyly with questions about Taylor in a *New York Times* story. (The *Times* reporter, Ira Berkow, was also made to sit through the promotional video before he could meet Trump.) "No one knows if we signed

him—actually only three people know—that's Lawrence, his agent, and me," Trump said.[389]

Interestingly, the incensed Giants immediately took action and basically bought out Trump's contract with Taylor—paying Trump his $1 million contract price *plus* an extra $750,000 and signing Taylor to a big raise in a new deal. A profitable negotiation for Trump, financially and promotionally.

This negotiation involves four main Trump agenda-control-related negotiation strategies, including:

- How to engage (in person versus by phone or email)
- Where to engage (my turf, your turf, or neutral turf)
- What to address, when, and in what order
- When and how to impose which deadlines (real, flexible, false/fake)

Before we analyze each, though, agenda control constitutes a critical element in all negotiations. In fact, it's my 5th Golden Rule of Negotiation: Control the Agenda. "If, when, where, how, and how long we address issues affects our results. So does setting the appropriate atmosphere in which to most effectively explore the substantive issues."[390]

Trump understands this. He consistently takes concrete, practical, agenda-related steps to give himself a leg up with tactics similar to those he used with Lawrence Taylor. Let's analyze how he controls—or attempts to control—the agenda in the Lawrence Taylor negotiation and others.

1. How to Engage—in Person vs. by Phone or Email

Trump wisely invited Lawrence Taylor to Trump Tower for a face-to-face meeting. Why not by phone? Or email? Because Trump had no previous relationship with Taylor and wanted to establish one and sign him immediately. Trump understood that you only make a first impression once. He thus used Trump Tower's opulence and grandeur (and his promotional video) to impress Taylor and set the stage.

Trump used classic agenda-control tactics to do this. Several factors impact this decision.

To Phone or Not to Phone

When should you negotiate in person and when over the phone? What about email versus letter? Text versus video conference? When should you start by letter, continue by phone and email, and finish in person? Or use some other order? Given the pace of technological change these days, who knows when the next communication device will reach out and touch us?

These various options require that we set up a strategic framework for this decision. Here's what I suggest.

RESEARCH: Determine what you want to accomplish with each communication. Then decide which method most appropriately accomplishes this goal. Map it out.

For instance, consider what you want to accomplish with your first communication. Often, parties want to start by establishing rapport and a relationship with their counterpart. This obviously helps with information gathering and sharing. If so, consider all the ways you can start. Examples include, from the most personal to the least personal: face-to-face…video conference…telephone…letter.

In making your decision, take into account the following factors as they relate to your goal: a) relationship, b) efficiency, and c) a written record.[391]

Let's examine each as if we were Donald Trump considering a meeting with Lawrence Taylor.

Relationship

The more your goal includes a long-term relationship, the more likely you should use the more personal communication methods (such as face-to-face, telephone, or handwritten note), at least to start. You don't want to initially negotiate with your business partner by exchanging emails. That would harm the relationship. For most people, it's also harder to establish a strong personal relationship over the phone or email than in person.

Likewise, when buying a computer or a large appliance you may do it all over the Internet because you don't care much about a relationship.

Consider also how the forum helps or hurts you. It's easier to say no on the telephone than in person. It's even easier by email or letter. The less personal and weaker the relationship, the easier to say no. It's also easier to be more competitive when you use less personal methods of communicating. I used to get some of the most adversarial letters I've ever seen from the opposing lawyers in some of my cases. Yet, they were entirely different in their in-person communications. (Of course, some were very adversarial in person, too.) It's easier to be adversarial in writing than in person.

My recommendation? If your proposal requires a significant change, making a personal oral presentation or setting up a meeting will increase its likelihood of acceptance.

Face-to-face negotiations also lessen the likelihood of misunderstanding and provide parties with the opportunity to observe body language, facial expressions, and behavioral cues. Accurately reading nonverbal signals can prevent crucial long-term problems. These can be substantial advantages or disadvantages, depending on your in-person skills.

Telephone negotiations also have advantages and disadvantages. Evaluate them. For instance, you can interpret verbal signals and inflections over the telephone, but not in a written document, yet you can't view your counterpart's facial expressions or other body language.

In short, consider your interest in a future relationship with your counterpart when deciding how to communicate.[392]

Trump's Considerations

Let's create a strategic plan for this agenda-control element as if we were Trump considering meeting with Taylor. Here are the factors to evaluate, along with likely Trump answers.

- Interest in long-term relationship with Taylor?   Trump: *Yes.*
- Ability to develop good relationship in person?   Trump: *Absolutely.*
- In-person setting help (seeking a "yes" there)?   Trump: *Yes.*
- Interest in a competitive/adversarial environment?   Trump: *No.*
- Seeking a significant decision at the time?   Trump: *Yes.*
- Possible misunderstandings in negotiation?   Trump: *Yes.*
  (There is a higher likelihood of misunderstandings due to no previous relationship between the parties. In-person meetings minimize this possibility.)
- Confidence in ability to read non-verbal cues?   Trump: *High.*

Every factor and response here points to a face-to-face meeting. Good strategic move by Trump to request one. (Trump did initially speak to Taylor on the phone, but only as a logistical precursor to the substantive Trump

Tower meeting. Taylor didn't even know what Trump wanted to discuss until they met.)

Contrast this with Trump's first communication with Diamond Shamrock's Chairman over his Boeing 727 purchase. Again, let's create a strategic plan for this element as if we were Trump.

- Interest in long-term relationship with Blackburn? Trump: *No.*

- Ability to develop good relationship in person? Trump: *Absolutely.*

- In-person setting help (seeking a "yes" there)? Trump: *Not for first meeting.*

- Interest in a competitive/adversarial environment? Trump: *Perhaps.*

- Seeking a significant decision at the time? Trump: *No.*

- Possible misunderstandings in negotiation? Trump: *Yes.*

- Confidence in ability to read non-verbal cues, etc.? Trump: *High.*

It's a closer call here, but the main factor relates to whether Trump anticipates a long-term relationship with Blackburn and the goal of his initial communication. On the relationship front, it's a transactional, one-time purchase.

And Trump's goal for his initial communication is solely to gather information about the plane. He could easily achieve this with a call. In fact, seeking an in-person meeting would have been *counterproductive*. It would have sent the "I really want your plane" message—weakening Trump's leverage.

The second factor in determining how to meet was also relevant: efficiency.

Efficiency

Efficiency often plays the largest role in how we communicate. That's one of email's greatest advantages. It's incredibly efficient. Sometimes, though, it's more efficient to meet in-person, especially if the negotiation involves multiple parties. Email is more efficient than the phone. The phone is often more efficient than face-to-face. Efficiency sometimes comes with a cost, though.

Efficiency-wise, Trump decided to meet face-to-face with Taylor and to phone Blackburn. Both were the right calls, from a relationship and an efficiency perspective.

But what about email for the 727 negotiation? Should Trump have emailed Blackburn? No. He gained a great deal of strategic information from rapport-building in his phone call (Shamrock's desperation to sell it quickly, interest in sending plane to New York for Trump to view, etc.). Trump would not have obtained this had he reached out by email.

What about a written record? You don't have it in face-to-face meetings or on the phone. There are advantages and disadvantages to initially communicating in writing.[393]

Written Record

In some negotiations you want to create a paper trail and get written commitments. There are advantages to making written offers at the start, especially when addressing complex issues.[394]

Trump should know. Almost all his negotiations involved complex real-estate and business deals and detailed legal issues. Every major issue in those deals, and most minor ones, were almost certainly reduced to writing, often early on.

I suspect Trump knows the awesome power of the written word well.

When, where, and how can negotiators harness the power of the written word (which has a disproportionate impact relating to offers and concessions and agenda-control)? Has Trump done this?

Here are some factors to consider in making these decisions and an evaluation of whether Trump has taken these into account.

First, written documents provide parties with more credibility, more legitimacy, and the appearance of being more definite and inflexible than equivalent oral statements. We believe what we read and see more than what we hear. Trump's years of working with the written media—and understanding its impact—tells us he fully appreciates this power.

Second, documents can be strategically designed to help accomplish your goals—or not. Sometimes putting an offer in writing can be counterproductive. In some negotiations you want an air of informality and flexibility. Written documents can counteract this. Trump gets this, too, as evidenced by his many face-to-face negotiations that did not appear to have any writing associated with them until later.

Third, jotting down notes can be productive, even if you don't use them. Writing helps me organize my ideas in a logical way and helps me fine-tune exactly what I want to communicate.

Fourth, written documents reduce the chance of a miscommunication destroying your negotiation and/or the trust you have developed. Writing confirmation letters to your counterpart after oral commitments have been made often makes sense. We don't have any evidence that Trump does this, although I suspect his lawyers and associates do this in many of his negotiations.

Do any of these advantages apply to the Lawrence Taylor or 727 initial communication/negotiation? Not really. And the disadvantage of making these initial meetings more formal would have outweighed them anyway. Trump wanted the opportunity in both meetings to develop rapport and gather information. Starting with a written communication would have undermined this goal.

He can also accomplish this goal, and others, by meeting in the appropriate place. Where? That's a significant strategic decision.

2. Where to Engage (my Turf, your Turf, or Neutral Turf)

Donald Trump loves Trump Tower. Not surprisingly, it's his default site of choice for face-to-face negotiations. His turf, right? Classic. As *Trump Revealed* notes, Trump "summon[s]" his counterparts there, calling it his "usual practice."[395]

The Apprentice creator Mark Burnett met Trump there. *Trump: The Game* creator Jeffrey Breslow met Trump there.[396] So did Lawrence Taylor.

Should Trump always negotiate on his turf? No. Does he? No. Why not? Because he knows it does not always provide a strategic benefit. Sometimes it helps him to meet on neutral turf. Sometimes, even, on his counterparts' turf.

Of course, he can't always choose. Strong leverage may lead to his counterparts dictating the place.

I faced this challenge many years ago when I interviewed for a law firm job. It was the end of the day when I was escorted into the corner office of the managing partner of the law firm. And he sat behind a large desk, in the power position. It was my last interview. If it went well, I hoped to receive a job offer.

So began our negotiation. Many negotiators would say I was already at a disadvantage. I was on his turf, in his office, at the mercy of his schedule, and he controlled the environment. I'm not so sure. While these factors can provide a leg up, I learned some crucial information about him from sitting in his office and soaking up his surroundings. For instance, I did not notice many family or personal pictures, and the environment was very businesslike. This information proved indispensable in the later stages of our negotiation.

Many negotiations begin with the turf battle: your place, my place, or a neutral ground. Sometimes the home court advantage provides a significant advantage. Other times it can work to your detriment. Neutral sites eliminate much of the bias. What factors impact this turf issue?

RESEARCH: When deciding or negotiating where to meet, consider:

- your control of the environment,
- the parties' psychological tendencies,
- information you want to share,
- efficiency and logistics, and
- the parties' expectations about the turf.[397]

Let's evaluate each and identify how Trump considered them in his negotiations.

Control the Environment

In Trump's office at Trump Tower, he controls the environment. While some limitations exist, he largely controls the seating and the office support functions that parties require. He might even control who attends, if this has not already been explicitly addressed. This control can provide a substantial advantage.

Years ago, I consulted with a large manufacturing company after it experienced a particularly challenging negotiation with one of its biggest customers. The prior year it was asked to send its team to negotiate at its customer's headquarters in the Midwest. Unexpectedly, when the company's negotiating team arrived they were told their biggest competitor was in the adjoining conference room. A bidding war ensued for the customer's business. This could not have happened without the customer's home-court advantage.

The company's mistake? They failed to address the question of who would be at the table *before* they traveled to their counterpart's turf.

Psychological Tendencies

Another big reason to negotiate on your home front relates to the psychological comfort many derive from their most familiar environment. If you're psychologically at ease you will be better able to make the moves necessary to maximize your negotiation effectiveness. Plus, we psychologically fight harder for what we want on our home front than elsewhere. Sports teams know this well. These psychological factors work in the reverse if you're heading to their place.

Some experienced negotiators downplay the relevance of this factor, saying it's no big deal. It may very well be true for them. If you're an extremely confident negotiator, you may be equally comfortable in many different environments. But your counterpart may not.

No one doubts Trump considers himself an extremely confident negotiator. But does it work for or against him to make his counterparts comfortable or uncomfortable? It depends. If it's going to be a tough, adversarial, zero-sum type negotiation with no future relationship between the parties, it will likely help to throw his counterparts off balance.

But if he wants a long-term business partnership and hopes to creatively explore satisfying mutual interests in a relaxed environment, a comfortable environment for everyone would be better. Maybe even meet at *their* offices.

Information Exchange

At your office you inevitably provide strategic information to your counterpart concerning who you are and how you approach situations. One of the first things I do when I meet someone in their office is analyze that individual's personal and business environment. Are they ego-driven, with awards and other exhibitions of their alleged expertise prominently displayed? Are they family- and relationship-oriented, with family pictures all over? Are they risk-takers, with skydiving pictures on the wall? What does it tell you if they have an organized, neat desk with sharpened pencils lined up on top? The list goes on.

You may or may not want to share this information. Evaluate this. Of course, you can always meet in a relatively sterile conference room, although your counterparts will still get a sense of the personality of your work environment.

Efficiency and Logistics

There's no travel cost in time or money if you're negotiating from your place. Plus, you can often deal more effectively with unexpected issues or emergencies. Your resources are right at hand. But if your office doesn't satisfy the parties' logistical needs, you may be forced to meet at your counterparts' place or at a neutral site. Efficiency and logistics often prove critical in deciding where to meet.

Expectations

Finally, expectations exist regarding the site. Tradition may drive this decision. Be wary of conceding on the location front, though, if you believe your counterpart will consider it a sign of weakness and reflective of your negotiating style.

How does Trump evaluate these factors? Let's analyze five Trump negotiations—two where they met on Trump's turf, one where they met on neutral ground, and two where Trump traveled to his counterparts' turf.

Trump Tower Turf

The Lawrence Taylor Negotiation

Donald Trump instructed his secretary to initially get Lawrence Taylor on the line for him. "Please hold for Mr. Trump," she said. Why not just call Taylor himself? A not-so-subtle message that a) Trump is higher up on the food chain (a team owner—not a player) and b) Trump's time is more valuable than Taylor's (who would have to wait to talk to Trump).

Trump then sent his limousine to pick up Taylor. Why? I suspect to impress Taylor *and* serve as an information-gathering and sharing effort (assuming Trump's personal driver picked up Taylor and could, on the drive, extol Trump's virtues, wealth, and importance to Taylor). Taylor was a captive audience.

Taylor then got to Trump's offices, where the USFL General's President Jim Gould greeted him. Again, the food chain issue: bottom rung—Taylor, next rung—Gould, top rung—Trump. Taylor was then shown the eight-minute promotional video/slide show on Trump the "visionary builder."

Trump scripted this. The slide show, we know, was standard practice for those meeting Trump (it was even shown to *The New York Times* reporter who interviewed Trump on the Taylor deal). Finally, Trump met with Taylor and the negotiation occurred.

Did Trump evaluate the turf factors for this negotiation? Here's his likely analysis.

- **Control the environment?** Yes—a likely dominant factor in Trump's thinking.

- **Psychological tendencies?** Yes—Trump wanted to keep Taylor guessing as to the purpose of the meeting and keep him off his game. Taylor can't prepare much if he doesn't even know why he's meeting. (Recall, his contract with the Giants at the time extended for several more years.)

- **Information exchange?** Yes—Trump liked to show his counterparts his office, filled with Trump-adorned magazine covers. Interestingly, this may have disadvantaged Trump given what visitors could then learn about him (if they hadn't already done their homework).

- **Efficiency and logistics?** Yes—Trump's time right up to the meeting could be utilized on other business. Taylor spent time and effort traveling and waiting—inefficient from his perspective.

- **Expectations?** Yes—traditionally an owner at that time would not travel to meet a potential player.

Trump's decision to meet Taylor at Trump Tower was a very strategic move. I would note, however, that some would consider some of Trump's tactics questionable, ethically and from an effectiveness perspective. For instance, I would not have recommended that Trump show his promotional video (too over-the-top and obvious in terms of its intent). I also would not have recommended all the "subtle" messages communicating Trump's relative importance. These often backfire when used with sophisticated negotiators.

The Subcontractors' Bully Meeting

In 1984, Trump met cabinetmaker Edward Friel and about nine other subcontractors who had worked on his Harrah's Casino. Why? To tell them he would not be paying their final bills. Where did they meet? At the Trump family offices at the casino. Trump's turf.

Did it make sense for Trump to meet there? Yes. Why?

- **Control the environment?** Yes—a likely dominant factor in Trump's thinking.

- **Psychological tendencies?** Yes—Trump wanted these subcontractors to feel uncomfortable and just accept his "offer" as a *fait accompli*.

- **Information exchange?** Yes—this would be more akin to a conference room at Trump Tower. He's not sharing any personal information or trying to impress them here. Just get them in and out.

- **Efficiency and logistics?** Yes—Trump's time before meeting could be utilized on other business. The subcontractors, though, spent time and effort traveling and waiting. It was also more efficient for Trump to meet them in a group.

- **Expectations?** Probably favors Trump's turf. Most negotiations between owners or general contractors and their subcontractors take place where the owner or general dictates.

Trump importantly held the upper hand leverage-wise in both these negotiations. That put him in the driver's seat in determining the place. He chose well.

Neutral Turf for the NFL

Trump sat in the passengers' seat, however, when he secretly met NFL head Pete Rozelle to negotiate over an NFL franchise team in March 1984. Where did they meet? A room at Manhattan's Pierre Hotel.[398] A neutral site. Why? They both likely would have objected to meeting at the others' offices. So, Trump suggested they meet at a neutral hotel.[399]

They met at the Pierre to a) keep it secret, and b) not provide either with a perceived strategic advantage due to being on their own turf (the controlled environment factor). None of the other factors likely made much difference. A good move from both their perspectives.

Trump here, importantly, had relatively weak leverage (only one head of the NFL). This might also have played into their decision to meet at a neutral site.

Counterparts' Turf

The Phillips–Van Heusen Licensing Deal—at its Shop

When Trump drove the turf decision, he set the negotiation for Trump Tower. When he sat in the passenger seat, he pushed for a neutral site. But when Trump sat in the back seat, he ended up on his counterparts' turf.

What do I mean? In mid-2003, just prior to the premier of *The Apprentice*, Trump reached out to a broker in the clothing licensing world named Mark Hager. Trump:

> envisioned that companies would pay to put his name on products showcased on the program. He told Hager that he would start with menswear - shirts, ties, and suits with the classic American executive look that had been his own uniform for decades. Then he would move to fragrance and water and anything else that could be sold under the Trump brand.[400]

Hager had his deputy Jeff Danzer pitch the idea to the apparel industry heavyweight Phillips-Van Heusen, which manufactured clothing for Calvin Klein.

The company's reaction, according to *Trump Revealed*? "The company's head of licensing laughed. The clothing executive, Danzer recalled, saw Trump not as the powerful titan of the boardroom that he played on TV, but as what he had been in the 1980s and 1990s—the tabloid playboy known for his bluster in the face of bankruptcies at several of his businesses. Who would want to dress like him?"[401]

This changed by April, after the season finale of *The Apprentice*. Trump's vision then proved prescient—as "no one [then] laughed at the idea of Trump-branded shirts, ties, cologne, water."

His new persona also changed Trump's vision. Where before he wanted to outsource it to Hager, he now brought it in-house, hiring licensing veteran Cathy Hoffman Glosser as a new executive vice president of global licensing.

But he still couldn't get in to Phillips–Van Heusen, as it was "wary because it had just discontinued a Regis Philbin line that had petered out quickly, despite the popularity of his TV show *Who Wants to Be a Millionaire*."[402]

What happened next reflects Trump's weak leverage *and* his willingness to depart from Trump Tower to achieve his goal, as described in *Trump Revealed*.

> In August 2004, Trump announced he wanted a meeting with the company's executives. Instead of summoning them to Trump Tower, his usual practice, he offered to visit the shirt manufacturer's Garment District headquarters. "I was taken aback," said Mark Weber, the company's CEO at the time. Sure enough, Trump arrived at the company's offices looking

just as he did on television, and full of flattery for his future business partners.

"I really respect and love Regis," Trump told Weber. "However, I'm a brand. I'm building a brand. Everything I do, I do with the best quality, the finest taste. That's why I want to do business with your company." The more insistent Weber was that the deal just wasn't going to work, the harder Trump pushed back. Both companies will make money. This will work, Trump told him.[403]

They got a deal. And they both made a lot of money. "For eleven years, Phillips-Van Heusen manufactured clothing for Trump, contracting with factories in China, Honduras, Bangladesh, and other countries, where low-wage workers stitched Trump's name into the collars of thousands of shirts. Trump put up no money. The clothing company paid him a percentage of sales, amounting to more than $1 million a year."[404]

Note three turf-related elements in this deal.

- Weber drove this deal from a leverage-perspective, as he only reluctantly wanted the deal and Trump kept pushing him for it. And the more Weber pushed him away, the stronger Trump pushed. (This reflects another psychological tendency articulated by social psychologist Robert Cialdini called The Scarcity Principle. Basically, it means we tend to want things more when the supply seems to be diminishing.)[405]

- Trump's leverage strengthened from *The Apprentice's* success, but not enough to get Phillips–Van Heusen to come to him at Trump Tower.

- Trump went to Weber's turf in the Garment District but showed up "looking just as he did on television," a smart move building on his new television brand and persona (in contrast to his 1980s and 1990s persona).

- Trump recognized his relatively weak leverage and went to the Garment District.

Trump made the right decision here. He would never have gotten a deal without driving downtown to negotiate on their turf. Even if he had to sit in the back seat.

The Workout Negotiations at Weil Gotshal—Their Turf

Trump said he initiated the meeting with the bankers to whom he owed $3.2 billion in 1990, with $833 million personally guaranteed and a net worth of around minus $300 million. Many of those debts arose from his casinos. And remember—this took place on his counterparts' lawyers' turf—at Weil Gotshal in the GM Building in Manhattan. I would place a big bet that Trump's "bluffing" on this one.

Let's analyze where Trump would prefer meeting, based on our factors.

- **Control the environment?** Yes—Trump would strongly prefer controlling the environment at Trump Tower to his counterparts' lawyers' conference room.

- **Psychological tendencies?** Yes—Trump wanted his bankers and their lawyers as uncomfortable as possible. And despite his confidence in his negotiation abilities, he is desperate, hoping no bank will put him into personal bankruptcy.

- **Information exchange?** No sharing information either way—they now will know his true financial situation.

- **Efficiency and logistics?** Yes—Trump is better off at Trump Tower, especially given the months this negotiation will take. The last place he wants to meet consistently is anywhere other than Trump Tower. Highly inefficient and a logistical hassle for Trump.

- **Expectations?** Probably favors the lawyers' turf or at one of the banks.

There's only one logical conclusion if you combine these factors with Trump's relatively weak leverage and strong preference to meet as often as possible at Trump Tower—the bankers summoned Trump to their turf. He had no choice. And he knew it. Just like with Phillips–Van Heusen.

Does Trump evaluate all these factors for each negotiation in a systematic, disciplined way? No. Few negotiators do. Does he intuitively take many of these factors into consideration? Almost certainly. I would bet on that, too.

3. What to Address, When, and in What Order

Donald Trump would not be President of the United States today if he did not know how to control what negotiation issues to address, when, and in what order. In his first major deal, the Commodore Hotel redevelopment, Trump faced a deal-breaker dilemma: he needed a major New York City tax break to make the deal financially viable. He also needed major financing to redevelop the hotel.

The dilemma? New York City required that he already have the financing to give him the tax break. And the banks required that he already have the tax break to get the financing. Trump's dilemma—he needed to get one of them committed first so he could get the other one. This deal would have failed otherwise, and, according to Trump, he likely would have ended up back in Brooklyn managing his father's apartment buildings. As he wrote, "If I hadn't managed to make one of those first projects happen…and then gone on to develop the Grand Hyatt [the old Commodore], I'd probably be back in Brooklyn today, collecting rents."[406]

How did he ensure the appropriate order of issues got addressed in this complex, multi-party negotiation? He pulled two fast ones on New York City. First, he inaccurately told the city he had the financing. They never confirmed. Here's what happened, according to *Trump Show*.

> Handwritten notes of a city official… scrawled at an early 1976 meeting that included [Trump and most of the negotiation parties from New York City] revealed that Donald's much ballyhooed "commitment" from Equitable Life to provide the long-term financing for the project was only "oral." When pressed for assurances about this loan, Donald would claim that "the lenders don't want to meet with officials," though he did offer confirmation of the commitment from broker Henry Pearce, who he said "could meet on behalf of the lenders."

> But Pearce was working for Donald, not the lenders, and the sixty-seven-year-old financial adviser had, in fact, spent months touring the boardrooms of the city without picking up a committed dollar. Equitable had actually delivered what Pearce would later call a "knockout blow," rejecting Donald's $75-million request, saying that the most they would lend was $25 million and insisting that Pearce find a lead bank to act as a joint venture partner.…

> Donald [eventually as a result] concluded that "the only way to get financing was if the city gave me a tax abatement." And the only way to get the abatement was to mislead the city into believing that he already had the elusive financing.[407]

Trump's first fast one related to the crucial order of issues in this negotiation—getting the city to believe he had the financing. His second? Creating the illusion that he controlled the Commodore Hotel site, another element the city needed to give him the tax abatement. How did he create this illusion? Again, *Trump Show*:

> As early as May of 1975 the *Daily News* quoted [Trump] as claiming that he had a "purchase contract" with Penn Central to buy the Commodore. In 1976, while the Board of Estimate was considering the abatement, the *[New York] Times* quoted him as saying that he had "an option—with no particular time limit—to buy the Commodore for $10 million from the railroad trustees."... When the city did ask Trump for a copy of the option he periodically claimed to have, he sent them one. **No one paid much attention to the fact that the option bore only Trump's signature**. While [the railway's representatives] did meet with [the city] and left the impression they planned to sell the hotel to Donald, **it wasn't until almost a full year after the abatement was granted that they signed an option.** [Emphasis added.][408]

Trump got his tax break. Then he got his control of the site and the financing.

Putting the ethical issue of his misrepresentations aside, this negotiation reflects Trump's appreciation of the importance of what negotiation issues to address when and in what order. Trump used similar tactics to get his financing for the Taj Mahal casino in his deal with Hilton.

What does the research suggest regarding these issues?

RESEARCH: Prepare a substantive and strategic agenda at the start of the negotiation process, mapping out what issues need to be addressed and in what order. Be prepared to negotiate the agenda, too, if necessary. Trump did both in his Commodore deal.

You should also evaluate what atmosphere—during the beginning, middle, and end of the negotiation—will most likely get you what you want. For instance, an agenda might include a) rapport-building, b) collaboratively working together to find shared and compatible interests, and then c) competing in a businesslike but friendly way over conflicting interests.

And don't forget to analyze why it also makes sense for your counterpart to adopt this agenda. It takes two to tango.[409]

You should also consider setting short- and long-term agendas.

Setting the Agenda for Short-Term Negotiations

In the early 1990s I represented a company being sued for allegedly stealing some trade secrets from another company. After litigating the matter for months, we scheduled a one-day negotiation session to try to resolve the case without going to trial.

Since my clients were not based in Arizona, they flew in for the session. I recommended that they come in early to prepare. When they arrived for our preparation session I gave them a written agenda that detailed our goals for the day and what we needed to accomplish. Our short-term preparation and focus on the agenda-control process helped us immeasurably in the negotiation.[410]

Does Trump prepare agendas for short-term negotiations? I expect his employees, colleagues, and lawyers sometimes prepare them for him. Does he follow them? Unknown but unlikely. He's incredibly intuitive and off-the-cuff in his overall approach. This would suggest he rarely follows a set written agenda. Plus, he doesn't do nearly the level of preparation and homework he did early in his career. Again, this suggests he doesn't create or adhere to written agendas overall, much less for short negotiations.

We do know, however, that he's disciplined and strategic when negotiating and communicating with the business-oriented media. At least in interviews. Here's how *TrumpNation* describes Trump's discipline with the media:

Control the Dialogue

Ask Donald about the series of failed deals from the 1980s— the Trump Shuttle, the Plaza Hotel, the USFL, the casinos— and he'll offer single-sentence responses. Press a little farther and he'll change the subject, often to the Wollman Rink [a success], or to the handsome new golf courses he's opened....

This works. Flooding an interviewer with a torrent of colorful remarks, flattering press clippings, and various other huzzahs related to the projects that he does want to talk about inevitably steers the conversation, and hence the subject matter, in that direction.

On matters personal, Donald jests, expounds, and responds with amusing, disarming candor to almost any question, no matter how intimate. **On matters of business and money, candor evaporates. Donald decides what he wants to talk about and then stays immovably on point....**

Going into most interviews, Donald maintains a small list of bullet points in his mind's eye, and he largely hews to those topics regardless of the questions he's asked. [Emphasis added.][411]

Does Trump control the agenda in dealing with the media? Yes. On the business side? Unclear. Trump has the skills to set and stick with a short-term agenda. How often did he do it in his business negotiations? In the latter stages of his business career, I suspect he most often winged it.

Setting the Long-Term Agenda

What about Trump's long-term agenda-setting skills? The value of controlling the agenda applies with equal force to longer-term negotiations played out over months or even years. The more parties involved and the longer the negotiation, the more crucial to control the agenda.[412]

We just don't have much recent evidence of Trump's longer-term agenda-control skills in the business arena. We do know that he engaged in several complex, months-long negotiations in the 1980s. More recently, however, his longer-term negotiations appear to have been relatively rare.

We do know, however, his level of intuitiveness toward the negotiation process. Since a longer-term agenda-control approach requires much *more* discipline than setting a short-term agenda, it's likely Trump does not do this well.

When to Address Issues, for How Long, and in What Order

What about the order of issues within the negotiations? Donald Trump seems to like to cut to the chase and jump right into the back-and-forth on financial issues. Just consider that the following negotiations took place in *one meeting* between Trump and his counterparts.

- NFL/Rozelle negotiation over a possible NFL franchise;
- *The Apprentice* negotiation with creator Mark Burnett;
- *Trump: The Game* negotiation with creator Jeffrey Breslow;
- Lawrence Taylor negotiation;

– And the list goes on.

And these were not marathon day-long sessions. They met. They negotiated. They likely went back-and-forth on one or more major deal points. They agreed (or didn't). The end. The rest, and the details, Trump delegated to his lawyers and associates.

Trump admittedly has relatively little patience. Recall what he said to Ned Eichler, one of his early negotiation counterparts, during a walk around New York City's Central Park during a break in their negotiations—the park was "merely the lawn in front of his future properties." Trump pointed to the buildings on Fifth Ave and Central Park South and said, "I'll be bigger than all of them. I'll be bigger than Helmsley **in five years**." [Emphasis added.][413]

And one of his earliest negotiation counterparts, Sally Goodgold, who sat across from Trump on a project in the late 1970s, learned the following about him.

> The experience [in a meeting with Trump and his then-lawyer Sandy Lindenbaum] taught her an important lesson about the contrasting styles of Donald and his lawyer—Lindenbaum had a sense of the long-term and was not about to burn his bridges, while his client [Trump] was a child of the moment, with neither a respect for the past nor an instinct for the future. **All he knew was what he needed right then.** [Emphasis added.][414]

Trump's long-term strategy? Not sure one existed. "Get it done *now*" seems to have been his mantra.

This has advantages, of course. It may be efficient. But it also has major disadvantages. It may lead to a) insufficient time and effort on due diligence in strategic preparation for major negotiations, b) lack of focus and information-gathering during a negotiation on the counterparts' interests, and c) a premature move agenda-wise into the offer-concession stage.

RESEARCH: Here are some more tactical agenda-control elements to evaluate—and my perception of whether Trump instinctively follows them.[415]

- Listeners remember the beginning and end of a presentation more than the middle.
  - *Trump almost certainly gets this.*
- Repetition of a message leads to learning and acceptance. The more you repeat, within reason, the more likely it will be accepted as true.
  - *Trump knows the power of repetition—especially in politics and with the public.*
- Stressing the similarity of positions and interests will be more likely to lead to acceptance than focusing on differences.
  - *Trump likely understands this fundamental element of negotiation.*
- You will be more likely to reach agreement on conflicting issues if you link them to issues on which agreement can be more easily reached.
  - *Unknown.*
- You can often generate positive momentum by starting with issues on which all sides can agree relatively easily and by leaving the more competitive, difficult, and conflict-oriented issues to the end. Develop a good, trusting working relationship first. Then use this to tackle the hardest issues. (This contrasts with those individuals who want to start negotiations with "deal-breakers," saying that "if we can't reach agreement on this issue, why waste our time?" While this latter strategy has the advantage of raising important issues early on and consistently emphasizing their value, this is largely counterproductive in complex negotiations involving multiple issues and long-term relationships between the parties.)[416]
  - *Trump may or may not put this into practice. He has a tendency to cut to the chase and appears to have little patience. And many of his negotiations have occurred in highly competitive contexts. On the other hand, he understands the value of rapport-building and building momentum in negotiations. I suspect he sometimes does this. Other times not.*

One thing Trump understands, though, are short deadlines. That's a crucial agenda-related element. And deadlines regularly pop up in Trump's negotiations.

4. When and How to Impose Deadlines

Trump gave Lawrence Taylor until the end of the day to sign and get $1 million wired into his account. Trump told NFL head Pete Rozelle in their secret meeting he needed to know right away whether he would accept Trump's "demand" for an NFL expansion franchise.[417] Trump gave the Resorts' board *one day* to accept his oral commitment to buy their company, an agreement negotiated over months that had not yet been presented to the board.[418]

Trump regularly used short deadlines—real and false—in his negotiations. He's also had deadlines imposed on him, like when Boston Safe Deposit and Trust gave him a deadline to pay *The Trump Princess*' insurance payment (and then paid it anyway). How well does he understand and effectively use deadlines?

To answer this question, first understand how deadlines impact parties' behavior (I call these "deadline dynamics"), the agenda, and the overall negotiation process. Then we can evaluate Trump's deadlines and their impact.

> **RESEARCH:** Deadlines generally impact parties in four ways: urgency, timing, concessions, and organization.[419]

Let's consider each in the context of my friend's home-buying negotiation years ago in Chicago. Here's what happened, and the impact of his aggressive deadline. It was 1999, and my friend made an offer on what he calls the Daddy Warbucks house, a house once owned by the creator of *Annie*. When he made this first offer, the house had been available for only a short time. Since he felt the house was priced below market, he worried that someone else might come in shortly after his offer and start a bidding war.

What did he do? He told the seller his offer would only remain valid through the end of the day. If not accepted within that time period, he said, he would withdraw it and offer *less* for the house. We call this the "take-away" in the negotiation world.[420]

What impact did this have on the seller in terms of urgency, timing, concessions, and organization?

Urgency Impact

Deadlines often create an increasing sense of urgency and pressure for all the parties, especially for those with weaker leverage. Deadlines tend to focus us on our weak leverage. Here the seller had weak leverage, with a need to sell quickly and no good alternative offer/Plan B at the time.

My friend, by contrast, had no real need to buy, and he had a decent alternative/Plan B. By imposing a deadline and combining it with the take-away he emphasized the transitory nature of his offer, increased the seller's sense of urgency, and focused the seller on her weak leverage.

Psychologically, deadlines also focus us on our tendency to want things more when the supply appears to be diminishing. After all, the supply, or the deal, disappears if the parties reach the deadline without an agreement. This feeling increases even more with short deadlines imposed by independent outside factors. Deadlines also increase the competitive nature of the process and create an increasingly tense atmosphere.

Of course, sometimes setting a deadline can backfire by unnecessarily ratcheting up the tension. Certain deadlines will be counterproductive if success depends upon parties creatively working together to resolve mutual problems. Pressure and tension can short circuit the creative process and lead to hard feelings, especially if one party attempts to impose a deadline on the other.

Timing Impact

The passage of time, noted earlier, usually helps or hurts parties' leverage. Deadlines cut this time short. How do parties take advantage of this? If delay and the passage of time hurts a party, setting short deadlines will help them. If delay helps a party, setting long or no deadlines will help them.

In my friend's negotiation, he felt that time would help the seller by presenting alternative buyers. This hurt him. He thus imposed a short deadline to minimize this possibility. It worked. He received a signed contract before his deadline expired.

Concession Impact

The closer you get to the end of the negotiation, the faster the concessions flow and the smaller they get. Deadlines greatly affect offer-concession behavior. This needs to be strategically considered as deadlines approach. Tracking such behavior near the end can be especially productive.

Organization Impact

Deadlines also often increase the likelihood that the negotiations will move along at a more organized and controlled pace. Creating a set time frame for the negotiation, or within which certain activities are to take place, often causes parties to behave in ways consistent with the deadline.

Deadlines impact the negotiation process in fairly predictable ways and patterns. Expert negotiators know these impacts and patterns and use them to gain an advantage.

Does Trump?

One thing we know—he often imposes short deadlines. He imposed one on Lawrence Taylor, and Taylor signed. It seemed effective. He imposed one on Pete Rozelle, and Rozelle pushed back and later said no. That may have backfired, although other factors also impacted that situation.

RESEARCH: Where and under what circumstances should Trump—and others—impose *short* deadlines?

- When the passage of time hurts you, especially leverage-wise (You have a good Plan B and are not sure how long it will last, and your counterpart has a bad Plan B and may be about to get a better one.)
- When you have little interest in a future relationship (The imposition of the pressurized environment resulting from short deadlines tells the other party, "I don't really care how you feel, nor do I want you to carefully consider all the factors involved—decide *now*.")
- The shorter the deadline, the more pressurized and competitive the environment. Short deadlines can thus harm future relationships.
- The longer the deadline (or having no deadline), the less pressure and the more problem-solving.[421]

My friend wanted pressure, tension, competition, and had no interest in a future relationship with the seller. Setting a short deadline made sense for him.

The Taylor and Rozelle Deadlines' Effectiveness

Did Trump want pressure, tension, competition, and no future relationship with Taylor or Rozelle? Actually, the opposite. He presumably wanted Taylor to play for the USFL Generals several years later. And he wanted to become an NFL owner—which would involve a future relationship with Rozelle.

Based on these goals and criteria, Trump's short deadlines backfired. Poor strategy.

"Hold on," you say. "Taylor signed, got $1 million wired to his account that same day, and Trump ended up $750,000 richer in the end when the Giants resigned Taylor. How is that a poor strategy?"

Excellent points. In fact, I suspect Trump cared *more* about the public relations bonanza he could get from a quick signing and less about a true relationship with Taylor. If he just wanted a quick public relations hit and some extra bucks, his short deadline worked well. Taylor also had strong leverage (His contract with the Giants lasted several more years.), so he likely didn't feel much pressure from the deadline anyway. As a result, the short deadline didn't come at much cost relationship-wise.

Trying to impose a short deadline on a savvy negotiator like Rozelle, though, was counterproductive. *First*, Trump had *weak* leverage—and Rozelle knew it. Rozelle thus likely felt little pressure from a Trump-imposed deadline. *Second*, neither party was hurt by several weeks' delay. Pushing for an answer right away didn't help Trump, either.

Finally, Rozelle likely recognized the tactic and ignored it. Trump would thus lose credibility if it came and went without any consequences. And Rozelle didn't give Trump an answer right away. His answer turned out to be no, too.

The Resorts' Board/Taj Deadline

Trump imposed an *effective* short deadline, however, on the Resorts' independent board members in his Taj deal. Recall that Trump needed these board members to approve the deal. Here's how *Trump Show* described the deadline:

> The contract [negotiated by the Resorts management with Trump] was essentially sprung on these [independent] directors, who finally acquiesced after a day of intense lobbying.

> Four conference-call meetings of the board were held on Sunday, March 8 [1987], starting at 10:45 a.m. and ending almost twelve hours later. [Resorts' management] worked relentlessly on the reluctant directors, reading sections of the proposed contract over the phone to them, promising that Trump would rescue a company [Resorts' president Jack] Davis suddenly warned was about to "run out of cash."

They explained the urgency with the claim that Donald's oral commitment to buy was only good if they had a written agreement *by the end of that day*. Though the directors had previously retained a penetrating financial consultant, David Schulte of Chilmark Partners, they were told there was no time for him to analyze the terms. [Emphasis added.][422]

Why was this short deadline effective where the Rozelle and possibly the Taylor ones were not?

1) Trump had strong leverage. (Trump didn't need the deal; Resorts did—and Resorts didn't have a good Plan B to Trump buying, and it was getting worse if they were truly "running out of cash.")

2) Trump's allies in Resorts' management worked the Trump-imposed deadline hard (adding their credibility to Trump's regarding the deadline's inflexibility).

3) Time could hurt Trump as the Resorts' board's financial expert could then analyze the actual terms of the deal and possibly recommend against it.

Smart deadline by Trump.

The NBC—New York City Deadline

Two months later Trump would impose another short deadline—this time on New York City to try to get a tax exemption for his Television City development. He said he needed it to prevent NBC from relocating to New Jersey. This deadline backfired, as noted in *Trump Show*.

Trump tried to increase the pressure with a panicky phone call to [New York City's Deputy Mayor for Economic Development Alair] Townsend in the middle of a Friday afternoon in early May [1987]. **He gave her a two-hour deadline to accept or reject his proposal, warning that NBC was "on the precipice of making a decision" and would otherwise be Jersey-bound.** Townsend pressed him for an estimate of the tax write-offs cost to the city, but Donald could offer none. The city quickly calculated it at a billion dollars. Although Townsend told Trump his proposal "was ridiculous," he met with NBC officials later that day "and left them with the impression that the city had approved this proposal." When the network called Koch the following Monday to confirm that the city had agreed in concept with the site-wide tax exemption, a distressed mayor replied that 'no such agreement' had been reached.

Townsend quickly wrote to Trump saying that the city's preliminary analysis indicated that its tax loss under Trump's plan would be "well in excess of what is needed and defensible" and would give Trump "tax benefits beyond those that would benefit NBC." She added that the city was determined to negotiate a deal directly with NBC, not with Trump. Donald responded with a furious memo, charging that Townsend's claim that the city had made "substantial progress" with NBC was "both incorrect and patently self-serving" and listing a dozen other major companies that had fled the city in the past year. **Citing the "extreme urgency" of the situation, he demanded that the city respond immediately....**

Koch was so irate over Trump's letter that he sent Townsend a note saying it exhibited Donald's "normal bullying self to the utmost" and urging a "very tough" reply. [Emphasis added.][423]

Why did Trump's short deadlines here fail where his Resorts' deadline succeeded?

1) Trump here, like with the Rozelle deadline, had weak leverage. He needed New York City more than it needed him. He also needed NBC, which he was seemingly representing in these negotiations. But NBC could negotiate directly with the city, and this was the city's and NBC's decent Plan Bs to Trump's Television City deal. Trump's Plan B? Another anchor tenant to his West Side land. Even with another big tenant, he still needed major tax benefits from the city to make it financially viable.

2) Trump appeared to arbitrarily create these super-short deadlines. Crucially, he had no backup from NBC to confirm their actual impact. He had this on the Resorts' deadline.

3) Trump's initial two-hour deadline was almost comically short and unrealistic. It undermined his credibility with New York City and created a highly pressurized, competitive environment with officials Trump needed for *any* development on that site.

4) Trump's name-calling and attempted bullying of New York City Mayor Ed Koch, with whom he had previously had a nasty public battle in a separate negotiation, came back to haunt him (the negative power of reciprocity). Trump's short deadlines fanned these flames.

Trump's Deadline Dynamics

Does Trump effectively use short deadlines? Overall, no. Why not?

- Trump commonly and seemingly arbitrarily imposed short and sometimes totally unrealistic deadlines, making them weak and ineffective.

- Trump indiscriminately used deadlines regardless of his leverage—strong or weak. Trump does not appear to target short deadlines only to leverage-related situations where they would most likely succeed (where he had strong leverage and could capitalize on a counterpart's short-term weak leverage).

- Trump set up deadlines as real and inflexible, with presumably negative impacts on his counterparts if they were not met. Yet Trump allowed several deadlines to pass without consequence to his counterparts. Trump thus signaled that a) the deadline was false (losing credibility), and b) it was engineered to pressure his counterparts into making ill-considered decisions (thus harming the relationship). This engendered major pushback from his counterparts.

- Trump aggressively set short deadlines even in situations involving counterparts with whom he wanted a future relationship (like New York City and Pete Rozelle). This misuse of deadlines—which created pressurized, competitive environments—damaged his relationships.

- The publicity surrounding his false deadlines, several of which were publicly reported, created a credibility problem for Trump in later negotiations. Future counterparts, if they did their homework, would be aware of Trump's lost deadline credibility. This undermined future Trump-imposed deadlines.

Agenda-Control "Games" Trump Plays

One final illustration of Trump's agenda-setting tactics. This example, shared by the business author and then writer for *CBS Moneywatch* Geoffrey James in May 2009 in *"Donald Trump's Negotiation Mind Games,"* involved Trump using many of these tactics.

> About a year ago, my friend was contacted by Trump's organization with a bid to acquire his company, a medium-sized startup in the health and beauty field. After a period

of due diligence and preliminary negotiation, my friend was invited to meet with Trump in order to iron out the final terms.

The meeting was held at the famous Trump Towers in New York City. My friend, though savvy at business, found it impossible not to be awed by the fact that he was riding the elevator featured in the television show *The Apprentice*.

Rather than meeting immediately with Trump (the original plan), my friend was taken to a conference room to discuss the final terms with some staffers.

A message was then brought to the meeting that Trump would be arriving at the meeting in a few minutes. A staffer took my friend aside and said: "You need to understand that Mr. Trump never shakes hands with anybody. So don't be offended if he doesn't offer his hand, and don't offer your hand when he comes in the room."

While my friend digested this tidbit, the staffer continued, "Mr. Trump is a very busy man and prefers to make decisions quickly. So if the meeting lasts less than five minutes, please don't take it amiss, because that's normal for him."

Finally, Trump makes his appearance. He walks right over to my friend and warmly shakes his hand. Then Trump proceeds to spend 40 minutes with my friend, discussing the business and then, at last, ironing out the final terms.

And those terms were, as you probably guessed, less advantageous than my friend might have hoped.[424]

Trump used a number of agenda-related tactics and "mind games" here. They worked.

- **Trump's Turf:** Trump set the meeting on his home turf at Trump Tower.

- **Trump's Timing and Subject Matters:** Trump and his team set the timing and the subject matters to be addressed in a meeting agenda in advance. It only included a meeting with Trump to negotiate the final terms of the deal—not his colleagues.

- **Trump's Importance:** Trump sent his staffers to meet with the seller first. A not-so-subtle message of Trump's relative importance. Keep the seller waiting—Trump's time is more important. And let the staffers initially negotiate with him. Again, Trump is higher up the food chain.

- **Trump's Leverage:** Trump acted as if he was in the driver's seat, leverage-wise. Probably not true. Trump contacted the seller initially, so he didn't start with strong leverage. He created the perception of it, though. Smart move.

- **Trump's Renegotiated Agenda:** Trump's staffers—now psychologically equivalent to the seller as they were negotiating deal points with him—then reset, reordered, and renegotiated the agenda's timing and subject matter. New meeting time with Trump—five minutes or less! And the seller should be happy with this!

- **Trump's New Short Deadline:** The new five-minute expected deadline—which Trump seemingly magnanimously extended to 40 minutes—was probably less than the *original* agenda's meeting time with Trump (James expected the original time set aside at one hour, as this was "a fairly significant business deal." Yet now the seller should be grateful to get 40 minutes?) I suspect he felt so grateful, too, due to the principle of reciprocity, that he conceded more to Trump than he would have otherwise.

- **Trump's Handshake:** Here's what James said about the handshake issue in his article.

  Now, when my friend told me this story, he kept talking about how impressed he'd been by the Trump Towers and how gracious Trump had been. "He even shook my hand!" he said, taking that as a sign of special privilege....

  The Unexpected Handshake... Trump is turning a common business courtesy—the handshake—into a negotiation advantage. My friend felt complimented that Trump shook his hand. Give me a break!

I agree. In fact, other than the handshake ploy, all these represent classic agenda-related power moves in competitive negotiations. CEOs and other VIPs, as James points out, have traditionally used many of these tactics in similar situations.

Trump, too.

LESSONS LEARNED	
Trump's Strategies and Tactics	Trump consistently seeks to control the agenda.
	Trump strategically decides where to meet but almost always defaults to his turf.
	Trump intuitively decides what to discuss, when, and in what order.
	Trump regularly sets short deadlines, often false. Sometimes they work. Other times—counterproductive.
	Trump plays agenda-control "games" to create the perception of power.
Lessons Learned	Determine what you want to accomplish with each communication and decide which method best accomplishes this goal.
	Strategically decide where to meet based on controlling the environment, the parties' psychological tendencies, information you want to share, efficiency and logistics, and parties' expectations of the turf.
	Strategically decide what to address, when, and in what order.
	Account for deadline dynamics in setting and evaluating short and long deadlines.

PART TWO

TRUMP'S PERSONAL SKILLS AND ETHICS

We now know *what* Donald Trump does in his business negotiations. His Top Ten. They include effective strategies like:

- aggressive goal-setting and expectations,
- exploring and satisfying his interests,
- engaging in puffery,
- exhibiting a deep, insightful understanding of leverage and using it to lock down favorable deals,
- demonstrating a sophisticated appreciation of the offer-concession "dance," and
- controlling the agenda on his turf and often on his terms.

He has also implemented counterproductive strategies, including:

- not doing his homework since the mid-1980s, except in select deals,
- viewing all negotiations as short-term, win–lose and taking a highly adversarial approach in situations involving future relationships,
- destroying deals and potential deals with personal and business threats, business bullying, and other overly aggressive leverage-related tactics,
- excessively using the legal system to punish counterparts,
- losing credibility by exaggerating too much,
- overly aggressively making moves and countermoves, and
- setting empty deadlines that backfire.

But we don't yet know *how* Donald Trump puts these strategies into practice. What personal skills have empowered him to close deals and have destroyed others?

And what about his honesty, trustworthiness, and credibility in his business negotiations? What strategies have raised important ethical issues?

Along the way, he has developed a negotiation reputation in business. What is that reputation? Reputations impact negotiation effectiveness. Has this been positive or negative?

How has Trump negotiated, personally and ethically? That's next.

CHAPTER 11

GRADING HIS PERSONAL NEGOTIATION SKILLS: As, Bs, OR ...?

"I was relentless, even in the face of total lack of encouragement, because much more often than you'd think, sheer persistence is the difference between success and failure."[425]

—Donald J. Trump

Has Donald Trump's assertiveness and sheer persistence helped him in negotiations? How about his empathy? What about his sociability or likability? How has his emotional intelligence affected his deals? What impact have these skills had on his success—and failure—in diverse negotiation environments?

We address these crucial questions here. And we provide the answers based on Trump's 40-plus years of negotiating and the experts' proven research. A fine line exists between *what* you do—your strategies and tactics—and *how* you do it—the skillset you use to put those strategies into practice. Both need to be analyzed for a complete picture of Trump's negotiation abilities. We can all learn from this, too.

What skills do the *most* effective negotiators put into practice?

RESEARCH: Marquette University Law School Professor Andrea Schneider has studied these skills and characteristics for over 25 years. Based on her and other negotiation experts' research, she has identified five separate skill areas to evaluate in negotiators.

- **Assertiveness**
- **Empathy**
- **Flexibility**
- **Social Intuition**
- **Ethicality**[426]

Before we evaluate Trump based on these skill areas, a few caveats:

- It's extremely rare for any individual to exhibit high levels of *all* of these skills. In fact, to some extent they conflict with one other. A person's extreme assertiveness rarely co-exists with an equally high level of empathy. A tension exists between them.

- These skills' effectiveness also exists on a spectrum. Schneider has helpfully judged each skill as *Minimum—Average—Best Practices*. To provide more detailed context, we will use a 1–10 scale, with *Minimum* a "1," *Average* a "5," and *Best Practices* a "10."

- Different skills are effective in different circumstances and with different negotiators. Some negotiation situations require more assertiveness and less flexibility. Others require more empathy and less assertiveness. Most, of course, require high levels of ethicality.

  Plus, some negotiators—like one-trick ponies—consistently use certain skills in some environments with a particular type of counterpart. The most effective negotiators, though, use different skills in different environments with different counterparts.

- These skills are innate tendencies *and* learned behavior. Nature *and* nurture. All negotiators exhibit a base level of these skills. That base, however, differs in each individual.

- Parties' effectiveness in each skill—because this is partially learned behavior—can be improved through better understanding, practice, implementation in real negotiations, and post-negotiation reflection of what works.

- Labels like these can't fully address the unlimited nuances inherent in our human characteristics. But they do help us understand, learn, and improve.

How one negotiates and the skills one uses in negotiations impact *what* one does and what that person's counterpart does in terms of strategies. Vice versa, too.

Assertiveness Level

What does it mean to have a "Best Practices" or "Minimum" assertiveness skills?

Professor Robert Mnookin, Chair of the Harvard Program on Negotiation and author of the excellent book *Bargaining with the Devil: When to Negotiate, When to Fight*, defines assertiveness in negotiations as "the ability to state clearly and confidently the interests and perspectives of one's own side."[427]

One example Mnookin uses to exemplify assertiveness comes from South Africa's extraordinary former leader, political prisoner and Nobel Peace Prize winner Nelson Mandela, who spent over 27 years in prison and then negotiated peace, an end to apartheid, a new constitution, and a transition to democracy with the white power structure that had imprisoned him.[428]

Mnookin calls Mandela *"the greatest negotiator of the twentieth century."*[429] How did Mandela exhibit assertiveness in those negotiations, and what does that mean? Mnookin describes Mandela deploying his skills in many ways.

One example involved Mandela's negotiation with his guards and prison authorities while locked up in horrific conditions at Robben Island. How did Mandela assert himself in this situation involving extremely weak leverage? Mnookin describes it in the following way, which includes some of Mandela's own words:

> From the very beginning, he became the leader of Robben Island's political prisoners, and he told them that the "struggle" in prison was no different from the struggle outside. With characteristic dignity, he insisted on proper treatment from his jailers and taught the other political prisoners to do the same. He complained about the inadequacies of the prison blankets, clothing, and food, but not in an adversarial spirit. He and his fellow prisoners *"adopted a policy of talking to the wardens and persuading them to treat us as human beings. And a lot of them did, and there were lots of things we could talk about. And the lesson was that one of our strongest weapons is dialogue. Sit down with a man [and] if you have prepared your case very well, that man... will never be the same again."*[430]

Mandela's assertiveness skills included: a) knowledge of the issues and interests, b) preparation of a "case," c) a non-adversarial spirit, and d) an ability to articulate and persuade.

Years later, Mandela made the case to South Africa's President F. W. de Klerk relating to his release from imprisonment. Interestingly, he made the case that he would *not* accept release except under certain conditions, again described by Mnookin:

> Mandela knew that his imprisonment was a stain on [de Klerk's] National Party's (NP's) reputation and that his release could help the NP. He was in a strong position to negotiate the terms of his own release and he drove a hard bargain. It made no sense, he told de Klerk, to release him while the ANC

[African National Congress—Mandela's exiled political party] was still officially illegal. Mandela had no intention of going into retirement, so the government would just have to arrest him again. The best plan, he said, was for the government to release the remaining political prisoners, allow exiles to return, lift the official ban on the ANC and other political organizations, and end the state of emergency. *Then* it could free Mandela....

About a month later, de Klerk stunned the country by announcing a set of decisions that met most of Mandela's conditions for release.[431]

What assertiveness skills did Mandela exhibit? The same ones as with his prison guards: a) knowledge of the issues and interests, b) preparation of a "case," c) a non-adversarial spirit, and c) an ability to articulate and persuade.

One final example of Mandela's assertiveness skills: The negotiations with South Africa's white minority apartheid government lasted four years and included tense periods of violence and impasse. Despite seemingly irreconcilable differences on the big political and economic issues, though, they ultimately reached agreement.

How? Mandela largely prevailed on the political side, and de Klerk largely prevailed on the economic side. A specific example of Mandela's assertiveness involved his reaching across the aisle to contact some extremist white political leaders to the right of de Klerk. Mnookin notes:

These stakeholders had to be brought around and de Klerk couldn't do it alone. The Volksfront, for example, was an extremist Afrikaner party headed by General Constand Viljoen. **Mandela built a relationship with Viljoen by inviting him to his home and talking openly with him. Viljoen was impressed by Mandela and appreciated his candor.** At one point Mandela told him, *"If you want to go to war, I must be honest and admit that we cannot stand up to you on the battlefield...[but] you cannot win because of our numbers: you cannot kill us all."* Ultimately, Viljoen and his party supported the interim constitution. [Emphasis added.][432]

Mandela's assertiveness, including his candor, directness, honesty, persuasiveness, inner power and strength, and frank but non-adversarial explanation of his leverage (We will lose on the battlefield, but you cannot win because of our numbers), played a significant role getting the support of perhaps his most challenging counterparts.

Mnookin concluded, "Mandela's achievement is unique in modern history, largely because of his extraordinary personal characteristics."[433]

Note that Mandela's personal characteristics and skills—while assertive—did *not* include a competitive win–lose mindset, a largely intuitive approach, name-calling, offensive and demeaning comments, an overtly adversarial tone or atmosphere, or threats and bullying.

Trump's Assertiveness Skill Level

How does Trump match up with Mandela and others on *his* assertiveness skills?

Trump has no shortage of confidence, and he's extremely aggressive and competitive. Everyone knows this. But confidence plus aggression and competitiveness do not necessarily equal effective assertiveness.

> **RESEARCH:** Effective assertiveness requires, as noted in Mandela's case:
> - preparation and knowledge of the parties' issues and interests,
> - ability to articulate, persuade, and make the case based on evidence, facts, and appropriate objective criteria,
> - engaging with relative candor,
> - inner power and strength,
> - the skill to set a firm but professional tone and the spirit with which to engage, and
> - frank and direct but non-adversarial explanations of leverage and power-related elements in the negotiation.

Schneider found that "the ability to assert yourself in a negotiation can depend on your alternatives, your goals, your research or knowledge in the area, and your ability to speak persuasively."[434]

She then goes on to define how to measure effective assertiveness, stating: "In order to assert oneself, a minimal skill might be some level of competence and knowledge. An average skill would be to have fully researched the situation and be well-prepared. Best practices would include confidence based on competence and knowledge."[435]

The dilemma with Trump: How can he be effectively assertive if he doesn't really know the issues and hasn't fully prepared? He can't.

Yet Trump, after his early deals, rarely appeared to do his due diligence for his negotiations. He certainly didn't in the late 1980s, when the banks were throwing money at him to buy the Plaza, Eastern Shuttle, casinos, and *The Trump Princess*, among other deals.

On the other hand, Trump exhibited relatively effective assertiveness skills around that time for the Resorts/Taj Mahal purchase, the Television City negotiation, and his workout negotiations with the banks in 1990.

How can we reconcile these seemingly conflicting Trumps? Actually, they don't conflict if we analyze a) the way he used his skills differently in those different negotiations, and b) how he asserted himself with regards to his different strategies.

For instance, Trump displayed effective assertiveness skills early on by learning the intricacies of the issues and interests, persuading city officials to give him tax breaks, preparing his "case" for the Resorts' deal with the board, negotiating to get out of his suffocating debt with the banks, and others. Early on, he was more effectively assertive than later.

Yet on these deals he combined effective assertiveness skills with skills that undermined his assertiveness effectiveness—the bullying and threatening, the name-calling, an overtly adversarial win–lose approach, and a highly aggressive and adversarial tone.

Even later, after his fame skyrocketed with *The Apprentice* and he started negotiating licensing deals, it doesn't appear Trump dug deep into the actual negotiations—except perhaps at the very start or end of the process.

He did, however, consistently display effective "best practices" assertiveness skills *as it relates to leverage* in almost all his negotiations.

Schneider sets the framework here:

> In measuring your [assertiveness] skills using the concept of [what I call Plan B], a minimal level of skill would be to know your [Plan B] in advance of a negotiation. The average skill level would be to then set your reservation price [what you would accept at a minimum in the negotiation] for the negotiation based on your [Plan B]. And best practices would be to work on improving your [Plan B] before and during the negotiation. You could also work to worsen their [Plan B].[436]

Trump consistently worked on improving his Plan B before and during his negotiations and worked to worsen his counterparts' Plan Bs.

Where would I score Trump on his overall assertiveness skills? About a seven, early on. About a three, later. It's extremely tough to be persuasively assertive when you implement it with strategies like threats, bullying, public name-calling, short arbitrary deadlines, a win–lose mindset, intuitive engagement, and a highly adversarial tone and communications approach.

Of course, this assessment does not mean Trump didn't negotiate some great deals. He did. It just means his assertiveness skills did not help him achieve those great deals.

Four other skills also impacted his negotiation success.

Empathy Level

Mnookin defines empathy as requiring "good listening skills and the ability to demonstrate an understanding of the other side's needs, interests and perspectives, without necessarily agreeing."[437]

Schneider expounds on this and provides detailed context for an evaluation of empathy.

> "Empathy is linked to success in a variety of careers. The skill of "empathic accuracy," according to William Ickes, is what creates "the most tactful advisors, the most diplomatic officials, [and] **the most effective negotiators**." Even lawyers and economists now recognize that separating decision-making from emotions is detrimental.
>
> **Being empathetic in a negotiation requires a complex mix of skills—a willingness to hear the other side, open-mindedness or curiosity, good questioning, and excellent listening, among others.**
>
> *First,* one needs the belief and understanding that your counterpart might have something to contribute….
>
> *Second,* one needs the skills to gather information about one's counterpart to build the relationship in order to work together substantively. [Emphasis added.][438]

Nelson Mandela describes the critical nature of listening skills and empathy, elements that he learned at an early age from his tribe as well as in British missionary schools:

"My later notions of leadership were profoundly influenced by observing the regent and his court," [Mandela] writes. The regent presided over tribal meetings that lasted for hours. He would open the meeting, thank everyone for coming, explain the issue at hand, and listen in silence until everyone else had spoken. Then he would summarize the points made and search for a consensus. Mandela followed these principles for the rest of his life. **"I have always endeavored to listen to what each and every person in a discussion had to say before venturing my own opinion."** [Emphasis added.][439]

Classic empathy skills. High assertiveness and high empathy. Extremely effective.

Does Trump exhibit high empathy skills? No. Few objective observers of Trump in business would describe him as an active listener or a questioner or someone who respects counterparts with whom he disagrees. Assertive? Yes.

Deep and respectful listener and questioner interested in his counterparts' needs and interests? No.

Of course, Trump would likely disagree. And I'm sure he deeply listens at times, especially to the media and when he has weak leverage (like when the banks considered throwing him into personal bankruptcy).

Gay Walch, a Hollywood TV writer hired to write a pilot show involving Trump, would also disagree. She commented that Trump was a "confident listener, acutely listening" in her interactions with him.[440]

But, over his entire business career, has he consistently and respectfully exhibited active listening and questioning skills, especially over an issue of disagreement? No. I expect he would agree with this.

Flexibility

Here's the challenge in negotiations relating to flexibility. Too much flexibility signals no core principles, no deal-breakers, no consistent strategy, and weak leverage. (I will say or do almost anything to get a deal.)

Yet too much *in*flexibility signals no give-and-take on any issue, unnecessarily adversarial positional rigidity, a one-size-fits-all strategy, and a weakening of parties' credibility. (Why negotiate if you won't move on anything?)

What's the perfect balance?

> **RESEARCH:** Relative inflexibility on core issues and interests and strategies—signaling a principled basis and strategy for the negotiation and the back-and-forth part of the process. Yet relative flexibility on strategy and style and moves where it's helpful to satisfy the parties' interests, including identifying and prioritizing issues and interests and creatively exploring ways to address them.

Longtime Trump lawyer George Ross recognizes the importance of this type of flexibility, writing, "I have observed time and again that inflexible negotiations are usually doomed to fail. You need to be able to 'go with the flow,' and to adjust your style to the people involved, the issues, and the sticking points you discover along the way. Remember the saying, 'If your only tool is a hammer, you see every problem as a nail.'"[441]

Ross also recommends that you "be a chameleon" and "adapt your negotiating style to the negotiating environment," a trait he finds Donald Trump exhibits, stating:

> Being a chameleon is a matter of displaying a particular negotiating style at a particular time. A chameleon always blends in with its surroundings. A good negotiator has the ability to blend in harmonious fashion with the tone, mood, and people in the room when it's in his best interest to do so but can quickly change tactics when necessary to achieve a desired effect.
>
> **For example, Donald Trump has impressive personal skills and he knows how to quickly assess the other side, to seize and recognize the mood, and to go with it when it suits his purposes.** [Emphasis added.][442]

While I agree with Ross regarding the importance of flexibly changing tactics and styles, I expect most would agree that Trump rarely—if ever—blends in with his surroundings. This is not a criticism. In fact, Trump admittedly loved the attention he generated for years.

Like Ross, however, I would assess Trump as fairly high on the flexibility scale (about a seven). He has demonstrated significant creativity to get a number of complex deals done, to strengthen his leverage, and to work with his counterparts to satisfy his interests. This occurred particularly frequently in his early deals, when he dug into the details sufficiently to explore these.

Interestingly, Trump was fairly creative *within* his early deals. But his overall mindset, strategic approach, and tactics have been remarkably consistent throughout his business career. His strategies do not reflect a negotiator that modifies their style to fit various negotiation environments.

Social Intuition

I have long been fascinated with the concept of emotional and social intelligence. Why? Individuals high in emotional and social intelligence achieve better negotiation results and lead more fulfilling and satisfying lives. We should all aspire to acquire and utilize such skills. Easy to say. Much harder to do.

Here's how Schneider describes these traits and connects them to the negotiation process. I emphasized areas that apply particularly to Trump.

> "We know that having a pleasant and welcoming personality helps effectiveness in life. The work of Daniel Goleman on emotional and social intelligence has made it clear that successful people manage their emotions and social skills in order to get along with others…. Social intelligence itself is defined as both social awareness (Much of this falls under empathy, discussed above.) and social facility, which includes interacting and presenting ourselves to others. **Others have also written about the importance of being nice and of the "No Asshole" rule in business as being exceedingly successful."**

> In a more specific negotiation context, we have seen this from several angles. **The research on tone in negotiation shows that positive moods can make people more creative and more likely to use integrative strategies.** The converse is also true—negotiators in bad moods are more likely to be competitive.

> **Similarly, in rating negotiators as effective, [my research] shows how many adjectives covering social skills fit into effectiveness: personable, rational, perceptive, self-controlled, sociable, helpful, smooth….** Unsurprisingly, these adjectives could be mapped onto a measure of social intelligence….

> In terms of setting rapport, for example, Leigh Thompson suggests that a "savvy negotiator increase[s her] effectiveness

by making themselves familiar to the other party." [Emphasis added.][443]

Rapport-building based on common personal and other interests, especially early in negotiations, represents a crucial social skill underlying negotiation effectiveness. At the least, effective information-gathering will not occur unless you create the appropriate atmosphere. If you initially come across in an adversarial fashion, your counterpart will likely respond in kind. Relevant information flow will be largely nonexistent. If you appear friendly, your counterpart will likely do the same. Relevant information flow then will likely take place.

My advice? Do the "big schmooze." Build rapport.

Does Donald Trump "schmooze," and, if so, to what extent? First, let's more fully understand what this means strategically and how expert negotiators do it. Then let's assess Trump's skills.

Strategic Rapport-Building

> **RESEARCH:** Studies have shown that we like others more when they exhibit similar characteristics. We tend to like others—and thus be more likely to say yes to them—when they look like us in clothing and appearance, share our beliefs, and display similar attitudes. Psychologist Robert Cialdini calls it the Liking Rule. "We most prefer to say yes to the requests of someone we know and like," he notes in *Influence: Science and Practice*.[444]

Knowing this, some sales professionals will mirror prospective customers in their expected appearance and attitude and attempt to find some similarity with them on a number of subjects. Interestingly, this usually works, even when recipients know it's occurring. Individuals still find it more difficult to say no to those with whom some true rapport has been established.

Individuals are also more likely to say yes if they negotiate over lunch, especially if it's at a club where they both belong. Why? They appear to share some interests, since they belong to the same club. And studies since the 1930s show we have more positive feelings toward people and things we experience while eating. Politicians learned this years ago. They rarely ask for money at fundraisers until *after* the food has been served.[445]

What should you do in negotiations to increase your likelihood of getting relevant information with stronger relationships? And has Trump done this?

RESEARCH: Here's what you should do:

- Start with the "big schmooze," and preferably do it over a meal.
- Research possible similarities with your counterpart before the negotiation starts.
- Show a genuine interest in your counterpart.
- Don't build rapport in a dishonest way.[446]

Nelson Mandela, not surprisingly, scores extremely high on social intuition. He had a series of secret meetings early on in his negotiations with a Special Committee of the South African government. He ultimately met with them 47 times. Here's how Mnookin describes it:

> Mandela felt that these meetings were essential in earning the trust of the Afrikaners (the white South Africans in the meetings). He knew that the white officials were afraid of what he represented and of what the future might hold for them as a white minority. **He treated them with respect and worked to make them comfortable.** Indeed, by all accounts, he dazzled them. At the first meeting between Mandela and [the head of South Africa's secret police Neil] Barnard, for example, the latter confessed: "I am not able to express myself in English as one is able to do in one's mother tongue." Mandela immediately put him at ease by saying, "I can follow Afrikaners quite well. If I don't understand something, I will ask you."
>
> **[Mandela] also tried to establish a "personal link" with each member of the committee.** The commissioner of prisons, Van der Merwe, was surprised and flattered that Mandela remembered him from some thirty years before, when they had argued opposite sides of a case. **The trust Mandela earned with these simple gestures "counted for far more than Mandela's policy position on any particular issue."** [Emphasis added.][447]

And Mandela's rapport, trust, and relationship-building didn't stop there. Mandela helped ensure later formal meetings with a larger group of officials started similarly. Again, Mnookin:

The first official talks between the ANC and the government, held in May 1990, did not tackle any of these fundamental [political or economic] issues. Instead, the parties focused on simply getting to know each other....

These talks, which lasted three days, had a powerful psychological impact on the participants. It was a first step in reversing their mutual demonization: As an ANC participant later told reporters, "each side had discovered that the other did not have horns."[448]

Former Presidents Ronald Reagan and Bill Clinton famously had similar skills. President Reagan regularly met with Democratic House Speaker Thomas "Tip" O'Neil and bonded over their joint Irish heritage.[449] And President Clinton regularly socialized with Members of Congress.[450] President George W. Bush also had high sociability skills, often described as someone fun to be around.[451]

President Barack Obama, with whom I was in law school and whom I taught as a Teaching Fellow at Harvard's Kennedy School of Government, is extremely intelligent and has many powerful traits—but does not have the same level of sociability skills as a Reagan or Clinton.[452]

Trump's Sociability-Skills Assessment

What about Trump? He gets this. In fact, his understanding of this, along with his family money and political connections, helped him get started. How? He first negotiated his way into an exclusive members only social club in New York City called Le Club. Here's how *Trump Revealed* described his effort to join:

In 1973, Le Club was a gathering spot for "some of the most successful men and the most beautiful women in the world," Trump wrote... But this young newcomer hardly qualified for such an exclusive venue. The club rejected him. Trump cajoled and pleaded with management. Acceptance was granted on one condition: he had to promise not to go after married women who came to the club. He boasted that he went there almost every night....

To Trump, the wish to belong was part of his quest for connections. He wanted to befriend those who held sway in New York City, the power brokers who moved easily between the dealmakers and the politicians.[453]

It was also where he met Roy Cohn, who mentored and greatly contributed to Trump's early success.

But does he *like* the sociability aspect of it? Yes and no. According to Random House's Peter Osnos, who edited *The Art of the Deal* and was quoted earlier, Trump "was not a big New York socialite, never was. He basically enjoyed going upstairs [in Trump Tower] and watching the tube."[454] According to *Trump Show* author Wayne Barrett "[Trump] had always prided himself on his incapacity for small talk,"[455] an important element of rapport-building.

Trump knew how to turn on the charm, though. Trump in perhaps the "biggest pay day in his life...peddled the St. Moritz Hotel...for $100 million more than he'd paid for it. The buyer, Australian magnate Alan Bond, agreed to lavishly overpay after a single dinner with the engaging Donald, apparently convinced he was getting the land as well when all Donald had to sell was the hotel's leasehold."[456]

And New York gossip columnist Liz Smith, who knew Trump for decades, said,

> "There's something about him that's ever juvenile. It's hard to believe he's a grown-up person who went to college," says Liz Smith, matriarch of New York's gossip columnists and a long-time chronicler of Donald's ups and downs. "He's a lot like a kid, and he's got that brash, narcissistic thing that works for him. He has enormous appeal to the masses because of that."

> "He once threatened to buy the *Daily News* so he could have me fired. **And yet I still go on liking him, no matter what you or I think about him taste-wise.**" [Emphasis added.][457]

Trump also loves golf, perhaps the most social sport in the world.

How would I rate Trump's social intuition? A seven. But he combines sociability with strategies that undermine its impact, including name-calling, demonization, threats, and bullying. And sometimes he does both within a very short timeframe, counteracting the benefits he derives from his sociability.

Ethicality

"Perceptions of a negotiator's ethicality—his trustworthiness and willingness to follow the ethical rules—has a direct impact on reputation. And reputation—the perception of ethicality—is directly linked to effectiveness in negotiation."[458]

—Professor Andrea Schneider

Where does Donald Trump fall on ethics? And how does this impact his negotiation effectiveness?

That's our next chapter.

LESSONS LEARNED	
Trump's Strategies and Tactics	Trump exhibits relatively strong assertiveness skills, but his tone diminishes his effectiveness.
	Trump's empathetic skills rate is extremely low.
	Flexibility is one of Trump's higher skill levels.
	Social intuition involves rapport-building, one of Trump's stronger traits, but he undermines its impact with other negative traits.
Lessons Learned	Effective assertiveness requires preparation and knowledge, ability to "make the case" and be relatively candid, inner power, skill to set the right tone, and non-adversarial explanations of leverage.
	Empathy increases negotiation effectiveness on many levels.
	Balance in flexibility is optimal.
	Social intuition and emotional intelligence involve being nice, personable, rational, perceptive, and other effective negotiator traits.

CHAPTER 12

ETHICS AND "ALTERNATIVE FACTS"

"I see myself as a very honest guy stationed in a very corrupt world."[459]

—Donald J. Trump

Is Donald Trump "very honest?" And should his honesty be evaluated relative to a "very corrupt world?" How do his business partners, colleagues, counterparts, and friends view his trustworthiness, honesty, and credibility? How does his reputation and ethicality impact his business negotiations and effectiveness? Does this differ based on the type of negotiation, industry, and geographical area or cultural background of those involved? What does the negotiation research conclude regarding these issues?

All these questions deserve serious analysis. Business and presidential historians will no doubt spend years dissecting and judging Trump on these issues. Most of these issues, though, fall outside our scope.

What is our scope? Here's what it is *not*.

- It is *not* an effort to morally evaluate Trump. Morality often revolves around deeply personal beliefs involving many of these issues. Philosophers, religious authorities, and other similar experts will no doubt weigh in on this question. We will not.

- It is *not* a legal analysis assessing whether Trump crossed the legal line in his negotiations. As noted earlier, Trump has been criminally investigated several times in his business career related to his negotiation tactics. There is no evidence he has ever been criminally indicted or charged. Civilly, Trump has been investigated and charged and has settled with the authorities. Trump has also been involved in thousands of lawsuits. He won some, lost some, and settled some. Regardless, Trump's past civil and/or criminal liability are well outside our scope. Our justice system was designed to address legal behavior. That is the appropriate forum for it.

- It is *not* exclusively about Trump's business negotiations. Why not? Because business and personal ethics, honesty, credibility, and trustworthiness inevitably intersect and impact each other. It's virtually impossible to separate business and personal in this area. Practically speaking, our personal attitudes toward ethics and honesty also influence and often direct our business negotiation strategies. This especially holds true for Trump, whose business and personal lives were inextricably interlinked for over forty years.

- It is *not* an exhaustive analysis of the ethical standards underlying negotiations in the business environments in which Trump negotiated. We cannot appropriately address all this here.

- It is *not* a treatise on negotiation ethics research. While we will identify the research as it relates to Trump and his negotiation reputation and effectiveness, we will limit our analysis to the ethics areas impacted by Trump and his strategies.

- Finally, it is *not* an evaluation of how those in politics or business may or may not lie or be more likely to engage in ethically challenging negotiation strategies. Some believe all politicians lie. Others believe all negotiators lie. And some find these beliefs justify their and others' ethically questionable behavior. We can't fully address this here.

So what *is* our scope?

First, we will identify the Trump business negotiation strategies and tactics that objectively raise questions related to his honesty, credibility, trust, and ethics.

Second, based on those, we will address how his negotiation counterparts view his honesty, credibility, trust, and ethics. Our counterparts' attitudes and comments *after* our negotiations produce our negotiation reputations.

Here's the crucial credibility factor when it comes to negotiating. Many negotiators apply a different ethical standard to negotiations than to other parts of their lives. Justifications abound. "Everyone lies in negotiations," some will say. Or, "It's just a white lie."

Here's the deal. Even the most competent and professional negotiations involve a certain amount of "salesmanship." In fact, a significant dynamic in many negotiations involves one party attempting to convince the other party that their bottom line is different than what it is in reality. Or that they have more leverage than is actually the case. Or they try to avoid answering certain questions or revealing strategically important information.

At the end of the day, deal or no deal, everyone will leave the negotiation with an impression of whether their counterparts dealt with them in a professional and honest fashion. If you gain a reputation as an honest and trustworthy negotiator you will be more likely to get what you want in the future. If not, you will lose credibility, fewer opportunities will come your way, and fewer negotiations will conclude with you achieving your goals.[460]

Finally, we will evaluate how Trump's reputation impacts his negotiation effectiveness, based on the experts' research.

Trump's Ethically Questionable Negotiation Strategies and Tactics

In the last fifty years, Trump has used many negotiation strategies and tactics. Some have been successful. Others not so much. Which ones were ethically questionable? Here are 10. There may be more. We don't know every strategy and tactic he has used, but these have consistently been identified by those involved as part of Trump's repertoire.

How can we *objectively* assess these as ethically problematic?

One, those of us in the negotiation teaching, researching, and consulting worlds—having analyzed and viewed thousands of negotiations—have found these tactics to raise ethically questionable issues.

And it's not just my expert opinion. Ohio State Business School Professor Roy Lewicki and Marquette University Law School Professor Andrea Schneider have independently reviewed whether these 10 tactics raise ethical issues. Both confirmed the ethically problematic nature of these strategies.

Two, these strategies cannot simply be passed off as commonly utilized in highly competitive, adversarial, negotiation situations. They're *not* common, based on the research. And each cross significant negotiation-ethics lines relating to honesty, trust, and credibility.

"Hold on," Trump might respond. *"These strategies work! And they're legal. End of story. I shouldn't have to tie my hands behind my back if these fall within the rules."*

In fact, Trump himself has stated, "I'll do nearly anything within legal bounds to win."[461]

Here's the problem with that analysis. The strategies' possible short-term effectiveness and legality do *not* change the fact that Trump's counterparts and the experts view these tactics as raising ethical red flags.

Plus, these strategies do not constitute normal, accepted, above-board ethical behavior in business negotiations. Few business counterparts would conclude that the person using these tactics deserves high ethical marks, and they certainly would not recommend others use these strategies.

Of course, the use of these strategies in most negotiation situations may not become well-known beyond those directly involved (and counterparts may never even learn what really happened). Even in our age of social media dominance and connections well beyond our traditional communities, counterparts rarely share their thoughts on their adversaries' negotiation ethics.

But the public history of Trump's negotiations, the investigative reporting of his entire career, and the breadth and scope of the litigation surrounding so many of his negotiations provide an unparalleled view into his negotiation strategies and tactics and, yes, his ethics, too.

So which Trump strategies raise significant issues related to his honesty, credibility, trust, and ethics?

1. LYING AND MATERIAL MISREPRESENTATIONS

Trump's first documented intentional misrepresentation about a material fact in a significant business-related negotiation occurred in the U.S. Justice Department's racial discrimination lawsuit against the Trump companies in 1973. Trump was 27. According to *Trump Show*:

> **Donald also debuted his talent [in this case] for manipulating the truth, sworn or otherwise.** In an attempt to put distance between himself and the discriminatory practices of the Trump companies, he repeatedly claimed he did not handle the rental of apartments. Asked if he "ever had anything to do with rental decisions in individual cases," he answered: "No, I really don't." Yet he told the state examiner for his brokerage license, according to written reports filed shortly after his deposition in the race case, that "he supervises and controls the renting of all apartments owned by the Trump organization." Indeed, he showed the examiner hundreds of files "containing leases and rental records for commercial and residential tenants, all of which contained [Trump's] signature and handwriting." Matthew Tosti, the longtime Trump attorney, also wrote state officials supporting

Donald's license application and contended that Donald had "negotiated numerous leases for apartments."

Another example of this penchant for misstatement drew the attention of his federal interrogators. He had complained to reporters when the lawsuit was announced by the Justice Department that he'd first learned about it on his car radio riding to work, when in fact, according to the government attorneys, he and the organization had both been notified both during the probe and at the time of the filing of the suit. [Emphasis added.][462]

Two years later, the Trumps negotiated a settlement. Here is what occurred in the final part of those negotiations in 1975.

Nearly two years of fighting was about to end, and the settlement was much like what the Trumps could initially have gotten. But Trump had one more ploy. He viewed the signing of a[n] [already negotiated] consent order as a new chance to negotiate, and he started haggling....

When government officials persisted [that Trump stick with its deal on advertising], Trump said, "Will you pay for it?" The government said the Trumps had to pay for the advertising.

On June 10, 1975, the Trumps signed a consent order prohibiting them from "discriminating against any person in the terms, conditions, or privileges of sale or rental of a dwelling".... The agreement also required the Trumps to buy the ads assuring minorities of their equal access to housing. [Emphasis added.][463]

Trump made similar misrepresentations in negotiations throughout his business career, as evidenced by the following chart reflecting a representative sample of his intentional misrepresentations in negotiations. Importantly, Trump has admitted to many of these misrepresentations, usually calling them inadvertent, irrelevant, or simply a mistake or an oversight.

He has also proudly pointed to some of his misrepresentations as examples of his creativity and negotiation expertise. For instance, he admitted sending an unsigned agreement to New York City as evidence of his confirmed option to buy the Commodore Hotel from Penn Central, as "Trump [publicly] announced [at a press conference in May 1975] that he had a signed contract with Penn Central to buy the hotel. It was signed, but only by him; he had yet to pay the $250,000. Then came a feat of misdirection he would later boast about. When a city official asked for proof of Penn Central's commitment, Trump sent what looked like an agreement with the sellers."[464]

No such agreement existed.

Trump also intentionally told New York City officials on several occasions he had the financing all lined up for this redevelopment—more intentional material falsehoods. "Donald had…made misrepresentations about the certainty of his financing" as he had concluded that he needed New York City to believe he already had the financing to get his tax abatement, according to *Trump Show*.[465]

Similar misrepresentations occurred surrounding negotiations involving the demolition of the site that would become Trump Tower. The first occurred during a meeting between Trump and Robert Miller, a nearby art gallery owner, and Penelope Hunter-Stiebel, a curator at the Metropolitan Museum of Art. The issue? What to do with the bronze grillwork above the building's entrance and two 15-foot sculptures of goddesses carved into the front of the building. The Metropolitan Museum wanted these pieces of art.

Hunter-Stiebel and Miller believed they had a deal where Trump would donate the friezes to the museum in exchange for a generous appraisal (estimated at more than $200,000) he could use as a tax write-off. Trump "appeared enthusiastic" about this, saying, "This is going to be a great deal," according to Hunter-Stiebel and Miller when they met at Trump's office.[466]

Shortly thereafter, Trump instructed his construction foreman to demolish the sculptures, according to *Trump Revealed*.

> "Developer Scraps Bonwit Sculptures," read the front-page headline on the next morning's *[New York] Times*. The article quoted 'John Baron,' a 'vice-president of the Trump organization,' explaining that the company had decided on demolition after three independent appraisers concluded that the sculptures were 'without artistic merit,' were worth less than $9,000, and would have cost $32,000 to move. John Barron—usually spelled with two r's—was a pseudonym that Trump often used when he did not want to identify himself to a reporter. Two days later Trump, using his real name, addressed the incident, saying that removing the sculptures could have cost more than $500,000. "My biggest concern was the safety of people on the street below," he insisted....
>
> Kent Barwick, chairman of New York's Landmarks Preservation Commission, said the demolition established Trump "as a bad guy. **Afterwards, rightly or wrongly, there was a question of trust**." [Emphasis added.][467]

How many misrepresentations occurred here? *One*, Miller and Hunter-Stiebel believed they had a deal based on what Trump told them. If they had one, Trump misrepresented to them that they had a deal, then breached it. If they didn't have one, he misled them into believing they had a deal. It could also have been a misunderstanding. Unlikely, though, based on what occurred later.

Two, assuming three independent appraisers actually evaluated this—the cost to remove the sculptures couldn't have been $32,000 *and* $500,000. Trump made *both* statements. One was untrue.

Three, no truly independent appraiser could have concluded the sculptures were "without artistic merit" if the Metropolitan Museum of Art wanted them. They might have found they had little merit, but not none.

Another negotiation-related misrepresentation involving Trump Tower occurred in the context of a labor lawsuit concerning the use of illegal Polish immigrant workers to demolish the site. Trump in that suit, according to *Trump Show*, claimed "in sworn testimony that he did not 'think' he knew anything about the Polish brigade [the illegal immigrant workers] 'until probably sometime after the demolition.'... **So fainthearted a claim of ignorance was transparently disingenuous**." [Emphasis added.][468]

What evidence suggests Trump lied about *when* he learned about these workers? *First*, Trump hired the demolition contractor himself after finding and inviting the contractor to bid. One reason he liked them? The contractor's super low bid was only possible because it paid these illegal workers "one-half to one-third those of the union scale."[469] Trump most certainly would have investigated why its bid was so low.

Second, Trump knew this contractor had *previously* used illegal Polish immigrants. How? This contractor had used illegal workers for interior demolition work next to the future Trump Tower site—another site owned by Trump. Again, *Trump Show*.

> Zbigniew Goryn, a Kacszycki [the demolition subcontractor] foreman on both jobs, said that Donald came to the 57th Street job once and said he "liked the way the men were working." Goryn recalled that Trump remarked that the "Polish guys" were "good, hard workers." In fact, Trump hired away from Bonwit a construction supervisor who'd overseen its 57th Street work, Tom Macari, and put him in charge of supervising the Fifth Avenue demolition [the Trump Tower site]. Macari, whose office was in Donald's suite, went to the Fifth Avenue site "twenty to thirty times" from March until

the job was finally finished in late August. One of only a half dozen or so Trump Organization officers at the time, Macari knew, according to the eventual findings of a federal judge, "that the Polish workers were working 'off the books,' that they were non-union, that they were paid substandard wages, and that they were paid irregularly if at all."[470]

Third, Trump's office at the time was in the Crown Building—directly across the street from the future Trump Tower site. Why should we care? "Trump's ignorance was even more improbable in light of Kacszycki's testimony that 'hundreds, thousands of workers from Poland and other countries' came to the Trump Tower site and 'stood in lines down the street, waiting, begging' for jobs. 'You could see that all the time,' Kacszycki said, 'five, six, ten, twenty times—all the time—come begging for jobs.'"[471]

And Trump said under oath he didn't think he knew about the workers until *after* the demolition? An intentional misrepresentation of fact under oath.

One final example of Trump's negotiation misrepresentations, this one from his former partners at Harrah's—who had partnered with him to build his first Atlantic City casino. After he had negotiated a great deal with Harrah's to partner in building and operating Harrah's at Trump Plaza, the partnership fell apart. Why? According to *Trump Revealed*:

> "[Its] debut was marred by malfunctioning slot machines and fire alarms, and the money didn't come rolling in as expected. The first year's results brought in half of projected profits. Trump blamed part of the problem on the name and began a campaign to eliminate the reference to Harrah's. He reasoned that gamblers confused the casino with the other Harrah's Atlantic City property.... **A Harrah's executive responded that Trump's 'unsupportable falsehoods' had undermined their partnership.** After lawsuits and countersuits, Harrah's sold its 50 percent stake." [Emphasis added.][472]

While some of these misrepresentations and those in the following chart might have been inadvertent, the consistent nature and pattern of these misrepresentations belies Trump's excuses. Regardless, each documented Trump intentional misrepresentation erodes his credibility for future negotiations and negatively impacts his reputation.

Here's the chart of a representative sample of Trump's documented business negotiation misrepresentations. Detailed descriptions of many of these can be found earlier in the book.

Negotiation Situation	*Intentional Misrepresentation*	Under Oath?
U.S. Department of Justice Racial Discrimination Lawsuit	Misrepresentation relating to his activity in renting apartments on behalf of the Trump companies.[473]	Yes
U.S. Department of Justice Racial Discrimination Lawsuit	Misrepresentation to reporters relating to how and when the U.S. Department of Justice informed him of the lawsuit.[474]	No
Fred C. Trump Convention Center	Misrepresentation to New York City's Peter Solomon regarding the size of his commission (informed Solomon it was $4.4 million when it was $500,000) in an effort to trade his commission for the naming rights to the convention center.	No
Commodore Hotel Redevelopment	Misrepresentation relating to his agreement to buy the hotel from Penn Central.[475]	No
Commodore Hotel Redevelopment	Misrepresentation to Penn Central that he had a deal with Hyatt. Trump *"assured Penn Central's negotiators that he a had a solid deal with Hyatt when he had no such thing."*[476]	No
Commodore Hotel Redevelopment	Misrepresentations relating to his financing for the redevelopment.[477]	No
Trump Tower Art Deco Deal	Misrepresentations relating to a deal with the Metropolitan Museum of Art to donate the Bonwit Teller frescos and explanations regarding it.[478]	No
Trump Tower Development	Misrepresentation regarding the timing of his knowledge of the Polish illegal immigrant workers on his Trump Tower demolition.[479]	Yes
Harrah's Casino Development Deal	Misrepresentations regarding Trump's financing for the casino deal: Trump claimed Harrah's had agreed to finance it as part of their deal in *The Art of the Deal*. But he conceded in court papers later that he was responsible for the financing. Either way, the financing was "lost" *after* he signed the Harrah's deal, forcing Harrah's to use its corporate guarantee to get the financing.[480]	No
New Jersey Casino Application	Failure to list previous documented criminal and civil investigations involving him and the Trump companies.[481]	Yes
New Jersey Casino Application	Failure to list associations with known mob-related individuals.[482]	Yes

Net worth in O'Brien Lawsuit and to reporters in other contexts	Misrepresentations regarding his net worth in connection with the Timothy O'Brien/ *TrumpNation* lawsuit.[483] Many other public misrepresentations regarding his net worth, albeit most were not under oath.	Yes
Mar-a-Lago purchase price and terms	Misrepresentation regarding his "all-cash purchase" of Mar-a-Lago and its purchase price. He admitted under oath later he financed all but $2,800 of it.[484]	No
Possible NBC/ Television City deal	Multiple Trump misrepresentations in his negotiations with New York City's lead negotiator Jay Biggins, who said in a memo to New York City Mayor Ed Koch, *"The kind of brinksmanship and misstatement of the facts we have seen is not the kind of conduct we can tolerate in a partner with so much at stake."* [485]	No
Trump University	Misrepresentations regarding his involvement in Trump University.[486]	No
Trump real-estate licensing deals in Mexico, Florida, and Hawaii	Misrepresentations regarding his involvement in real-estate developments around the world. Trump licensed his name and sometimes managed the properties but did not develop them despite public representations to buyers to the contrary.[487]	Unknown

2. BUSINESS BULLYING

Stiffing contractors in direct contravention of legally valid signed executed agreements reflecting Trump's promises in writing—simply because you can—represents a fundamental ethical issue regarding fairness, honesty, and credibility.

Trump has a history of doing this. Not every time. But enough times to reflect a pattern and to negatively impact his reputation.

3. PERSONAL AND BUSINESS THREATS—ESPECIALLY EMPTY THREATS AND BLUFFS

Trump loves to threaten his counterparts. Just ask Pete Rozelle, Ed Koch, Jim Brady, Peter Goldmark, Liz Smith, Marvin Roffman, Timothy O'Brien, and the list goes on.

Threats raise at least two ethical issues. *One*, certain types of threats, like explicit personal ones, have no place in ethical negotiations. Personal ones include threatening an individual with unspecified future problems—like losing their job—unrelated to the business negotiation issues on the table.

And, *two*, empty threats—those made but not carried out—destroy the maker's credibility. While an empty business threat may not be unethical per se, it undermines a person's credibility if the maker does not carry it out. This has ethical consequences.

Trump falls into both categories, having regularly made explicit personal threats and empty threats. A double whammy to his reputation.

Here are a few of them. Trump denies most of these.

Explicit Personal Threats

- Trump to World Trade Center executive Peter Goldmark: "You wouldn't last in your job very long if Governor Carey decided you weren't doing the right thing on this…. You should know I have a lot of weight in Albany."[488]

- Trump to gossip columnist Liz Smith: "[Trump] once threatened to buy the *Daily News* so he could have me fired."[489]

- Trump to casino gaming analyst Marvin Roffman's employer (in a fax): "You will be hearing shortly from my lawyers unless Mr. Roffman is immediately dismissed or apologizes."[490]

- Trump on issue of suing reporter and author Timothy O'Brien: "'I spent a couple of bucks on legal fees and they spent a whole lot more. **I did it to make his life miserable, which I'm happy about**,' Trump bragged. It was a comment that fit cozily within his philosophy of revenge." [Emphasis added.][491] [This action is more about carrying out a personal threat through litigation, which raises ethical issues but not credibility ones.]

Empty Threats

- All the above personal threats, except those involving Marvin Roffman and Timothy O'Brien.

- Trump to *New York Post* gossip-page editor Jim Brady: "[Trump] was cursing me with every four-letter word…. You SOB. You *bleeping* this. You *bleeping* that. I'm going to sue you. I'm going to sue the Post. I'm going to sue Murdoch [the Post's owner]. I'm going to sue everyone."[492] (Trump's lawyer Roy Cohn then phoned Brady and told him no suit would be forthcoming as this was just Trump letting off steam.)

- Trump to author Wayne Barrett: "'I've broken one writer.... You and I've been friends and all, but if your story damages my reputation, I want you to know I'll sue."[493]

- Trump's threat to finance a New York City mayoral candidate versus New York City Mayor Ed Koch.[494]

Explicit personal threats and empty threats—common Trump moves. Both undermine his credibility, ethics, and negatively impact his reputation.

4. OFFERING BRIBE-LIKE PERSONAL FINANCIAL BENEFITS TO HIS COUNTERPARTS

Donald Trump has never been indicted or convicted of any bribery-type offense, but he has been investigated several times by federal officials for providing monetary and other value to his counterparts during or shortly after their negotiations concluded.

Let me be clear: I am not suggesting Trump engaged in any criminal activity, although it's possible. (Just because prosecutors didn't find sufficient evidence to indict or convict does not mean the criminal activity did not occur.)

Instead, I am simply suggesting the timing and appearances involved make Trump's offers and actions highly unethical. Which instances? Here are five, each described earlier.

- Trump joined David Berger's $100-million lawsuit against nine major oil companies shortly after Berger dropped his opposition to Penn Central's selling the Commodore Hotel to Trump. (This was the subject of a federal investigation.)[495]

- Trump sent the Penn Central representative a television set as a Christmas gift while negotiating with him to purchase the Commodore Hotel site from Penn Central. The Penn Central representative, apparently recognizing the unethical nature of the gift, returned it.[496]

- Trump said to *Village Voice* reporter Wayne Barrett, "I could get you an apartment" [in a nicer part of town than where he lived].[497]

- Trump and his lawyer Roy Cohn seemed to arrange for New York City Deputy Mayor Stanley Friedman to receive a high-paying job at Cohn's law firm and to become the Bronx Party Democratic Leader after helping Trump close the Commodore Hotel deal.[498]

- Trump apparently arranged for labor racketeer John Cody's girlfriend to get three large duplexes on two Trump Tower floors, just under Trump's penthouse, including Trump Tower's only indoor swimming pool and, "Cody invested $100,000 in [Hixon's] apartments…stayed there often…and Trump helped the woman get a $3 million mortgage to pay for the three apartments….She said she got the mortgage from a bank that Trump recommended she use, without filling out a loan application or showing financials."[499] Despite other developers experiencing work stoppages from Cody's union members that summer, Trump Tower's work never stopped. (This was the subject of a federal investigation.)

These were not isolated instances of Trump offering his negotiation counterparts items of personal value in exchange for something Trump wanted. "The repeated wooing or retention of critical public or legal opponents [was] a lifelong hallmark of the Trump style… [and was] a pattern of Donald's business life," according to *Trump Show*. [500]

In fact, *Trump Show* summarized Trump's attitude toward many of his counterparts and his regular and continuous financial—and unethical—wooing of them, stating:

> [Trump] had prided himself on never having met a public official, a banker, a lawyer, a reporter, or a prosecutor he couldn't seduce. Some he owned, and others he merely manipulated. As he saw it, it was not just that everyone had a price, it was that he knew what the price was. He believed he could look across a table and compute the price, then move on to another table and borrow the money to pay it. "Everybody tries to get some money" was his assessment in one unpublished interview of what motivates the people he dealt with. It was his one-sentence summary of human nature. Yet he believed that a lifetime of such seductions—from hiring the governor's son to a federal prosecutor's brother—hadn't cheapened him.[501]

5. INTENTIONALLY HIDING THE BALL WITH MISLEADING STATEMENTS AND ACTIONS

Intentionally misrepresenting material facts is a clear ethical no-no in negotiations. Making statements and taking actions that significantly mislead your counterpart into falsely believing a material element in the negotiation is true or untrue—another clear no-no. Trump does both.

Interestingly, Trump himself trots out perhaps the most infamous example of his misleading and "hide the ball" efforts in *The Art of the Deal*. There, he describes how he misled his future casino partners—Harrah's—into thinking his construction site was making a lot of progress when almost no construction had actually taken place. He did this to impress Harrah's with his ability to manage complex construction efforts and bring in major projects under budget and on time. His illusion worked. It was also admittedly a blatant falsehood.[502]

His sale of the St. Moritz Hotel to Australian Alan Bond also was based on Bond falsely believing Trump owned the highly valuable Manhattan real estate on which the hotel rested, according to *Trump Show*. But Trump only had the leasehold to sell. Trump made $100 million on that sale.[503]

Trump also reportedly reprised his illusion of activity with more misdirection in his sale of Resorts to *Wheel of Fortune*'s Merv Griffin, as "a former Trump executive, who'd gone to work for Merv [Griffin], claimed [in a later lawsuit] that Donald had tricked Griffin into believing that the old Resorts casino was in better shape than it was by having painters and carpenters refurbish a small section of the hotel where [Griffin] was taken on a very guided tour."[504]

Trump also misled governmental entities and others by filling out multiple financial forms, under oath, in an incomplete and inaccurate way. In fact, "by the end of the [1980s] Trump's evasive responses on these forms had become a decade-long routine," according to *Trump Show*.[505]

And, in perhaps the greatest feat of misleading and hiding the ball by Trump in his entire business career, Trump convinced numerous banks and financial institutions in the 1980s to lend him over $3 billion based on assets and collateral valued at a lot less.

As one example of his misleading statements, which borders on a misstatement, he said the following to the New Jersey Casino Control Commission in 1988 relating to the bank financing he could get for refinancing the Taj. "The banks call me all the time—can we loan you money, can we this, can we that. There is tremendous liquidity if you have a good statement and you're solid. The banks, they want to throw money at you. I can give them security on their loan, **100 percent certainty**. With me, they know they would get their interest." [Emphasis added.][506]

We know what happened to the banks shortly thereafter.

And recall the misleading nature of his mortgage submission to the bank and his directing his employee Blanche Sprague to justify a $220 million mortgage loan with highly inaccurate and unsupportable sales projections.

"Wait a second," you might respond. "Isn't this actually a prime example of Trump's **brilliant** negotiating? Isn't some level of misdirection a staple of negotiating—including ethical negotiating? And why blame Trump 100 percent? Even if he misled them, the banks and financial institutions owed a moral, ethical, and legal obligation to their shareholders to do their due diligence and figure out the truth about Trump's financial condition *before* loaning him money. Trump didn't have an ethical obligation to point out the weakness of his own negotiating position to his opponents, did he?"

Excellent points. Let's address them.

The "Appropriate" Level of Misdirection

How much misdirection is ethically problematic? This is not an easy question. On the one hand, some misdirection is expected and warranted in almost all negotiations. If my client is desperate to sell his business, I would not share this with a potential buyer.

In fact, most negotiations involve a certain acceptable element of misdirection that all the parties understand, accept, and practice.

If I'm negotiating to buy an allegedly rare artifact in an open marketplace in Mexico City, I'm not going to wear a suit, an expensive watch and volunteer that I'm a U.S. lawyer. Am I a U.S. lawyer? Yes. But I'm not going to share it. Instead, I will try to create a different reality for that shopkeeper in the world of perception and expectations. And he'll try to do the same for me. That's the playing field for most negotiations.

On the other hand, parties do have an ethical and legal obligation to share certain material facts and circumstances involved in the negotiation process and not to go overboard in trying to mislead their counterparts.

The key here revolves around the parties' *expectations* in different negotiation environments of what to share and how much misleading is ethically appropriate. If my client is desperate to sell his business, my counterpart does not *expect* me to tell them, *"Oh, by the way, my client is **desperate** to sell his business."* In fact, I might be guilty of negotiation malpractice if I said this. Instead, my counterpart *expects* I will mislead *about this issue* (and maybe even make a misrepresentation regarding it).

Likewise, the Mexico City vendor selling an allegedly rare artifact in an open marketplace does not *expect* that my "normal" clothing and general appearance will definitively tag me as being unable to afford his artifact. Again, it's about the parties' expectations in those negotiation environments.

Of course, this analysis puts the legal issue aside.

How can you decide what to do? Evaluate what your counterpart would say about the misdirection/misleading if they later found out about it. If they expected it, they would likely say *"No big deal. Everyone does it."* But if they would react later by saying, *"That's sleazy. I never would have done the deal had I known he was that misleading,"* then don't do it.

Remember, your negotiation reputation for honesty, trust, credibility, and ethics will be created by your counterparts. Consider what your counterparts would say after. Too much misleading and misdirection leads to a reputation as a dishonest, untrustworthy, sleazy, and unethical negotiator.

What about Trump's level of misleading/misdirection in the earlier examples? We know how Harrah's feels about Trump's misleading and misdirection efforts. An executive said their partnership fell apart due to Trump's "unsupportable falsehoods." Lawsuits were also filed—always a bad sign regarding what our counterparts might say.

What about Alan Bond on the St. Moritz Hotel deal? We don't know, but I suspect he didn't praise Trump's negotiation honesty and ethics after that deal. At the least, I suspect he felt "played" and considered Trump's misdirection sleazy. On the other hand, perhaps he expected this type of misleading to occur in these types of transactions. If so, he might just chalk it up to experience. But he still likely wouldn't praise Trump's ethics after the deal.

Merv Griffin sued Trump on his Resorts' deal, making many allegations about Trump's misstatements and misleading efforts connected to their negotiations.

What about the bankers and financial institutions? Remember, they were surprised to learn of the others when they first compared notes about Trump's collective financial obligations and assets. They almost certainly felt Trump had not dealt with them openly, honestly, and ethically.

The Banks' Independent Obligation to Figure Out Trump's True Financials

The financial institutions did share in the culpability, though, because they did *not* do their due diligence. Nor, apparently, did Alan Bond, at least until later.

However, their shared culpability does *not* change the ethically problematic nature of Trump's misleading efforts. Just because he was dealing with sophisticated parties that shared the blame does not mean his intentional misleading actions were above-board and ethically acceptable. Whether his counterparts believed him or did their homework goes to whether his misleading efforts *worked*. Not whether they were ethically inappropriate in the first place.

In fact, ironically, Trump probably ended up far better off in the end *because* the banks shared the blame for their enormous losses. How? They shared an interest in keeping their mutual culpability and malfeasance quiet. According to *Trump Show*:

> From the outset of Trump's crisis, Citibank and the rest of the banks behaved as if they and Donald had at least one common concern: to keep a lid on the story of his demise. Bankers leaked to the [*WSJ's*] Neil Barsky, but only for tactical advantage in the table games of June, when the restructuring was negotiated. When he [Barsky] subsequently pursued a fraud story, they were as tightlipped as the target [Trump]. When the [U.S. Congress'] House Banking Committee announced hearings into the Trump fiasco, the bankers and Donald were equally resolved not to cooperate with the probe, and it died.[507]

While the truth would have laid bare Trump's misleading conduct (at the least), it would have also shone a light on the banks' possible malfeasance in giving Trump billions without requiring a sufficient showing of financial strength. The congressional probe died.

Trump's Independent Ethical Obligation Not to Mislead

Finally, does Donald Trump have an independent ethical obligation not to engage in significant misleading actions in negotiations? Negotiation ethics experts would answer "yes." We might quibble as to *where* to draw the ethical line. But everyone would agree a line exists. There is a level of unethical, inappropriate misleading that just should not take place.

Negotiation is *not* an activity where "anything goes" as long as you don't cross the legal line.

Trump's line appears to be "as long as it's legal, it's okay." That's not okay from an ethical perspective. And it's certainly not okay for most negotiators. They are the ones who create reputations.

6. SLIPPING IN SIGNIFICANT CHANGES AFTER THE DEAL'S DONE (THE NIBBLE)

Donald Trump got a great tax abatement deal from New York City on his first major development, the Commodore Hotel. But it wasn't enough. Shortly after the opening of the new Grand Hyatt Hotel, Trump pulled a fast one on the city, according to *Trump Revealed*.

> As hotel visitors rolled in, [Trump] tightened his grip on one of the few concessions he'd made to land his tax break. In 1987, Trump told his accountants to change their reporting methods, limiting the amount that the Grand Hyatt's profit-sharing deal would deliver to the city government. When the city's auditor general, Karen Burstein, [later] reviewed hotel records, she found that "aberrant" accounting practices had shortchanged the city by millions of dollars in taxes. Asked years later about the changes, Trump said he did not remember the investigation.[508]

Not uncovered until 1990, the newly elected New York City Mayor David Dinkins administration described Trump's actions in legal motions submitted to a state judge as "fraud."[509]

It wasn't the only time Trump pulled a similar stunt. In 1984, Trump Plaza on Third Ave opened, and longtime Trump advisor Louise Sunshine—who had contributed greatly to his early success by introducing him around New York to her political and other connections—owned a 5 percent stake in it. He repaid her, according to *Trump Show*, by:

> ...structur[ing] the profit-and-loss accounting for the building in a way that left her owing a million dollars in taxes on her tiny part of it, and when she objected he tried to buy her out cheap. She hired a lawyer, forced Donald to pay her three times his initial offer, and quit, saying the man she'd helped invent had 'used his money as a power tool over me.'[510]

A third example of Trump inserting a major benefit to himself into a deal—without the agreement of the other side—occurred in his sale of

Resorts to Merv Griffin. There, Trump "slipped a costly little item into the agreement, unnoticed by Griffin until it was too late," as described by *Trump Show*.[511] What happened?

- Trump—shortly before the Resorts' sale closed and Griffin took control—awarded Resorts' [then] executive Jack Davis a $600,000 annual lifetime pension starting slightly over a year after his three-year million-dollar contract expired.

- Davis's wife Caroline would become eligible for this $600,000 annual lifetime pension after he died. (He was 63 at the time and in great health.)

- The value of this pension was conservatively estimated to be $20 million.

- Griffin, upon learning of the change—asked Trump to pay part of it. Trump refused.

- Griffin later fired Davis and legally contested the pension.

- During the legal dispute, Trump hired Davis as president of the Taj and his wife Caroline as a high-paid special-events coordinator.[512]

Some would think Trump would be embarrassed by this sleazy maneuver. Nope. After the deal closed, *Trump Show* described how he highlighted this move as an example of his negotiation prowess.

> Trump waved the pension in the face of some journalists as another example of how he had prevailed over the hapless Griffin. He even wrote a letter to *People*, which had profiled Griffin, charging that its statement that Griffin had become a billionaire by virtue of the Resorts deal was "a total joke." The magazine, said Trump, had "failed to deduct the approximately $1 billion in debt" Merv incurred, meaning that Griffin "won't even be a millionaire." While "everyone tries to beat Donald Trump," he wrote of himself, "not too many have succeeded."[513]

Slipping in unnoticed benefits to himself and his team. Trying to screw long-time aides. Nibbling for more at the end. All represent unethical acts reflecting poorly on negotiators—and negatively impacting their reputations.

Trump even went after Griffin personally after the deal by reaching out to reporters to try to rub his "win" as a big loss for Griffin.

That's another Trump modus operandi: Personally attack your negotiation counterparts, publicly.

7. NAME-CALLING AND PERSONALLY DEMEANING HIS COUNTERPARTS

Donald Trump—amid negotiations with New York City over tax benefits he needed to lure NBC to his Television City site—publicly called New York City Mayor Ed Koch:

- A *"disaster waiting to explode,"*

- A *"moron,"*

- Someone *"who can't hack it anymore"* and who has *"absolutely no sense of economic development,"* and

- Someone who should resign.

Several months later, well after this public spat had seemingly run its course, Trump lit back into Koch and called him:

- An *"idiot,"*

- *"The pits,"* and

- *"Incompetent."*[514]

These public statements, detailed in *Trump Show*, occurred **at the same time** that Trump was actively seeking major New York City tax abatements and zoning changes needed to get NBC to Television City. If successful, Trump could have built the world's tallest building and made hundreds of millions of dollars on a huge development project.

Koch—the top New York City decision-maker with veto power over any project—ultimately rejected *any and all* NBC–Trump proposals. No surprise, right?

Of course, Koch gave back as good as he got. Their public feud was anything but one-sided. But Trump needed Koch and New York City more than Koch and New York City needed Trump.

This relationship had also gotten off to a rocky start before Koch even became mayor. While a longshot mayoral candidate, Koch had called Trump asking for a political contribution. Trump refused and engaged in such a tirade that Koch later told his campaign treasurer Bernie Rome, months later, that he *"could still hear Trump yelling in my ear."*[515]

Trump's temper and impolitic name-calling was not limited to New York City, a place infamous for its rough-and-tumble business and political climate.

He also got into a public feud with fellow gaming titan Steve Wynn in the mid-1980s and later. Here is how *TrumpNation* described the feud, along with some of the choice words exchanged. Keep in mind that competitors Trump and Wynn were also negotiation counterparts at times.

Trump called Wynn:

- *"Disgraceful,"*
- A *"blowhard,"*
- A *"scumbag,"* and
- *"Nutty."*[516]

Trump further expounded on these labels, saying of Wynn, *"'You know, I think Steve's got a lot of psychological problems,'* Donald told a New York magazine writer during a heated exchange with Wynn in 1998. *'I think he's quite disturbed. That's just my feeling. I think he's a very disturbed person.'"*[517]

And Wynn—like Koch—hit back hard over the years, calling Trump:

- A *"lightweight, second-string adolescent,"*
- A *"half-baked mentality,"*
- A *"cartoon,"* and
- A *"perverse exaggeration."*

Wynn also expounded on these labels, saying of Trump:

"Because he doesn't understand the gaming industry, he's capable of being confused. He's obsessed with being king of the hill, and he's probably threatened on more than one level, Wynn once said of Donald in *Fortune* magazine...."

"[Trump's] statements to people like you [reporters], whether they concern us and our projects, or our motivations, or his own reality, or his own future, or his own present, you have seen over the years have no relation to truth or fact. And if you need me to remind you of that, then we're both in trouble. He's a fool."[518]

Interestingly, Trump and Wynn patched up their relationship in 2005, after this name-calling went on for years.[519]

Let's not forget Trump's nasty personal and public feud with USFL Commissioner Chet Simmons and his fellow USFL owners after buying the New Jersey Generals. As quoted earlier, Tampa Bay Bandits owner John Bassett noted Trump's "personal abuse of the commissioner."[520]

At the end of the day, Trump's name-calling and personally demeaning comments about his negotiation colleagues and counterparts significantly damaged his negotiation reputation. They also undermined his negotiation effectiveness and potentially cost him, at least on the Television City/NBC deal, hundreds of millions of dollars.

Unethical, too? Of course.

8. EXCESSIVE PUFFERY

Chapter Three addressed Trump's tendency toward over-the-top puffery in his business negotiations. The superlatives just seem never-ending in Trump's world, at least regarding his developments, deals, golf courses, products, and casinos.

What ethical considerations arise from his serial exaggerations?

In two words—lost credibility. How so?

If *everything* someone says about matters involving themselves include excessive adjectives like great, incredible, amazing, brilliant, wonderful, fantastic, and so on, listeners discount the statements right off the bat. *Not everything* can be that awesome, at least not in the real world. So listeners presume the speaker must be exaggerating or lying. Either way, the person loses credibility. Either way, listeners conclude the person is *not* a straight-shooter—a very effective trait in a negotiator.

Parties in negotiations gain credibility in part by differentiating between the issues and interests on the table. "This tech company has some incredibly profitable products, including..." an investment banker might state. "Of course, it also has two divisions that have not yet produced the profitability it wants."

If the investment banker instead lumped every division of the tech company together and called every division awesome or great, a possible purchaser simply would not believe him.

Lost credibility.

Of course, I'm not suggesting Donald Trump exaggerated *everything* about himself and his products in his business negotiations. He's too smart for this. But does he regularly use over-the-top exaggerations and rhetoric to describe elements in his negotiations? Yes.

He thus loses credibility due to the frequency and level of his exaggerations.

9. SUPER-SHORT, FALSE DEADLINES

The fundamental problem with false deadlines—where you set a seemingly drop-dead, inflexible deadline and then ignore it by negotiating afterward—relates to credibility. It's gone.

Parties might try a few excuses, like, "circumstances have changed since we set the deadline," but sophisticated counterparts will likely just laugh in the parties' faces (not literally, of course).

I strongly suspect Pete Rozelle inwardly laughed when Trump told him he needed an answer to his demand for an NFL franchise right away. It was a blatantly transparent Trump effort to impose time pressure on Rozelle. It almost certainly backfired.

I also strongly suspect Deputy New York City Mayor for Economic Development Alair Townsend and her team did not believe Trump's two-hour deadline to accept or reject his proposal relating to NBC's move to Television City. His contention that NBC was "on the precipice of making a decision" and would otherwise be Jersey-bound in two hours just doesn't pass the straight-face test—especially as he did not formally represent NBC.

Both these Trump deadlines turned out to be false. As have others. Each false deadline imposed, and ignored, eats away at Trump's credibility. Especially public ones.

Of course, Trump also imposed real deadlines and stuck with them. He gave one to the Resorts' board, and they basically caved. He also gave one to Lawrence Taylor. That worked, too.

But here's the problem. Once *any* false deadline gets publicly known, as did the New York City one and others, Trump's deadline-based credibility takes a serious hit. That significantly and negatively impacts his ability to impose real deadlines in the future.

Why believe him then if multiple deadlines of his proved false in the past?

Credibility lost. Again.

10. SCOPE AND BREADTH OF LITIGATION—WHERE THERE'S SMOKE, THERE'S FIRE

Perhaps the most incredible statistic about Donald Trump relates to the number of litigation matters in which he has been involved. As noted earlier, Trump has been a party in over 4,000 litigation matters in his lifetime prior to becoming President.[521]

I don't know any litigators—even those who have practiced law for over 40 years—who have been involved in that many litigation matters. And they litigate for a living.

What does this tell us about Trump and ethics and credibility? Where there's smoke, there's almost certainly fire. Parties and businesses do not generally litigate for fun. It's an expensive, time-consuming, energy-draining, inefficient, and psychologically difficult process. And it usually only occurs as a last resort when parties have lost complete trust and credibility with their colleagues and/or counterparts.

Do we as a society need it and rely on it to resolve certain intractable disputes and enforce appropriate behavior on bad actors? Of course. But is it the first, second or even third choice of ethical business professionals to resolve disputes? No. It's almost always a last resort. And it should be.

But not for Trump. Why not? Because he doesn't seem to really care about his lost trust and credibility in business relationships. His business bullying serves as the prime example. He cares about winning, and litigation feeds his win–lose mindset.

It has, however, served as a last resort for most of his counterparts—those sued and those suing. But they have nevertheless engaged. Why? Some didn't have a choice, as Trump sued them. Others sued him. In almost all those 4,000 instances, the parties and Trump had likely lost sufficient trust and credibility in each other to resort to this admittedly painful and expensive process.

Who is to blame for that lost trust and credibility? Litigation is designed to answer this question. With that many litigation matters over almost 50 years of negotiating, there's plenty of fire there—not just smoke.

Those cases collectively and negatively impact Trump's credibility, ethics, and reputation.

Trump's Negotiation Reputation Relating to Ethics and Credibility

What can we conclude about Trump's negotiation reputation relating to ethics and credibility, based on these 10 ethical issues and his Top Ten Trump Business Negotiation Strategies? It's not a pretty picture.

What about his friends? George Ross, his longtime lawyer, writes many complimentary things about his ethics and credibility. But Ross rarely sat *across* the table from Trump. He worked and negotiated *for* him. He had a significant interest in portraying Trump in the most positive ethical light.

Trump's partners, ex-partners, and counterparts, on the other hand, personally experienced the full Trump negotiation treatment. What they have said about him—good and bad—has largely determined his negotiation reputation.

What have they said? Many of their views and comments have been described and quoted earlier. Some comments were publicly reported in newspapers and magazines. Others were in interviews with investigative reporters or authors. And some were in the context of litigation. I won't repeat them here, other than listing his counterparts.

Many also had multiple negotiations and interactions with Trump—so their body of knowledge of him spanned years, not hours or days. In some cases, I have also grouped some counterparts together as they, in effect, negotiated collectively with Trump. Many also worked for Trump for years as employees of his various entities.

Here's the list. To see their specific comments and to understand the context of the negotiations in which they were made, I've listed the page numbers where their comments appear. These are basically in chronological order, starting with Trump's counterparts in the 1970s.

- New York City zoning and real-estate–related bureaucrats	82
- Penn Central trustee selling Commodore Hotel site	51
- Trump collaborator on the Commodore Hotel deal and later NBC representative Michael Bailkin	82
- UDC Chair Richard Ravitch	25
- World Trade Center executive Peter Goldmark	72
- Metropolitan Museum of Art curator Penelope Hunter-Stiebel	230
- Art gallery owner Robert Miller	230
- Harrah's executives	232

On a scale of 1 to 10, 10 being the highest ethics score and 1 constituting the least ethical, where would I rate Trump's reputation for negotiation ethics? Around a 2.

Trump's likely response?

> "I beat all these folks in negotiations. I won. They lost. Of course they'll say mean things about me. Plus, I've been negotiating major deals for over 40 years. It's inevitable that some folks won't like what I've said or done. Negotiating is rough-and-tumble and not for the faint of heart. It's not a popularity contest. Some of these folks just weren't cut out for it.
>
> I was also involved in litigation with a bunch of them. They probably blame me for beating them. And the list is not even a representative sample of all my counterparts. Most don't even know me well.
>
> And what about those who would have positive things to say about my negotiation ethics? Most haven't publicly spouted off. Why should they? They have no ax to grind.
>
> Bottom line—these folks are jealous. I won. They've got sour grapes. I'll bet most are Democrats, anyway."

Excellent points, again. Let's address them.

I won—they lost, "sour grapes" issue

No question—many of these counterparts may be jealous or have an ax to grind. And some did end up with the short end of the stick in their negotiations with Trump. Others did well, though. Regardless, an objective evaluation of Trump's negotiation ethics must account for these factors.

On the other hand, these factors account for elements in *everyone's* negotiation reputation. The nature of the negotiation process—and how our reputations derive from it—necessarily result from what our counterparts say about us after our negotiations conclude. And those who "lose" don't always trash their counterparts' ethics or reputation.

Since some of these statements have also been made under oath, there's a huge incentive for them to be accurate and truthful. Many comments are not just unsupported opinion and feelings about Trump based on jealousy or having "lost" a negotiation. Instead, they're based on objective evidence of what Trump did and said in their negotiations, some of which Trump has admitted and even highlighted (like his illusion with Harrah's board and his "slipping in" the pension issue with Merv Griffin).

Facts matter.

Inevitably some counterparts will dislike and criticize him

Yes—a wealthy and powerful real-estate, gaming, and business negotiator will inevitably ruffle feathers and leave some bad feelings and perhaps even enemies in his or her wake. Especially when they largely operate in areas like New York and New Jersey where business professionals sometimes pride themselves on their toughness.

And those same business negotiators may make more negotiation enemies than others if they use multiple business bankruptcies to legally discharge millions of dollars of debts, as did Trump.

But the breadth and scope of Trump's counterparts and the consistency of their comments about Trump's ethics, credibility, and trustworthiness speaks volumes about their accuracy. These comments span almost 50 years of Trump's business career. They also include counterparts who worked for Trump for years. Their opinions should carry more weight than others. And they do.

Plus, none of these factors suggest that even his enemies would feel so strongly about him that they would publicly comment on his ethical issues. Many, though, have done exactly this. And they have climbed out on the proverbial limb to do it, given Trump's proclivity to sue.

Is it inevitable we could find some Trump counterparts to disparage his negotiation ethics? Of course. But that doesn't fully undermine the scope and accuracy of his counterparts' statements.

Not a statistically accurate and representative sample

I don't know how many negotiations Trump has engaged in over the last 40-plus years, and I don't know the exact number of his negotiation counterparts. No one does. A safe guess would be in the hundreds—if not, thousands—for both.

If so, how can this list constitute a statistically accurate and representative sample of all his counterparts. It can't. The data just isn't available.

Unfortunately, this represents the reality of reputations. Reputations—for negotiation and otherwise—do not arise from statistically accurate and representative samples of all the individuals with whom we have interacted. Instead, they derive from statistically inaccurate comments made by those who usually feel the strongest about us. If it's just a normal negotiation, why take the time and effort to publicly comment?

That is true here, too. But Trump is unique. He invariably generated strong business feelings among his partners and counterparts. Almost all his major deals have been publicly and extensively reported. Unusually, many of his counterparts were even interviewed at the time.

In fact, this list includes colleagues and/or counterparts and stories involving almost every major Trump deal and many minor ones. The reputation he generated from these negotiations and others matters. We rely on them.

That's the nature of reputations.

Many counterparts are litigation adversaries

It's unfair to rely on Trump's litigation adversaries to ascertain his reputation, isn't it? Many have spent thousands of dollars fighting Trump tooth and nail. They could never be objective.

Is it fair? Perhaps not. Are they objective? No. But our reputations—fair or not—impact our negotiations. Given the volume of Trump's litigation, if you eliminated Trump's negotiations that ended up in litigation, relatively few counterparts would be left.

Regarding objectivity, it's not our counterparts' objectivity that matters. In fact, you don't want them to be objective. They have expressed their personal, subjective opinions about Trump. Instead, it's our challenge to objectively evaluate their statements and feelings and draw a conclusion from them.

Finally, the litigation issue cuts both ways. Yes, they've fought Trump. But they ended up in litigation for a reason. Something caused their lost trust and credibility issues. That led to the litigation, which likely formed the basis for their comments about him.

Don't know me well—they're probably Democrats anyway

Trump's friends' opinions contribute to his reputation, too, right? Absolutely. They know him better than many of his counterparts, right? Yes. So why not list them?

Because they have rarely been on the other side of the table from him in negotiations. And if they have been there, they haven't spoken about it. They certainly haven't spoken about his ethics. Like Ross, they would have a great incentive, especially now that Trump is President, to speak nicely about him. *That* bias would be overwhelming.

On the political-ax-to-grind front, every counterpart listed, and every negotiation described here except the Trump University settlement negotiations, involved negotiations *prior* to Trump announcing his candidacy for President. We have not yet addressed Trump's political reputation. The conclusions in this chapter relate solely to his ethical reputation in business negotiations.

One final point. Assume that all his counterparts have lied about what happened in their negotiations with him. Further assume that Trump, despite his statements and all the statements of his counterparts, has:

- Never lied nor made a material misrepresentation in a negotiation,

- Never engaged in business bullying,

- Never made business or personal empty threats nor bluffed,

- Never offered bribe-like personal financial benefits to his counterparts,

- Never intentionally hid the ball with misleading statements and actions,

- Never slipped in significant changes after a deal was done,

- Never used name-calling or personally demeaning comments in a negotiation,

- Never used puffery,

- Never imposed short, false deadlines, and

- Never was involved in over 4,000 pieces of litigation.

Assume he's never done any of this stuff and all his counterparts have been lying all along. Yet they've still made all their statements. In that case, Trump *still* has a problem reputation-wise from a negotiation-ethics perspective. Why? Because reputations, regardless of the underlying truth, depend on what others say about us and what we say, too. Good or bad, that is the reality.

Trump knows this better than almost everyone. A master promoter, he has spent millions of dollars over the years creating and protecting his reputation.

Trump's Ace Card

In fact, Trump's incredible self-promotion and branding skills have been his ace card in the hole, and he has expertly played it. Despite engaging in all the unethical conduct described here, and despite his counterparts regularly discussing this conduct publicly, and despite all the litigation, for years Trump has enjoyed a general reputation with the public as a topnotch and tough but ethical negotiator.

Where does this leave his business-related negotiation ethics reputation? Objectively speaking, and *not* accounting for Trump's promotional activities, not good. I would still grade it a 2 on a 1-to-10 scale, 1 being the worst and 10 being the best. The scope and breadth of his unethical conduct is overwhelming.

Trump might say, *"Who cares? I'm President of the United States. I'm the most powerful man in the world."* Yes, he's President. And yes, he's the most powerful man in the world. But *everyone* should care, including Trump. His reputation for negotiation ethics impacts his credibility and trustworthiness, and his credibility and trustworthiness impact his negotiation effectiveness.

Only now that reputation impacts his negotiation effectiveness *as President of the United States.* How much? That's next.

The Impact of Trump's Reputation on his Negotiation Effectiveness

RESEARCH: University of Pennsylvania Wharton School of Business Professor G. Richard Shell, Director of the Wharton Executive Negotiation Workshop and one of the world's leading scholars on negotiation, writes in his book *Bargaining for Advantage: Negotiation Strategies for Reasonable People*, that:

Effective negotiators are reliable. They keep their promises, avoid lying, and do not raise hopes they have no intention of fulfilling.

The research on this is reassuring. Skilled negotiators prize their reputations for straightforward dealing very highly. That makes sense. Given a choice, would you want to do business with someone you could trust or someone who might be trying to cheat you? [Emphasis added.][522]

Research also shows that the extent that parties mutually trust each other leads to maximum success in many negotiation contexts.

Ohio State Business School Professor Roy Lewicki, another top scholar in the field and author of the bestselling negotiation textbook in business schools worldwide, writes in his *Handbook on Negotiation*, co-authored with Beth Polin, in a section entitled *"Why Is Trust Integral to Negotiation?"* that:

> The need for trust arises because of each party's interdependence with the other in achieving [their opposing interests.] Negotiators depend on each other to help them achieve their goals and objectives—primarily by depending on the amount and accuracy of the information presented by the other party, on the outcomes to which the parties commit throughout the negotiation process, and on the other party delivering on those commitments.
>
> ...Of course, trust in a negotiation is more efficacious than a situation with distrust.[523]

Lewicki and Polin, in a section entitled *"What Are the Consequences of Broken Trust for Negotiators?"* continue: "the short- and long-term consequences of using deception and engaging in other trust-breaking behaviors [are such that]: while short-term defection can lead to enhanced payoffs, **the long-term consequences are a significant decline in trust and poor individual and joint gain in the future."** [Emphasis added.][524]

Marquette University Law School Professor Andrea Schneider concurs.

Bottom line: Studies show the extent that parties trust each other leads to maximum negotiation success in many negotiation contexts.

The opposite is true, too. Parties' distrust leads to lack of information sharing (a crucial element of negotiation effectiveness), inefficiencies, wasted time, high transaction costs, implementation problems, and lost deals.

Without trust, I will be less willing to work with you to satisfy our mutual and sometimes competing interests. We may not even engage, leaving us with a suboptimal resolution to a problem we both face.

Assume I'm looking for a contractor to build an addition to my house. I get several bids. XYZ's bid, after our initial negotiation, is the lowest by $10,000, and his references say he does excellent work.

But I also reach out to my LinkedIn and Facebook networks to research his reputation. One mutual connection tells me XYZ orally promised her certain prices on changes that arose during her renovation. He reneged. The other emails me XYZ used cheap piping despite promising top quality.

I will likely go with the next-lowest contractor. XYZ lost my business. And I paid more for my addition. Lose–lose, due to lack of trust and credibility.

Or let's say I still go with XYZ, but I end up spending a ton of time detailing the parts used, every possible contingency, and negotiate everything into a contract with airtight provisions relating to every possible breach. It may still be better than my alternative/Plan B, given the cost difference and risk involved, but we both lost time and effort having to dot every "i" and cross every "t."

Trust and credibility also disproportionately and negatively impact negotiations involving parties expecting future relationships.

A little while ago, I was involved in a nine-month negotiation involving a long-term partnership between a business owner and a serial entrepreneur interested in further funding and managing it. Neither party would have closed had either heard a hint the other party had trust or credibility issues.

By contrast, many years ago I raised some money for my e-learning digital company. I had an investor willing to put in $100,000. But my research turned up a fraud-related problem on his SEC record. I turned down his money. Too risky.

I eventually closed that round, but it took more of my time and effort. He lost out, too.

The research is clear: Trust, credibility, and an honest reputation lead to more successful negotiations and better deals.

Trump does not enjoy that reputation. So, how much of a problem does he face in his negotiations given his negotiation-ethics reputation?

At this point, he's not negotiating business deals; he is negotiating with Congress and internationally on behalf of the United States. To evaluate that impact, we would need to evaluate his political negotiation ethics reputation along with his business one.

The short answer to the impact of his business reputation on his current effectiveness? We don't know. Overall, though, it's not positive. He's been negotiating in business for almost 50 years. His political negotiation history? A year or so.

If he continues to negotiate as President the way he negotiated in business—and early indications suggest this to be the case—he will have a much harder time achieving his goals.

Another reason he will face challenges in his presidential negotiations? Significant differences exist between business and presidential negotiations. His business negotiation strategies—even if hugely successful in business—may be counterproductive in presidential negotiations.

How should we evaluate this? That's next.

LESSONS LEARNED	
Trump's Strategies and Tactics	1. Lying and material misrepresentations
	2. Business bullying
	3. Personal and business threats—especially empty threats and bluffs
	4. Offering bribe-like personal financial benefits to his counterparts
	5. Intentionally hiding the ball with misleading statements and actions
	6. Slipping in significant changes after the deal's done (the nibble)
	7. Name-calling and personally demeaning his counterparts
	8. Excessive puffery
	9. Super-short, false deadlines
	10. Scope and breadth of litigation—where there's smoke, there's fire
Lessons Learned	Negotiation ethics reputation directly impacts negotiation effectiveness.
	Trust and credibility between parties leads to better negotiation results and disproportionately impacts parties with future relationships.

PART THREE

THE TRUMP TRANSITION: BUSINESS TO PRESIDENTIAL NEGOTIATIONS

Donald Trump has negotiated business deals for almost 50 years. Now he's President of the United States. And his negotiation skills and strategies will not just put money in his pocket, they will impact billions of people. Some will be better off financially due to his negotiation strategies, some worse. Some will live better lives. And some will lose their lives.

Given these stakes, we need to address: a) whether *President* Trump has negotiated differently than he has in business for nearly 50 years, b) how his skills and strategies translated into the different world of presidential negotiations, and c) the extent he has used presidential negotiation strategies aligned with the experts' research.

Initially, we will identify the strategic differences between Trump's business negotiations and presidential negotiations.

Every new president comes to the job with different history, experiences, and expertise. And President Trump comes to the job with even *greater* differences than his predecessors, given that he has never held political office. Will this help or hurt him in his negotiations?

How has he done so far? We will evaluate two of his major campaign promises and negotiations that took place in Year One of the Trump Presidency: his negotiation to get Mexico to pay for an enhanced border wall, and his negotiations to repeal and replace Obamacare.

I chose these because:

- Trump personally negotiated in each,
- both started and ended during his first year as President,
- each represented a core Trump campaign promise,

- one involved a straightforward zero-sum–type negotiation—where one dollar more from Mexico to pay for the wall necessarily translates to one dollar less from the U.S.—and one involved a hugely complex, interconnected set of issues impacting almost 20 percent of the U.S. economy, and

- one involved international diplomacy and illegal immigration, perhaps the most polarizing foreign policy issue in the campaign—and the other a domestic negotiation with Congress and 535 political power centers with their own interests.

One thing we know: His job as President is different from every other job he has ever held. In fact, it's different from every other job in the world. Yes—he is in the early stages of this job, and we don't know what will happen the rest of his presidency. He could still get Mexico to pay for the wall. He could still repeal and replace Obamacare. But we can already see what and how he is doing negotiation-wise on these issues and on others. Can he pivot and change? Let's see if he has so far.

CHAPTER 13

BUSINESS v. PRESIDENTIAL NEGOTIATIONS: COMPARING THE BOARDROOM AND THE OVAL OFFICE

Negotiation is negotiation, right? Right. And wrong.

What do I mean?

Fundamental building blocks underlie all negotiations:

1. Information Is Power—So Get It!

2. Maximize Your Leverage

3. Employ "Fair" Objective Criteria

4. Design an Offer-Concession Strategy

5. Control the Agenda

In all negotiations, effective parties should understand and implement these Five Golden Rules.

Donald Trump intuitively understands and implements many of these, some more effectively than others. To be most effective, all should be implemented with the skills and ethics identified in Chapters 11 and 12. Stronger skills and better ethics lead to more effective negotiations.

But different negotiation environments require implementing these in different ways. Assume it's Thursday night and you just finished a hard workday. You just want to eat a relaxing dinner and catch up on reading and sleep. Unfortunately, your spouse or significant other wants you to meet your new neighbors and attend a play you don't want to see.

So begins one of the most difficult types of negotiation. Negotiating with loved ones and/or with long-term business partners and friends can pose unique challenges. Certainly, this dynamic requires different strategies than negotiating with a stranger over the price of an allegedly rare artifact in a foreign market. What are these different negotiation strategies, and when and where should we apply them?

> **RESEARCH:** While an unlimited number of negotiation strategies exist, two overall strategies tend to be the most dominant in practice and in the negotiation literature: *Competitive Strategies* and *Problem-Solving Strategies*. Each occupies opposite ends of a strategic spectrum and requires that we implement my Five Golden Rules in different ways. Since these strategies fall on a spectrum, an unlimited number of strategies fall in between these extremes.

Business and Presidential Negotiations Require Different Strategies

Why do we care and how do these strategies relate to the differences between Trump's business and presidential negotiations? Because Trump's Top Ten Business Negotiation Strategies closely track classic Competitive Strategies, while many presidential negotiations fall on the Problem-Solving end of the spectrum.

In other words, Trump's success in many of his presidential negotiations will depend on his pivoting *away* from the business negotiation strategies he has been using for almost 50 years. While his Competitive Strategies have succeeded at times in his highly adversarial business environments, these same strategies will crash and burn in the world of presidential negotiations.

To fully understand the differences between Trump's business and presidential negotiations, we must first appreciate the differences between Competitive and Problem-Solving Strategies.

In describing these, we will look back to Trump's Top Ten Business Negotiation Strategies. By doing so, it will become apparent where Trump the business negotiator stands on this spectrum.

As we address these, we will also illustrate how Trump's business negotiations differ from presidential negotiations, using this Competitive/Problem-Solving framework.

Competitive Strategies

Let's say Jill, a wealthy U.S. businesswoman, wants to purchase that allegedly rare artifact in a foreign market and price is the only issue on the table.

Classic Competitive Strategies will work best. How should Jill implement my Five Golden Rules using Competitive Strategies?[525]

Golden Rule One: Information Is Power—So Get It!

What information should Jill share with the foreign shop owner? The minimum amount sufficient to accomplish her goal—learning as much as she can about the artifact so she can buy it for the lowest possible price.

- *Substantial Information Bargaining—Share a Little and Get a Lot.* Jill should not share that she's a wealthy American businesswoman nor her significant interest in the artifact. Instead, she should play her cards close to her vest.

Trump's Strategies: Aggressive Information Bargaining

Trump the business negotiator set extremely aggressive goals and played his cards very close to his vest. Recall all his information hiding and misleading efforts.

Classic and aggressive information bargaining.

Golden Rule Two: Maximize Your Leverage

The full range of leverage tactics will be on display between Jill and the shopkeeper in their negotiations for this allegedly rare artifact. Several walkouts by Jill will likely dominate this process. And the shopkeeper will likely emphasize his *unique* artifact (suggesting Jill has a bad Plan B).

- *Open Conflict on Leverage.* Competitive Strategies often revolve around leverage. Threats. Walkouts. Bluffing. "Take it or leave it" offers.

Trump's Strategies: Highly Aggressive Leverage Moves

Trump has aggressively sought to maximize leverage in almost every one of his business negotiations. Chapters 5, 6, and 7 about Trump's bluffs, walkouts, threats, and bullying detail numerous examples of his sophisticated leverage moves. Open conflict on leverage is bread and butter to him. Another hallmark of highly Competitive Strategies.

Golden Rule Three: Employ "Fair" Objective Criteria

Independent standards like market value and experts constantly crop up with those using Competitive Strategies. But they rarely supplant leverage as the dominant negotiation element. Instead, parties largely use them as tools to change the other side's perception of their leverage.

Jill here might point to the shopkeeper's likely high profit margin to justify a lower price. But it would have little impact. Minimal *reliance* on independent standards characterizes Competitive Strategies.

Trump's Strategies: Only Use Standards That Help

Chapter 8 describes Trump's use of "independent" standards. If they help him, highlight them. If they hurt him, hide them. And if his counterparts find ones that help them—undermine them. Competitive negotiators are committed to themselves first, second, and third. "Fair" equals what helps *them*. Competitive Strategies all the way.

Golden Rule Four: Design an Offer-Concession Strategy

The full range of offer-concession tactics will be on display in situations involving Competitive Strategies. The shopkeeper would start extremely high and Jill would counter super low. Lots of back-and-forth here.

- *Most Aggressive Offer-Concession Moves and Tactics*. Parties use very aggressive offer-concession moves here, often including a first offer well outside the range of reasonable standards.

Trump's Strategies: Most Aggressive Offer-Concession Moves

$18 million per episode for *The Apprentice's* second season. $5 million for the luxurious Boeing 727. *No* taxes for 99 years for the Commodore Hotel. *Decreasing* offers for Mar-a-Lago.

Chapter 9's title says it all: *Outrageous Moves and Countermoves*. Aggressively Competitive Strategies.

Golden Rule Five: Control the Agenda

The agenda will be hotly contested in Competitive Strategies situations.

- *Overt and Biased Agenda-Control Tactics*. Timing and deadlines with the shopkeeper will dominate. If Jill has a flight leaving that day, her deadline will drive the process.

Trump's Strategies: My Agenda Controls

Short, inflexible deadlines. Trump's turf. Shaking hands as a concession. Psychological "games" to make his counterparts *feel* less powerful. Typical Trump agenda-control tactics. Typical Competitive Strategies.

Two final notes regarding Competitive Strategies. *One*, they do not necessarily involve a hostile tone or style. Just because these moves involve aggressive strategies does not mean the environment includes mean-spirited communications. It simply means you hold your cards close to your vest, aggressively exercise leverage, and so forth. Of course, the atmosphere may be really tense. But not always.

And, *two*, effective Competitive Strategies do not inherently include unethical negotiation conduct like name-calling and misstatements of material facts. Such conduct is more likely to occur, though, in Competitive environments.

Here's a chart detailing the characteristics of "end of the spectrum" Competitive Strategies matched to Trump's negotiations. These fit Donald Trump the business negotiator like a glove.[526]

COMPETITIVE STRATEGIES		
Golden Rules	**Characteristics of Strategy**	**Trump's Business Negotiations**
1. Information Is Power—So Get It!	Substantial information bargaining—share a little and get a lot.	Yes
2. Maximize Your Leverage	Open conflict on leverage.	Yes
3. Employ "Fair" Objective Criteria	Minimal reliance on independent standards. Mask self-serving criteria as "fair."	Yes
4. Design an Offer-Concession Strategy	Most aggressive offer-concession moves and tactics.	Yes
5. Control the Agenda	Overt and biased agenda-control tactics.	Yes

Problem-Solving Strategies

Remember the negotiation where you come home tired and your spouse or significant other wants to go to a play you don't want to see? The experts do *not* recommend Competitive Strategies.

Instead, use Problem-Solving Strategies, those focused on building trust, strengthening relationships and promoting an atmosphere in which the parties can work together in search of a mutually satisfactory solution.

How? Implement my Five Golden Rules in the following way, which generally occupy the *opposite* end of the strategic spectrum to Competitive Strategies.

Again, we will match Trump's typical strategies to these moves.

Golden Rule One: Information Is Power—So Get It!

When you negotiate with your spouse or significant other, should you hide information about your true feelings and interests? What about the atmosphere—adversarial or collaborative?

- *Mutually Share Critical Information Openly and Honestly*. Parties mutually share their true goals, issues, and fundamental interests when using Problem-Solving Strategies.

- *Actions and Atmosphere Confirm Trust and a Valued Relationship*. Trusting environments dominate here, where the parties value the relationship and feel comfortable sharing critical information.

Trump's Strategies: Carrots Satisfy the Personal Interests of His Counterparts

Trump understands parties' interests. He knows his own goals and interests and has often explored his counterparts' interests, especially their personal interests.

However, he typically only shared what he needed to share and regularly hid, misled, and misstated—hallmarks of highly Competitive Strategies.

Does he sometimes find creative solutions to satisfy the parties' mutual interests? Of course. But he rarely engaged in true information-related Problem-Solving Strategies. These strategies form the fundamental basis for what's sometimes referred to as "win–win" negotiations. Parties—by virtue of *how* they negotiate and their focus on satisfying the parties' *mutual* interests—create a *bigger* pie and *more* value for *all* the parties.

Why has Trump *not* engaged in this way? Three main reasons.

One, Trump's win–lose, zero-sum mindset is antithetical to win–win. He perceives his counterparts as enemies out to win at his expense. He lives in a zero-sum world—where more for him necessarily means less for his counterparts and vice versa.

Of course, many of his business counterparts *were* competitors. And many of his negotiations were tough, zero-sum efforts. But Trump even viewed his partners as adversaries. Recall how he interacted with his fellow USFL owners, partners with a shared goal to get into the NFL.

Remember him saying, *"I'm not big on compromise. I understand compromise. Sometimes compromise is the right answer, but oftentimes compromise is the equivalent of defeat, and I don't like being defeated."*[527]

Trump even threw his partners under the bus, even when they had been indispensable to his success. He saddled Louise Sunshine, who opened many doors to political power for him, with a huge tax bill in one of his early developments. And he changed the accounting method on the Commodore Hotel in a way that cost New York City millions despite already getting a 99-year tax abatement. His Harrah's partnership also deteriorated quickly due to trust and other issues.

These do not reflect Problem-Solving Strategies designed to find options to satisfy mutual interests. These are win–lose strategies meant solely to cut the pie so Trump gets the biggest piece at the expense of others at the table.

Importantly, his extreme Competitive approach also resulted in his leaving significant value on the table where his strategy proved counterproductive. Television City likely cost Trump hundreds of millions of dollars. A less adversarial and competitive dynamic with New York City and Mayor Ed Koch would almost certainly have brought that deal home, a likelihood Trump implicitly acknowledged later.

Two, another reason Trump doesn't share critical information in Problem-Solving Strategies—a prerequisite to finding a mutual "win–win"—involves trust. Sharing information about your true interests and needs involves information risk, even if you dole it out in small chunks. Your counterparts might use that information against you.

But *not* sharing carries risk, too. That risk is you never find the mutual value.

Trump doesn't trust much, if at all. He's naturally suspicious of others' motives. A person who trusts others—even a little—does not believe *"man is the most vicious of animals, and life is a series of battles ending in victory or defeat. You can't let people make a sucker out of you."*[528]

Finally, true "win–win" and information-sharing about fundamental interests requires skills Trump has not exhibited much: empathy, deep listening skills, a belief that the knowledge you learn can help everyone, and that win–win even exists. Not Trump's strengths.

Golden Rule Two: Maximize Your Leverage

How often should you threaten your spouse, significant other, or business partner? Most avoid such overt leverage tactics in family negotiations and business partnerships. Such tactics harm stable, long-term relationships.

- *Leverage Downplayed, but Still There.* Parties here avoid the brinksmanship that accompanies high-pressure leverage tactics. Instead, they honestly share information about their leverage-related wants and needs and often shy away from even discussing their alternative/Plan B. If it makes sense to discuss it, they address it in a plain, factual, and non-aggressive way.

Trump's Strategies: Leverage Dominates

To Trump, negotiations with downplayed leverage would be akin to life without breathing. Leverage dominates Trump's negotiation world. And not just matter-of-fact explanations of leverage, but super-aggressive, high-pressure leverage tactics like threats, bullying, walkouts, and bluffing.

These can be effective. But not in situations calling for Problem-Solving Strategies. *Don't* use these on your spouse or long-term business partner.

Golden Rule Three: Employ "Fair" Objective Criteria

- *Frequently Rely on Independent Standards.* Parties often *rely* on independent standards here because doing so let's both sides accept the result as "fair and reasonable" based on the mutually agreeable standard. Independent standards dominate Problem-Solving like leverage dominates Competitive Strategies. Deals revolve around them. And they often even become the deal.

Trump's Strategies: Only Use Standards that Help

Trump doesn't trust or rely on independent standards like precedent and experts unless they help him. That's not how Problem-Solving Strategies work effectively.

Golden Rule Four: Design an Offer-Concession Strategy

Should you lowball a family member or business partner, like Trump did to Louise Sunshine? No. Least-aggressive offer-concession moves will prove most successful. Problem-Solving offer-concession strategies are characterized by relatively reasonable moves.

Trump's Strategies: Most Aggressive Moves

Donald Trump almost always starts with outrageously aggressive offer-concession moves and does a lot of dancing here. The list is legendary, as detailed in Chapter 9.

Golden Rule Five: Control the Agenda

Overtly controlling the agenda for most family negotiations is overkill. Instead, parties here rely on mutually agreeable agendas and agenda-control tactics. And they stay away from tension-increasing tactics like deadlines and one-sided agendas.

Trump's Strategies: I Control the Agenda

Donald Trump doesn't cede control of the agenda to his counterparts if he can help it. Meet on my turf at Trump Tower. Watch my promotional video. Negotiate with my underlings until I'm ready to make my entrance. And short deadlines with tension-creating agendas favoring Trump.

Competitive Agenda-Control Strategies all the way—not Problem-Solving Strategies.

Here's a chart detailing the extent Trump the business negotiator used Problem-Solving Strategies. [529]

PROBLEM-SOLVING STRATEGIES		
Golden Rules	**Characteristics of Strategy**	**Trump's Business Negotiations**
1. Information Is Power—So Get It!	Mutually share critical information openly and liberally. Actions and atmosphere confirm trust and a valued relationship.	No
2. Maximize Your Leverage	Leverage downplayed, but still there.	No
3. Employ "Fair" Objective Criteria	Frequently rely on independent standards.	No
4. Design an Offer-Concession Strategy	Least aggressive offer-concession moves and tactics.	No
5. Control the Agenda	Mutually agreeable agenda and agenda-control tactics.	No

Some might be thinking that, even if Trump is ill-suited to engage in Problem-Solving Strategies, these strategies don't describe all presidential negotiations. After all, they don't describe negotiations with the U.S.'s traditional adversaries like China, Russia, Iran, and North Korea. And they don't describe the extremely polarized and adversarial negotiation environment in Congress. Trump the Competitive Strategies negotiator should be *well*-suited to engage in these, right?

Great points. We will address them. But before we do, we must identify a framework to evaluate where and under what circumstances the research recommends Problem-Solving versus Competitive Strategies. Many types of presidential negotiations exist, in addition to those with our adversaries and between Democrats and Republicans.

Only by doing this can we accurately evaluate how well Trump's negotiation mindset and skillset will translate into the presidential negotiation world.

The Framework—Competitive vs. Problem-Solving Strategies

> **RESEARCH:** Four factors should be considered to determine the extent Competitive Strategies versus Problem-Solving Strategies should be used.
> - The Relationship Factor
> - The Number Factor
> - The Zero-Sum Factor
> - The Mutuality Factor[530]

Let's analyze each. I will also identify here how they interact with the major differences between business and presidential negotiations.

The Relationship Factor

Your strategy should fundamentally change based on the extent you expect a future relationship with your counterpart. The more you see potential interests satisfied with a future relationship, the more likely you should use Problem-Solving Strategies.

Conversely, the *less* you see your potential interests and long-term goals satisfied with a future relationship, the more likely you should use Competitive Strategies.

Trump's Strategies Don't Differ Based on Future Relationships

Donald Trump has been remarkably consistent in how he has negotiated over the last 40-plus years. There is great value in being consistent in many environments. Negotiating the same way regardless of your future relationship with your counterparts is *not* one of them.

How has this impacted Trump's negotiation effectiveness?

His most *effective* negotiations almost all involved one-shot deals with no ongoing future working relationships. In fact, most of Trump's deals did not involve future relationships between the parties. As a result, Competitive Strategies make sense.

Just look at his most effective negotiations: Commodore Hotel, Trump Tower, Mar-a-Lago, Boeing 727, Casino License Applications, St. Regis Hotel, Bank Workout Negotiations in 1990, 40 Wall Street. One common characteristic—no future working relationship with his counterparts.

Where Trump's deals involved future relationships, and he still used Competitive Strategies, it proved problematic. Consider these *ineffective* Trump negotiations: USFL Negotiations with his fellow owners and then with Pete Rozelle, Harrah's, Television City, his business bullying negotiations, Resorts Management Negotiations, 100 Central Park South Tenants. One common characteristic—the post-negotiation relationship went into the gutter.

What about his long-term success with *The Apprentice,* his licensing negotiations, and his lengthy relationships with the media?

Yes and no. His *Apprentice* relationship lasted 14 years and the show enjoyed enormous success. Did he have a positive working relationship with NBC? Unclear. Anecdotal evidence exists that working with Trump was extremely challenging, which would be consistent with his reputation in the gaming world. But we don't know.

Trump's licensing deals didn't involve ongoing working relationships, with his involvement limited to promotional activities and collecting licensing fees.

Regarding his media relationships, carrots *and* sticks.

One final note. Trump's unethical strategies caused his ineffectiveness in some negotiations. They don't help when Competitive Strategies should be used, but they're toxic in negotiations involving future relationships, as they can kill the deal and even prevent a deal from getting presented.

Remember Steve Ifshin, who felt played when Trump refused to negotiate with the buyer he brought to the table? Ifshin decided to never deal with Trump again. Trump may have lost many deals as a result.

What about presidential negotiations? Do they involve ongoing future relationships between the parties? Usually. This differentiates Trump's business from his presidential negotiations. Presidential negotiations, while sometimes extremely competitive, often require the use of mostly Problem-Solving Strategies.

Major Difference #1:
Future Working Relationships with the Same Counterparts

Trump will be negotiating with the same 535 Members of Congress for his first two years as U.S. President and, if history holds, the overall turnover at the 2018 mid-term election will be relatively low. Republicans also currently control the House, Senate, and Executive Branch. This suggests strategies on the Problem-Solving end of the spectrum as they should enjoy a natural partnership.

Contrast this with the domestic negotiation environment in the latter years of President Barack Obama's administration. There, Republicans controlled Congress with a Democratic president. Competitive Strategies appropriately dominated. Neither side *wanted* a future relationship and sought to undermine each other's efficacy. They didn't want to negotiate with each other—but they had to. The polarized nature of politics further contributed to that Competitive dynamic.

The Senate Republicans' extremely narrow control today further suggests Problem-Solving Strategies will be more effective. Trump can't lose more than one Republican on each vote or nothing will get done.

Note that Problem-Solving Strategies are neither Democratic nor Republican-oriented. They solely relate to the four factors identified earlier. President Ronald Reagan largely used Problem-Solving Strategies to achieve tax reform in 1986.

Two U.S. Senators—both longtime effective negotiators and on different sides of the political aisle—also confirmed to me the general impact of these types of strategies.

U.S. Senators Jon Kyl and Joe Manchin's Top Strategies

I was in the Washington, D.C. airport a few years back waiting to return home and noticed former U.S. Sen. Jon Kyl (R-AZ) nearby. Since he enjoyed an excellent reputation as a negotiator in his many years in the U.S. Senate and House, I asked him to share his "pearls of wisdom."

Fortuitously, in the middle of our conversation we were joined by former West Virginia Governor and current U.S. Sen. Joe Manchin (D-WV), so I asked him to also share his negotiation lessons.

Here are a few they shared. Note how these, a) apply to presidential negotiations with those in Congress, b) may or may not match up with Trump's Top Ten Business Negotiation Strategies and with his personal skills and ethics, and c) relate to the relationships and negotiations between a president and House and Senate members.

Former Sen. Jon Kyl

- Relationships matter. "You have to work together if you want to get anything done."
- You need to "get trust with the other side."
- Do what works best for you, but it usually "doesn't pay to be a jerk."
- Get "good intel" and develop a plan in advance. You need information to start.
- Be wary of those always asking for "one more thing." If they do, say no.
- "Everyone needs to get something out of it [the negotiation]."
- It usually doesn't pay to bluff. Sen. Kyl recalled former Sen. Phil Gramm (R-TX) once telling him, "Never take a hostage if you're not willing to shoot."
- "Take what you can" and don't hold out for everything or you may get nothing.

Sen. Joe Manchin

- "First, build the relationship."
- Trust is crucial.
- Never put your colleagues in an embarrassing position. They need something out of the negotiation, too.
- "Leave a little meat on the bone for the next dog," Sen. Manchin recalled his "granddaddy telling me."
- Beware of personalities and egos messing up deals. Sen. Manchin recalled a negotiation between the Teamsters and a company when he was governor and he was asked to help resolve an impasse. He said he immediately recognized that the contested issue—while relatively minor—had become a big problem because of two personalities in the room. Each had become personally vested in winning that issue—and neither would give the other side a win. What did Manchin do? He asked the two individuals at loggerheads to leave the room. The other parties quickly resolved the issue.

Sens. Kyl and Manchin—across the political divide—both mentioned the importance of trust and credibility.[531] Relationships go hand-in-hand with these. To most effectively negotiate, presidents need these, too.

Internationally, Trump will also largely be negotiating with the same leaders for his first term and possibly his second.

Of course, Trump can't choose these counterparts, like he did in business. Once he did his deal with Alan Bond, Trump could choose never to work with him again. Bond could also choose. That doesn't happen in presidential negotiations. Mitch McConnell. Chuck Schumer. Nancy Pelosi. Angela Merkel. Xi Jinping. Ongoing relationships, whether Trump likes it or not.

Major Difference #2:
Relationships Involve Multiple *Unrelated* Negotiations

These longer-term relationships will also involve multiple *unrelated* negotiations. Strategies used in the health care negotiations will impact Trump's negotiation effectiveness over immigration. Long-term ramifications for Trump's strategies.

This did occur somewhat in Trump's business negotiations. His negotiations with New York City over the Commodore Hotel impacted his negotiations over Television City. But this was relatively rare, and we know how this turned out.

President Lyndon B. Johnson mastered this relationship-oriented negotiation environment when he negotiated to pass the Civil Rights Act and the Great Society programs. Importantly, Johnson had built strong working relationships with those in Congress in his 24 years of serving in the House and Senate. These proved crucial to his negotiation successes.

Of course, President Johnson knew when and where and how to exercise leverage with his former colleagues—and did it aggressively. He also mastered the offer-concession horse-trading necessary to round up votes. These strategies fall more on the Competitive end of the spectrum.

But Johnson truly understood the power of his relationships and expertly exercised it.

Multiple Pulitzer Prize–winning biographer Robert Caro, who spent decades studying and writing about Johnson, noted how Johnson's appreciation of the power of relationships enabled him to achieve his negotiation goals.

> Among [Johnson's] many techniques [to get close to powerful people], one…was especially striking. With powerful men,

he made himself what his friends called a "professional son."
In each institution in which he worked, he found an older
man who had great power, who had no son of his own, and
who was lonely.... In the House of Representatives, it was the
Speaker, Sam Rayburn; in the Senate, it was the leader of the
Southern block, Richard Russell of Georgia. In each case, he
attached himself to the man, kept reminding him that his
own father was dead and that he was looking on him as his
new "Daddy." Rayburn and Russell were bachelors; Johnson
made them part of his family, constantly inviting them over
for meals. Sundays were very important in this technique: On
Sundays, Johnson would have Russell to brunch, Rayburn to
dinner.[532]

Of course, this was highly manipulative. But it reflected a master
negotiator's understanding of the power of relationships in political and
presidential negotiations.

The Number Factor

The second factor affecting the choice of negotiation strategy—the number
factor—relates to the number of issues and interests on the table and the
number of parties around the table.

The more issues, interests and parties, the more likely you should
use Problem-Solving Strategies. The fewer issues, interests, and parties,
the more likely you should use Competitive Strategies.[533]

Typical Problem-Solving negotiations in business involve mergers where
the principals and employees need a future working relationship to ensure
the merged company succeeds. Typical Competitive negotiations in business
involve the purchase or sale of an asset where the price issue dominates and
only a few principals sit around the table.

Trump's Strategies Don't Differ Based on the Number of Issues and Parties

Trump negotiated with his business partner Harrah's after his initial
deal—where issues and interests cropped up every day—*the same way* as in
his negotiation to buy 40 Wall Street: Competitive Strategies.

It worked brilliantly with 40 Wall Street. Not so with Harrah's (nor New
York City nor his USFL fellow owners).

"Wait," Trump might say. "I spent months working through a 65-page contract on the Commodore Hotel and bought and sold Resorts. A huge number of issues were involved in each. I did really well in both. I also spent years on those deals and on Trump Tower, negotiating every day with our subcontractors."

That is largely correct. But none of those negotiations also involved ongoing working relationships with his counterparts, except for his purchase of Resorts. Trump moved on after closing those deals. And while he had an ongoing relationship with Resorts and the Taj, it didn't work out well.

Most of Trump's really complex deals with the most issues also took place early in his career. How many major issues cropped up in his negotiations with Mark Burnett for his 50 percent share of *The Apprentice*? One. How many major issues did Trump negotiate on his licensing deals? Two. His fee and his promotional commitments.

Of course, Trump supervised hundreds of additional legal details that his lawyers and other colleagues negotiated. And he may have taken an active role on some, but he likely only got heavily involved in a few.

And he alone controlled his side.

This Number Factor and related elements, importantly, form the basis for three more major differences between Trump's business and presidential negotiations.

Major Difference #3:
The Number of Issues and Interests on the Table

Major Difference #4:
The Number of Parties at the Table/Coalition-Building

Major Difference #5:
Negotiating on *Two* Levels: Behind the Table and Across the Table

How many issues and interests need to be negotiated on health care? Immigration? The budget?

How many parties will be sitting at these tables, each with his or her own substantive political issues and interests?

Many other parties will also impact these negotiations. And most won't even have a formal seat at the table. Interest groups. Corporations. Nonprofits. Lobbyists. Bureaucrats. The courts. Local and state political leaders. Think tanks. Academic experts. Political consultants. And individual citizens, who will sometimes determine the ultimate success of these negotiations at the ballot box.

These parties also do not share the same goals, interests, and needs. In fact, they come from incredibly diverse backgrounds and exhibit widely diverse and strongly held views.

Business negotiations, while challenging and difficult in their own right, pale in comparison to presidential negotiations in this regard. In fact, presidential and political negotiations—domestically and internationally—probably constitute the most challenging negotiations in the world.

RESEARCH: Harvard Program on Negotiation Chair Robert Mnookin notes that effective political negotiations also require the negotiator to manage the tension between:

...what is going on across the table with your adversary and what is happening behind the table among your constituents. [Harvard University Public Policy Professor] Robert Putnam has called this a 'two-level game' in which a leader must negotiate in both directions. This requires enormous skill. History is full of political leaders who have failed this test, especially when dealing with violent ethnic conflicts.[534]

How do presidents effectively negotiate in two directions in these complex environments with an almost unlimited number of parts and parties? The following two strategies are crucial, at a minimum: 1) effectively managing the process, and 2) coalition-building behind and across the table.

Effectively Managing the Process

James Madison's Brilliant Political Negotiation

Over two hundred years ago, Constitutional Convention delegate and later President James Madison faced an enormous negotiation challenge—

how to revise our new country's failing Articles of Confederation into an effective governing system. He was just 36 years old.

Here's how our "Father of the Constitution" negotiated the fundamental democratic nature of our country. Without his negotiating brilliance, as described in Harvard Business School Professor Deepak Malhotra's well-researched and insightful book *Negotiating the Impossible*, we would have a very different country today:

> Madison arrived in Philadelphia…11 days before the Constitutional Convention was scheduled to start…[and] got straight to work. The task ahead, as Madison saw it, was to convince the other delegates that the Articles of Confederation needed to be thrown out completely.…
>
> Madison understood that the greatest barrier to the drastic change he wanted was the default process that was in place as the Articles of Confederation were going to be the starting point of any conversation. As long as the Articles served as the template to be revised, they would be too powerful an anchor in every discussion of how to structure government appropriately.…
>
> Madison, working with George Washington and other like-minded delegates from Pennsylvania and Virginia, started to draft an alternative document [known as the Virginia Plan] that could serve as the starting point for discussion.…
>
> The convention finally started on May 25. Only four days later, Virginia Governor Edmund Randolph presented the Virginia Plan. Reactions ranged from enthusiastic support to shock and anger but the die was cast, and all of the debates to follow would take place in the shadow of the Virginia Plan.[535]

Madison's extraordinary negotiation involved three particularly relevant elements due to their differentiation from Trump's business negotiations.

One, 55 delegates attended the Constitutional Convention. Each had a voice and a vote. Presidents today negotiate legislation with 535 "delegates."

Two, our Constitution included numerous challenging issues on the table. Not just several. Donald Trump has never negotiated deals with that many issues and parties, and the only significant coalition he built involved the USFL, which ended poorly.

And, *three*, Madison had comprehensively prepared *before* going to Philadelphia, as "not even the considerable talent gathered in Philadelphia in May 1787 could have created... [the Virginia Plan] without the exhaustive preparation Madison had undertaken before setting foot in Philadelphia."[536]

Malhotra concluded that "what truly exemplifies Madison's genius is not merely the extent of his preparedness, but the focus of it. Whereas most people know to prepare for the substantive discussions that will eventually occur, Madison understood the power of **shaping the process** that will ultimately determine whether, when, and how the substantive discussions will take place."[537]

This level of preparation and the power it provides is *especially* crucial in presidential negotiations involving large numbers of parties and issues, as Malhotra notes.

> Madison understood the power that comes from being the most prepared person in the room. **It was this quality that inspired him to conduct his scholarly research before the convention and to reach out to other Virginia delegates asking them to arrive early to draft "some materials for the work of the Convention."** He brought the same quality into the Convention itself. [Delegate] William Pierce...referred to Madison as someone who "always comes forward as the best-informed Man of any point in the debate." ... [Emphasis added.][538]

Trump has *not* been that man in most of his business negotiations; instead, he tends to wing it. His now friend Steve Wynn told a story about Trump to *TrumpNation* author Timothy O'Brien that illustrates Trump's lack of interest, preparation, and attention to detail. It occurred on a golf course shortly after Trump lost two top casino executives in a tragic helicopter crash:

> As the two men teed off on Saturday morning, Donald got right to the point.
>
> "I don't know what to do. I'm lost. I don't even know the names of the people working for me in the casinos," he told Wynn.
>
> "Go back to Atlantic City and bring in your department heads at each casino and tell them, 'Hey, guys, I need your help. I need to learn,'" Wynn replied. "If you spend two full days at each hotel, you'll learn everything you need to know."

Wynn said Donald looked blankly back at him, without any enthusiasm.

"I could see in his own eyes that wasn't what he wanted to do. That wasn't his thing. His heart wasn't in it and he didn't go for it," Wynn told me. "He doesn't deny that's how he felt about it. So now you've got what you've got: A casino company that has his name on the door but doesn't have his heart inside. And that doesn't work....

Atlantic City is a gritty, operational place where you have to bear down every day, and that's not what Donald's about.[539]

Trump owned three casinos—yet didn't know the ins and outs of the business.

This was confirmed in *Making Trump*:

...[where] competitors (and even executives who worked for Trump) loved to swap stories about what he didn't know about the gambling business, from the odds of specific bets to the internal controls required to make sure no cash was skimmed off the top when the day's winnings were counted.... As Wynn and other casino executives knew, Trump did not understand the math of the games any more than he seemed to understand casino and hotel operations.[540]

Problem-Solving Strategies, like those used by Madison, require understanding the nitty-gritty details of the issues and interests.

Malhotra recommends:

...in a truly important situation…you want to be a Madison: someone who has all the facts at your fingertips, who can anticipate the arguments and reservations of the other parties, and who has carefully examined not just the strengths but also the weaknesses of your own argument. This is the person who is hardest to ignore or push around, to whom others are most likely to give deference, and who will most easily shape or reshape the process and the substantive negotiations effectively.[541]

The impact of this takes on exponentially greater significance as the number of parties, interests, and issues increases.

Coalition-Building on Both Sides of the Table

Madison not only fully prepared, he started building coalitions *before* the Convention. This is another difference between Trump's business and presidential negotiations.

How did Madison build his coalitions? He almost certainly started by focusing on shared and compatible interests with his natural allies and then expanded his interest-based focus to involve more and more parties. In short, Problem-Solving Strategies.

Presidents must build coalitions in negotiating with Congress.

Internationally, this can be extraordinarily complex. You can effectively negotiate a great deal with multiple adversaries, but still need Congress to ratify it. Practically speaking, presidents must negotiate international deals while *simultaneously* negotiating with Congress.

Effective coalitions—which necessarily involve trusting, reliable political and international partners—serve as *the* primary driver of these negotiations. Without coalitions, presidential negotiations will fail.

In business, Trump could decide yea or nay on a deal. He was the decider-in-chief. In effect, he needed to negotiate only one way—across the table. No one sat behind him at the table.

Presidents need partners. Trump needs to be the negotiator-in-chief in both directions. That's a challenge he has not faced.

In his first ten months as President, Donald Trump successfully achieved one significant congressional deal (Neil Gorsuch's confirmation only involved the Senate): extending the debt ceiling and financing the government from mid-September through mid-December 2017.

How many issues were on the table? Two big ones—the length of the extension and short-term emergency hurricane aid. How many decision-makers were involved? Effectively, five. Trump, Senate Minority Leader Chuck Schumer, House Minority Leader Nancy Pelosi, House Speaker Paul Ryan, and Senate Majority Leader Mitch McConnell. How long did this negotiation last? Not long. Where did it take place? On Trump's turf in the Oval Office. When did it happen? Days away from the debt ceiling deadline—where the U.S. would not be able to pay its bills, potentially throwing the U.S. financial and economic system into chaos.

What happened? Trump's Treasury Secretary Steven Mnuchin and his seeming partners in Congress—Senate Majority Leader Mitch McConnell (R-KY) and House Speaker Paul Ryan (R-WI)—planned to push hard for an 18-month extension. In the meeting, the three of them did just this. And the Democrats pushed for a three-month extension.

But then, Trump turned to the Democrats and did a three-month deal. By doing so, he threw his own team and Republican partners under the bus as he:

- undermined his Treasury Secretary,

- damaged his relationship with his partners, the Republican leaders, and

- negatively impacted his partners' credibility with the other congressional Republicans.

Here's how the *WSJ* described its ramifications for Trump:

> Mr. Trump's decision to align with Democrats over the objections of GOP leaders and a member of his cabinet is likely to inflame tensions between the president and his fellow Republicans. Just hours earlier, House Speaker Paul Ryan (R-WI) had called Democrats' proposal to combine Harvey aid and a three-month debt limit increase "ridiculous" and "unworkable."

> Former Senate Majority Leader Trent Lott (R-MS) said it was "terrible" for Mr. Trump to undercut his fellow Republicans, particularly when their partisan adversaries were witnesses to it. "The president should not do that," Mr. Lott, a Republican, said. "It is embarrassing to Republican leadership and it shows a split."[542]

Did President Trump get a deal and avert a major economic disaster? Yes. Did he start to build a relationship with the Democratic leaders? Possibly. But at what cost to his Republican partners? Did he prepare with his team—in his Cabinet and his partner Republicans in Congress—to make these moves? No. Instead, he blindsided them.

Did he effectively negotiate, short- and long-term? No.

Compared to Madison, how did Trump do? Poorly. Of course, it's probably unfair to compare Trump to Madison. But he did the *opposite* of Madison. He used extreme Competitive Strategies. That's the issue.

That's another difference between Trump's business and presidential negotiations—the substantive knowledge and process-oriented strategic preparation that underlies every great presidential negotiator.

Trump got by without learning the details in his business negotiations. That won't work if he aspires to be a great presidential negotiator.

Major Difference #6: The Knowledge to Effectively Engage

The Zero-Sum Factor

Creativity sets apart some of the greatest negotiators in the world. Yet, even the most creative negotiators can't add value if the negotiation involves only zero-sum issues—where more for one side necessarily means less for the other.

The nature of the issues involved is the third factor impacting the "Competitive versus Problem-Solving Strategies" decision. The more zero-sum–type issues exist, the more likely you should use Competitive Strategies. The less zero-sum–type issues—with greater opportunities for creativity and finding nontraditional solutions—the more likely you should use Problem-Solving Strategies.[543]

How can you evaluate this? Two keys govern this decision.

The Interest Key

The most important key involves the nature of the parties' fundamental interests. Parties' interests can be shared, compatible, or conflicting. The more the parties enjoy shared or compatible interests, the more likely they can develop options that satisfy those interests. Thus, the more likely they should use Problem-Solving Strategies.

The Timing Key

The second key involves the timing of the strategy decision. The issues may initially appear zero-sum, so the parties use Competitive Strategies and don't share their strategically crucial interests. But their initial assumption and strategy may be wrong. If so, and if creative options exist that would provide value to both parties, they will likely leave this on the table.

Why? Competitive Strategies will not create the right environment in which to find their mutual interests. Nor will it create the atmosphere that would allow them to explore value-added situations. This is the classic "expand the pie" scenario, and they will go hungry.

Parties should thus find out as much as they can about parties' fundamental interests *before* deciding which strategy to use.

Trump's Strategies: Zero-Sum Issues Rule

Donald Trump has rarely, if ever, explored parties' fundamental interests *before* making his overall strategy decision. His Competitive Strategy win–lose mindset comes first. Zero-sum issues have also dominated Donald Trump's business negotiations for almost 50 years. The amount Trump paid for the option right to the Commodore Hotel's land? Zero-sum. The financial benefit he received for his tax abatements? Zero-sum. His "allowance" from the banks in 1990? Zero-sum.

Sometimes, zero-sum issues *should* dominate, and Competitive Strategies make sense. But not always. Importantly, negotiators like Trump never find out about the possible mutual interests because they start Competitive.

Of course, zero-sum issues don't *always* dominate business negotiations. Many, if not most, include mutual interests, some obvious and others hidden.

But zero-sum rules in Trump's world, and his consistent use of Competitive Strategies in all types of negotiations confirms his worldview.

Major Difference #7: Non-Zero-Sum Issues and Interests Dominate Many *Presidential* Negotiations

To what extent do zero-sum issues dominate *presidential* negotiations? Rarely, especially after the end of the Cold War. What do I mean?

Coalitions drive most presidential negotiations. Presidents can only do so much alone, by executive order, regulatory changes, or through appointments. Everything else involves negotiations. The only way to build coalitions is through negotiations *based on shared and compatible interests*. The reason Senator A will join a coalition with President B relates to whether they enjoy mutual interests. These interests might be political, ideological, strategic, tactical, or even personal.

Political parties—a large coalition—include individuals who share or have compatible *interests*. Not on every issue, but overall. Let's analyze this in terms of international and domestic negotiations.

International Negotiations Now Require Coalitions and Problem-Solving Strategies

During the Cold War between the U.S. and Soviet Union, conflicting interests dominated international negotiations. Competitive Strategies, not surprisingly, also dominated.

Since the Cold War ended, however, coalitions have dominated. Why? To achieve significant international movement on almost any issue—like the environment, trade, sanctions, even military action—you now basically need a coalition. Of course, sometimes countries go it alone. But often that will be substantially *less* effective than banding together to achieve their goals.

The best example of this? The brilliant negotiation led by President George H.W. Bush and Secretary of State James A. Baker III in 1990 to build an international coalition of countries to militarily push back Iraq after it invaded Kuwait. The largest military alliance since World War II, this was the first major coalition created after the U.S. became the world's sole superpower.

How did they do it? By focusing on shared and compatible interests with allies and former adversaries alike. Problem-Solving Strategies. Not that they didn't twist arms and recognize conflicting interests. They did. But they focused on making it in their potential partner's *interest* to join.

As noted in a PBS documentary on Baker and its website, "When it came to the Soviets, Baker and Bush set about doing what Baker did best: solving the other party's problems in order to solve their own. Baker later explained: 'It's so important to understand the political constraints of the person across the table.'"[544]

Political constraints = exploring and addressing the other party's political interests.

The documentary's site also describes Bush and Baker's masterful coalition-building against Iraq:

> Iraq had been a client state of the Soviet Union for much of the Cold War. But when Baker heard news of the invasion, his thoughts turned to Moscow. If the Soviets could be convinced to condemn Hussein's invasion, it would add legitimacy to the United States' position against Hussein. Immediately following the invasion, Baker flew to Moscow for an emergency meeting with Soviet foreign minister Eduard Shevardnadze.

"It was a fairly contentious meeting," Baker recalled. "We kicked it around for 90 minutes. Finally, though, he agreed." ...

Baker [also] believed that the United States should not jump into a military conflict in the Middle East without first winning the consent of Iraq's Arab neighbors. He set out to build an international coalition....

Before Baker could finish building a coalition, Hussein upped the ante. Hussein sent oil tankers into the Persian Gulf, a clear violation of U.N. sanctions. Most of Bush's advisors wanted the United States to take immediate military action against the ships, but Baker advised against it. He knew that if the U.S. acted alone, they would lose the support of the Soviets and other coalition members.... The president trusted his old friend's advice, and that trust was rewarded: Shevardnadze did get Hussein to turn the ships around. The Soviets were not alienated from the coalition against Hussein.[545]

Bush and Baker knew the Soviets and the other Arab Gulf nations shared interests with the United States to stop Iraq's aggression and send a signal to the world about countries' sovereignty.

Even the Syrian and Afghanistan armed conflicts today—as competitive as they are—largely depend on leading coalitions of countries with varied interests.

Malhotra, and Jonathan Powell, chief-of-staff to former British Prime Minister Tony Blair and author of *Talking to Terrorists*, also emphasized the non-zero-sum, interest-based nature of international negotiations, stating:

They lose does not equal you win. Trump tells us, "I beat China all the time," and promises to "beat Mexico," "beat Japan," and so on. **The underlying belief, that negotiation is fundamentally a zero-sum game in which only one side wins, is dangerously misplaced in the context of protracted conflicts and complex international deal-making.** When you negotiate with newly elected individuals on the other side of a trade or security deal, for example, you are not just their adversary [with whom you have conflicting interests]; you are also a partner whose job is to help them think more creatively, overcome mistrust, and, most importantly, sell the agreement to their constituents....

No deal with Iran, Russia, or China on any foreseeable issue, however, will be devoid of mutual interests, and in no negotiation with them will it be possible to judge U.S. success on the basis of how badly we "beat" the other side. [Emphasis added.][546]

Domestic Negotiations between Republicans Should Involve Problem-Solving Strategies

What about domestic negotiations? To what extent should they involve similar coalition-building and Problem-Solving Strategies? Interestingly, negotiations between Congressional Democrats and Republicans (and between a Democratic President and Congressional Republicans) have gone the *opposite* way. Increasingly, they have become competitive due to the increasing *conflicting* interests of Congress.

More and more ideologically rigid members—due to gerrymandering and other issues better analyzed by political scientists—enjoy less mutual and more conflicting interests than previously. The *New York Times* bestseller *It's Even Worse Than It Looks: How the American Constitutional System Collided with the New Politics of Extremism*, by political scientist Thomas E. Mann and congressional expert Norman J. Ornstein, describes this change well.[547]

This, however, describes the negotiations *between* Democrats and Republicans. The election of President Trump created a *new* domestic dynamic. Republicans now control every branch. President Trump only needs to negotiate with his fellow Republicans, with whom he should enjoy mostly mutual interests.

RESEARCH: Trump should thus use mostly Problem-Solving Strategies with his partner Republicans in Congress, based on the experts' proven research.

This runs up against, however, Trump's 40-plus year business history of using Competitive Strategies with everyone.

It also runs up against Trump's history of largely dealing with fairly straightforward zero-sum financial, real-estate, gaming, and licensing issues in business. And this is another major difference between Trump's business and presidential negotiations.

Major Difference #8:
The Complexity and Interconnected Nature of the Issues and Interests

This is not to downplay the challenging nature of Trump's business negotiations. Many involved big deals and tough, hard-nosed negotiations.

Many were complex with extensively negotiated terms and conditions. But in business negotiations generally, as noted by Malhotra and Powell, "Your job is to figure out how much money is on the table, to consider all the ways in which the deal could be structured, and to find an agreement that will allow you to capture more or most of the value that is being created."[548]

This is straightforward compared to presidential negotiations, which involve complex and interconnected personal, political, economic, domestic, and international issues and interests. The unpredictable nature of the impacts of various moves in these negotiations also make them exponentially more challenging.

And it makes it more likely that Problem-Solving Strategies will be more effective.

As Malhotra and Powell note, the type of negotiations in which Trump has engaged is **not** how it works in presidential negotiations:

> ...when you're negotiating a high-stakes, protracted, multiparty conflict that has escalated to potentially devastating levels. There will not be multiple solutions from which to choose. If you're lucky, there is **one** deal that everyone can live with—and there are countless barriers standing in the way of achieving even that. Your job is not to convince or threaten the other side into accepting your preferred solution, but rather to use everything at your disposal to knock down the barriers that are making the conflict seem unsolvable. **In most cases you are not trying to beat the other side; you are trying, often in collaboration, to reach the one and only deal that can avoid disaster.**
>
> This difference between buying real estate, for example, and ending wars, building coalitions, structuring global agreements, and balancing military and diplomatic leverage has serious implications for the kind of negotiator a president should be. [Emphasis added.][549]

Nothing like even Trump's most complex business negotiations.

As Carnegie Mellon's Institute for Politics and Strategy Professor Baruch Fischhoff noted, "In politics, compared to business, there are potentially many more people and issues that can affect how decisions are made and things turn out."[550]

Extremely different from Trump's business negotiations.

Major Difference #9:
The Nature of the Unknowns

Presidential negotiations not only involve extraordinarily complex and interconnected issues—they also involve issues with a high degree of unknown and sometimes unknowable risks and predictions. This also differs from Trump's business negotiations.

When Trump negotiated in business, he dealt with unknowns. How will the real-estate market grow in Manhattan? What demand exists for his products? How big can gaming get in Atlantic City?

Presidential negotiations, by contrast, involve a much *higher* degree of uncertainty given the number of unknowns and the type and scope of factors involved. What will happen to the uninsured if Obamacare becomes law? How many will sign up, and how many will pay the penalty? Will part of it be considered unconstitutional? If so, will its interconnected parts fail?

How much will it cost—in treasure and lives—if the U.S. invades Iraq due to a belief that it has weapons of mass destruction? How will this impact Syria, Afghanistan, Iran?

As Cale Guthrie Weissman, a *Fast Company* business, technology and leadership reporter, explains:

> In business, it's easy to understand the risks—the business could lose or gain money or partners, etc. But things aren't so easy to analyze when it comes to politics. **Political decision making, explains [Professor] Fischhoff, goes from the realm of economics analysis to a new realm where there's no way to predict overall ramifications.** Which is to say, the political actors need to know that there are myriad unknown elements to consider when making any moves. The stakes are higher. **Political analyses, he says, are "much harder**

**calculations than the ones entrepreneurs need to make."
When a president makes a seemingly small move, it could
alter relationships with a key ally. Understanding the
potential risks when making political negotiations is at
once impossible but necessary.** [Emphasis added.][551]

Of course, all new presidents must learn on the job. But Trump starts this
job with experience in the *opposite* type of negotiations, and no real experience
in political negotiations, to say nothing of presidential negotiations.

The Mutuality Factor

The final factor involving what strategy to use is whether both sides will use
Problem-Solving Strategies. Does mutuality exist?

Let's say you believe: 1) both sides want a future relationship;
2) many issues need to be resolved; and 3) few zero-sum issues exist with
creativity potentially adding value to everyone based on mutual interests.
All factors point to Problem-Solving Strategies. You use Problem-Solving
Strategies, right?

Wrong. At this point, it's still premature to decide. To effectively
use Problem-Solving Strategies, all parties must use them. If you
share strategic information and your counterpart doesn't reciprocate,
you lose power. And if your counterpart engages in leverage games
designed to make you feel defeated, and you don't fight back, you will be
perceived as weak.[552]

In short, if you Problem-Solve and your counterpart Competes, you will
be on the losing end of a win–lose negotiation.

The solution? Start by Problem-Solving in small increments. Share a
little strategic information and see if they reciprocate. If they don't, and you
can't get them to Problem-Solve, match their Competitive Strategies until
they realize everyone loses with this approach.

The key is to deeply understand your counterpart's goals, interests, and
needs. Knowing what drives their strategy, especially whether they care
about a future relationship, will help you determine how to most effectively
negotiate.

In the majority of Trump's business negotiations, he could probably
figure out most of the interests. The details and priorities may vary, sometimes
significantly, but business counterparts' main interests often come to the fore.

Presidential counterparts tend to be far more difficult to fully understand. Why? Internationally, major cultural differences impact this evaluation. In fact, a major role of U.S. diplomats worldwide is to make this evaluation. What makes North Korean Leader Kim Jong-Un tick? What about German Chancellor Angela Merkel?

Major Difference #10:
Counterparts' Cultural and Political Background

That's the final major difference between Trump's business and presidential negotiations—the diverse cultural and political nature of the president's counterparts.

Trump's business counterparts, even foreign ones, live in different negotiation worlds than his presidential ones on both the domestic and diplomatic fronts. Different backgrounds, mindsets, instincts, traditions, political systems, negotiation styles and histories, ways of communicating, philosophies, and priorities. And sometimes radically different ways of viewing negotiations and the world at large.

Negotiating with a Middle Eastern military dictator like Syrian President Bashar al-Assad or the President of a tribal-based country like Afghanistan—or a U.S. Senator like Rand Paul—present wholly different challenges than negotiating the purchase or sale of a casino.

The U.S. came closer to a nuclear war during the Cuban Missile Crisis in 1962 than at any other time in our history. President John F. Kennedy (JFK) negotiated our way back from the brink.

Kennedy's power of empathy and understanding of Soviet Premier Nikita Khrushchev played a crucial role, according to Malhotra in *Negotiating the Impossible*. Here's what happened. Then we will evaluate the negotiation elements.

- In October 1962, American spy planes over Cuba discovered Soviet Union–aided construction of missile sites capable of launching nuclear weapons.

- JFK immediately convened his advisors, eventually called the Executive Committee of the President of the United States (or ExComm), to secretly meet and assess how to respond.

- The ExComm developed two primary options to address the danger: a) an *aggressive* option involving immediate air strikes to destroy the missile sites plus a possible land invasion of Cuba; and b) a *gradual* option involving a blockade preventing additional military equipment from reaching Cuba, plus diplomacy and coalition building in the United Nations (and where a military strike remained on the table as a last resort).[553]

Note that these two options generally track Competitive and Problem-Solving Strategies—although imperfectly. The aggressive alternative focused on a military response—largely a leverage-related element. By contrast, the gradual option included diplomacy and coalition-building, elements largely reflecting Problem-Solving Strategies.

What happened? The initial reaction of the ExComm strongly favored the aggressive option, but most of the members over several days concluded the gradual option was better.

The initial response by the ExComm, not surprisingly, appeared fairly instinctive and visceral. A few days later, Congress' initial reaction, when JFK briefed them on it, was similar, as "members of Congress lambasted the president's strategy as insufficient, too weak, and likely to embolden further Soviet aggression."[554]

But JFK understood Congress' immediate reaction, as it paralleled the initial feelings of his own advisors. As Robert Kennedy noted about his brother JFK, "He was upset by the time the (congressional) meeting ended. When we discussed it later he was more philosophical, pointing out that the Congressional leaders' reaction to what we should do, although more militant than his, was much the same as our first reaction when we first heard about the missiles the previous Tuesday."[555]

JFK then also noted that the ExComm had been "given many days— behind closed doors—to think about the problem, to debate it, to change their minds, to sleep on it, and to grapple with the complexities of seemingly straightforward choices."[556]

At least two elements reflect differences between presidential negotiations and Trump's business negotiations. With the inclusion of Congress in the discussion, the number of parties involved increased substantially. Plus, the "complexities of seemingly straightforward choices" also differentiates this from Trump's business negotiations.

Fortunately for the world, JFK chose the gradual option. Why? According to Malhotra:

From a historical perspective, almost everyone agrees that the shift from aggressive to gradual was wise. The reason is that we have learned a lot since 1962 about what was happening at the time in the Soviet Union and Cuba, and almost **every** piece of new information suggests that an aggressive (air-strikes/invasion) strategy would have been even more disastrous than the ExComm had imagined.[557]

In fact, it could easily have led to the mutual use of nuclear weapons and the destruction of the planet.

What reflects relatively unique elements of presidential negotiations? The unknowns and the radically incorrect and dangerous assumptions about what would occur with the aggressive option. This lack of accurate information, and the unpredictability of other actors' actions, make presidential negotiations extremely challenging. Trump has never faced anything remotely similar in his business negotiations.

What happened? The U.S. initiated a naval blockade of Cuba and then, with a growing coalition of allies, and the possibility of military escalation, the U.S. pressured the Soviet Union to resolve the crisis.[558]

The final negotiated agreement included:

- the Soviet Union removing the missile sites under monitoring by the UN;
- the U.S. ending the quarantine and promising a) it would not invade Cuba, and b) it would dismantle its own nuclear-capable missiles in Turkey and Italy. (This last element was kept secret so the United States would not *look* weak.)[559]

The secrecy element was crucial politically—and it represented another difference with Trump's business negotiations. JFK needed to look strong *behind the table* to the U.S. public.

The key, according to Malhotra? "JFK's willingness to consider Khrushchev's point of view, and to investigate precisely why the Soviet Union felt compelled to transfer nuclear weapons to Cuba even when it risked starting a war. There were, it turns out, a number of such reasons—and understanding them was pivotal."[560]

The final difference between presidential negotiations and Trump's business negotiations involves the nature of presidential counterparts and how to truly empathize and understand their concerns. It's easy to demonize counterparts in an environment rife with distrust and distaste. It's better to understand them.

Robert Kennedy described this component of presidential negotiations as critical for future generations:

> The final lesson of the Cuban missile crisis is the importance of putting ourselves in the other country's shoes. During the crisis, President Kennedy spent more time trying to determine the effect of a particular course of action on Khrushchev or the Russians than on any other phase of what he was doing. What guided his deliberations was an effort not to disgrace Khrushchev, not to humiliate the Soviet Union.[561]

Has Trump done the same in dealing with North Korea's Kim Jong-Un? No. It's not surprising. He hasn't exhibited this trait in his 40-plus years of business negotiations.

Of course, history is only a guide. And every living president will attest to the fact that the presidency changed them. Trump has changed, too.

How much? We will next evaluate what changes, if any, he exhibited in negotiating with Mexico to pay for the wall and negotiating with Congress to repeal and replace Obamacare.

LESSONS LEARNED	
Trump's Strategies and Tactics	Trump consistently uses highly Competitive Strategies, including extremely aggressive: <ul><li>information bargaining</li><li>leverage moves</li><li>standards only if they help</li><li>offer-concession moves</li><li>agenda-control tactics</li></ul>
	Trump rarely uses Problem-Solving Strategies.
	Trump's strategies don't differ based on future relationships.
	Trump's strategies don't differ based on the number of issues.
	Trump rarely prepares and digs deep into the details.

	Trump has not exhibited much coalition-building skill nor been involved in negotiations involving 20 plus parties and hundreds of issues.
	Leverage and zero-sum issues dominated Trump's business negotiations.
Lessons Learned	Domestic presidential negotiations between members of the same political party require largely Problem-Solving Strategies.
	Effective domestic presidential negotiations require high levels of trust and credibility with members of Congress.
	Many international negotiations now require coalition-building and largely Problem-Solving Strategies.
	Major differences exist between Trump's business negotiations and presidential negotiations, including: 1. Future working relationships with the same counterparts 2. Long-term relationships involve multiple *unrelated* negotiations 3. The number of issues and interests on the table 4. The number of parties at the table/coalition-building 5. Negotiating on two levels: behind the table and across the table 6. The knowledge to effectively engage 7. Non-zero-sum issues and interests dominate many presidential negotiations 8. The complexity and interconnected nature of the issues and interests 9. The nature of the unknowns 10. Counterparts' cultural and political background

CHAPTER 14

THE U.S.-MEXICAN
BORDER NEGOTIATION

Trump's negotiation to get Mexico to pay for a newly enhanced border wall ended almost before it began. What happened?

To start, some context.

One, perhaps Trump's most popular line during his campaign—delivered hundreds of times in his stump speech and proving hugely important to his supporters—involved two elements: 1) building a "beautiful" wall along the Mexico–U.S. border designed to reduce illegal immigration and drug and weapons trafficking, and 2) Mexico would pay for it.

Two, Mexico's president Enrique Peña Nieto repeatedly stated—prior to Trump's election—that Mexico did not believe in and would *not* pay for such a wall.

Three, many Mexicans shared Nieto's position and viewed Trump negatively due to this issue and Trump's characterizations of undocumented Mexican immigrants in the United States. The perception of Trump in Mexico—and its political impact on Nieto—would prove to be a significant "behind the table" element in their negotiations.

Four, this "wall" negotiation did not exist in a historical vacuum. According to the *WSJ* in *"Trump Moves Shake Deep U.S.–Mexico Relationship,"* Trump's actions follow a "quarter-century of bipartisan policies aimed at fostering greater integration between the two neighbors."[562]

And, *finally*, Mexico and Canada are the U.S.'s two most important trading partners, linked on trade through the North American Free Trade Agreement (NAFTA). Trump also denigrated NAFTA and proposed renegotiating this 25-year agreement, calling it the worst free-trade deal in U.S. history.[563]

So what happened in this border wall negotiation? Trump took the lead from the start and predictably used highly Competitive Strategies. Let's analyze how, by evaluating:

- how aggressively he implemented my Five Golden Rules of Negotiation;

- the extent that his strategies matched up with his Top Ten Business Negotiation Strategies and ethics; and

- the different and more challenging nature of this presidential negotiation relative to Trump's business negotiations.

Golden Rule 1:
Information Is Power—So Get It!

Trump set his goal—get Mexico to pay for the entire wall—impossibly high. Not surprising, given his history and its wild popularity on the campaign. And not just an aggressive goal. Unattainable.

His goal also concerned one zero-sum issue (at least how he framed it), where one dollar more from Mexico to pay for the wall necessarily meant one dollar less from the United States.

Of course, Trump might respond "that was the campaign. And it served my larger purpose of getting elected. Plus, that was really just an extremely aggressive first offer. I fully intended to accept less than 100% payment from Mexico."

Perhaps. But the impact of his rhetoric and impossibly high goal still caused major problems *for President Nieto*—who felt the need during Trump's campaign to repeatedly and publicly disavow any intention of paying for the wall. This harmed Trump's chances of success.[564]

Plus, given the frequency and popularity of Trump's statement that Mexico would pay for it, he risked losing substantial credibility if—once elected—he accepted less than 100 percent.

The result of these diametrically opposed positions on a Trump-created zero-sum issue? Both parties publicly dug in hard and only tangentially addressed other options that might satisfy their mutual interests. (They shared interests in reducing illegal immigration and drug and weapons trafficking over their 1,954-mile joint border.)

Golden Rule 2:
Maximize Your Leverage

How strong was Trump's leverage? Not strong. Trump regularly communicated during the campaign the high importance to him of this issue. He *really* needed it. How much did Nieto need a deal? Not as much. Advantage Nieto.

What about their Plan Bs? This gets tricky due to the unknowns, a characteristic of presidential negotiations versus Trump's business negotiations. What do I mean? If Mexico holds firm on not paying for the wall (Trump's Plan B), Trump loses credibility. And Nieto loses nothing (his Plan B, too). Mexico is not currently paying anything. In fact, Nieto could gain politically by not doing a deal, as it shows he is standing up to Trump. Bad Plan B for Trump. Good Plan B for Nieto. This translates to stronger leverage for Nieto.

But Trump could have strengthened his leverage. How? By combining the wall funding negotiation with renegotiating NAFTA. He wanted to renegotiate NAFTA or had threatened to terminate it. And a ton of issues on the table relate to NAFTA and U.S.–Mexican trade, many of which also relate to the wall, although indirectly. This could potentially change Mexico's Plan B, which goes from pretty good politically to pretty bad economically. A leverage-enhancing move.

On the other hand, if Trump took a hardline in renegotiating NAFTA or terminated it, the U.S.–Mexican trade relationship could go down the tubes. Economically, that also hurts the U.S. In fact, it turns into a classic lose–lose. But, at least from Trump's perspective, it strengthens his leverage in a situation where he had little.

Of course, we don't *know* what would actually happen. And given Trump's reputation and lack of credibility in following through on his threats, it makes this Plan B/alternative very uncertain.

This would be bad for Trump and the U.S. *and* bad for Nieto and Mexico. Neither have a good Plan B if you add NAFTA to the mix, especially economically.

Now maybe Trump says that, politically, *he* has a good Plan B. This is his "behind the table" negotiation. Perhaps his supporters would love it if Trump pulls out of NAFTA. But what if that pullout then harms the U.S. economy and his supporters lose jobs. They might blame him. Not great for Trump, behind the table.

What about Nieto's Plan B behind the table? Mexico has presidential elections in 2018. If Nieto agrees to pay for any part of a wall (his Plan A), he might create even greater political problems than he already has. And it would be hard for his political problems at home to get *worse*. According to the *WSJ*:

> Nieto [in 2017 was] extremely unpopular at home, registering the lowest approval ratings of any Mexican president in recent memory…. [And relating to how Mexicans viewed Trump, making it even tougher for Nieto to do any deal with him,] Mexicans felt repeatedly insulted and humiliated during the presidential campaign by Mr. Trump, including his description of Mexican migrants to the U.S. as including criminals and rapists, his repeated bashing of trade as a job killer in the U.S., and his pledge at rallies to make Mexico pay for a border wall.
>
> A recent poll showed 89% of Mexicans have a "bad" or "very bad" image of the new U.S. president.[565]

So Nieto's Plan B—not paying for any wall—is almost certainly *much better* than his Plan A. Again, this translates to stronger leverage.

On the other hand, if Trump pulls out of NAFTA and it negatively impacts the Mexican economy—bad Plan B for Nieto.

Once again, an uncertain and likely bad Plan B for Trump. And perhaps a pretty strong Plan B for Nieto behind the table. But perhaps a bad Plan B longer-term regarding his economy. Still, advantage Nieto.

Once you evaluate all these factors, including the behind-the-table Plan Bs and NAFTA, this translates to relatively strong leverage for Nieto. Bottom line—Nieto has sufficient leverage to stay firm on *not* paying for any portion of a wall. Even if you include NAFTA in the mix.

No matter how you slice and dice it, Trump doesn't have strong leverage. But he acts like he does, just like he did in business, with threats on NAFTA and the wall. But a lot of unknowns and uncertainty. Typical presidential negotiations. Highly Competitive Strategies from Trump, on leverage. Counterproductive.

Golden Rule 3:
Employ "Fair" Objective Criteria

How much will the wall cost? Expert estimates vary, significantly. These are "independent" standards. According to *Reuters*, Trump during the campaign estimated $12 billion. Senate Majority Leader Mitch McConnell and House Speaker Paul Ryan put it at $15 billion. The U.S. Department of Homeland Security estimated $21.6 billion.[566]

And the Democratic staff on the Senate Homeland Security and Governmental Affairs Committee estimated $70 billion, according to *The New York Times*.[567]

Other standards also relate to NAFTA and trade. According to the *WSJ*, the following is at stake in this negotiation for both countries.

- 'NAFTA fundamentally reshaped North American economic relations, driving an unprecedented integration between Canada and the United States' developed economies and Mexico, a developing country,' the Council on Foreign Relations wrote in a January 2017 report [an independent standard].

- Regional trade between the U.S. and Mexico had more than tripled to over $1.1 trillion with some components going back and forth multiple times before integrating into finished products.

- U.S. foreign investment, according to the Council on Foreign Relations report, had grown sevenfold to over $100 billion.

- The United States is Mexico's largest trading partner.

- Mexico is only behind Canada and China in terms of trade with the United States.

- $340.8 billion worth of goods were transported by truck and rail across the U.S.–Mexico border through November 2016, which was up 16 percent in the previous two years (according to the U.S. Bureau of Transportation Statistics (another independent standard).[568]

How do these standards impact the negotiation between Trump and Nieto? The cost issue will likely have minimal impact. Cost does not appear to be the main issue. The main issue appears to be philosophical and political.

But the wall cost will impact Trump's behind-the-table negotiations with Congressional Republicans and Democrats. After all, Trump has asked Congress to fund the wall, until he can get Mexico to pay for it.

Not surprisingly, Trump offered the lowest estimate and the Democrats the highest. Highly partisan standards. And the use of extreme Competitive Strategies.

How much does the economies' interconnected nature impact the Trump–Nieto negotiations over NAFTA? Trump hasn't spoken much about this, not surprisingly, except to focus on American jobs lost to Mexico (and his efforts, like in Indiana with Carrier, to keep American jobs in the U.S.).

Why avoid talking about the trade numbers and the interconnected nature of the economies? The more interconnected—the bigger the problem if he pulls out of NAFTA. So Trump ignores these standards. Sometimes, though, he will threaten to terminate NAFTA, shifting the conversation off standards and back to leverage. Typical Trump. Typical also of extremely Competitive Strategies.

Golden Rule 4:
Design an Offer-Concession Strategy

Trump says Mexico will pay for the wall. An extremely aggressive first move. Not that it would share it 50/50. Not that it would pay a portion based on some economic formula. He wants 100 percent.

Nieto says no. But not just no. He says, "Mexico doesn't believe in walls. I've said it once and again: Mexico won't pay for any wall."[569] Nieto is *philosophically* opposed—a harder line and more difficult to move off later.

Opposites on paying for the wall. No wiggle room in their rhetoric. Both have boxed themselves in and can't concede without losing credibility.

Very aggressive offer-concession moves. On both sides.

Again; typical Trump. Typical Competitive Strategies.

Golden Rule 5:
Control the Agenda

The agenda for this presidential negotiation began in August 2016, during the campaign. At that time, Mexican secretary of foreign affairs Luis Videgaray—who knew Trump's son-in-law and close advisor Jared Kushner through mutual friends in the financial world—convinced Nieto to invite Trump and Hillary Clinton to separate meetings in Mexico City. Trump accepted. Clinton declined.

Trump met Nieto in Mexico City on August 31, and reports of their meeting were generally positive. Later that same day, however, Trump delivered a blistering anti-immigrant speech in Phoenix.

The meeting and Trump's Phoenix speech exacerbated a major problem for Nieto involving Nieto's behind-the-table negotiation with his constituents and his "political constraints" and interests, as master negotiator and former U.S. Secretary of State James Baker might say.

The reaction, according to an analysis of the wall negotiation in the Harvard Program on Negotiation May 2017 *Negotiation Briefings* newsletter (Harvard's *Briefings*):

> Many Mexicans were outraged that the meeting with their president took place at all…. Peña Nieto [afterward] fired Videgaray in an attempt to appease the pubic. Nevertheless, Videgaray remained in close contact with Kushner, even flying to New York to meet with him. And after Trump won the election, Peña Nieto rehired Videgaray, hoping once again to capitalize on Videgaray's ties to the U.S. president-elect.[570]

The timing of Trump's Phoenix speech also likely humiliated and embarrassed Nieto, helping move him in the *opposite* direction.

It also wasn't the last time Trump would take timing-related steps to make a negotiated agreement with Nieto *less* likely.

What else did Trump do that *worsened* his ability to get a deal with Nieto? It happened shortly after Trump became president.

Traditionally, U.S. presidents meet with their Mexican counterparts shortly after taking office. Kushner worked hard to make this happen. And he succeeded, with a Trump–Nieto meeting scheduled for the White House on January 31. An initial meeting was also scheduled for January 25 involving high-level officials from both countries to start the negotiations on trade, immigration, and border security.

On January 23, leading up to the meeting, Nieto in a speech once again stated his position on the wall, indicating, "Mexico does not believe in walls. Our country believes in bridges.... The solution is neither confrontation nor submission. The solution is dialogue and negotiation."[571]

This sounds like he was open to Problem-Solving Strategies. How did Trump and the White House respond? Here is how the *WSJ* described the White House's plans for January 25 and Mexicans reactions to public reports of it.

> Mexicans reacted angrily to news U.S. President Donald Trump would unveil details Wednesday [the 25th] of his plan to build a border wall between both nations, particularly since the announcement comes on the day top Mexican officials meet with U.S. administration representatives to discuss the troubled bilateral relationship.
>
> "This is an insult to those Mexican officials, to the president of Mexico and to all Mexicans," Jorge Castaneda, a former foreign minister, said in a televised interview. "It's a way of making them negotiate under threat, under insults, and it should lead (Mexican) President (Enrique) Peña Nieto to cancel his trip next week."[572]

Later, on the 25th, after Trump had signed two executive orders detailing his border-wall plans and imposing other Mexican-border security and deportation measures, the *WSJ* reported that the Mexican delegation had indicated *prior* to the signing that it would be impossible for Nieto to meet Trump if Trump mentioned in his signing ceremony that he would get Mexico to pay for the wall.[573]

Videgaray and Kushner reportedly communicated this to Trump in an Oval Office meeting the morning of the 25th. There, the three of them negotiated a compromise agreement in which the executive orders would be signed but Trump would say nothing about the wall funding. They further agreed that Trump would say positive things in the ceremony about Mexico, according to the *The Washington Post*.[574]

Trump did not mention Mexico paying for the wall in his signing ceremony. And he did say nice things about Mexico at the ceremony. ("I truly believe that we can enhance the relation between our two nations to a degree not seen before in a very, very long time.")[575]

Trump kept their agreement. But then, in a move that *worsened* U.S.–Mexican relations and led to the termination of even any discussion of the issue, Harvard's *Briefings* noted that:

> In an interview **that night** with ABC News, Trump said that planning for the wall was "starting immediately," with construction to begin within months. According to Trump, federal funds would be used to pay for the wall and then the U.S. government would seek reimbursement from Mexico. "I'm telling you there will be a payment," Trump said, as reported by CNN. "It will be in a form, perhaps a complicated form." [Emphasis added.][576]

This move by Trump effectively ended the negotiation before it even began. Again, Harvard's *Briefings*.

> Peña Nieto, still in Mexico, [then] went on TV to issue an emotional statement condemning Trump's orders. "Mexico will not pay for any wall," he declared [again], and hinted that he might cancel his trip to Washington.

> The following morning, Trump wrote on Twitter, "If Mexico is unwilling to pay for the badly needed wall, then it would be better to cancel the upcoming meeting." Peña Nieto then canceled, and his negotiating team returned to Mexico. The incident is said to have "maximally embarrassed" Videgaray, potentially closing off one of the few links between the two governments, according to the *New Yorker*.

> The next day, January 27, White House press secretary Sean Spicer told reporters that the president was considering a 20 percent tax on imports from Mexico to pay for the border wall. Both Democrats and Republicans in Congress immediately objected, saying that American citizens would end up paying for the wall through their purchases of Mexican goods. Within hours, White House chief of staff Reince Preibus walked back Spicer's statement, saying the proposal was just one funding idea among several.[577]

A postscript to the canceled negotiation meeting: Trump and Nieto had an hour-long telephone call on January 27 to patch things up. Both characterized it as productive and cordial, according to *The New York Times*. They also then apparently agreed not to speak publicly about the wall issue for a while.[578]

[A] Mexican government official told *[The New York] Times* that the leaders planned to allow their relationship to "cool off" before talking further. However, they did reportedly authorize their teams to reconvene negotiations on trade, immigration, and border security. As for the border wall and its funding, they took the issue off the table for the time being, "in effect quarantining it so that it did not contaminate conversations about other issues," according to the *[New York] Times.*[579]

How Did Trump Do in the Border-Wall–Funding Negotiation?

Trump made numerous negotiation missteps that underscored his ineffectiveness in this negotiation. In fact, he failed on almost all fronts, including not getting Mexico to fund any element of a wall. Unfortunately, his moves were largely predictable based on his Top Ten Business Negotiation Tactics, personal skills, ethics, and the strategic differences between presidential and Trump's business negotiations. What were they?

- Trump used extremely Competitive Strategies, consistent with the strategies he has used for years with his business negotiation counterparts. In contrast to many of his business negotiations, he should have been on the Problem-Solving Strategies end of the spectrum. Why? Based on the Four Factor test: 1) he was negotiating with a partner nation with whom the U.S. had enjoyed a long-time bipartisan and bilateral trade relationship that the U.S. presumably wished to continue; 2) the renegotiation of NAFTA involved a ton of issues, even if the border-wall–funding issue only involved one; 3) many NAFTA issues were non-zero-sum and open to possible creative solutions; and 4) Mexico was interested in negotiation and working with the U.S. on revising NAFTA if not on the border wall funding issue. After all, Mexico invited Trump to meet in August in Mexico City, and Nieto agreed to meet Trump on January 31 after already meeting him the previous August, again communicating an interest in finding a mutually beneficial solution.

- Trump also made many strategic mistakes in his implementation of extremely Competitive Strategies, including:

  o Setting an impossible and unrealizable goal, not only during the campaign (That was understandable, given how campaigns work and his overarching goal to get elected.), but continuing *after* he became president, when he could have moderated it or been less publicly strident about it.

As Harvard's *Briefings* concluded, "**Avoid extreme public demands.** Trump's declarations about the border wall served him well on the campaign trail but could prove hard to deliver now that he's in office. Though there's nothing wrong with setting ambitious goals, make sure they're not impossibly high."[580]

o Acting as if he had much stronger leverage than he had, at least on the wall-funding issue, losing credibility.

o Threatening, humiliating, and embarrassing the U.S.'s close ally Mexico and President Nieto and his constituents, making Nieto's behind-the-table negotiation virtually impossible (and not empathizing and making it *easier* on Nieto, which Secretary Baker would no doubt have recommended).

o Engaging in extremely aggressive offer-concession moves and rhetoric on trade and wall-funding issues after his election (this differs from his impossible goal as this also encompasses his proposal to impose a 20 percent tax on Mexican imports to pay for the wall, a proposal Chief of Staff Priebus "walked back" shortly after it was publicly floated).

o Agenda- and timing-wise, planning and delivering a blistering anti-immigrant speech in Phoenix *the same day* he met with Nieto in Mexico City, undermining Nieto and any more diplomatic message he may have communicated in that earlier meeting.

o Scheduling the signing of two executive orders on immigration *the same day* his team first met with Mexican officials in the White House and just six days before a scheduled summit with Mexico's president, inflaming already high tensions between the two countries. This reflected poor planning for the negotiation, described in the Harvard *Briefings* as "a failure to coordinate a unified strategy within his administration."[581] Coordinating large numbers of parties and issues was a major difference between Trump's business negotiations and presidential negotiations.

o Giving an interview with ABC and using heated rhetoric on the wall-funding issue *after* agreeing not to mention in his

signing ceremony his position that Mexico pay for the wall.
This inflamed the issue, ensuring reciprocation from Nieto
that led to the canceled meeting.

- Not understanding or ignoring the behind-the-table negotiations for himself and Nieto.

- Violating the spirit of the "won't talk about Mexico paying for the wall" agreement reached with Kushner and Videgary in his Oval Office meeting in the ABC News interview.

- Undermining the credibility of Kushner and the U.S. negotiating team that organized the January 31 summit meeting by Tweeting an implicit threat to Nieto to cancel the meeting solely on the wall funding issue. His entire team lost credibility when Nieto predictably canceled.

- Failing to coordinate an overall negotiation team strategy with Kushner and others regarding the timing of the border-related executive orders. This, like Trump's other mistakes, was predictable given Trump's business-negotiation history (now with a lot more people, more issues, behind-the-table elements, NAFTA, and a lot more uncertainty involved).

- Engaging in high-stakes complex diplomacy with a long-time ally through what appeared to be a wholly instinctive use of the limited characters of Twitter, seemingly without any review by his foreign policy experts, which damaged the long-term relationship between the U.S. and Mexico as a result.

- Threatening through his press secretary to impose a 20 percent tax on Mexican imports without building a coalition and coordinating with his Congressional partners (his behind-the-table negotiations). This also may have illustrated an ignorance on the details relating to the policy and politics of this issue and understanding its impact on Mexico and the U.S.

Of course, Trump might respond that 1) this negotiation has just begun and he will still get Mexico to pay for it, 2) he appeared tough and his supporters will love what he did, and 3) he ended with a good conversation with Nieto and expects the U.S. to continue its strong relationship with Mexico.

If Trump's goal related solely to the attitude of his supporters, he may be correct. But I would be very surprised if Mexico would ever agree to pay for any portion of a wall after what happened here. I also believe Trump could have negotiated a significant payment from Mexico for some part of a wall had he used more effective negotiation strategies from the start.

While the U.S. and Mexico will likely continue its mutually beneficial trade and other relationships, Trump's strategies damaged the relationship.

Did Trump do anything right here? Of course. *One*, he immediately contacted President Nieto after Nieto canceled their meeting and reset their relationship. As the Harvard *Briefings* noted, "**Regroup quickly after failure. If talks collapse, reach out to your counterpart and make plans to regroup after a suitable cooling-off period.**"[582]

And, *two*, both leaders recognized that the wall issue had become toxic to the countries' entire relationship. They smartly decided to take this issue off the table temporarily. As the Harvard *Briefings* noted, "**Quarantine hot-button issues.** Though it's usually beneficial to discuss all relevant issues simultaneously, there are times when quarantining a particularly controversial issue will allow you to make headway—and build trust—on more manageable matters."[583]

This analysis may seem overly critical of Trump. And yes, almost all this occurred in the first week after Trump became president. "Cut him some slack," you might say. "He just became president. He will learn. In fact, he has learned."

Hold on. Trump is President of the United States. The most powerful person in the world. He had his finger on the nuclear button and could immediately impact our economic health and welfare from Day One. And he got elected in part on his promise to be an expert negotiator on our behalf. We can't afford to cut him slack.

Regarding whether and how much he is learning on-the-job, let's analyze his negotiations with Congress to repeal and replace Obamacare. These lasted well into his first year.

How effectively did he engage in those negotiations? Did he use similar strategies to the wall negotiation? Were they similar to his business negotiations? We know how they ended. The important question here—how did he get there?

CHAPTER 15

THE "REPEAL-AND-REPLACE OBAMACARE" NEGOTIATION

"Repeal and replace Obamacare." Another Trump stump speech staple. Hugely popular with his supporters, too. And who doesn't want better healthcare and benefits, lower premiums, with no one losing their insurance? Win–win–win, right? One problem: It's another almost impossible goal, like getting Mexico to pay for the wall. A predictable pattern—and another major negotiation challenge.

What happened? Trump lost. Again.

This time, though, the negotiation sharply contrasted with his border-wall–funding negotiation. This time, the negotiation involved:

- 535 Members of Congress, 50 Governors, hundreds of state and local elected officials, the elected officials' staffs, federal and state insurance regulators, lobbyists galore, lawsuits and constitutional lawyers, congressional budget officials, tons of healthcare-related interest groups, liberal and conservative think tanks, academic experts, religious institutions, media personalities—with late-night comics even weighing in with serious commentary, and significant grassroots individual involvement,

- an enormously complex and detailed issue with thousands of interconnected and moving parts,

- significant issues relating to the federal and state government's roles,

- a wedge issue with major philosophical differences between various factions *within* the Republican Party,

- perhaps the defining element of President Barack Obama and Democrats' accomplishments in the previous eight years,

- the health, welfare, and lives of millions of U.S. citizens and non-citizens,

- the pocketbooks and taxes of millions of U.S. residents,

- millions of jobs in a growing sector of the U.S. economy,

- millions of dollars in interest-group advertising across the country,

- a benefit that thousands of organizations voluntarily provide their employees, and

- huge amounts of uncertainty and unpredictability relating to its financial, economic, and health impact.

It also impacted almost 20 percent of the U.S. economy and represented a core promise that many Republican Members of Congress primarily used to get elected and re-elected in the previous four election cycles.

Wow. Huge differences with Trump's bilateral negotiation with Mexico over the wall. But the same result.

What happened, and how did President Trump negotiate?

First, here is a brief history of Obamacare, as it set the stage for Trump's negotiations. It will also provide a study in contrasts from how President Obama got healthcare reform passed—which also involved almost all these challenges.

Then we will analyze what happened in the negotiations between President Trump and Congress.

Some brief history:

- Obamacare was passed by the U.S. Senate on December 24, 2009, with no votes to spare after passing the U.S. House with just a few extra votes. The votes occurred after over a year of hearings, changes, and negotiations in multiple congressional committees.

- The effort under President Obama started as a significant campaign promise by Obama and many other Democrats, but the negotiations included many meetings between Democrats and Republicans in which both sides tried to achieve a bipartisan solution.

- The final version was generally opposed by liberal Democrats, who pushed hard for a public option to be included.

- The Democratic leaders in Congress, House Speaker Nancy Pelosi and Senate Majority Leader Harry Reid, were seasoned congressional negotiators. And President Obama's Chief of Staff Rahm Emanuel previously served in the House as an important member and skilled negotiator on Pelosi's leadership team.

- Democrats had been working to pass healthcare reform for years, and the latest significant effort had crashed and burned in the early 1990s due in part to the secretive process used to develop the plan.

- The public generally supported healthcare reform at the beginning of the process in part due to rising healthcare premiums.

- The Democrats tried to sell Obamacare as a reform effort that would improve the health of all Americans while maintaining health care choice, largely be cost-neutral or less costly due to the savings generated by additional efficiencies, and substantially increase the number of insured.

- The Republicans' aggressive political and public relations efforts had largely turned the American public against Obamacare before it passed.

- Many healthcare-related interest groups supported Obamacare, including the major health-insurance companies and doctors' groups.

- Obamacare was passed solely with Democratic votes against the united opposition of Republicans using a technical procedural maneuver.

- Obamacare transformed the healthcare economy but remained incredibly controversial.

- Congressional Republicans, after first gaining control of the House in 2010 and then the Senate in 2014, passed legislation repealing and replacing Obamacare over 50 times. But they could not overcome President Obama's veto.

- Obamacare never enjoyed significant public support until 2017, when many of its beneficiaries faced losing it.[584]

Enter President Donald Trump in 2016, who took up the Republican mantra in the campaign to repeal and replace it. Yet, he neither offered a detailed proposal for it during the campaign, nor did he demonstrate any significant substantive knowledge regarding the issue during the campaign.

So, what happened in President Trump's negotiation with Congress?

Let's analyze President Trump's role in these negotiations, by evaluating:

- how aggressively he, Speaker of the House Paul Ryan, and Senate Majority Leader Mitch McConnell implemented my Five Golden Rules of Negotiation;

- the extent that Trump's strategies matched up with his Top Ten Business Negotiation Strategies and ethics; and

- the different and more challenging nature of this presidential negotiation relative to Trump's business negotiations.

Keep in mind that these negotiations—if successful—would involve a minimum of four separate but related negotiations, all of which needed to be successful for their reform effort to become law: 1) negotiations with the U.S. House, 2) negotiations with the U.S. Senate, 3) negotiations with a joint House-Senate Conference Committee if the House and Senate couldn't pass identical bills, and 4) President Trump's agreement/signature (assuming Congress could not generate veto-proof majorities). Enormously complex and challenging, to say the least.

As we know, Trump failed in his initial effort to get House support before successfully getting the House to pass repeal and replace legislation. It then failed in the Senate. To analyze Trump's role, let's view these as three "sub-negotiations:"

1) **Trump's role in failing to get an initial House bill passed,**

2) **Trump's successful second effort in getting a House bill passed, and**

3) **Trump's Senate effort, which failed by one vote.**

Along the way we will focus on President Trump's role in each of these negotiations, contrasting it where appropriate with how President Obama addressed this similarly challenging issue. We will not, however, address the substantive healthcare elements except where necessary to highlight President Trump's negotiation moves.

Three further caveats. Trump's moves in the earlier negotiations impacted his later negotiations. In other words, even though the House passed repeal and replace on his second try, the way he negotiated in the first failed effort impacted his second effort in the House and his final failed negotiation in the Senate.

Plus, many of Trump's mistakes during the initial House negotiations—which were consistent with his 40-plus years of business negotiating—also comprised mistakes in his Senate negotiations.

Finally, while this negotiation effort failed, healthcare reform continues to be a moving target. So even though Trump failed in his first year to repeal and replace Obamacare, he and his fellow Republicans might still succeed.

Trump's Role in Failing to Get an Initial House Bill Passed

Golden Rule 1:
Information Is Power—So Get It!

Hundreds of parties. Thousands of issues. At-the-table and behind-the-table negotiations with crucial constituencies. Huge complexity. Where did President Trump start? With his campaign promises, reflected in his negotiation goals.

Trump's Unrealistic Healthcare Goals

Trump repeatedly claimed the ability to accomplish the following main healthcare-related goals, some of which Trump and his team reiterated after the election, according to the *WSJ* in *"Where Donald Trump's Health-Care Promises Stand Now."*

"We're going to have insurance for everybody."

"I want to keep pre-existing conditions."

"There will be no cuts to Social Security, Medicare & Medicaid."

"It's going to be much better for the people at the bottom, people that don't have any money."

"Nobody will be worse off financially." (Trump's Health and Human Services Secretary Tom Price).

"I will sign the first bill and give Americans many choices and much lower rates." [585]

Are these realistic and aggressive, as recommended by the research? No. Are they consistent with how he set his business goals? Yes. Counterproductive here, though, in presidential negotiations. Of course, many were campaign promises—we expect exaggeration there—but Trump got elected in part due to his *not* promising like a typical politician. "Drain the swamp," he repeated over and over during the campaign.

Of course, President Obama also made healthcare promises that weren't kept. As noted in that same *WSJ* article, Obama said, "'If you like the plan you have, you can keep it. If you like the doctor you have, you can keep your doctor, too. The only change you'll see are falling costs,' as Obamacare rolled out. This didn't turn out to be true. Mr. Obama also promised that the typical family's health insurance premium would drop by $2,500. This was not the case, either."[586]

From a negotiation perspective, Trump's campaign promises and goals created an extremely challenging behind-the-table negotiation with his constituents. In business, it wasn't a big deal to set aggressive unrealistic goals. Trump was only accountable to himself. No real downside risk existed. In presidential negotiations, Trump's publicly articulated aggressive goals made his negotiations more difficult.

Extreme goal-setting also represents the first step in an aggressive Competitive Strategies approach. Trump's approach—to be successful—would need to be practically perfect. As former House Republican Speaker John Boehner said at a healthcare conference early in 2017, "In the 25 years that I served in the United States Congress, Republicans never, ever, one time agreed on what a health-care proposal should look like. Not once."[587]

Trump's extreme and unrealistic goal-setting started this extraordinarily challenging negotiation off on the wrong foot.

Trump Gives Lead Negotiator Role to Ryan and McConnell

One of Trump's first strategic negotiation steps? In contrast to the Mexican wall-funding negotiation and all his business negotiations, he passed the lead role to Republican House Speaker Paul Ryan and, later, to Senate Majority Leader Mitch McConnell.

Why? This is what happened, according to the *WSJ* in *"Donald Trump Plays Background Role in Health-Care Battle"*:

> The course of Donald Trump's presidency will be defined by his ability to seal a deal to rework the U.S. health-care system, but so far, he has outsourced the job of hammering out the details to about a dozen Republican leaders and White House advisers while he serves in the background as a pitchman.
>
> It is an approach that suggests the White House intends to use its most potent weapon—the bully pulpit—sparingly in the initial stages of what could be a protracted battle to replace the Affordable Care Act. Mr. Trump instead is using White House meetings to prod recalcitrant lawmakers, grass-roots groups and industry leaders to embrace the legislation, offering sympathy for their concerns even if they are in conflict.
>
> A fight over scaling back funding for Medicaid, a program offering health care to the poor, for instance, is growing more

complex after competing interests became convinced they each have the president's support.[588]

Four significant Trump negotiation mistakes relate to this strategic decision.

1. Trump's Lack of Detailed Knowledge Undermined His Negotiation Effectiveness

President Trump could not have led this negotiation even if he had wanted. He didn't have the knowledge, expertise, or experience to take that role. As he himself famously said at the time to a group of Republican governors after meeting with them and insurers, *"Nobody knew that healthcare could be so complicated."*[589]

This statement highlighted his lack of knowledge of this issue *and*— by publicly saying it—undermined his credibility to substantively negotiate those issues later. This Trump liability has already been extensively addressed. It caused problems for Trump here.

Of course, Trump would likely suggest that giving Ryan the lead made strategic sense. As the *WSJ* noted:

> 'Mr. Trump's inclination to let Mr. Ryan guide the initial process by educating members—and the public—about the details of the proposal and its conservative credentials is the correct one,' said Tom Scully, a former Medicare and Medicaid administrator who cobbled together support for health-care laws under previous Republican presidents. 'Ryan knows health-care policy cold, and knows the House,' Mr. Scully said. 'The president is smart to let him do this. If you need Trump, then call him in for the final push.'[590]

Unfortunately for Trump, his lack of knowledge also impacted his ability to make the "final push." Here's how Harvard's *Briefings* described this Trump liability:

> Following a budget meeting at the White House, House Freedom Caucus [the Republican group of 30 or so very conservative House members that Trump and Ryan needed for passage] leaders Mark Meadows and Jim Jordan nabbed an impromptu meeting with the president and complained that Ryan wasn't soliciting their input on the Obamacare repeal and replace bill. Trump assured them that he himself was open to their ideas.

The president began courting House Republicans with invitations to the White House and unannounced phone calls. Speaking to *Politico*, congressmen recounted 'colorful' talks full of "exaggerations and foul language and hilariously off-topic anecdotes."

Trump seemed to relish the schmoozing and arm-twisting, **but the details eluded him.** As a business executive, "He's really not used to getting involved himself," one senior House GOP aide told *Politico*.

"If this was about personalities, we'd already be at 'yes,'" Meadows later told the *[Washington] Post*. Calling Trump 'charming,' he added, **"but this is about policy, and we're not going to make it about anything else."**

Representative Dave Brat of Virginia recalled an unexpected phone call he got from Trump. "He's selling. The salesman in sell mode. On that, he's the best. Humor, heart, personality." But with his policy concerns unaddressed, Brat was unable to get behind the bill. [Emphasis added.][591]

One final push occurred on the day of the scheduled vote. Again, Trump's lack of policy knowledge proved a liability. Here's what happened, according to Harvard's *Briefings*:

On the day of the scheduled vote, March 23, Trump told Freedom Caucus leaders at the White House that he was willing to go along with their proposed cuts to so-called essential benefits—including outpatient visits, mental-health services, and maternity care. But Meadows and others wanted deeper cuts, which were even more likely to turn off Tuesday Group members [more moderate House members] and perhaps doom the bill in the Senate.

House members left the meeting with the impression that Trump hadn't learned enough about health-care policy to know how to put together a package that could win in the House, let alone the Senate. [Emphasis added.][592]

Trump's failure to learn the policy nitty-gritty contributed to the bill's initial failure in the House. This reflected a pattern in Trump's business negotiations ever since the mid-1980s. Early on, he learned the details. Later, he did not. Predictable liability in his presidential negotiations, where this knowledge had an even greater negotiation impact given the number of parties, interests, issues, and moving parts.

2. President Trump and the Republican Team Were Inexperienced in Presidential Negotiations

Another problem with giving Ryan the lead role was that Ryan had only been elevated to speaker in October 2015, shortly after Speaker Boehner was forced out by his fellow Republicans. Crucially, Ryan had never pushed significant domestic legislation into law. While he may know healthcare policy and the House cold, this negotiation effort involved a lot more than just House members, as noted earlier.

Plus, neither Trump nor critical members of his administration had substantial experience or expertise in presidential negotiations. They certainly had no specific expertise building coalitions around an incredibly complex issue like healthcare reform. Trump's Chief of Staff Reince Priebus had never served in congress, with a background solely in campaigns and party politics. Trump's Health and Human Services Secretary Tom Price understood the complex healthcare issues, but he had never been involved in this level of coalition-building, much less presidential-style.

Here's how the problems were described in Harvard's *Briefings*, in *"How the 'Party of No' Didn't Get to Yes"*:

> The trouble began with the way the Republican health-care bill was drafted. House Speaker Paul Ryan and his team put together the American Health Care Act (AHCA) in "secretive locations at the Capitol" with input from White House Chief of Staff Reince Priebus, writes Tim Alberta for *Politico*. Trump himself stayed out of the fray, marveling publicly that health-care had proven to be an "unbelievably complex subject." After being leaked, the AHCA was released unceremoniously on March 6 as a take-it-or-leave-it document.
>
> **Apparently, assuming congressional Republicans would rally around the bill, Ryan didn't develop a clear strategy for selling it to them or to the American people. He was reportedly unprepared when conservative pundits trashed the bill as "Obamacare Lite" and moderates objected that it would harm millions, including many Trump voters....**

The debacle serves as a warning to negotiators preparing for complex multiparty talks of the need to plan carefully and dig deep into the details. [Emphasis added.][593]

Neither Trump nor the entire Republican team had prepared sufficiently for these complex multiparty talks nor dug deep into the details.

3. Trump's Zero-Sum Win–Lose Business Approach—and Failure to Focus on the Multiple Parties' Fundamental Policy Interests—Ignored a Crucial Path to Victory

What details did President Trump and the Republican leadership team *not* take into account? Classic interests underlying their positions. Where Trump predictably looked to their political interests (addressed later in terms of leverage), he seemed to never learn nor care much about the House members' true policy interests and needs. Another classic characteristic of Competitive Strategies—and one destined to make this negotiation involving thousands of interconnected issues—far more challenging.

Here is how the *WSJ's* Chief Economics Commentator Greg Ip described the problem *"In Health-Care Failure, a Lesson on Treating Politics like Business."* Notice the contrasts Ip draws between business and presidential negotiations:

> Investors have greeted Donald Trump's presidency with optimism rooted in great part in the business credentials of his administration. **They may want to reconsider that optimism after Mr. Trump's humbling defeat on healthcare, due in no small part to treating politics like business.**
>
> In business, deals usually live or die because of money. Even things that aren't ostensibly about money—who will run a merged company, whose property gets seized, the terms of a license—can usually be resolved with money. This makes success binary [a very win–lose, zero-sum dynamic]: Either one party pays a price that the other, whether a merger partner, a lender, a supplier, a union, or a government, can accept, or the deal does not happen.
>
> In politics, by contrast, deals involve multiple parties whose priorities include not just money but ideology, power, loyalty and respect, among other things. Even when the fight seems to be over money, it often isn't: The Freedom Caucus Republicans who scuttled their party's proposed Obamacare replacement object not just to the cost but to the very notion of expanding

the welfare state. In politics, definitions of success are both elusive and often mutually exclusive: Pleasing moderates on healthcare meant angering conservatives, and vice versa.

"No one expected a businessman to completely understand the nuances, the complicated ins and outs of Washington and its legislative process," *Fox News* commentator Jeanine Pirro said Saturday. This supposed defense of Mr. Trump ignores his own pitch to voters that his dealmaking prowess could succeed where career politicians failed.

By approaching Obamacare the way he approached business [using Competitive Strategies with a win–lose mindset], Mr. Trump hobbled himself. With scant interest in the underlying details, he did not appreciate the motivations [true interests] of many players, from congressmen in varying Republican factions to Democrats, governors, insurance companies, and of course the uninsured. Lacking any policy goal of his own, he defined success in a binary way, simply as passage of a bill. That rang hollow for those in Congress who disliked its substance. [Emphasis added.][594]

Three major issues here. *One*, Trump's Competitive Strategies business-oriented, win–lose, zero-sum mindset—what Ip calls a binary approach—proved counterproductive in these presidential negotiations.

Two, Trump did not understand the nuances, motivations, and true interests of the parties. Nor did he seem to really want to discover them. For example, Trump overestimated the loyalty interests of House Freedom Caucus Republicans. He apparently believed that Republican team loyalty and getting anything passed would trump their policy-oriented interests.

But a cursory review of these Freedom Caucus members' history of Republican loyalty and ideological rigidity would have raised serious questions of the efficacy of this strategy. After all, these were the same members who shut down the government several years prior over the objections of most mainstream Republicans.

As Congressman Adam Kinzinger (R-IL) stated in an opinion piece in *The New York Times*, "It's what they do: They move the goal posts, and once that happens, they still refuse to play. We are the Charlie Brown party, hoping that this time, things will be different. But time and again, the Freedom

Caucus is Lucy—pulling the ball out from under us, letting us take the fall and smiling to themselves for making a splash."[595]

Loyalty and "taking one for the team" is not really in their playbook. Not fully understanding these fundamental interests and not doing his due diligence undermined Trump's negotiation effectiveness.

And, *three*, Trump seemed to care little about the actual policies involved—his only goal appeared to want to "win" a vote. This proved counterproductive with philosophically driven members of Congress. As Ip noted, Trump was "lacking any policy goal of his own…[and] defined success simply as passage of a bill."

In business, Trump defined "wins" by closing deals and in monetary terms. As president, he just wanted a win, any win. This undermined his negotiation effectiveness with ideologically driven counterparts.

One final note from the *WSJ*'s Ip, who contrasted Trump's approach with that of President Obama's:

> Sen. Tom Cotton, an ally of Mr. Trump, is no friend of Obamacare. Yet in explaining what Mr. Trump and Paul Ryan…did wrong, he cited the Democrats' contrasting approach with Obamacare: "They didn't pass it for over a year in President Barack Obama's first term," the Arkansas Republican said on CBS' *Face the Nation* Sunday. "So it went through very public hearings, and took testimony, developed a fact-based foundation of knowledge. President Obama traveled around the country, held town halls, spoke to a joint session of Congress."
>
> The complexity of the resulting bill was no accident; it reflected the excruciatingly delicate balance among so many competing priorities.[596]

Some additional differences to note here relating to Trump's versus Obama's negotiations.

- Obama used classic Problem-Solving Strategies with Congress.
- Obama dug into the policy and political details of healthcare and demonstrated a deep understanding of the parties' interests involved.
- Obama had spent his entire political career in a legislative and political negotiation environment versus a business negotiation environment.

- The House and Senate Democratic leaders were skilled and experienced negotiators in the congressional/presidential environment. Speaker Ryan was not. And McConnell had never been Majority Leader with a Republican President, having become Majority Leader in 2014.

- Obama's Chief of Staff Rahm Emanuel had significant experience in Congress.

Even with all these differences, Obama still only got healthcare reform passed by the slimmest of margins. In fact, it almost failed in the House after initially passing the House and then getting revised and passed in the Senate.

Here's how the *WSJ* described what happened, including Obama's role. This foreshadowed some of what happened to the Trump–Ryan efforts:

> Nearly a decade ago, House Democrats passed a version of [Obamacare] that was more pleasing to its liberal wing, but the bill had to be revised to more middle ground in the Senate. Then-Speaker Nancy Pelosi, out of options and with no prospect of Republican support, had to persuade House Democrats to back it anyway and relied heavily on Mr. Obama to personally win them over, one-by-one, to cross the finish line.[597]

4. Trump's Early Lack of Commitment Caused Problems

One final negotiation mistake Trump made in connection to "delegating" the lead to Ryan: He psychologically signaled he wasn't all in, at least early on, and did this publicly. By giving his own proposal lukewarm support, he caused even greater problems.

As the *WSJ* reported in *"GOP's Health Plan Draws Skepticism on Capitol Hill"*:

> Mr. Trump endorsed the legislation [drafted by House Republican leaders and crafted with White House support] but left open the question of whether he would lobby personally and forcefully for it. Mr. Trump met with House lawmakers responsible for gathering votes for the bill and urged them to move swiftly. But he signaled that the task, at least for now, fell to congressional leaders.
>
> ...Senior White House officials have said they see Congress as holding the primary responsibility for undoing the health

law but that they are willing to work publicly and privately to help.[598]

President Trump was quoted by *The New York Times* as asking his advisers, *after* this Trump–Ryan bill was rolled out on March 6, *"Is this really a good bill?"*[599]

This was *his* plan and *his* first big legislation introduced in congress after getting elected. The Republicans needed the president fully engaged to pass it. Here is how Congressman Dennis Ross (R-FL), a member of the House GOP whip team (which is charged with rounding up votes) described their need, according to the *WSJ*: "The president's going to be very pivotal in this. He's got to go into these districts and give air cover to these members who are weak-kneed on some of these issues."[600]

You can't get air cover from a president who's not all in.

Importantly, though, the bill already faced major problems within the Republican caucus, reflecting the lack of coalition-building by Trump, Ryan, and their leadership teams.

All these problems combined to cause major negotiation problems right off the bat, as detailed in the *WSJ*'s *"GOP's New Plan to Repeal Obamacare: Dare Fellow Republicans to Block Effort"*:

> An array of conservative lawmakers and activist groups on Tuesday attacked a proposal by House GOP leaders to overturn the 2010 health law, posing the first major test to President Donald Trump's White House of its ability to broker deals among Republicans in Congress.
>
> Members of two conservative House caucuses, at least three right-leaning GOP senators and a set of allied groups outside Congress signaled their dissatisfaction with the health plan published Monday [the previous day] by House Republican leaders **and crafted with White House support**....
>
> Late Tuesday, AARP, an advocacy group for older adults, announced that it also opposed the plan. The group said the bill would raise costs "for those who can least afford higher insurance premiums."
>
> ...Inside the White House, [some] members of the president's team privately expressed surprise that Republican leaders needed Mr. Trump to spend political capital to deliver votes from the conservative Freedom Caucus. "Nobody over here

ever felt that it was going to be incumbent on the president to put it upon his shoulders," one senior White House aide said. [Emphasis added.][601]

The start of President Trump's first major domestic legislative effort—an effort requiring masterful presidential negotiation and coalition-building skills—was close to a disaster. While not dead on arrival, Trump and his Republican colleagues faced a steep uphill climb.

How did they proceed? Leverage played a major role.

Golden Rule 2:
Maximize Your Leverage

Like the Republicans in 2009 and early 2010, the opposition Democrats united and mobilized many of the affected interest groups against Trump and the Republicans' efforts to repeal and replace Obamacare. And they did it effectively. This weakened Trump and the Republican leadership's leverage with the Republican holdouts and contributed substantially to the eventual demise of repeal and replace.

Even many Republicans and traditionally Republican interest groups opposed this effort.

What happened? Trump and his team—not even fully in place due to delays in getting congressional approval of his political appointees—faced an aggressive public-relations and coalition-building effort organized by the Democrats and their healthcare allies to defeat any repeal and replace plan.

It succeeded with the public, according to the *WSJ*'s *"Trump Calls Health Care 'So Complicated,' but Vows to Replace Law,"* noting "[a] spirited campaign by Democrats to preserve the law by warning that repealing it would be catastrophic has boosted support for it and led to raucous town-hall meetings held by members of Congress across the country. That has rattled some GOP lawmakers whose votes the party cannot afford to lose."[602]

Polls reflected this, striking at the core of Republicans' survivalist political interests.[603]

How did this weaken their leverage, especially as the Republicans determined early on they would get no votes from the Democrats? Assume you are a moderate Republican House member and face a "raucous town-hall meeting" where hundreds of your constituents confront you over their possible loss of health insurance.

Even though you know the vast majority are likely Democrats, you will certainly consider whether a vote to fulfill your promise to repeal and replace—your Plan A deal—is better than your promise to ensure your constituents maintain their health insurance—your Plan B/alternative to a deal (assume Trump's plan doesn't include provisions you *also* promised your constituents). In effect, you're caught between two promises, and you have a lot of angry constituents pushing for your Plan B saying they will not vote for you if you vote to repeal and replace.

As a result of these town-hall meetings, your Plan A just got worse relative to your Plan B. This weakened Trump's leverage with you.

What do you do? Hold out and push for a better Plan A.

But here's the rub for Trump and Ryan—the very conservative Republican members also don't like Trump and Ryan's Plan A. Why? It doesn't give them all they and their conservative constituents want. They call it Obamacare Lite. They hold out, too.

How can Trump and the Republican leaders change this leverage? With their own PR campaign. And Trump is a master of this, right?

Here's the problem. Ryan got blindsided by Republican opposition to his plan. He started late, and Trump wasn't ready to jump full bore into it. Trump had the bully pulpit, but he ineffectively used it. Plus, his approval rating was pretty low, further weakening his leverage with his fellow Republicans. The higher his approval rating, the greater Trump's potential impact on these congressmen's constituents.

So here, Trump and Ryan lost leverage and ceded the PR ground to the Democrats and other Republican opposition groups. Not effective.

Here's how Harvard's *Briefings* described their dilemma regarding leverage:

> To pass a bill in the House and move it on to the Senate, Ryan and Trump faced the daunting task of winning votes from two factions that disliked the bill for opposite reasons. Members of the conservative House Freedom Caucus wanted a more complete rollback of Obamacare. Meanwhile, some of the members of the more moderate Tuesday Group, many of whom were spooked by the angry constituents who had been

protesting the proposed repeal at town-hall meetings, felt the new bill needed greater consumer protections.

What tools of persuasion [leverage] did Ryan and Trump have available to win some votes? Because a 2011 ban on federal earmarks remains in effect in Congress, Ryan couldn't try to win over members with promises of pork-barrel spending in their districts. Throughout the negotiations, Trump hinted that he would work to keep "no" voters from being reelected in 2018, but in light of his low approval ratings, lawmakers seemed to shrug off these threats.[604]

Bottom line: Trump and Ryan had relatively weak leverage due to the Democrats and other opposition groups' grassroots efforts. And they didn't do much to change it.

Of course, Trump might have been able to get sufficient House Republican votes if he had built up public support for the bill's major provisions and built coalitions among the involved interest groups.

This could have led those Freedom Caucus members to believe their constituents would have been better off with the final bill and/or would have used this issue to vote against them in two years. This would have directly addressed what many believe to be a politician's most crucial interest—re-election.

But the bill, according to polling, only had a 17 percent public approval rating.[605] And almost every major interest group, from the conservative Koch brothers to doctors to every liberal group, opposed it, and many spent millions on ads trashing it.[606] No coalition-building by the Republicans here.

This didn't, however, stop Trump from making threats, a regular Trump business strategy, but they proved ineffective, given his weak leverage. Again, Harvard's *Briefings*:

> In mid-March, Trump entertained [Freedom Caucus leader Mark] Meadows at his private club in Florida. Back at the Capitol for a meeting the following Tuesday, March 21, the president told the Freedom Caucus that he expected them to support the bill as-is. Trump singled out Meadows, saying he would "come after" him if he voted no.
>
> The threat may have been a deal breaker for Meadows, whom some Freedom Caucus members perceived as already being too close to Trump. "Mark desperately wanted to get to yes,

and Trump made it impossible for him," one caucus member told *Politico*. "If he flipped after that he would look incredibly weak."[607]

Ineffective threat based on weak leverage.

The next day, Trump again threatened, this time after he conceded to one of their principal demands, when the Freedom Caucus leaders asked for more. According to Harvard's *Briefing*:

> ...eventually, Trump cut off the discussion. 'Forget about the little [stuff],' he said, as reported by *Politico* [referencing the substantive policy details on the negotiation table]. 'Let's focus on the big picture here.' Fretting about how the bill's defeat would affect his reelection chances in 2020, the president warned the attendees that this would be the only chance he'd give them to reform healthcare—and that their constituents would punish them if they didn't get the job done.[608]

As we now know, this was an empty threat as Trump and Ryan later brought healthcare reform up again. This also reflected Trump's effort to move the negotiation from policy—not his comfort zone—to leverage. He ended up losing credibility.

This was one of Trump's and Ryan's four significant negotiation mistakes, according to Harvard's *Briefings*.

> When preparing for multiparty talks on contentious topics, you would be wise to learn from Trump's and Ryan's mistakes:
>
> - **Look for early, easy wins.** When negotiating with new partners, try to build momentum and rapport by discussing issues in which disagreement is low before moving on to more contentious ones.
>
> - **Involve others from the start.** Instead of presenting fully formed plans, enlist interested constituents in the planning process to get their input and begin shaping a deal that everyone can agree on.
>
> - **Prepare, prepare, prepare**. Charm and flattery will get you only so far. Immerse yourself in the details of the issues at stake so that you can make informed tradeoffs and win over potential deal spoilers.
>
> - **Make sure your threats have teeth.** For a threat to be effective, it has to be motivating and you must be willing

> to follow through on it. When you're negotiating from
> a place of weakness, a threat could backfire.[609]

Trump's threats backfired. It should come as no surprise. Many of his business threats backfired over the years, too.

One final note on leverage in Trump's initial negotiation with the House. Public opinion on Obamacare and healthcare reform was rapidly changing during this time—and it was getting worse and worse for Republicans. This changed the Republicans' leverage. In fact, it partially drove the Republicans' timeline and their efforts to develop it behind closed doors.

How? They felt that developing repeal and replace in public with hearings—which Obama had done ten years earlier—would generate a great deal of public opposition. After all, *any* reform effort would invariably involve the painful taking away of constituents' Obamacare benefits. The Democrats and their allies would use this to generate opposition in all the Republican members' districts, weakening Republicans' leverage.

Plus, any plan developed in public would highlight the fissures and competing interests of the Republican factions. This might drive a further wedge between them, making any compromise even more challenging.

Trump and Ryan had weak leverage. Sometimes when you have weak leverage, you focus on independent standards that favor you. Trump the business negotiator understood this.

Here, that worked against Trump and Ryan.

Golden Rule 3:
Employ "Fair" Objective Criteria

One powerful independent standard predominates presidential and congressional budget negotiations—the non-partisan independent federal agency called the Congressional Budget Office (CBO). The CBO serves within the legislative branch and is widely recognized by economists across the political spectrum as providing accurate and nonpartisan analysis. And its director, Keith Hall, was a Republican appointed by the Republican Congressional leadership in 2015.

In other words, Democrats and Republicans alike rely on the CBO's analysis and conclusions concerning the budgetary impact of proposed legislation.

Unfortunately for Trump and Ryan, CBO's analysis of their healthcare reform proposal undermined their ability to get to yes.

How? Here is a list of Trump's promises/goals compared with the CBO's estimate of whether the Trump–Ryan healthcare reform bill would accomplish them. Each promise was popular—and each CBO estimate showed the bill falling far short. This provided fuel for the opposition and helped strengthen their leverage. These quotes come from the *WSJ*'s *"Where Donald Trump's Health-Care Promises Stand Now."*[610]

1. Trump: *"We're going to have insurance for everybody."*

   - CBO per the *WSJ*: "...the number of Americans without health insurance would grow by 24 million by 2026 under the House GOP's effort to change [Obamacare]."

2. Trump: *"There will be no cuts to Social Security, Medicare & Medicaid."*

   - CBO per the *WSJ*: "The CBO estimated the cost cuts to Medicaid would be $880 billion over 10 years."

3. Trump: *"It's going to be much better for the people at the bottom, people that don't have any money."*

   - CBO per the *WSJ*: "The CBO estimates that for a single individual with an income level of $26,000, premiums would increase."

4. Trump's Health and Human Services Secretary Tom Price: *"Nobody will be worse off financially."*

   - CBO per the *WSJ*: "The CBO estimates that premiums would increase before 2020, up to 20 percent higher than under [Obamacare]....But then it estimates that premiums would fall, to 10 percent lower than under the current law by 2026."

These CBO estimates fueled the oppositions' ability to publicly undermine the Trump-Ryan health care bill.

Of course, true to form and consistent with Competitive Strategies, Trump attempted to undermine the CBO's conclusions. How? By indicating The White House "strenuously disagreed" with the CBO's estimate of how many would become newly uninsured under their bill.[611]

In this negotiation, however, the CBO had such credibility—with House members and the public—that Trump's effort did not appear to have much impact.

Golden Rule 4:
Design an Offer-Concession Strategy

In ideal negotiations, your goals drive your offer-concession strategy and provide a principled basis for your moves and where you end. Here, however, Trump's goals were impossible to achieve, at least according to the CBO. And he didn't appear to have any firm principled basis for his positions or interests, other than to achieve a "win."

Further, neither he nor Ryan had dug into the details of their counterparts' interests sufficiently to find options that may satisfy them. Typical for Trump. And typical for Competitive Strategies.

Trump also had weak leverage with few prospects of strengthening it in a short period of time.

What did Trump and Ryan do—after their March 6 release of their "take-it-or-leave-it" document? According to Harvard's *Briefings*:

> With few carrots [to satisfy interests] and sticks [given their weak leverage], the leaders were left to tinker with the contents of the bill, writes Paul Kane in *The Washington Post*. But that didn't offer a clear path to victory, either. If they offered too many concessions to the right wing of the party, moderates would never sign on—and vice versa. "Every concession made to win conservatives...was destined to result in the loss of moderates," *Politico* concluded. As for trying to pick off a few Democrats, Trump and Ryan didn't see a point in even trying.[612]

Yet they still continually gave concessions to the conservative Freedom Caucus, even giving up essential health benefits near the end, and the Freedom Caucus members kept nibbling for more.

Trump and Ryan's offer-concession strategy—to the extent they even planned it—proved ineffective. *First*, believing that their initial "take-it-or-leave-it" offer would simply be accepted by sufficient House Republicans proved wildly inaccurate. By moving off it, though, they lost credibility.

Second, Trump's policy ignorance hampered his ability to substantively engage on these complex issues and to craft offers that might satisfy his counterparts' interests. Of course, presidents don't need to be detailed policy experts to negotiate great deals, and regularly delegate policy details to others, but it's crucial to be able to substantively engage in a back-and-forth discussion about significant issues. An inability to do so even at a high level will be detrimental to achieving negotiation success.

Here's an example. Near the end of the negotiations, Trump offered to eliminate "essential health benefits" like requiring insurance to cover pregnancy and doctor's visits. He felt this would bring House Freedom Caucus members on board.

But offering this without also eliminating the requirement to cover pre-existing conditions could have led to a collapse of the insurance markets. Expert House members knew this. So giving in on the benefits issue actually made it *less* appealing to some of these members, not more. And by doing this, he also lost the votes of some moderate House Republicans, who liked those provisions.

Third, Trump's untrustworthiness negatively impacted his ability to cut side deals—a staple of presidential negotiating that Trump did not have in his business toolbox. *Business Insider* senior editor and commentator and former founding correspondent for "The Upshot" section at *The New York Times* Josh Barro described this issue:

Trump is too untrustworthy to make credible side deals

Usually, a legislative negotiation isn't just about what's in a bill.

Often, a member of Congress agrees to vote for the president's pet piece of legislation, and the president promises to advance the member's favorite regulatory initiative, or to advocate another piece of legislation later, or to campaign for that member's reelection.

Trump might be making such promises. But because he has a decades-long reputation for reneging on his promises to counterparties, members are unlikely to trust Trump when he does so. This limits his negotiating toolbox; because Trump can't be trusted, his promises have to be made good in the bill text itself.

Trump's assurance that the bill's limitations—for example, its limited impact on insurance regulations under Obamacare— will be addressed through executive action and future legislation do not seem to be convincing enough of his party's own representatives to get this bill passed.

In a way, this is similar to the way Trump alienated the mainstream banks with his reputation for not repaying debts, forcing him to seek increasingly creative means of financing his businesses. Screwing your partner in one deal makes it harder to get the next deal done.[613]

Trump's lack of credibility and trustworthiness in business impacted his negotiation effectiveness over healthcare reform. Not surprising, given his business-negotiation history and the research on reputation, credibility, and trustworthiness impacting negotiation effectiveness.

Golden Rule 5:
Control the Agenda

Trump and Ryan pursued a secretly developed, high-risk, tension-filled, deadline-driven, "now or never" effort to control the agenda to get repeal and replace passed in the House. Why? Partly to get a deal done before their leverage further weakened. And partly it reflected Trump's typical deadline-driven Competitive Strategies self.

It also reflected a practical recognition of the extremely difficult nature of rounding up sufficient votes exclusively from a highly divided House Republican caucus and later an equally divided Senate Republican caucus. Here is how the *WSJ* described the strategy shortly before Trump and Ryan unveiled their substantive proposal:

> Republican leaders are betting that the only way for Congress to repeal [Obamacare] is to set a bill in motion and gamble that fellow GOP lawmakers won't dare to block it.
>
> Party leaders are poised to act on the strategy as early as this week, after it has become obvious they can't craft a proposal that will carry an easy majority in either chamber....
>
> Republican leaders pursuing the "now or never" approach see it as their best chance to break through irreconcilable demands by Republican centrists and conservatives over issues ranging from tax credits to the future of Medicaid....
>
> Republicans can afford to lose no more than two GOP votes in the Senate and 22 in the House, assuming they get no support from Democrats. That means any GOP faction could torpedo

the repeal effort by withholding support—and members of each have threatened as much.

Advocates of the strategy hope that knife's-edge math will be an asset rather than a liability. They are betting different groups of Republican lawmakers can be pacified with a handful of concessions, then will swallow hard and vote for a longstanding repeal pledge, first in the House, then in the Senate.[614]

This agenda had its upside. But it also had a significant downside, as described in the Harvard *Briefings* earlier relating to Trump and Ryan's mistakes: a) no early easy wins and momentum among interested parties, and b) freezing out crucial stakeholders from the start, preventing them from having an important process role. This was especially crucial for those who see value in working together in a bipartisan fashion to develop a solution impacting almost 20 percent of the U.S. economy.

Trump also made some of the same meeting-related agenda mistakes he made in the Mexico-wall–funding negotiation. One day before the scheduled House vote, Trump invited the Freedom Caucus members to the White House. Here's what happened, according to Harvard's *Briefings*:

> With the vote on the AHCA just one day away, Meadows joined other caucus members at the White House expecting to talk policy with the president. To their dismay, they instead found themselves stuck in a "pep rally" led by Vice President Mike Pence and top Trump aides, according to *Politico*. The message? "Take one for the team." After White House chief strategist Steve Bannon [another top White House aide inexperienced in these types of presidential negotiations] repeated the phrase, one congressman reportedly snapped at him not to talk to them like children. An awkward silence followed.[615]

Trump's counterparts felt blindsided—like the Mexican officials meeting in the White House just prior to the scheduled Trump–Nieto summit. At the least, the Trump team poorly managed their expectations for this negotiation.

Of course, this could have been planned. After all, Trump invited the businessman selling his company to meet at Trump Tower to wrap up the negotiation with him personally. But then, when that businessman arrived, he spent most of his time negotiating with Trump's underlings.

Finally, Trump and Ryan—members of the same team with the same interests—did not see eye to eye on crucial agenda-related items. And their disagreements spilled over publicly, harming their future ability to work together to accomplish their shared goals. What happened?

First, on the day of the originally scheduled vote on the bill, Ryan postponed it for a day as he did not have the votes to pass it. But later that same day, "reporters caught Trump off guard with the news that Ryan had postponed the vote until the following day."[616]

Whether Ryan planned this or not, Trump must have been embarrassed to be out of the loop with his own partner.

And, *second*, as described by Harvard's *Briefings*:

> With the bill seemingly headed toward failure, the major players switched into damage-control mode. Ryan's allies began referring to Trump as "the Closer." Trump aides told the *[New York] Times* that the president regretted going along with Ryan's idea of putting health-care overhaul before tax reform.
>
> That night, Trump instructed House Republicans to hold a vote…even if they knew it would fail, apparently aiming to publicly identify and shame those who voted to leave [Obamacare] in place. Trump again warned that he would not try to negotiate an Obamacare repeal again. That night, the entire House Republican Conference convened and tried in vain to resolve their disagreements.
>
> The next day, after concluding that he didn't have enough votes, Ryan visited the White House and convinced Trump that pulling the bill was their best option. In a contrite public statement, Ryan said that Obamacare would remain "the law of the land."[617]

These agenda-related issues should not be surprising. In business Trump rarely partnered in his negotiations. Remember his Harrah's partnership. And he demonstrated a repeated lack of ability to work and partner with others. Blaming and undermining his partners—as he sought to do here with Ryan—caused these problems.

These actions tend to be particularly counterproductive in presidential negotiations. Trump will need the House Republican leader to get any future legislation passed.

Trump's and Ryan's false deadlines and calling this their last effort to repeal Obamacare also came back to haunt them. Fortunately for them, they passed it on their second try despite their lost credibility.

Trump and the House Republicans' Successful Strategies in Round #2

What did Trump and Ryan do differently that led to its passage in round two?

According to Gerald Seib in the *WSJ*'s *"The Balance Sheet for Republicans after Big Health Care Vote,"* Trump and Ryan did the following—which highlights both effective strategies they had *not* used in round one and ineffective strategies they *continued* to use.

> **President Donald Trump** showed he'll get down in the legislative trenches for his party. Mr. Trump at first seemed indifferent to the health debate roiling his party but **ultimately did the grinding presidential work of pulling lawmakers along one by one.** Some doubted he had the interest or patience to do that. He does, if only because he likes to win....

> [On the other hand], **lawmakers don't really fear Mr. Trump. The president tried to both coerce and cajole House Republicans into voting for the pending legislation, implying at various points that he would either go after them or go around them by working with Democrats.** Neither approach seemed sufficiently alarming to move some fellow Republicans.

> **House Speaker Paul Ryan** and House Republicans succeeded only after a giant initial failure followed by weeks of fits, starts and defections from conservatives and moderates in turn. To get across the finish line, the Republican majority violated some of the very principles it pledged to follow in running Congress: The vote happened so quickly after a final compromise was negotiated that there wasn't time to study the bill or for the congressional accounting arm [CBO] to estimate its costs and impact. So it was ugly....

> Democrats engaged in some whatever-it-takes maneuvering of their own to pass Obamacare in the first place, so perhaps it's no surprise Republicans did the same to unwind it. [Emphasis added.][618]

The New York Times also described what happened, focusing on separate negotiation strategies.

> By leaning on members to vote for a bill that many fear will leave millions of people unable to afford health care, Mr. Ryan has exposed moderate Republicans to withering political attacks. This is especially true in the roughly two dozen districts represented by Republicans where Hillary Clinton prevailed over Mr. Trump in November, but it is also the case in places where [Obamacare's] popularity has been increasing....
>
> In reshaping the bill, **Mr. Ryan worked with an attentive White House,** edging out the committee chairmen who helped write the original measure and turning to conservative lawmakers, moving the bill significantly to the right in the process. It also empowered conservatives who many Republican leaders had hoped to marginalize in an era of Mr. Trump....
>
> To get his victory, Mr. Ryan cast aside many promises he made when he became speaker about transparency and moving bills through committees and a process. Instead, he threw together bills without hearings, made back-room side deals to buy off individual lawmakers, and held votes on measures before the [CBO] could put a price tag on them.
>
> The process alienated committee chairmen, whose work took a back seat to the efforts of the elusive Chairman of the House Freedom Caucus, Representative Mark Meadows, Republican of North Carolina, and it chipped away at their authority. **Mr. Meadows and his fellow conservatives, who have toiled for years as philosophical bomb throwers in the legislative process, got the attention of the White House, which worked hard to meet their needs and pressure moderates to come along.**[619]

What exactly happened negotiation-wise? Six significant elements.

1. Trump–Ryan Moved Away from Extreme Competitive Strategies
2. Trump–Ryan Engaged in Coalition-Building
3. Leverage Remained Weak
4. The CBO Got Undermined
5. One-on-One Flexible Moves

6.   Ryan Controlled the Timing and Deadlines

Let's see how each impacted the result, analyzing them within my Five Golden Rules structure.

Golden Rule 1:
Information Is Power—So Get It!

---

1. Trump–Ryan Moved Away from Extreme Competitive Strategies

Trump jumped into these negotiations and fully committed himself to their success. Where he previously held back, this time he went in hook, line, and sinker. Ryan also went to the mat. His reputation as a speaker who could get something substantial done was at risk.

The result? They did anything and everything they could to pass a bill.

What did they do? Trump did more one-on-one negotiating. This meant he likely dug more into the details of the members' various interests. It's tough to engage like this without learning some details. It appears his interest in "winning" overcame his disinterest in learning the details.

Ryan also did more individual negotiating, and *made back-room side deals to buy off individual lawmakers.* You can't do this if you don't learn their interests and needs.

Overall, it appears both Trump and Ryan moved away from the extreme Competitive Strategies, the hallmark of Trump's business negotiations. And instead they moved toward the center of this strategic spectrum, a more effective strategy in presidential negotiations.

In other words, in the first round they used extreme Competitive Strategies, like:

- holding their cards close to their vests (developing their plan in secret) and paying less attention to all their counterparts' interests (largely ignoring the Freedom Caucus),

- hitting hard on leverage (with explicit and implicit threats),

- trying to undermine standards like the CBO,

- using extremely aggressive offer-concession strategies (take-it-or-leave-it), and

- overtly controlling the agenda (setting short, inflexible high-stress–inducing deadlines).

In round two, they used more Problem-Solving-type Strategies (but still pretty Competitive), like:

- sharing more information about their needs and interests (developing the bill in talks with the Freedom Caucus and other members—not just the committee chairs and leadership), and finding out their members' interests, coalition-building step-by-step;

- less focus on leverage and threats (although still some),

- delegitimizing the CBO (voting before it could complete its analysis),

- less-aggressive offer-concession strategies (more back-and-forth with individual members meant to satisfy their interests), and

- still controlling the agenda (but no more short, inflexible high-stress deadlines).

2. Trump–Ryan Engaged in Coalition-Building

Perhaps the most critical shift occurred when Ryan moved from secretly creating a take-it-or-leave-it proposal to jointly working with individual members to find options that may satisfy their mutual interests. Coalition-building.

And the first coalition Trump and Ryan built by listening to their concerns and interests? The Freedom Caucus. Interestingly, the Freedom Caucus effectively forced Trump and Ryan in round one to bring them to the table in round two. They kept holding out for more—perhaps because of the Trump threats—knowing Trump and Ryan needed them more than they needed Trump and Ryan. (That's strong leverage.)

Ironically, Ryan thus violated numerous commitments he had made as incoming speaker to a more transparent, committee-driven process. Ryan desperately needed a bill, so he paid this cost. It also cost him relationship-wise with those committee chairs, as he bypassed them to make these deals.

Short-term, Ryan probably needed to do this to get a win. Long-term, however, this strategy could have bitten him. His credibility took another hit, given his backtracking on his promises of an open, transparent committee-driven process. And his fast-tracking effort delegitimized the result in some members' eyes, potentially causing problems if a revised bill passed the Senate and returned for final passage.

Trump and Ryan also moved far right politically to build the coalition with the Freedom Caucus. And they creatively explored options to satisfy their interests *that had not been explored previously*.

They thus expanded their coalition in unexpected ways. According to the *WSJ*'s *"House GOP Health Insurance Plan Gains New Life,"* "conservatives applauded the changes [suggested by some moderates], saying they would lower premium costs by reducing regulations on insurers. The Club for Growth, Freedom Partners and Heritage Action, three conservative groups which had initially drummed up right-wing resistance to the bill, dropped their opposition."[620]

After Trump and Ryan got the Freedom Caucus on board, a moderate Tuesday Group leader flexed his muscles. But Trump and Ryan then satisfied *his* interests, too, adding the final members needed to their coalition.

Importantly, they fixed in round two the main negotiation issues Harvard's *Briefings* had called mistakes, as they:

- Built momentum early on,
- Involved the Freedom Caucus and others from the start, and
- Prepared themselves on the details so they could make informed tradeoffs.

While these adjustments solved their short-term issues, long-term they still had problems. While some moderates joined the coalition, their leverage remained weak. The bill's moderate supporters would still face angry constituents.

Their move to the right would also cause significant challenges in the Senate.

Golden Rule 2:
Maximize Your Leverage

---

3. Leverage Remained Weak

Why did their leverage remain weak in round two? As the *WSJ* reported one week before their new vote in *"New Plan, Same Hurdle in GOP's Quest to Gut Obamacare"*:

> Fifty-one percent of Americans now say [Obamacare] is either working well or needs minor modifications, according to an

April *NBC News/WSJ* poll. Those figures were considerably lower before the law appeared to be in jeopardy.

[Obamacare] has become "part of the daily fabric of people's lives," said Rep. Tom Rooney (R. Fla.), who nonetheless said the law wasn't sustainable. "A lot of people are very afraid out there of losing coverage, getting sick and not being able to afford to try to get better."

Mr. Rooney is leaning toward supporting the current GOP bill. "The problem is we haven't done a good job of explaining why our plan's better," he said.[621]

Trump and Ryan—like Obama before them—continued to fail to effectively make the public case for their solution.

But Trump did dial back his public threats against House members, and that gave them better cover to support his bill. As Seim in the *WSJ* noted earlier, House members didn't fear his threats. Counterproductive, just like often occurred in his business career.

The Democrats, however, were sitting pretty, politically. Their 2018 midterm elections were looking better and better.

Golden Rule 3:
Employ "Fair" Objective Criteria

---

4. The CBO Got Undermined

What happened to the CBO? Ryan threw it under the bus and set the bill for a vote before the CBO could complete its analysis. In other words, the House voted on a bill that would transform a huge element of the U.S. economy *without an official estimate of how it would impact healthcare's cost and coverage.*

Why? Ryan knew the CBO estimates would undermine the bill's support.

Short-term—this move helped them get a "win." Long-term—it potentially gave Democrats an important issue in the 2018 midterms.

Golden Rule 4:
Design an Offer-Concession Strategy

---

5. One-on-One Flexible Moves

Trump and Ryan engaged in hand-to-hand negotiation combat in round two—no broad-brush take-it-or-leave-it moves. Smart. More traditional back-and-forth dynamics in a presidential and congressional negotiation environment. More Problem-Solving Strategies.

Golden Rule 5:
Control the Agenda

---

6. Ryan Controlled the Timing and Deadlines

Where impatience ruled the day in round one, patience took over in round two. They learned their lesson.

Of course, it wasn't perfect. And the Trump–Ryan relationship continued to have rocky moments. As reported in the *WSJ*'s *"Trump Pushing for Vote on Health Bill but Stumbling Blocks Remain"*:

> The health-care bill has taken on a significance beyond the specific policies involved, as a symbol for whether Mr. Trump's team has learned how to work with Congress. The past two weeks suggest relations still aren't smooth.

> Some Republican aides have complained they are being set up to fail after members of Mr. Trump's team had previously predicted a House vote was going to take place last Wednesday.

> At the time of the suggestion, members of Congress were scattered across the country and the world for a recess, making it impossible for leaders to accurately count votes.[622]

Not on the same page. Again. More coordinated? Yes. But conflict amongst the team still.

They got the bill passed, 217–213. A big "win" for Trump and Ryan. More effective negotiations for each, too. They had learned significant lessons.

Next step? The Senate. Did Trump and Majority Leader McConnell apply these lessons learned? No.

The Senate Votes Down Repeal and Replace

Round three. The Senate. How do they start? The same way the House did—with a secret process. And with President Trump taking a hands-off approach. Trump starts in with his threats. Again. And finally, Trump doesn't do his homework, throws Ryan and the House under the bus, undermining his partners, and faced a reputation problem based on having previously demeaned a crucial partner. Again. These six mistakes led to the Senate failure.

1. The Senate's Secret Process

Here's how Harvard's *Briefings* described the original Senate secret approach.

> Senate Republicans repeated many of the House's mistakes when they tried and failed to pass their own version of the bill in July:
>
> - **A secretive process.** House Speaker Paul Ryan and his staff drafted [their bill] in secret, then released it on March 6 as a fait accompli. Similarly, after the bill moved to the Senate, Majority Leader Mitch McConnell invited a small group of Republican senators—all of them white men—to work on the redrafting, which they did in utmost secrecy.[623]

A problem? Yes. Here's how *The New York Times* described this in *"5 Takeaways from the Failed Senate Effort to Repeal Obamacare"*:

> Republicans grumbled about the secretive manner in which the majority leader, Senator Mitch McConnell of Kentucky, put together his repeal bill. There were no public hearings or formal bill-drafting sessions, and Republicans used a fast-track procedure meant for budget matters as they tried to enact complex health policy and avoid a filibuster.
>
> Mr. McCain was an outspoken critic. In June, asked about his comfort level with the process, he cut off a reporter. "None," he said.
>
> The final hours of the repeal effort seemed worse than ever: Republican leaders unveiled their bill and then expected their members to vote for it hours later, and in the middle of the night, no less.[624]

Negotiation Mistake Number One. This was McConnell's mistake, not Trump's. Of course, President Trump could have negotiated to help develop the bill—James Madison would never have let a crucial drafting effort take place in a negotiation without his active participation.

2. Trump's Hands-Off Strategy

Instead of actively participating, what did Trump do for the entire Senate effort? The *WSJ* in *"Trump Implores GOP Senators to Come Together Over Troubled Health Bill,"* describes his role up until the last week:

> ...before this week, the president had been less active in the negotiations in the Senate than he was in helping pass health-care legislation in the House.
>
> The question is whether his late intervention can turn the tide. Some Republicans have been quietly skeptical of the president's arms-length approach to Senate negotiations, though others have said he has been smart to hold back.[625]

Incredibly, Trump not only stayed away—the Senators kept him and his team away. *Not the mark of an effective negotiator.* Here is how the *WSJ* described a meeting involving Trump's Chief of Staff Reince Priebus.

> About 20 GOP senators huddled for more than two hours Wednesday night.... White House Chief of Staff Reince Priebus came to the meeting but was asked to stay in a room separate from the one where the senators held their discussion because some lawmakers wanted to speak privately, an aide said. 'We're at our best when we're amongst ourselves,' said Sen. John Kennedy (R., LA).[626]

Would the Senate have ever frozen out President Johnson's Chief of Staff from any meeting, much less one involving a critical bill on his legislative agenda?

Negotiation Mistake Number Two: A Hands-Off Approach. Had Trump learned from his House mistakes *and* the mistakes he made in the Mexican-wall–funding negotiation, he could have played a productive role here. He didn't. The Senate Republicans were thus left with no presidential role in most of these negotiations. That's a gaping problem as presidents can bring significant power to the negotiation table.

3. Trump's Threats Start Again

But perhaps this was smart. After all, what did Trump start doing that last week? Threats. And Republicans still had relatively weak leverage in terms of public opinion. Here's how the *WSJ* described Trump's actions: "'Any senator who votes against starting debate is really telling America that you're fine with Obamacare,' Mr. Trump said before a lunch with the senators Wednesday. He gestured at one wavering GOP lawmaker, Dean Heller of Nevada, saying, 'He wants to remain a senator, doesn't he?' and warned lawmakers not to leave town in August without a deal."[627]

Negotiation Mistake Number Three: More Trump threats. And it characterized his approach as his threats got more aggressive near the end. Trump apparently did not learn from his House mistake. Harvard's *Briefings*, in *"In Senate health care defeat, it's déjà vu all over again"* noted this:

- **Unintimidating threats.** President Donald Trump reportedly threatened certain House members that he'd fight their reelection efforts if they didn't vote for [their health care bill the first time around]. Most seemed unfazed by the threat. In a similar manner, Interior Secretary Ryan Zinke reportedly warned Alaska senator Lisa Murkowski that the Trump administration would not support key projects in her state if she voted against the bill. Murkowski, who oversees the Interior Department's funding in the Senate, voted against it anyway.[628]

Trump also went after Murkowski on Twitter after she voted against starting debate on the measure. But he needed her vote later. Big mistake. She later voted against the final bill—one of three Republicans who killed it.

4. Trump Failed to Do His Homework

Trump also failed to learn the details of health policy here, putting into question whether he really learned much in the House effort. As *The New York Times* noted, "In public, [Trump] did not show much fluency in the basics of health policy, let alone the ability to persuade Republicans on complicated issues like the growth rate of Medicaid payments. And he did himself no favors by changing his demands about exactly what he wanted the Senate to do."[629]

This was confirmed in another *New York Times* article entitled *"On Senate Health Bill, Trump Falters in the Closer's Role"*:

> A [Republican] senator who supports the bill left the meeting at the White House with a sense that the president did not have a grasp of the basic elements of the Senate plan—and seemed especially confused when a moderate Republican complained that opponents of the bill would cast it as a massive tax break for the wealthy, according to an aide who received a detailed readout of the exchange....

> [And when] asked by reporters clustered on the blacktop outside the West Wing if Mr. Trump had command of the details of the negotiations [after a meeting with the President and all 52 Republican Senators], Mr. McConnell ignored the question and smiled blandly.[630]

Negotiation Mistake Number Four: Trump didn't do his homework. Again.

5. Trump Throws Ryan and the House Under the Bus— Undermining His Effort in the Senate

Perhaps it shouldn't be a surprise that the Senators, wary of Trump's negotiation skills despite his House effort and unaffected by his threats, froze him out. After all, shortly after the House successfully voted their bill out and the Senate started developing its own plan, Trump threw Ryan and his House partners under the bus.

According to *Fox News* in *"Trump tells senators House health care bill is 'mean,' sources say"* (and many other media outlets also reported this):

> President Trump told Republican senators Tuesday that the bill passed by the House to repeal and replace ObamaCare is "mean" and "harsh," multiple GOP and Senate sources have told *Fox News*. The sources added that Trump told the group of 15 Republicans that they should build a "more generous" and "more kind" version of the American Health Care Act.

> Trump's remarks, made during a White House lunch, were a surprising critique of the House measure whose passage he lobbied for and praised. At a Rose Garden ceremony minutes after the bill's narrow House passage last month, Trump called it "a great plan."[631]

Negotiation Mistake Number Five.

6. Trump's Name-Calling Comes Back to Haunt Him

One final Trump mistake here—one that predates this specific negotiation and one that illustrates that reputation and past tactics matter.

On July 17, 2015, Trump got into a personal feud with Sen. John McCain, who threw the first salvo by saying Trump had "fired up the crazies," the "very extreme element within our Republican Party."[632]

Trump, who famously likes to counterpunch, then called McCain a "loser" for failing to win the White House in 2008. He then questioned McCain's credentials as a war hero. Trump said of McCain, who had been imprisoned and tortured for five years during the Vietnam War, "He was a war hero because he was captured. I like people who weren't captured."[633]

Negotiation Mistake Number Six: Name-calling and demeaning potential partners and true war heroes. Counterproductive.

Did Trump's name-calling and demeaning comments impact McCain as he considered joining his two Republican colleagues in killing Trump's signature domestic effort? He would deny it. But if you're on the fence on an issue, and one choice involves going against someone who called you a "loser," personally attacked you on a core patriotism issue, and whom you don't respect, will it impact your decision, perhaps just a little? Intangibles like this make a difference, if only subconsciously.

McCain killed Trump's repeal and replace due to process problems. As he said, in former Reagan White House speechwriter Peggy Noonan's *WSJ* column, *Trump, ObamaCare and the Art of the Fail*:

> ...one of the major problems with Obamacare was that it was written on a strict party-line basis and driven through Congress without a single Republican vote. As this law continues to crumble in Arizona and states across the country, we must not repeat the original mistakes that led to Obamacare's failure. [Congress must return to regular order, hold hearings, work across party lines,] and heed the recommendations of our nation's governors.[634]

The negotiation process matters.

CONCLUSION

Donald Trump's former campaign manager Corey Lewandowski called him *"the greatest dealmaker our country's ever seen."*

True? No.

How good is he? He negotiated some great business deals. The Commodore Hotel redevelopment. Trump Tower. Mar-a-Lago. The St. Regis Hotel. The Harrah's partnership. His Boeing 727. His workout negotiations with the banks. 40 Wall Street.

But he also negotiated some pretty bad business deals. The USFL Generals and the NFL/Pete Rozelle negotiation. The Eastern Airlines/Trump Shuttle purchase. *The Trump Princess*. The Plaza Hotel. Television City/NBC. 100 Central Park South Tenants.

He also lost almost all his assets in 1990, when his failed negotiations came back to haunt him and resulted in multiple corporate bankruptcies. He even came within a whisker of personal bankruptcy, at one point owing $3.2 billion and having personally guaranteed $833 million of his debt. He was then underwater by around $300 million.

Despite this, he came back to build a very valuable international brand. How valuable? We don't know. But it's worth hundreds of millions and potentially a lot more.

How did he do this? And how much of his financial successes and failures can we attribute to his negotiation abilities?

His detractors would suggest he started with a big inheritance and would be nowhere without his family's bailout 20-plus years ago. They could point, with some legitimacy, to what he could have earned had he simply put his entire starting fortune in the stock market in 1982—the first year he made the Fortune 400 list of wealthiest U.S. individuals. Had he put his $100 million in the Standard & Poor's Market Index at that time, it would be worth, assuming reinvested dividends, over $5 billion at the end of 2017.[635] This would have required zero negotiation skills—good or bad. This should be the baseline on which we should evaluate his true negotiation abilities, they would suggest.

His supporters would disagree. Strenuously. They would point to his great deals and suggest they didn't just happen—he *made* them happen. Regarding his bad deals, they would note that even the best negotiators have bad days and the ups and downs of the economy, including the gaming economy, drove his business failures. They would also point to his current assets and business success and international brand as proof positive of his tremendous negotiation skills.

What is the *reality* of his deals?

First, Trump has consistently used the same negotiation strategies and tactics for nearly 50 years. Of course, there's been some variation. But very little, overall. Specifically, what has he done? Trump's Top Ten Business Negotiation Strategies include:

- Bringing to the table an instinctive win–lose mindset
- Setting extremely aggressive goals and passionately expecting to succeed
- Using over-the-top exaggeration
- Offering carrots to satisfy his counterparts' interests
- Bluffing or walking when "enough is enough"
- Threatening a lot
- Business bullying
- Identifying aggressive standards when they help
- Making outrageous demands and moves
- Overtly controlling the agenda with aggressive tactics

Some of these strategies and tactics have worked. Others have failed. But he *believes* all of these worked. Otherwise he wouldn't keep using them.

Second, he has *not* exhibited personal skills associated with highly effective negotiators like Nelson Mandela and others. While he has relatively high assertiveness skills and moderate creativity, his empathy is super low. On social intuition, above average. Not the skills you would associate with a great negotiator. Overall, below average.

Third, he has repeatedly failed to demonstrate even a minimum level of ethics in his negotiations. Specifically, he has *consistently* used the following highly unethical negotiation strategies and tactics:

- Lying and material misrepresentations
- Business bullying
- Personal and business threats, especially empty threats and bluffs

- Offering bribe-like personal financial benefits to his counterparts
- Intentionally hiding the ball with misleading statements and actions
- Slipping in significant changes *after* the deal's done (nibbling)
- Name-calling and personally demeaning his counterparts
- Excessive puffery
- Super-short, *false* deadlines
- Almost unbelievable scope and breadth of litigation—"where's there's smoke, there's fire"

These tactics proved toxic to his business negotiation effectiveness. In fact, it's impossible to calculate the true negative impact of these strategies. Why? Because he has never even been presented with deals that—absent his use of these tactics—he could have done. Just ask Steve Ifshin, the New York City real-estate broker.

In fact, once he developed a reputation in the business community for the use of these tactics, and many of these were widely reported, it substantially limited his negotiation effectiveness.

It's no coincidence that his most effective negotiations largely took place early in his career, before he became associated with these unethical tactics. And even then, his negotiation effectiveness was largely limited to either a) one-shot, zero-sum negotiations involving no future relationship, few issues and dominated by leverage (like buying, selling or developing commercial or residential real estate), or b) other negotiations that later blew up due to his using these tactics (the Harrah's partnership and then later the Television City/NBC lost opportunity).

But what about his licensing and other business deals since he became a television star on *The Apprentice*? He's made a ton of money since, right?

Right. But his increased wealth has not largely come from his negotiation skills. Instead, his counterparts bought into the power of his celebrity and branding and believed that Donald Trump the businessman was the highly successful business titan he played on TV.

Trump is a master promoter. *The Apprentice* gave him and his business the perfect promotional platform. He smartly and profitably took advantage of this. Even with this platform, his negotiations only involved the licensing of his name and brand and his participation in promotions. Few, if any, active partnerships.

The reality, of course, was different than what he portrayed on TV.

We have now seen this play out in his first year as president. Presidential negotiations require vastly different types of negotiation skills and strategies than in Trump's business negotiations. Why? Because they occur in vastly different circumstances. Presidential negotiations involve situations with:

- Future working relationships with the same counterparts again and again
- Long-term relationships involving multiple unrelated negotiations
- Great numbers of issues and interests on the table
- Many parties at the table and complex coalition-building
- Negotiating on *two* levels: behind the table and across the table
- A premium for substantive knowledge of the issues
- Dominant non-zero-sum issues and interests
- Complex and interconnected issues and interests
- Massive unknowns
- Diverse cultural and political backgrounds of counterparts

Despite these differences, President Trump so far has negotiated the same way he negotiated in business—with extreme Competitive Strategies. In fact, he perfectly illustrated this in two of his major negotiations in year one: the border-wall–funding negotiation and the healthcare negotiation.

Since President Trump failed in each, will he learn?

Doubtful. He has not yet taken any responsibility for these failed negotiations despite his significant personal involvement in each. Instead, he has publicly blamed his Republican partners—the leadership *and* the rank-and-file—and the Democrats.

Donald Trump wrote in *Crippled America: How to Make America Great Again* that *"A great leader has to be savvy at negotiations so we don't drown every bill in pork-barrel bridges to nowhere. I know how to stand my ground—but I also know that Republicans and Democrats need to find common ground to stand on as well."*[636]

With one exception, Trump has not sought that common ground—yet.

Where will Donald Trump's negotiations lead us and the world? Will he find the common ground he seeks between Republicans and Democrats? How about finding common ground with our traditional allies and adversaries?

Analyzing and understanding Trump's negotiation history through the lens of the negotiation research has given us some clues. But they are only clues. We don't know what the future will hold.

In the end, history will judge Donald J. Trump's negotiation effectiveness as president.

*That will be the final evaluation of the **real** Trump deal.*

END NOTES

PART 1
CHAPTER 1

1 *Lewandowski quote:* Fox News Insider, quoting "Fox & Friends Weekend," April 22, 2017.

2 *in the genes:* Donald Trump with Tony Schwartz, *Trump: The Art of the Deal* (New York: Ballantine Books, 1987), 45.

3 Roger Fisher and William Ury, Getting to Yes: Negotiating Agreement without Giving In (Simon & Schuster, 1981).

4 *denigrating your competition:* Donald Trump with Tony Schwartz, Trump: The Art of the Deal (New York: Ballantine Books, 1987), 108.

5 *"Deals are my art form":* Donald Trump, Twitter account, December 29, 2014, 8:39 am; Art of the Deal (1987), 1.

6 *"Some people have an ability to negotiate":* Lois Romano, "Donald Trump, Holding All the Cards, The Tower! The Team! The Money! The Future! *The Washington Post,* November 15, 1984; Michael Kranish and Marc Fisher, *Trump Revealed, The Definitive Biography of the 45th President* (Scribner, 2016), 276.

7 *The Apprentice negotiation:* Donald Trump interview with Marc Fisher, December 2015, in *Trump Revealed* (2016), 211–12.

8 *"you have an instinct and you go with it":* Maggie Haberman, "Donald Trump Unfiltered, From His New York Times Interviews," *New York Times,* July 20, 2015.

9 *Bally's takeover effort and Lee quote:* Wayne Barrett, *Trump: The Greatest Show on Earth* (Regan Arts, 1992), 389–90.

10 *"It would take an hour and a half to learn everything there is to learn about missiles":* Trump Revealed (2016), 276, *citing* Lois Romano, "Donald Trump, Holding All the Cards, The Tower! The Team! The Money! The Future! *The Washington Post,* November 15, 1984.

11 *Preparation:* Robert Mnookin, *Bargaining with the Devil: When to Negotiate, When to Fight* (Simon & Schuster, 2010), 203.

12 *Preparation:* Martin E. Latz, *Gain the Edge! Negotiating to Get What You Want* (St. Martin's Press, 2004), 5–6.

13 *Trump's preparation:* George H. Ross, *Trump-Style Negotiation: Powerful Strategies and Tactics for Mastering Every Deal* (John Wiley & Sons, 2006), 60.

14 *Penn Central deal: The Greatest Show* (1992), 90.

15 *Trump not being detailed in mid- to late 1980s: The Greatest Show* (1992), 429.

16 *Quote on delegating: Trump-Style Negotiation* (2006), 47.

17 *Preparation:* Roy Lewicki, David Saunders, and Bruce Barry, *Negotiation* (McGraw Hill, 7th Ed., 2015), 593.

18 *"start winning again":* Rebecca Shabad, "Donald Trump goes on epic rant about winning," *CBS News,* June 18, 2016.

19 *"winning temperament":* Katie Zezima, "Trump: My strongest asset 'is my temperament,'" *The Washington Post,* September 27, 2016.

20 *"not big on compromise": Life,* Vol. 12 (January 1989), iii.

21 *"We [the U.S.] don't win anymore":* Rebecca Shabad, "Donald Trump goes on epic rant about winning," *CBS News,* June 18, 2016.

22 *"I always win":* Timothy L. O'Brien, *TrumpNation: The Art of Being the Donald* (Grand Central Publishing, 2005), 4; *quoting* Interview, December 20, 2004.

23 *"we're going to win at everything":* Paul Bedard, "Trump: 'Gonna win so much people will say we can't take it anymore,'" *Washington Examiner,* May 20, 2016.

24 *"my life has been about winning":* Matthew Boyle, "Donald Trump Shames the Doubters: My Life Has Been about Winning," *Breitbart News,* January 11, 2016.

25 *Merriam-Webster definition of "win":* www.merriam-webster.com.

26 *"Donald's competitive drive": Trump Revealed* (2016), 40.

27 *Dobias:* Michael D'Antonio, *The Truth about Trump* (St. Martin's Griffin, 2016), 43.

28 *Dobias:* Michael D'Antonio, *The Truth about Trump* (St. Martin's Griffin, 2016), 43.

29 *Formative experiences:* Michael D'Antonio, *The Truth about Trump* (2016), 47.

30 *Sports always held a special place: Trump Revealed* (2016), 175.

31 *High-profile NFL negotiations: Trump Revealed* (2016), 173; *The Greatest Show* (1992), 331.

32 *"I hire a general manager to help run a billion-dollar business":* Ira Berkow, "Trump Building the Generals in His Own Style," *New York Times,* January 1, 1984; *Trump Revealed* (2016), 176.

33 *USFL policy: The Greatest Show* (1992), 331; David Cay Johnston, *The Making of Donald Trump* (2016), 52.

34 *Taube and Tanenbaum quotes: The Greatest Show* (1992), 331.

35 *Devastating for USFL as a whole: The Greatest Show* (1992), 331.

36 *Exclusive right to Taylor: The Greatest Show* (1992), 332.

37 *Flutie salary cap and USFL rules: The Making of Donald Trump* (2016), 53.

38 *Overspent comment: Trump Revealed* (2016), 180, *quoting* Jim Byrne, *The $1 League: Rise and Fall of the United States Football League* (Prentice Hall Press, 1986), 293.

39 *Trump goals to get into the NFL: The Greatest Show* (1992), 328.

40 *Not going to be a failure: Trump Revealed* (2016), 174.

41 *Bassett letter to Trump: Trump Revealed* (2016), 179, *quoting* Matt Bonesteel, "Donald Trump Was Such a USFL Bully That a Fellow Owner Threatened to Punch Him, *The Washington Post,* March 3, 2016.

42 *McKinsey recommendation: Trump Revealed* (2016), 179 (*citing* McKinsey & Company report, USFL internal documents);

43 *End of USFL and McKinsey study: Trump Revealed* (2016), 179 (*citing* McKinsey & Company report, USFL internal documents); *The Greatest Show* (1992), 337.

44 *Rozelle–Trump meeting: The Greatest Show* (1992), 335; *Trump Revealed* (2016), 184–5, *citing* Pete Rozelle testimony, *USFL v. NFL* court records.

45 *Rozelle–Trump testimony: The Greatest Show* (1992), 335; *Trump Revealed* (2016), 184–5, *citing* Pete Rozelle testimony, *USFL v. NFL* court records.

46 *Sued 3500 times: Making of Donald Trump* (2016), 22; *more than 4,000 times:* "Donald Trump: Three Decades, 4,095 lawsuits," *USA Today,* June 9, 2016.

47 Cohn and McCarthyism: *Trump Revealed* (2016), 62–63.

48 *Better man quote: Trump Revealed* (2016), *quoting* Sidney Zion, *The Autobiography of Roy Cohn* (Lyle Stuart, 1988), 81.

49 *Hard-boiled tactics: Trump Revealed* (2016), 62–63.

50 *Best-known fixer: The Greatest Show* (1992), 81

51 *go to hell: Trump Revealed* (2016), 64.

52 *Esquire on Cohn:* Ken Auletta, "Don't Mess with Roy Cohn," *Esquire,* December 1978, *reprinted in Esquire,* July 13, 2016.

53 *Trump on Cohn:* Ken Auletta, "Don't Mess with Roy Cohn," *Esquire,* December 1978, *reprinted in Esquire,* July 13, 2016.

54 *Myerson one-man crime wave:* Arnold H. Lubasch, "70 Months for Lawyer in Tax Fraud," *New York Times,* November 14, 1992.

55 *Jury quote on USFL verdict and description: Trump Revealed* (2016), *quoting* from Patricia Sibilia interview with Will Hobson, April 2016.

56 *Court opinion summary: Making of Trump* (2016), 56.

57 *Trump quotes re: USFL:* Donald Trump with Tony Schwartz, *Trump: The Art of the Deal* (New York: Ballantine Books, 1987), 48 and 276.

58 *Recurring theme: Trump-Style Negotiation* (2006), 254.

59 *Trust and rapport: Trump-Style Negotiation* (2006), 259.

60 Trump's estimate in court papers he lost $22 million on this effort: *Trump Revealed* (2016), 187, *citing* Gwenda Blair, *The Trumps: Three Generations That Built an Empire* (2000), 333.

61 *NFL alternative: Trump Revealed* (2016), 187; Mike Ozanian: *The Most Valuable Teams in the NFL, Forbes,* September 15, 2015.

62 *Cowboys quote: Trump Revealed* (2016), 175, from "Trump Building the Generals in His Own Style," *New York Times,* January 1, 1984.

63 *O'Donnell on Trump's win–lose mindset: Trump Revealed* (2016), 145, John R. O'Donnell, *Trumped!: The Inside Story of the Real Donald Trump—His Cunning Rise and Spectacular Fall* (Simon & Schuster, 1991).

64 *Vicious quote: Trump Revealed* (201 *information is power: Gain the Edge!* (2004), 13.6), 94.

Chapter 2

65 *Goals? Quote: The Greatest Show* (1992), 29.

66 *Unrealistic time frames:* Peter Economy, "21 Donald Trump Quotes to Inspire Your Success," *Inc.,* August 6, 2015.

67 *Information is power: Gain the Edge!* (2004), 13. For ease of reading and because these citations come from my own previous book *Gain the Edge!,* I cite them in the end notes, but do not block quote or use quotations for them in the text (which I do for all the other sources and cites).

68 *Fred Trump business: Trump Revealed* (2016), 70.

69 *Central Park: The Greatest Show* (1992), 90–91.

70 *Bigger than Helmsley: Greatest Show* (1992), 91.

71 *34ᵗʰ St. property: Trump Revealed* (2016), 72.

72 *Solomon quote: TrumpNation* (2005), 60 quoting *New York Times,* August 26, 1980.

73 *Estimated $400 million: Trump Revealed* (2016), 75.

74 *Ravitch quote: Trump Revealed* (2016), 76, *citing* 2016 interview with Richard Ravitch.

75 *Bailkin quote: TrumpNation* (2005), 63, *quoting* interview January 24, 2005.

76 *Got his tax break: TrumpNation* (2005), 63, *quoting* interview January 24, 2005.

77 *Trump Tower option negotiation: The Greatest Show* (1992), 171.

78 *29-year lease: The Greatest Show* (1992), 171.

79 *Other developers offered higher prices for option: TrumpNation* (2005), 68, *quoting* interview January 12, 2005.

80 *Trump Tower inspired business deal: TrumpNation* (2005), 102.

81 *Shopping spree quote: TrumpNation* (2005), 81.

82 *Plaza Hotel purchase: TrumpNation* (2005), 99.

83 *Flip of hotel to Trump: TrumpNation* (2005), 100; *citing* William H. Meyers, "Stalking the Plaza," *New York Times Magazine* (1988).

84 *Plaza the ultimate trophy quote: TrumpNation* (2005), 103, *quoting New York Times,* April 12, 1995.

85 *Plaza Hotel Trump quotes: TrumpNation* (2005), 100, 101, *quoting Surviving at the Top* (1990), 113.

86 *New York magazine ad as reported in Trump Revealed* (2016), 190.

87 *$300 million mortgage: TrumpNation* (2005), 101.

88 *Cash flow debt issue: The Greatest Show* (1992), 418.

89 *Room rate calculation and fact that he paid tens of millions more than next highest bid: Trump Revealed* (2016), 190.

90 *Tens of millions more: Trump Revealed* (2016), 174.

91 *Barbara Res quote: TrumpNation* (2005), 102, *quoting* interview, January 5, 2004.

92 *"as is" nature of deal and demanding renovations: The Greatest Show* (1992), 418.

93 *Trump Shuttle value: TrumpNation* (2005), 103, *citing The Washington Post*, October 23, 1988; State of New Jersey, *Preliminary Report on the Financial Condition of the Donald J. Trump Organization*, August 13, 1990, p. 101.

94 *Trump Shuttle value: TrumpNation* (2005), 103, *citing The Washington Post*, October 23, 1988; State of New Jersey, *Preliminary Report on the Financial Condition of the Donald J. Trump Organization*, August 13, 1990, p. 101.

95 *Trump quote Mona Lisa: TrumpNation* (2005), 103, *quoting The Washington Post*, October 23, 1998.

96 *Shuttle financials: The Greatest Show* (1992), 418.

97 *Strike and market share: The Greatest Show* (1992), 418.

98 *Trump Shuttle operating costs: The Greatest Show* (1992), 419.

99 *Leventhal report: The Making of Donald Trump* (2016), 89.

100 *Trump quote on minus 900 million: TrumpNation* (2005), 145, *quoting* interview February 16, 2005.

101 *$450,000/month: Trump Revealed* (2016), 195.

102 *Just phenomenal: The Making of Trump* (2016), 90.

103 *"greatest deal I ever made": Trump Revealed* (2016), 196.

104 *Don't be too aggressive quote: Gain the Edge!* (2004), 27-28.

105 *Business failures: TrumpNation* (2005), 143–146, *quoting* interviews from April 1, 2005, March 1, 2005, August 11, 2004, February 16, 2005, March 5, 2005.

106 *Loan from family: TrumpNation* (2005), 144, *quoting* interview March 1, 2005.

107 *Remarkably resilient; gumption in spades TrumpNation* (2005), 145–46.

108 *Quote re: unreasonable goals bordering on lunacy:* Donald J. Trump with Meredith McIver, *Trump: Think Like a Billionaire: Everything You Need to Know about Success, Real Estate, and Life*, Ballantine Books, 2005), xvi.

109 *Passion absolutely necessary:* Donald J. Trump with Meredith McIver, *Trump 101: The Way to Success* (2006), Chapter 1.

110 *Nothing great without passion:*, Donald Trump attributed, *Social Networking for Authors: Untapped Possibilities for Wealth* (Volkin Associates, 2009); Peter Economy, "21 Donald Trump Quotes to Inspire Your Success," *Inc.*, August 6, 2015.

111 Norman Vincent Peale, *The Power of Positive Thinking* (Simon and Schuster, 2003).

112 *Best outcomes: Trump Revealed* (2016), 81.

113 *Peale and Trump quotes: Trump Revealed* (2016), 81 *citing New York Times*, August 7, 1983.

114 *Profound streak of honest humility: TrumpNation* (2005), 49.

115 *Accentuate the positive: TrumpNation* (2005), 48.

116 *Confidence is a magnet:* Dan Spainhour, *Coach Yourself: A Motivational Guide for Coaches and Leaders* (Educational Coaching & Business Communications, 2007), 174.

117 *Barbara Res quote on self-confidence: Trump Revealed* (2016), 109 *citing* interview with Res.

118 *Quote on Expect to Succeed: Gain the Edge!* (2004), 29–30.

119 *Trump perseveres quote:* Dan Schawbel "Donald Trump Has the Midas Touch," *Forbes*, October 3, 2011.

120 *Falcons negotiations:* Leigh Steinberg with Michael D'Orso, *Winning With Integrity: Getting What You're Worth Without Selling Your Soul* (Three Rivers Press, 1998), 190.

121 Martin E. Latz, "Effective Negotiators Exhibit Patience," *Arizona Republic*, September 5, 2003.

122 *Trump buying up airlines, department store chains: The Greatest Show* (1992), 429.

CHAPTER 3

123 *Trump truthful hyperbole quote: Art of the Deal* (1987), 58.

124 *Barrett on BS capabilities: Trump Revealed* (2016), 105.

125 *Trump quote fantasy: Art of the Deal* (1987), 181.

126 *Trump Tower condos sale: Trump Revealed* (2016), 94.

127 *Trump quote hottest ticket in town: Art of the Deal* (1987), 181.

128 *Philbin quote: TrumpNation* (2005), 71, *quoting* interview, March 2, 2005.

129 *New face of Manhattan: TrumpNation* (2005), 71.

130 *Rumor didn't hurt us: Trump Revealed* (2016), 95.

131 *Corcoran quote: TrumpNation* (2005), 74, *quoting* interview with Timothy L. O'Brien, Jan. 18, 2005.

132 *Puffery: Black's Law Dictionary* (2nd Ed.).

133 *elements of fraud: Restatement (Second) of Torts* § 525 (1977).

CHAPTER 4

134 *Name in print amazing quote: Trump Revealed* (2016), 42 *quoting* Michael D'Antonio, *Never Enough: Donald Trump and the Pursuit of Success* (Thomas Dunne Books, 2015), 46.

135 Magazine articles in Trump's office: *Trump Revealed* (2016), 120.

136 *Trump strategy with Barrett: Trump Revealed* (2016), 103, *quoting* Wayne Barrett, "Like Father like Son: Anatomy of a Young Power Broker, *The Village Voice,* January 15, 1979.

137 *Quotes on media strategy: Art of the Deal* (2016), 56–57.

138 *Osnos quote: Trump Revealed* (2016), 99, *quoting* Gwenda Blair, *Donald Trump: The Candidate* (Simon & Schuster, 2007), xiii.

139 *Breslow and Trump: The Game interaction with Trump: Trump Revealed* (2016),110–111, *citing* Jeff Breslow interview with Marc Fisher, *The Washington Post,* April 2016.

140 *Walking into room: Trump Revealed* (2016), 110, *quoting* John Taylor interview with Will Hobson, *The Washington Post,* April 2016.

141 *Morning routine: Trump Revealed* (2016), 107–108.

142 *Press hungry for a good story: Art of the Deal* (1987), 56.

143 *Res quote on Trump getting anything into print: Trump Revealed* (2016), 109, quoting author's interview with Res.

144 *Media timeliness: Trump Revealed* (2016), 108.

145 *Divorce not a pleasant thing: Trump Revealed* (2016), 121, *quoting* Neil Barsky and Pauline Yoshihashi, "Trump Is Betting That Taj Majal Casino Will Hit Golden Jackpot in Atlantic City," *The Wall Street Journal,* March 20, 1990, B1.

146 *Commodore Hotel negotiation – showing Penn Central representative Fred Trump's properties: The Greatest Show* (1992).

147 *Commodore Hotel negotiation –television set: Trump Revealed* (2016), 71.

148 *Beame comment: The Greatest Show* (1992), 90.

149 *Buying a Senator: The Greatest Show* (1992), 91.

150 *"a lot higher than mine": Art of the Deal* (1987), 108.

151 *Starrett: The Greatest Show* (1992), 93.

152 *Quote re: Berger payoff: Trump Revealed* (2016), 71–72.

153 *Wooing quote: The Greatest Show* (1992), 98.

154 *Friedman inducement quote: The Greatest Show* (1992), 137.

155 *Trump as one of Friedman's best-paying clients: The Greatest Show* (1992), 142.

156 *Hyatt and Fred financial guarantee: The Greatest Show* (1992), 140.

157 *Cody racketeer: Trump Revealed* (2016), 90.

158 *Trump on Cody: Trump Revealed* (2016), *citing* Robert O'Harrow Jr., "Trump Swam in Mob-Infested Waters in Early Years as an NYC Developer," *The Washington Post,* October 16, 2015.

159 *Construction didn't miss a beat: Trump Revealed* (2016), 90.

160 *Hixon got her upgrades: Trump Revealed* (2016), 90, *citing* Verna Hixon deposition, May 8, 1986.

161 *Deal through Cohn: Trump Revealed* (2016), 91.

162 *Res interview: TrumpNation* (2005), 70; *quoting* interview on Jan. 5, 2005.

163 *Cody racketeer: Trump Revealed* (2016), 90, *citing* Robert O'Harrow Jr., "Trump Swam in Mob-Infested Waters in Early Years as an NYC Developer," *The Washington Post,* October 16, 2015.

164 *Trump/Hixon litigation: The Making of Donald Trump* (2016), 47.

165 *Getting to Yes: Negotiating Agreement Without Giving In* (Penguin Group, 1981).

166 *Fundamental interests underlying positions: Gain the Edge!* (2004), 36–37.

167 *Fundamental interests underlying positions: Gain the Edge!* (2004), 36–37.

168 *"within legal bounds": Art of the Deal* (1987), 108.

CHAPTER 5

169 *Trump dead quote: Art of the Deal* (1987), 53.

170 *Leverage elements: Gain the Edge!* (2004), 69.

171 *Leverage definition: Gain the Edge!* (2004), 69.

172 *Cannot do without: Art of the Deal* (1987), 37.

173 *Enough is enough: Larry Kim,* "17 Donald Trump Quotes That Are Surprisingly Brilliant," *Inc.,* August 24, 2015.

174 *Relative needs: Gain the Edge!* (2004), 70-71.

175 *Perception definition: Gain the Edge!* (2004), 71.

176 *Fluid leverage definition: Gain the Edge!* (2004), 75.

177 *Fluid leverage definition: Gain the Edge!* (2004), 75.

178 *Leverage quote: Art of the Deal* (1987), 54.

179 *Xanadu quote: The Greatest Show* (1992), 202.

180 *Preserving options quote: The Greatest Show* (1992), 202.

181 *Trump quote re balls in air: Art of the Deal* (1987), 50.

182 *New York City gambling alternative and quotes: The Greatest Show* (1992), 202–203.

183 *Resorts negotiation description: The Greatest Show* (1992), 208.

184 *Unescrowed deal: The Greatest Show* (1992), 209.

185 *Casino Control Commission approval: Trump Revealed* (2016), 127.

186 *Leverage and timing: Gain the Edge!* (2004), 80–82.

187 *Strike when leverage is hot: Gain the Edge!* (2004), 80–82.

188 *Most lucrative negotiation: The Making of Donald Trump* (2016), 41.

189 NJ *process: The Making of Donald Trump* (2016), 41–42.

190 *Trump want expedited approval process: The Making of Donald Trump* (2016), 42.

191 *Casino license approval process: The Making of Donald Trump* (2016), 41–42.

192 *Strictly enforce casino license standard: The Making of Donald Trump* (2016), 44.

193 *Degnan meeting: The Making of Donald Trump* (2016), 42; *Art of the Deal* (1987), 207.

194 *Degnan meeting: The Making of Donald Trump* (2016), 42

195 *NJ desperately needed the white knight: The Greatest Show* (1992), 217.

196 *Trump fishing for financing everywhere: The Greatest Show* (1992), 228.

197 *Trump illusion at casino site: Trump Revealed* (2016), 127–128; *citing Art of the Deal* (1987), 143.

198 *Trump literally out of money: The Greatest Show* (1992), 228.

199 *Single best deal quote: The Greatest Show* (1992), 228.

200 *Trump lost his financing and Harrah's did it: The Greatest Show* (1992), 229.

201 *Milken quote: The Greatest Show* (1992), 228.

202 *Proven formula for success quote: The Greatest Show* (1992), 229.

203 *Trump boast about ethics Penn Central deal when didn't have it: Trump Revealed* (2016), 75.

CHAPTER 6

204 *Next-highest bid: Trump Revealed* (2016), 190, *citing* interviews with *The Washington Post.*

205 *Sunshine quote: Trump Revealed* (2016), 72; *citing* 2016 interview with Sunshine.

206 *not shy: Trump Revealed* (2016), 72.

207 *contributions: Trump Revealed* (2016), 72–73.

208 *The Godfather quote:* Francis Ford Coppola (director), and Robert Evans (producer), and Francis Ford Coppola and Mario Puzo (screenplay), *The Godfather* (Paramount Home Entertainment, 1972), from Mario Puzo, *The Godfather* (New York: Putnam, 1971).

209 *Goldmark Trump threat quote: Trump Revealed* (2016), 72–73; 2016 Goldmark interview.

210 *Rozelle description of Trump threat: The Greatest Show* (1992), 336.

211 *Reporter threat: Trump Revealed* (2016), 108–109, from Digiacamo gossip column.

212 *definition of threat:* Adam D. Galinsky and Katie A. Liljenquist, "Putting on the Pressure: How to Make Threats in Negotiations," *Negotiation* (Harvard, December 2004), 4.

213 *combine promises with threats: Ibid.*

214 *consequences of anger: Ibid.,* 5; see also Keith G. Allred et al., "The Influence of Anger and Compassion on Negotiation Performance," 70 *Organizational Behav. & Hum. Decision Processes* 175, 181 (1997).

215 Clark Freshman, "Lie Detection and the Negotiation Within," 16 *Harv. Negot. L. Rev.* 263 (2011).

216 *three circumstances:* Galinsky & Liljenquist at 4–5; *see also* Anne L. Lytle, Jeanne M. Brett and Debra L. Shapiro, *The Strategic Use of Interests, Rights, and Power to Resolve Disputes* (1999).

217 *negative consequences of threats:* Galinsky & Liljenquist at 5.

218 *Obama and Syria:* Peter Baker and Jonathan Weisman, "Obama Seeks Approval by Congress for Strike in Syria," *New York Times,* August 31, 2013.

219 *effective threats:* Galinsky & Liljenquist at 4–5; *see also* Anne L. Lytle, Jeanne M. Brett and Debra L. Shapiro, *The Strategic Use of Interests, Rights, and Power to Resolve Disputes* (1999).

220 *effective threats:* Galinsky & Liljenquist at 4–5; *see also* Anne L. Lytle, Jeanne M. Brett and Debra L. Shapiro, *The Strategic Use of Interests, Rights, and Power to Resolve Disputes* (1999).

221 *Reagan and air traffic controllers:* Galinsky & Liljenquist at 4.

222 *Trump replaced the wood on the Commodore: Trump Revealed* (2016), 76, *citing* Michael D'Antonio, *Never Enough: Donald Trump and the Pursuit of Success* (Thomas Dunne Books, 2015), 103.

223 *Tiffany's air rights: Gain the Edge!* (2004), 91–92; *citing* G. Richard Shell, *Bargaining for Advantage* (Viking, 1999), 103, *citing Art of the Deal* (1987), 103–104.

224 *Television City name by Trump: TrumpNation* (2005), 91, *citing* Associated Press, May 10, 1987.

225 *Extended quote re Trump strategy/threat on NBC: The Greatest Show* (1992), 310–311.

226 *Trump letter to Koch, May 26, 1987 quoted in TrumpNation* (2005), 92.

227 *Koch letter to Trump, May 28, 1987 quoted in TrumpNation* (2005), 92–93.

228 *Bailkin quote: The Greatest Show* (1992), 380.

229 *Trump advertising threat quote: The Greatest Show* (1992), 385.

230 *happenstance Koch-Trump meeting: The Greatest Show* (1992), 385.

231 *Koch nailed him again on priority of projects: The Greatest Show* (1992), 385–386.

232 *NBC tax benefits: The Greatest Show* (1992), 380.

233 *$98 million value: TrumpNation* (2005), 96, *citing New York Newsday,* November 13, 1988.

234 *Bailkin conclusion on value of deal: The Greatest Show* (1992), 381.

235 *Trump quote on Television City: Art of the Deal* (1987), 353–354.

236 *Trump walkout: Bargaining for Advantage* (1999), 183, citing David Johnson, "In Taj deal Trump used an old tactic," *The Philadelphia Inquirer*, November 18, 1990, p. D1.

CHAPTER 7

237 *Katrina negotiation leverage:* Martin E. Latz, "You May Be Stronger, but Be Savvy in Using Leverage," *Arizona Republic*, April 6, 2007.

238 *suit vs. O'Brien: The Making of Donald Trump* (2016), 147–148; *quoting* Paul Farhi, "What Really Gets Under Trump's Skin? Questioning His Net Worth," *The Washington Post*, March 8, 2016.

239 *quote on O'Brien suit: Trump Revealed* (2016), 304, *citing* Trump interview with Harwell, O'Harrow, Boburg, Goldstein, and Markon.

240 *Bloomberg Business: Trump Revealed* (2016), 298, *quoting* Bloomberg Business News, "40 Wall Street Is Sold to Trump," *New York Times,* December 7, 1995.

241 *40 Wall St. great deal: Trump Revealed* (2016), 298–299, *citing* Steve Cuozzo, "Donald Trump Could Sell 40 Wall St. to Fund His Campaign," *New York Post*, May 23, 2016.

242 *example of litigation as business strategy: Trump Revealed* (2016), 299–300, *citing* Nick Penzenstadler and Susan Page, "Exclusive: Trump's 3,500 Lawsuits Unprecedented for a Presidential Nominee," *USA Today,* June 2, 2016.

243 *threats: Trump Revealed* (2016), 300.

244 *Trump quote re: cut them:* Alexandra Berzon, "Donald Trump's Business Plan Left a Trail of Unpaid Bills," *Wall Street Journal,* June 9, 2016.

245 *court filings in 33 states:* Alexandra Berzon, "Donald Trump's Business Plan Left a Trail of Unpaid Bills," *Wall Street Journal,* June 9, 2016.

246 *when he pays:* Alexandra Berzon, "Donald Trump's Business Plan Left a Trail of Unpaid Bills," *Wall Street Journal,* June 9, 2016.

247 *court filings in 33 states:* Alexandra Berzon, "Donald Trump's Business Plan Left a Trail of Unpaid Bills," *Wall Street Journal,* June 9, 2016.

248 "Hundreds allege Donald Trump doesn't pay his bills" *USA Today,* June 9, 2016.

249 Ibid.

250 Ibid.

251 *USA Today* "dimes on the dollar" quote, ibid. Chap. 3.

252 "Hundreds allege Donald Trump doesn't pay his bills" *USA Today,* June 9, 2016.

253 "Hundreds allege Donald Trump doesn't pay his bills" *USA Today,* June 9, 2016.

254 "Hundreds allege Donald Trump doesn't pay his bills" *USA Today,* June 9, 2016.

255 "Hundreds allege Donald Trump doesn't pay his bills" *USA Today,* June 9, 2016.

256 O'Donnell quote: Alexandra Berzon, "Donald Trump's Business Plan Left a Trail of Unpaid Bills," *Wall Street Journal,* June 9, 2016.

257 *Details on Trump's Taj Mahal facility: Trump Revealed* (2016), 147–149.

258 *"couldn't count it fast enough":* Tim Golden, "Taj Majal's Slot Machines Halt, Overcome by Success," *New York Times,* April 9, 1990.

259 *Taj opening description: Trump Revealed* (2016), 151, *citing* Daniel Heneghan and David J. Spatz, "Trump Opens Taj with Flourish," *Press of Atlantic City,* April 6, 1990; Robin Leach, host, *Lifestyles of the Rich and Famous,* April 1990.

260 *Taj contractors getting stiffed: USA Today,* June 9, 2016.

261 *Trump response to Taj contractors getting stiffed, "wouldn't have had jobs":* Alexandra Berzon, "Donald Trump's Business Plan Left a Trail of Unpaid Bills," *Wall Street Journal,* June 9, 2016.

262 *Trump response to Taj contractors getting stiffed, "wouldn't have had jobs":* Alexandra Berzon, "Donald Trump's Business Plan Left a Trail of Unpaid Bills," *Wall Street Journal,* June 9, 2016.

263 Catalina Draperies dispute: Alexandra Berzon, "Donald Trump's Business Plan Left a Trail of Unpaid Bills," *Wall Street Journal*, June 9, 2016.

264 Catalina Draperies dispute: Alexandra Berzon, "Donald Trump's Business Plan Left a Trail of Unpaid Bills," *Wall Street Journal*, June 9, 2016.

265 Catalina Draperies dispute: Alexandra Berzon, "Donald Trump's Business Plan Left a Trail of Unpaid Bills," *Wall Street Journal*, June 9, 2016.

266 *unhappy with his work:* Alexandra Berzon, "Donald Trump's Business Plan Left a Trail of Unpaid Bills," *Wall Street Journal*, June 9, 2016.

267 "Donald Trump's Business Plan Left a Trail of Unpaid Bills," *Wall Street Journal*, June 9, 2016.

268 "Hundreds allege Donald Trump doesn't pay his bills" *USA Today*, June 9, 2016.

269 Author's conversation with business colleague whose family is in New York and New Jersey, May 10, 2017.

270 *Nelson quote: USA Today, ibid.*

271 *Wayne Rivers quote: Wall Street Journal, ibid.*

272 *Selzer quote:* Alexandra Berzon, "Donald Trump's Business Plan Left a Trail of Unpaid Bills," *Wall Street Journal*, June 9, 2016.

273 "Why U.S. Law Makes It Easy for Donald Trump to Stiff Contractors," *Fortune Magazine,* September 30, 2016.

274 Roger Parloff, "Why U.S. Law Makes It Easy for Donald Trump to Stiff Contractors," *Fortune Magazine,* September 30, 2016.

CHAPTER 8

275 Donald J. Trump to a CNN reporter, January 11, 2017.

276 *independent standards: Gain the Edge!* (2004), 105.

277 *Midas quote: Making of Donald Trump* (2016), 78.

278 *I'm really rich quote and central to presidency run quote: Trump Revealed* (2016), 293.

279 *"keep score" tweet: Trump Revealed* (2016), 294, *quoting* Donald Trump Twitter account, September 13, 2014.

280 *Forbes inclusion in 1982: Forbes*

281 *Forbes ranking: Trump Revealed* (2016), 294-5; *quoting* Jennifer Wang, "The Ups and Downs of Donald Trump: Three Decades on and Off the Forbes 400," *Forbes*, March 14, 2016

282 *intense lobbying: TrumpNation* (2005), 152.

283 *topic of net worth always coming up: TrumpNation* (2005), 152–156, *citing* interview March 5, 2005.

284 *topic of net worth always coming up: TrumpNation* (2005), 152–156, *citing Playboy*, March 1990.

285 *Princess purchase: Trump Revealed* (2016), 132, *citing* Harry Hurt III, Lost Tycoon, The Many Lives of Donald J. Trump (London: Orion Books, 1994), 228; David Johnston and Michael Schurman, "Trump's Ship Comes in—to Cheers," *Philadelphia Inquirer,* July 10, 1988.

286 *market value: Gain the Edge!* (2004), 107.

287 *40 Wall Street value: TrumpNation* (2005), *citing* interview with Allen Weisselberg, April 21, 2005.

288 *precedent: Gain the Edge!* (2004), 112.

289 *Commodore Hotel tax break,* Art of the Deal (1987), 135.

290 *NBC tax break:* TrumpNation (2005), 96, *citing New York Newsday,* November 13, 1988.

291 *costs and profits power: Gain the Edge!* (2004), 119–120.

292 *Mar-a-Lago purchase: Trump Revealed* (2016), 161, *citing* interview with Trump, November 2015.

293 *Mar-a-Lago furnishings cost: Art of the Deal* (1987), 26.

294 *paid cash for Mar-a-Lago: Art of the Deal* (1987), 26.

295 *Mar-a-Lago transaction: The Making of Donald Trump* (2016), 81–82.

296 *local tax authorities: The Making of Donald Trump* (2016), 81–82.

297 *expert power: Gain the Edge!* (2004), 116–117.

298 *Resorts negotiation and Taj cost: The Greatest Show* (1992), 393, 395.

299 *independent experts' usage: The Greatest Show* (1992), 401.

300 *Wallach example: Trump Revealed* (2016), 297–298, *quoting* Wallach interview and unpublished manuscript provided to *The Washington Post.*

301 *quote on not hiring number crunchers: Art of the Deal* (1987), 51.

302 *status power: Gain the Edge!* (2004), 126, *quoting* Roger Dawson, *Secrets of Power Negotiating: Inside Secrets from a Master Negotiator,* 2ⁿᵈ Ed. (Franklin Lakes, NJ, Career Press, 2001), 279–280; *Webster's New Collegiate Dictionary* (Springfield, Mass." G. & C. Merriam Company, 1979), 1128.

303 *Trump University: Trump Revealed* (2016), 225, *quoting* Tom Hamburger and Rosalind S. Helderman, "Trump Involved in Crafting Controversial Trump University Ads, Executive Testified," *The Washington Post,* May 31, 2016.

304 *Depressed market: Trump Revealed* (2016), 225.

305 *Develop curriculum: Trump Revealed* (2016), 227.

306 *Handpick teachers: Trump Revealed* (2016), 227.

307 *Donate to charity: Trump Revealed* (2016), 227.

308 *Ad text: Trump Revealed* (2016), 225.

309 *Tuition: Trump Revealed* (2016), 226.

310 *Facts revealed in lawsuit: Trump Revealed* (2016), 227.

311 *Trump's response to lawsuit claims: Trump Revealed* (2016), 227.

312 *Student satisfaction: Trump Revealed* (2016), 227.

313 *Refunds: Trump Revealed* (2016), 227.

314 *Trump University Settlement:* US Dist. Judge Gonzalo Curiel statement, *cited in* Josh Gersten, Judge Approves $25 Million Trump University Settlement," *Politico,* March 31, 2017.

315 *Spring 1990 financial problems: Trump Revealed* (2016), 192, 206.

316 *In the red: The Making of Trump* (2016), 89.

317 *Less than zero: The Making of Trump* (2016), 89.

318 *Devaluing rapidly: TrumpNation* (2005), 156–157, *citing* State of New Jersey, Casino Control Commission, Report on the Financial Position of Donald J. Trump, April 11, 1991, 5.

319 *Sale price of yacht: Trump Revealed* (2016), 206.

320 *Trump go-go days quote: Trump Revealed* (2016), 205, *citing* Trump interview with Amy Goldstein and Jerry Markon.

321 *Weil Gotshal meeting description: Trump Revealed* (2016), 193, *citing* interviews with bankers, including Alan Pomerantz and Robert McSween, with Jerry Markon, *The Washington Post,* April 2016.

322 *Bollenbach quote: TrumpNation* (2005), 158, *citing* interview, February 10, 2005.

323 *Bankers' knowledge: The Making of Trump* (2016), 83.

324 *Bankers Trust story of loan: The Greatest Show* (1992), 428.

325 *Not recorded: Making of Donald Trump* (2016), 82.

326 *Sprague example of inflating sales price lists: The Greatest Show* (1992), 431.

327 *Banks' behavior: The Greatest Show* (1992), 427–428.

328 *Suffer together quote: Trump Revealed* (2016), 195, *citing* interviews with three bankers familiar with the negotiations with Jarry Markon, *The Washington Post,* May 2016.

329 *Trump "greatest deal ever" quote, Trump Revealed* (2016), 196, *citing Surviving at the Top* (1990), interview with McSween.

330 Workout negotiations results, *Trump Revealed* (2016).

331 *Ivana $10 million check: Trump Revealed* (2016), 203–204, *citing* interview with Alan Pomerantz.

332 *What are they going to do: Trump Revealed* (2016), 204.

333 *The Trump Princess deadline with Boston Bank: TrumpNation* (2005), 158, *citing* interview, February 10, 2005.

334 *2005 TrumpNation lawsuit: The Making of Donald Trump* (2016), 78.

335 2005 *TrumpNation Trump testimony: The Making of Donald Trump* (2016), 78, *citing Trump v. Timothy L. O'Brien, et al.* No. CAM-L-545-06. Superior Court of New Jersey.

336 *Discrepancies: The Making of Donald Trump* (2016), 81.

337 *The Making of Donald Trump* (2016), 77, *citing* Peter S. Goodman, "Trump Suit Claiming Defamation is Dismissed," *New York Times,* July 15, 2009.

338 *The Making of Donald Trump* (2016), 80, *citing Trump v Timothy L. O'Brien, et al.* Superior Court of New Jersey, Appellate Division Docket No. A-6141-08T3, Decided 9/7/2001.

339 *Court of Appeals decision quote: Trump Revealed* (2016), 304, *citing Trump v. O'Brien et al.,* Appellate Division decision September 7, 2011.

340 *Roffman VP of research background: Trump Revealed* (2016), 134.

341 *Undermining Roffman: Trump Revealed* (2016), 145–47.

342 *Roffman quote: Trump Revealed* (2016), 145–46, *citing* Neil Barsky and Pauline Yoshihashi, "Trump Is Betting That Taj Mahal Casino Will Hit Golden Jackpot in Atlantic City," *Wall Street Journal,* March 20, 1990.

343 *Standards dance: Gain the Edge!* (2004), 140–141.

344 Martin E. Latz, "Buyer Taking a Hard Line Shows Leverage Trumps Fair, Reasonable, *Arizona Republic,* January 6, 2014.

345 *Trump's recovery: Trump Revealed* (2016), 206-207, *citing* "Trump Gets $295 Million in Sale of Stock, Debt," *St. Louis Post-Dispatch,* June 8, 1995; "Trump Pays 15.5% in Junk Bond Sale," *New York Times,* June 8, 1995; Timothy L. O'Brien, "What's He Really Worth?" *New York Times,* October 23, 2005.

346 *Personal Trump did great, public company lost millions: Trump Revealed* (2016), 207–208, *citing* Russ Buettner and Charles v. Bagli, "How Donald Trump Bankrupted His Atlantic City Casinos, But Still Earned Millions," *New York Times,* June 11, 2016.

347 *Raise money from public company offering: Trump Revealed* (2016), 206, *citing* David Cay Johnston, "Trump Walks a Tightrope in Plan to Sell Casino Stock," *New York Times,* April 3, 1995

348 *overpay for Castle quote: Trump Revealed* (2016), 207, *citing* James Sterngold, "Long Odds for the Shares of Trump's Casino Company," *New York Times,* March 9, 1997.

349 *Deal details—personal Trump benefit: Trump Revealed* (2016), 206–209.

350 *Trump quote re entrepreneurially speaking: Trump Revealed* (2016), 208–209, *citing* Daniel Roth, "The Trophy Life: You Think Donald Trump's Hit Reality Show Is a Circus? Spend a Few Weeks Watching Him Work," *Fortune,* April 19, 2004.

351 *Forbes in 2004 assessment: Trump Revealed* (2016), 208–209, *citing* Jennifer Wang, "The Ups and Downs of Donald Trump: Three Decades On and Off the Forbes 400," *Forbes,* March 14, 2016.

CHAPTER 9

352 *Asked for $18 million per episode: TrumpNation* (2005), 33, *quoting The Wall Street Journal,* July 27, 2004.

353 *"aim very high...": Art of the Deal* (1987), 45.

354 *Zoom in for the jackpot: TrumpNation* (2005), 33.

355 *The Apprentice negotiation and standards: TrumpNation* (2005), 33, *citing* interview May 11, 2005.

356 *Deal was confidential: TrumpNation* (2005), 33, *citing* interview May 11, 2005.

357 *NBC Jeff Zucker on The Apprentice negotiation*: Dorothy Wickenham, "Jeff Zucker Talks To David Remnick About Putting Trump on TV," *The New Yorker,* May 1, 2017.

358 *Trump made $214 million overall from The Apprentice: Trump Revealed* (2016), 299, *citing* Trump financial disclosure form.

359 *Jimmy Carter quote: Art of the Deal* (1987), 60.

360 *Barbizon deal: Trump Revealed* (2016), 91, *citing* William E. Geist, "The Expanding Empire of Donald Trump," *New York Times,* April 8, 1994.

361 *Harass tenants: The Greatest Show* (1992), 254.

362 *Force the tenants: The Greatest Show* (1992), 254.

363 *Verbally intimidating: The Greatest Show* (1992), 254.

364 *Tenant resolution: Trump Revealed* (2016), 91.

365 *On Ifshin: Trump Revealed* (2016), 92-93, *citing* Stephen Ifshin interview with Bob Woodward, *The Washington Post,* May 2016, confirmed by Trump in an interview with Fisher and Kranish, *The Washington Post,* June 2016.

366 *Think in reverse: Trump-Style Negotiation* (2006), 9.

367 *Where to start: Gain the Edge!* (2004), 158–159.

368 *First offer expectations: Gain the Edge!* (2004), 160-161.

369 *Goals: Gain the Edge!* (2004), 161.

370 *Aggressive but realistic standards: Gain the Edge!* (2004), 164.

371 *Room to move gamesmanship: Gain the Edge!* (2004), 165.

372 *Think in reverse: Trump-Style Negotiation* (2006), 9.

373 *Offer-concession patterns: Gain the Edge!* (2004), 146–147.

374 *Offer-concession patterns: Gain the Edge!* (2004), 146–147.

375 *Mar-a-Lago offer-concession strategy: Art of the Deal* (1987), 25–26.

376 *First offers: Gain the Edge!* (2004), 150–151.

377 *First offers: Gain the Edge!* (2004), 150–151.

378 *Negotiating for 727: Art of the Deal* (1987), 365–366.

379 *Freund quote: Gain the Edge!* (2004), 151–152, quoting James C. Freund, *Smart Negotiating: How to Make Good Deals in the Real World* (New York: Simon & Schuster, 1992), 114-115.

380 *First offer expectations: Gain the Edge!* (2004), 151–152.

381 *Lack information to set first offer: Gain the Edge!* (2004), 155, *citing* Donald G. Gifford, *Legal Negotiation Theory and Applications* (St. Paul, MN: West Publishing Co., 1989).

382 *Tony Schwartz quote: The Greatest Show* (1992), 324–325.

383 *When to assert standard: Gain the Edge!* (2004), 185.

384 *Tying moves to standards: Gain the Edge!* (2004), 184–185.

385 *Reciprocity principle: Gain the Edge!* (2004), 123.

386 *Reciprocity principle: Gain the Edge!* (2004), 123.

387 *Trump's political activity in contributions: Trump Revealed* (2016), 273, *citing* George Arzt and Cindy Darrison interviews with Shawn Boburg, *The Washington Post,* May 18, 2016.

388 *Cialdini on reciprocity principle, holiday card quote: Gain the Edge!* (2004), 177, *citing* Robert B. Cialdini, *Influence: Science and Practice,* 4th Ed. (Allyn & Bacon, 2001), 20.

CHAPTER 10

389 *Lawrence Taylor negotiation: Trump Revealed* (2016), 177-178, *citing* Gerald Eskenazi, "Taylor Buys Out Generals' Pact," *New York Times,* January 18, 1984.

390 *Agenda control: Gain the Edge!* (2004), 214.

391 *Phone vs. email: Gain the Edge!* (2004), 230-231.

392 *Relationship factors: Gain the Edge!* (2004), 230–231.

393 *Efficiency factor: Gain the Edge!* (2004), 231.

394 *Put it in writing: Gain the Edge!* (2004), 188.

395 *Meeting at Trump Tower: Trump Revealed* (2016), 223.

396 *Breslow meeting at Trump Tower: Trump Revealed* (2016), 110, *citing* Jeffrey Breslow interview with Marc Fisher, *The Washington Post,* April 2016.

397 *Control the turf factors: Gain the Edge!* (2004), 227.

398 *NFL Meeting place at Pierre Hotel in Manhattan: Trump Revealed* (2016), 184, *citing* Donald Trump testimony, *USFL v. NFL* court records.

399 *Trump requested NFL meeting at Pierre: The Greatest Show* (1992), 335.

400 *Hager licensing deal: Trump Revealed* (2016), 221–222, *citing* Deposition of Mark Hager, March 3, 2011, *ALM International Corp. v. Donald J. Trump,* 12.

401 *Phillips licensing guy laughing: Trump Revealed* (2016), 222, *citing* Testimony of Jeff Danzer, April 15, 2013, *ALM International Corp. v. Donald J. Trump,* trial transcript, 593.

402 *Phillips wary of Trump deal, Trump Revealed* (2016), 223, *citing* Deposition of Hager, 50.

403 *Weber visit: Trump Revealed* (2016), 207.

404 *Money made from deal: Trump Revealed* (2016), 223, *citing* Executive Branch Personal Public Financial Disclosure Report (OGE Form 278e), Donald J. Trump, July 22, 2015, 21.

405 *Cialdini scarcity effect: Influence: Science and Practice* (2001), 205.

406 *Back to Brooklyn: Art of the Deal* (1987), 107.

407 *Fast ones with NYC: The Greatest Show* (1992), 117–118.

408 *Second fast one: The Greatest Show* (1992), 118.

409 *Substantive and atmospheric agenda: Gain the Edge!* (2004), 215–216.

410 *Short-term agenda setting: Gain the Edge!* (2004), 215–216.

411 *Control the dialogue, TrumpNation* (2005), 226.

412 *Long-term agenda setting: Gain the Edge!* (2004), 216.

413 *Central Park: The Greatest Show* (1992), 90–91.

414 *Goodgold attitude toward Trump: The Greatest Show* (1992), 107.

415 *Agenda-control factors: Gain the Edge!* (2004), 218.

416 *Agenda-control list of tactics: Gain the Edge!* (2004), 218.

417 *Rozelle must decide "right away": The Greatest Show* (1992), 336.

418 *Trump on Resorts' deal deadline: The Greatest Show* (1992), 395.

419 *Deadline impact: Gain the Edge!* (2004), 220-21.

420 *Daddy Warbucks house deadline: Gain the Edge!* (2004), 220.

421 *Deadline duration: Gain the Edge!* (2004), 222.

422 *Resorts board one day deadline: The Greatest Show* (1992), 395–97.

423 *Trump deadline to NYC on NBC deal: The Greatest Show* (1992), 373–374.

424 Geoffrey James, Donald Trump's Negotiation Mind Games, *Moneywatch,* May 8, 2009.

PART 2
CHAPTER 11

425 *Persistence quote, Art of the Deal,* (1987), 147.

426 Andrea Kupfer Schneider, "Teaching a New Negotiation Skills Paradigm," 39 *Wash. U. J. L. & Pol'y* 13, 25–35 (2012).

427 *Definition of assertiveness: Bargaining with the Devil* (2010), 134.

428 *Mandela's negotiation for a political system: Bargaining with the Devil* (2010), 128, 132.

429 *Mandela greatest negotiator: Bargaining with the Devil* (2010), 135.

430 *Robben Island conditions description: Bargaining with the Devil* (2010), 119–120.

431 *Mandela – de Klerk: Bargaining with the Devil* (2010), 126.

432 *Reaching across the table: Bargaining with the Devil* (2010), 133.

433 *Mandela's characteristics: Bargaining with the Devil* (2010), 133.

434 *"ability to assert yourself":* Andrea Kupfer Schneider, "Teaching a New Negotiation Skills Paradigm," 39 *Wash. U. J. L. & Pol'y* 13, 28 (2012).

435 *Competence and knowledge:* Andrea Kupfer Schneider, "Teaching a New Negotiation Skills Paradigm," 39 *Wash. U. J. L. & Pol'y* 13, 28 (2012).

436 *Assertiveness skills measured by leverage element:* Andrea Kupfer Schneider, "Teaching a New Negotiation Skills Paradigm," 39 *Wash. U. J. L. & Pol'y* 13, 28 (2012).

437 *Empathy definition:* Bargaining with the Devil (2010), 134.

438 *Schneider on empathy:* Andrea Kupfer Schneider, "Teaching a New Negotiation Skills Paradigm," 39 *Wash. U. J. L. & Pol'y* 13, 29–30 (2012).

439 *Mandela quote on listening: Bargaining with the Devil* (2010), 109.

440 *Walch comment on Trump listening skills: Trump Revealed* (2016), 219.

441 *Flexibility: Trump-Style Negotiation* (2006), 30, 32.

442 *Trump's chameleon-like qualities: Trump-Style Negotiation* (2006), 33.

443 *Schneider on social intuition:* Andrea Kupfer Schneider, "Teaching a New Negotiation Skills Paradigm," 39 *Wash. U. J. L. & Pol'y* 13, 31–33 (2012).

444 *Rapport-building: Gain the Edge!* (2004), 52–53, including Cialdini's Liking Rule, *Influence: Science and Practice* (2001), 44.

445 *Positive associations with food: Gain the Edge!* (2004), 53.

446 *Rapport-building tips: Gain the Edge!* (2004), 53-54.

447 *Mandela rapport-building: Bargaining with the Devil* (2010), 123–124.

448 *2Mandela first official talks quote: Bargaining with the Devil* (2010), 129.

449 *Reagan and Tip O'Neil rapport-building:* John Cassidy, "Can Donald Trump Learn from Ronald Reagan and Tip O'Neill? *The New Yorker,* March 28, 2017.

450 *Bill Clinton social person:* Kenneth T. Walsh, "Obama and Clinton Share Personality Traits: Clinton may have upstaged Obama but their relationship could be beneficial," *U.S. News & World Report,* December 23, 2010.

451 *George W. Bush an everyday sort of social person:* Ben Feller, "Bush's Personality Shapes His Legacy," *NBC News,* January 3, 2009.

452 *Barack Obama a bit of an introvert:* Damon Brown, "The Leader of the Free World Is an Introvert. Here's How Obama Leads," *Inc.,* July 5, 2016.

453 *Le Club: Trump Revealed* (2016), 60–61.

454 *Osnos quote: Trump Revealed* (2016), 99.

455 *Small talk: The Greatest Show* (1992), 12.

456 *Bond purchase of the St. Moritz: The Greatest Show* (1992), 418.

457 *Smith quote: TrumpNation* (2005), 214.

458 *Schneider on ethicality:* Andrea Kupfer Schneider, "Teaching a New Negotiation Skills Paradigm," 39 *Wash. U. J. L. & Pol'y* 13, 33–35 (2012).

CHAPTER 12

459 *"corrupt world": TrumpNation* (2005), 211, *citing The Washington Times,* April 18, 1995.

460 *Credibility:* Martin E. Latz, *Gain the Edge! Negotiating to Get What You Want* (St. Martin's Press, 2004), 6–7.

461 *"within legal bounds": Art of the Deal* (1987), 108.

462 *Racial discrimination quote/lie: The Greatest Show* (1992) 83–84.

463 *Settlement with Trumps and Trump's nibble: Trump Revealed* (2016), 67.

464 *Unsigned option contract to NYC officials: Trump Revealed* (2016), 75.

465 *Misrepresentation about financing: The Greatest Show* (1992), 118.

466 *Hunter-Stiebel and Miller quotes: Trump Revealed* (2016) 86–87.

467 *Question of trust quote: Trump Revealed* (2016), 87.

468 *Polish brigade quote: The Greatest Show* (1992), 181–182.

469 *Low bid: The Greatest Show* (1992), 182.

470 *Paid irregularly if at all: The Greatest Show* (1992), 182.

471 *Begging for jobs: The Greatest Show* (1992), 182.

472 *Harrah's partnership fell apart quote: Trump Revealed* (2016), 128.

473 DOJ racial discrimination lawsuit misrepresentation re: rentals: *The Greatest Show* (1992) 83–84.

474 DOJ racial discrimination lawsuit misrepresentation re: knowledge: *The Greatest Show* (1992) 83–84.

475 Misrepresentation re: agreement to buy Commodore from Penn Central: *Trump Revealed* (2016).

476 Misrepresentation to Penn Central re: Hyatt deal: *Trump Revealed* (2016), 75.

477 Misrepresentation re: financing for Commodore redevelopment: *Trump Revealed* (2016).

478 Art Deco Deal misrepresentation: *Trump Revealed* (2016) 86–87.

479 Trump Tower development misrepresentation: *The Greatest Show* (1992), 181–182.

480 Misrepresentations re: Harrah's financing: *Art of the Deal* (1987) 214–215.

481 New Jersey casino application failure to list civil and criminal investigations: *The Making of Donald Trump* (2016), 41–43.

482 New Jersey casino application failure to list mob-related associations: *The Making of Donald Trump* (2016), 44.

483 Net worth misrepresentations: *TrumpNation* (2005); Trump testimony: *The Making of Donald Trump* (2016), 78, citing *Trump v Timothy L. O'Brien, et al.* No. CAM-L-545-06. Superior Court of New Jersey.

484 Mar-a-Lago purchase price and terms misrepresentations: *Art of the Deal* (1987), 26; *The Making of Donald Trump* (2016), 81–82; Trump Revealed *(2016)*, 161, citing interview with Trump, November 2015.

485 Biggins quote re: Television City: *The Greatest Show* (1992), 377.

486 Trump University misrepresentations: *Trump Revealed (2016)*, 225, quoting Tom Hamburger and Rosalind S. Helderman, "Trump Involved in Crafting Controversial Trump University Ads, Executive Testified," The Washington Post, May 31, 2016; US Dist Judge Gonzalo Curiel statement, cited in Josh Gersten, Judge Approves $25 Million Trump University Settlement," Politico, March 31, 2017.

487 real-estate licensing deals: *The Making of Donald Trump* (2016), 167–175.

488 threat to Peter Goldmark, Trump Revealed (2016), 72–73; 2016 Goldmark interview.

489 threat to Liz Smith: TrumpNation (2005), 213–214, quoting Interview August 26, 2004.

490 threat to Marvin Roffman: Trump Revealed (2016), 146, citing Roffman interview with Robert O'Harrow, The Washington Post, November 16, 2015; Take Charge of Your Financial Future: Straight Talk on Managing Your Money from the Financial Analyst Who Defied Donald Trump (Carol Publishing Group, 1994).

491 threat re O'Brien: The Making of Donald Trump (2016), 147–148.

492 threat to Jim Brady: Trump Revealed (2016), 108-109, from Digiacamo gossip column.

493 threat to Wayne Barrett: Trump Revealed (2016), 103, citing Wayne Barrett, "Like Father like Son: Anatomy of a Young Power Broker, The Village Voice, January 15, 1979.

494 threat to Mayor Ed Koch: The Greatest Show (1992), 384.

495 bribe-like to David Berger: Trump Revealed (2016), 71–72.

496 bribe-like to Penn Central rep with television set: Trump Revealed (2016), 71.

497 bribe-like to Wayne Barrett: Trump Revealed (2016), 103, citing Wayne Barrett, "Like Father like Son: Anatomy of a Young Power Broker, The Village Voice, January 15, 1979.

498 bribe-like to Stanley Friedman: The Greatest Show (1992), 137.

499 *bribe-like to Cody: Trump Revealed* (2016), *citing* Robert O'Harrow Jr., "Trump Swam in Mob-Infested Waters in Early Years as an NYC Developer," *The Washington Post,* October 16, 2015.; *construction didn't miss a beat: Trump Revealed* (2016), 90; *Hixon got her upgrades: Trump Revealed* (2016), 90, *citing* Verna Hixon deposition, May 8, 1986.

500 *Wooing quote: The Greatest Show* (1992), 98.

501 *Never having met a public official…he couldn't seduce: The Greatest Show* (1992), 433–434.

502 *Misleading Harrah's board: Art of the Deal* (1987), 212.

503 *St. Moritz sale misleading: The Greatest Show* (1992), 428.

504 *Griffin "very guided tour": The Greatest Show* (1992), 413.

505 *Decade-long evasiveness: The Greatest Show* (1992), 431.

506 *Casino Control Commission, ease of getting bank loans: The Greatest Show* (1992), 405.

507 *House Banking Committee quote: The Greatest Show* (1992), 435.

508 *Shortchanging New York City on taxes: Trump Revealed* (2016), 84.

509 *Mayor Dinkins description of fraud: The Greatest Show* (1992), 430.

510 *Sunshine split: The Greatest Show* (1992), 200.

511 *Griffin: The Greatest Show* (1992), 412–416.

512 *Davis pension trick: The Greatest Show* (1992), 412–413.

513 *Griffin won't even be a millionaire: The Greatest Show* (1992), 413.

514 *Trump personal attacks on Koch: The Greatest Show* (1992), 378.

515 *Koch could hear Trump yelling in his ear: The Greatest Show* (1992), 169.

516 *Trump calling Wynn names: TrumpNation* (2005), 124, *citing Fortune,* July 22, 1996.

517 *Trump saying Wynn has psychological problems: TrumpNation* (2005), 124, *quoting New York,* February 16, 1998.

518 *Trump and Wynn quotes about each other: TrumpNation* (2005), 124; *quoting New York,* February 16, 1998.

519 *Trump and Wynn resolved their differences: TrumpNation* (2005), 123, *quoting* interviews February 25, 2005 and March 4, 2005.

520 *USFL Bassett letter to Trump: Trump Revealed* (2016), 179.

521 *Over 4,000 litigation matters:* "Donald Trump: Three Decades, 4,095 lawsuits," *USA Today,* June 9, 2016.

522 *Quote re: effectiveness: Bargaining for Advantage* (1999), 17–18.

523 *Importance of trust:* Roy J. Lewicki and Beth Polin, *Handbook of Research on Negotiation* (2013).

524 *Consequences of broken trust:* Roy J. Lewicki and Beth Polin, *Handbook of Research on Negotiation* (2013).

PART 3
CHAPTER 13

525 *Competitive vs. problem-solving strategies: Gain the Edge!* (2004), 255.

526 *Competitive strategies, Five Golden Rules framework: Gain the Edge!* (2004), 260–265

527 *"not big on compromise": Life,* Vol. 12 (January 1989), iii.

528 *Vicious quote: Trump Revealed* (2016), 94.

529 *Problem-solving strategies, Five Golden Rules framework: Gain the Edge!* (2004), 256–260.

530 *Four Factor framework: Gain the Edge!* (2004), 266–278.

531 *Sen. Kyl and Sen. Manchin negotiation strategies:* Martin E. Latz, "Negotiation Lessons from Politics," April 14, 2016.

532 *Quote re: President Johnson:* Diane Coutu, "Lessons in Power: Lyndon Johnson Revealed," *Harvard Business Review,* April 2006.

533 *Number factor: Gain the Edge!* (2004), 271–272.

534 *"two-level game": Bargaining with the Devil* (2010), 133–134.

535 *James Madison story:* Deepak Malhotra, *Negotiating the Impossible: How to Break Deadlocks and Resolve Ugly Conflicts (Without Money or Muscle)* (Harvard Business School, 2016), 62.

536 *Madison preparation: Negotiating the Impossible* (2016), 63.

537 *Shaping the process: Negotiating the Impossible* (2016), 63.

538 *Preparation: Negotiating the Impossible* (2016), 67.

539 *Wynn quote: TrumpNation* (2005), 109–10, *citing* interview with Wynn, February 25, 2005 and interview with Trump, March 1, 2005.

540 *Trump didn't know the business: The Making of Donald Trump* (2016), 178.

541 *Facts at your fingertips: Negotiating the Impossible* (2016), 67.

542 *Debt deal:* Kristina Peterson, Siobhan Hughes, and Louise Radnofsky, "Trump Stuns GOP by Dealing with Democrats on Debt, Harvey Aid," *Wall Street Journal,* October 13, 2017.

543 *Zero-sum factor: Gain the Edge!* (2004), 274–276.

544 Bush and Baker coalition-building: "James Baker as a Coalition Builder," http://jamesbaker.thinkport.org/index.html

545 *coalition building against Iraq:* "James Baker as a Coalition Builder," http://jamesbaker.thinkport.org/index.html

546 *they lose does not equal you win:* Deepak Malhotra and Jonathan Powell, "What Donald Trump Doesn't Understand about Negotiation," Harvard Business Review, April 8, 2016, 3.

547 *More conflicting interests:* Thomas E. Mann and Norman J. Ornstein, *It's Even Worse Than It Looks: How the American Constitutional System Collided with the New Politics of Extremism* (Basic Books, 2012).

548 *How much money is on the table:* Deepak Malhotra and Jonathan Powell, "What Donald Trump Doesn't Understand about Negotiation," Harvard Business Review, April 8, 2016.

549 *Collaboration to avoid disaster:* Deepak Malhotra and Jonathan Powell, "What Donald Trump Doesn't Understand about Negotiation," Harvard Business Review, April 8, 2016.

550 *Fischhoff quote:* Cale Guthrie Weissman, "The Huge Difference Between Business and Political Strategies," *FastCompany,* January 13, 2017.

551 *Political calculations harder:* Cale Guthrie Weissman, "The Huge Difference Between Business and Political Strategies," *FastCompany,* January 13, 2017.

552 *Mutuality factor: Gain the Edge!* (2004), 277.

553 *Cuban Missile Crisis: Negotiating the Impossible* (2016), 122–123.

554 *Cuban Missile Crisis—Congressional Response: Negotiating the Impossible* (2016), 132.

555 *RFK recollection: Negotiating the Impossible* (2016), 132.

556 *ExComm: Negotiating the Impossible* (2016), 132.

557 *Shift from aggressive to gradual: Negotiating the Impossible* (2016), 123.

558 *Naval blockade and resolution: Negotiating the Impossible* (2016), 124.

559 *Ending quarantine: Negotiating the Impossible* (2016), 124.

560 *Khrushchev's point of view: Negotiating the Impossible* (2016), 124.

561 *Final lessons: Negotiating the Impossible* (2016), 124–125.

CHAPTER 14

562 *Quarter-century historical context:* Jose de Cordoba, "Trump Moves Shake Deep U.S.—Mexico Relationship," *Wall Street Journal,* January 25, 2017.

563 *Worst free-trade deal:* Jose de Cordoba, "Trump Moves Shake Deep U.S.—Mexico Relationship," *Wall Street Journal,* January 25, 2017.

564 *Nieto's political problems in Mexico:* Jose de Cordoba, "Trump Border Wall Announcement Builds More Resentment in Mexico," *Wall Street Journal,* January 25, 2017.

565 *Mexican poll re: image of Trump:* Jose de Cordoba, "Trump Border Wall Announcement Builds More Resentment in Mexico," *Wall Street Journal,* January 25, 2017.

566 *Estimate of cost for DHS vs. Trump campaign:* Julia Edwards Ainsley, "Trump border 'wall' to cost $21.6 billion, take 3.5 years to build: internal report," Reuters, February 9, 2017; Ron Nixon, "Border Wall Could Cost 3 Times Estimates, Senate Democrats' Report Says," *New York Times,* April 18, 2017.

567 *Estimate of cost for DHS vs. Trump campaign:* Julia Edwards Ainsley, "Trump border 'wall' to cost $21.6 billion, take 3.5 years to build: internal report," Reuters, February 9, 2017; Ron Nixon, "Border Wall Could Cost 3 Times Estimates, Senate Democrats' Report Says," *New York Times,* April 18, 2017.

568 *Trade statistics:* "Trump Moves Shake Deep U.S.—Mexico Relationship," *Wall Street Journal,* January 25, 2017.

569 *Nieto quote re: not believe in walls:* Jose de Cordoba, "Trump Border Wall Announcement Builds More Resentment in Mexico," *Wall Street Journal,* January 25, 2017.

570 *Mexicans outraged:* "How the U.S.–Mexico negotiations collapsed before they started," *Negotiation Briefings* (Harvard Program on Negotiation), May 2017, 6.

571 *Mexico does not believe in walls quote:* "How the U.S.–Mexico negotiations collapsed before they started," *Negotiation Briefings* (Harvard Program on Negotiation), May 2017, 6.

572 *Mexicans' reaction to border wall plans:* Jose de Cordoba, "Trump Border Wall Announcement Builds More Resentment in Mexico," Wall Street Journal, January 25, 2017

573 *wall funding:* "Trump Moves Shake Deep U.S.—Mexico Relationship," *Wall Street Journal,* January 25, 2017.

574 *Compromise agreement:* Philip Rucker, Ashley Parker and Joshua Partlow, "Jared Kushner proves to be a shadow diplomat on U.S.-Mexico talks," *The Washington Post,* February 10, 2017.

575 *Ceremony quote:* "Jared Kushner proves to be a shadow diplomat on U.S.-Mexico talks," *The Washington Post,* February 10, 2017.

576 *ABC news interview:* "How the U.S.–Mexico negotiations collapsed before they started," *Negotiation Briefings* (Harvard Program on Negotiation), May 2017, 7.

577 *Nieto statement:* "How the U.S.–Mexico negotiations collapsed before they started," *Negotiation Briefings* (Harvard Program on Negotiation), May 2017, 7.

578 *phone call:* "How the U.S.–Mexico negotiations collapsed before they started," *Negotiation Briefings* (Harvard Program on Negotiation), May 2017, 7.

579 *cool off:* "How the U.S.–Mexico negotiations collapsed before they started," *Negotiation Briefings* (Harvard Program on Negotiation), May 2017, 7.

580 *avoid extreme public demands:* "How the U.S.–Mexico negotiations collapsed before they started," *Negotiation Briefings* (Harvard Program on Negotiation), May 2017, 7.

581 *failure to coordinate unified strategy:* "How the U.S.–Mexico negotiations collapsed before they started," *Negotiation Briefings* (Harvard Program on Negotiation), May 2017, 6.

582 *regroup quickly after failure; quarantine hot-button issues:* "How the U.S.–Mexico negotiations collapsed before they started," *Negotiation Briefings* (Harvard Program on Negotiation), May 2017, 7.

583 *quarantine hot-button issues:* "How the U.S.–Mexico negotiations collapsed before they started," *Negotiation Briefings* (Harvard Program on Negotiation), May 2017, 7.

CHAPTER 15

584 *Affordable Care Act historical context:* Judith Burns, Obama Presses Parties on Health, *Wall Street Journal,* February 20, 2010; Louise Radnofsky and Michael C. Bender, "Donald Trump Plays Background Role in Health-Care Battle," *Wall Street Journal,* March 10, 2017; Naftali Bendavid, "Why Obamacare Passed but the GOP Health Bill Failed," *Wall Street Journal,* July 18, 2017.

585 *Trump's goals:* Natalie Andrews, "Where Donald Trump's Health-Care Promises Stand Now," *Wall Street Journal,* March 14, 2017.

586 *Obama promises:* Natalie Andrews, "Where Donald Trump's Health-Care Promises Stand Now," *Wall Street Journal,* March 14, 2017.

587 *Rep. Boehner quote:* Louise Radnofsky, Kristina Peterson, and Stephanie Armour, "GOP's New Plan to Repeal Obamacare: Dare Fellow Republicans to Block Effort," *Wall Street Journal,* February 27, 2017.

588 *outsourcing lead role:* Louise Radnofsky and Michael C. Bender, "Donald Trump Plays Background Role in Health-Care Battle," *Wall Street Journal,* March 10, 2017.

589 *Nobody knew health care could be so complicated"*: Louise Radmofsky, Anna Wilde Mathews and Michelle Hackman, "Trump Calls Health Care 'So Complicated,' but Vows to Replace Law," *Wall Street Journal*, February 27, 2017.

590 *final push:* Louise Radnofsky and Michael C. Bender, "Donald Trump Plays Background Role in Health-Care Battle," *Wall Street Journal*, March 10, 2017.

591 *Trump's inability to make final push:* "How the 'Party of No' Didn't Get to Yes," *Negotiation Briefings* (Harvard Program on Negotiation, July 2017), 7.

592 *Trump's lack of knowledge:* "How the 'Party of No' Didn't Get to Yes," *Negotiation Briefings* (Harvard Program on Negotiation, July 2017), 7.

593 *contrasts between business and presidential negotiations:* Greg Ip, "In Health-Care Failure, a Lesson on Treating Politics Like Business," *Wall Street Journal*, March 27, 2017.

594 *contrasts between business and presidential negotiations:* Greg Ip, "In Health-Care Failure, a Lesson on Treating Politics Like Business," *Wall Street Journal*, March 27, 2017.

595 *Charlie Brown party:* Adam Kinziger, "How the Freedom Caucus is Undermining the G.O.P.," *New York Times*, March 31, 2017.

596 *balance with competing priorities:* Louise Radnofsky and Michael C. Bender, "Donald Trump Plays Background Role in Health-Care Battle," *Wall Street Journal*, March 10, 2017.

597 *President Obama getting the ACA past the finish line:* Louise Radnofsky and Michael C. Bender, "Donald Trump Plays Background Role in Health-Care Battle," *Wall Street Journal*, March 10, 2017.

598 *Trump endorsed but left open whether he would lobby:* Louise Radnofsky, Kristina Peterson, and Siobhan Hughes, "GOP's Health Plan Draws Skepticism on Capitol Hill, *Wall Street Journal*, March 7, 2017

599 *really a good bill?:* "How the 'Party of No' Didn't Get to Yes," *Negotiation Briefings* (Harvard Program on Negotiation, July 2017), 6, *quoting New York Times.*

600 *Congressman Ross quote:* Louise Radnofsky, Kristina Peterson, and Stephanie Armour, "GOP's New Plan to Repeal Obamacare: Dare Fellow Republicans to Block Effort," *Wall Street Journal*, February 27, 2017.

601 *polls showing increasing support for Obamacare:* Louise Radnofsky, Kristina Peterson, and Stephanie Armour, "GOP's New Plan to Repeal Obamacare: Dare Fellow Republicans to Block Effort," *Wall Street Journal*, February 27, 2017.

602 *Nobody knew health care could be so complicated":* Louise Radnofsky, Anna Wilde Mathews and Michelle Hackman, "Trump Calls Health Care 'So Complicated,' but Vows to Replace Law," *Wall Street Journal*, February 27, 2017.

603 *polls:* Dan Mangan, "The GOP's health-care bill is a polling disaster, with voters much more likely to punish Senators who support it," *CNBC*, May 26, 2017.

604 *daunting task:* "How the 'Party of No' Didn't Get to Yes," *Negotiation Briefings* (Harvard Program on Negotiation, July 2017), 6.

605 17%: Bob Bryan, "Only 17% of Americans support 'Trumpcare' in new poll," *Business Insider*, March 23, 2017.

606 *interest groups opposing plan:* Louise Radnofsky, Kristina Peterson and Siobhan Hughes, "GOP's Health Plan Draws Skepticism on Capitol Hill," *Wall Street Journal*, March 7, 2017.

607 *Trump and Meadows:* "How the 'Party of No' Didn't Get to Yes," *Negotiation Briefings* (Harvard Program on Negotiation, July 2017), 6.

608 *Forget about the little stuf:* "How the 'Party of No' Didn't Get to Yes," *Negotiation Briefings* (Harvard Program on Negotiation, July 2017), 7.

609 *Trump's goals compared with CBO's estimate:* Natalie Andrews, "Where Donald Trump's Health-Care Promises Stand Now," *Wall Street Journal*, March 14, 2017.

610 *Trump's goals compared with CBO's estimate:* Natalie Andrews, "Where Donald Trump's Health-Care Promises Stand Now," *Wall Street Journal*, March 14, 2017.

611 *strenuously disagree:* Fox News - Politics, "Trump administration disagrees with CBO report on health care," March 13, 2017.

612 *few carrots and sticks:* "How the 'Party of No' Didn't Get to Yes," *Negotiation Briefings* (Harvard Program on Negotiation, July 2017), 6.

613 *offer-concession:* Josh Barro, "The Republican Healthcare Plan Just Failed Because Trump Is Bad at Making Deals," *Business Insider,* March 24, 2017.

614 *agenda control:* Louise Radnofsky, Kristina Peterson, and Stephanie Armour, "GOP's New Plan to Repeal Obamacare: Dare Fellow Republicans to Block Effort," *Wall Street Journal,* February 27, 2017.

615 *Trump and Meadows:* "How the 'Party of No' Didn't Get to Yes," *Negotiation Briefings* (Harvard Program on Negotiation, July 2017), 6–7.

616 *caught off guard:* "How the 'Party of No' Didn't Get to Yes," *Negotiation Briefings* (Harvard Program on Negotiation, July 2017), 7.

617 *damage-control mode:* "How the 'Party of No' Didn't Get to Yes," *Negotiation Briefings* (Harvard Program on Negotiation, July 2017), 7.

618 *What Trump and Ryan did differently:* Gerald F. Seib, "The Balance Sheet for Republicans after Big Health Vote," *Wall Street Journal,* May 4, 2017.

619 *What Trump and Ryan did differently:* Jennifer Steinhauer, "Republicans Get Their Health Bill. But It May Cost Them," *New York Times,* May 4, 2017.

620 *expanded coalition:* Stephanie Armour, "House GOP Health Insurance Plan Gains New Life," *Wall Street Journal,* April 27, 2017.

621 *leverage remained weak:* Stephanie Armour and Kristina Peterson, "New Plan, Same Hurdle in GOP's Quest to Gut Obamacare," *Wall Street Journal,* April 28, 2017.

622 *continued trouble:* Louise Radnofsky and Kristina Peterson, "Trump Pushing for Vote on Health Bill but Stumbling Blocks Remain," *Wall Street Journal,* April 30, 2017.

623 *secretive drafting:* "How the 'Party of No' Didn't Get to Yes," *Negotiation Briefings* (Harvard Program on Negotiation, July 2017), 6; Thomas Kaplan, "5 Takeaways from the Failed Senate Effort to Repeal Obamacare," *New York Times,* July 28, 2017.

624 *late intervention:* Louise Radnofsky, Kristina Peterson, and Stephanie Armour "Trump Implores GOP Senators to Come Together Over Troubled Heath Bill," *Wall Street Journal,* July 19, 2017.

625 *kept Trump at a distance:* Louise Radmonfsky, Kristina Peterson, and Stephanie Armour "Trump Implores GOP Senators to Come Together Over Troubled Heath Bill," Wall Street Journal, July 19, 2017.

626 *kept Trump at a distance:* Louise Radnofsky, Kristina Peterson, and Stephanie Armour "Trump Implores GOP Senators to Come Together Over Troubled Heath Bill," Wall Street Journal, July 19, 2017.

627 *Threats: Louise Radnofsky, Kristina Peterson, and Stephanie Armour "Trump Implores GOP Senators to Come Together Over Troubled Heath Bill," Wall Street Journal, July 19, 2017.*

628 *repeated mistake:* "In Senate health care defeat, it's déjà vu all over again," *Negotiation Briefings* (Harvard Program on Negotiation, October 2017), 7.

629 *failure to do homework:* Glenn Thrush and Jonathan Martin, "On Senate Health Bill, Trump Falters in the Closer's Role," *New York Times,* June 27, 2017.

630 *smiled blandly:* Glenn Thrush and Jonathan Martin, "On Senate Health Bill, Trump Falters in the Closer's Role," *New York Times,* June 27, 2017.

631 *Throwing House under the bus:* Serafin Gomez and Mike Emanuel, "Trump Tells Senators Health Care Bill is "Mean," Sources Say," *FOX News,* June 13, 2017.

632 *fired up the crazies:* "John McCain Has a Few Things to Say About Donald Trump," *The New Yorker,* July 16, 2015.

633 *people who weren't captured:* Donald Trump, 2015 Family Leadership Summit, July 19, 2015.

634 *process problems:* Peggy Noonan, "Trump, ObamaCare and the Art of the Fail," *Wall Street Journal,* July 20, 2017.

Conclusion

635 Michael Casey, Senior Manager for Investment Firm in the Midwest with more than 20 years' experience in the investment business.

636 *savvy at negotiations*: Donald J. Trump, Crippled America: How to Make America Great Again (2015), 96

ACKNOWLEDGMENTS

This book was not my idea. My colleague John Fechter suggested that everyone would benefit from a book evaluating President Donald Trump's negotiation abilities. The moment he said it I knew I had to do it. It just felt right. That started this journey, and I am extremely grateful to John for his great idea. I am also grateful for his team that has also worked on this effort, especially Rhonda Moret—a marketing and public relations professional extraordinaire.

I am also extremely grateful for my academic colleagues who gave this manuscript a close and careful read. Ohio State Business School Professor Roy Lewicki—a prolific author, researcher and giant in the field—spent many hours reading the manuscript and making extremely helpful suggestions and edits, including how to streamline and improve it.

University of California-Hastings Law Professor Clark Freshman, a negotiation expert specializing in lie detection, also offered extremely productive ideas to make it better and more likely to resonate with readers. Marquette University Law Professor Andrea Schneider, Arizona State University Law Professor Art Hinshaw, and Stanford Law Lecturer Megan Karsh also provided very insightful and helpful comments. The result? A much better book. Thank you!

Many family and friends also spent countless hours reading the manuscript and pointing out how to improve it, including my parents, sister Shari Rothman, my in-laws June and Gary Beier, Pat Braatz, John Fechter, Rhonda Moret, and Ann Rayson. All looked at an early draft with critical eyes that improved the book.

PCI Publishing Group as well as Mona Gambetta and her team also deserve great appreciation for believing in this concept and taking this effort to the next level. Special appreciation goes to Laura Rutt and Kellie Coppola.

The following authors of Trump biographies also deserve appreciation for the extraordinary effort and resources they devoted to uncovering the facts, details and strategies surrounding Trump's negotiations over the last 50 years. This book could not have been written without their thousands of hours of research and hundreds of interviews of Trump and those who interacted with him over the years. They have done the world a real service in providing us with incredible insights into Trump the person. And they have allowed me to overlay a negotiation analysis on top of their original research.

Special thanks go out to: Wayne Barrett, *Trump: The Greatest Show on Earth*; Michael Kranish and Marc Fisher, *Trump Revealed, The Definitive Biography of the 45th President;* David Cay Johnston, *The Making of Donald Trump;* and Timothy L. O'Brien, *TrumpNation: The Art of Being The Donald.*

And where would this book be without my colleague Tricia Schafer, who cheerfully tackles every task I ask of her (including informally editing this book and painstakingly putting together the End Notes) and completes them in a professional fashion? I appreciate all your hard work.

Finally, I want to thank—again—my incredible wife Linda, who made many excellent suggestions on how to improve my book. She's a great writer and thinker in her own right, and this book would not be the same without her significant contributions. My son Jason and daughter Valerie also deserve special thanks. They also experienced firsthand the long hours that inevitably accompanied writing this book. I do what I do in part to make them proud and to make their lives easier and better and to make this world a better place in which to live. I hope this effort will help them—and help you—toward that end.

Thank you. I appreciate it.

Martin E. Latz

ABOUT THE AUTHOR

 MARTIN E. LATZ is the founder of Latz Negotiation, an internationally recognized negotiation expert, and author of *Gain the Edge! Negotiating to Get What You Want*. Latz has taught more than 100,000 lawyers and business professionals around the world to negotiate more effectively, including in many Fortune 100 companies and the world's largest law firms.

A Harvard Law honors graduate, Latz also founded an e-learning negotiation software company, served as an adjunct professor at Arizona State University College of Law, and regularly consults on negotiations involving the sale of private businesses. Latz also negotiated for The White House nationally and internationally on The White House Advance Teams and has appeared as a negotiation expert on many national shows, including on CBS, CNN, and FOX. He has also written a negotiation column for various newspapers since 1999 that is now emailed to approximately 40,000 recipients each month.

A former Teaching Fellow at Harvard's Kennedy School of Government, one of his students was President Barack Obama.

Latz and his wife and two kids live in Scottsdale, Arizona.

To learn more about LATZ Negotiation, to receive his free monthly negotiation column, or to view his public seminar schedule visit
LatzNegotiation.com

NOTES

NOTES

NOTES